Partners in Conflict

Next Wave New Directions in Women's Studies

A series edited by Inderpal Grewal, Caren Kaplan,

and Robyn Wiegman

Heidi Tinsman

Partners in Conflict

The Politics of Gender, Sexuality, and Labor

in the Chilean Agrarian Reform, 1950–1973

Duke University Press Durham & London 2002

© 2002 Duke University Press

All rights reserved

Printed in the United States of America on acid-free paper ∞

Designed by C. H. Westmoreland

Typeset in Bembo with Frutiger display by Tseng Information Systems, Inc.

Library of Congress Cataloging-in-Publication Data appear on the last
printed page of this book.

For Erik

contents

maps and tables

preface

This book started as one thing and became something else. In the summer of 1991, I was contemplating dropping out of history graduate school to pursue what, at the time, I supposed would be a more meaningful career in law. Thanks to a series of lucky accidents, I ended up working as a legal researcher in rural Chile for a nonprofit organization called the Casa del Temporero, which had assisted in the creation of Chile's first union of temporary fruit workers in the Aconcagua Valley county of Santa María. General Augusto Pinochet's seventeen-year dictatorship had formally ended just the previous year with the inauguration of Chile's first democratically elected president since Salvador Allende.

The countryside, especially the Aconcagua Valley, still reeled from the ways military rule had dramatically transformed it. Fresh-fruit exports of grapes, apples, and peaches had become Chile's third most lucrative source of foreign currency. Aconcagua was the heart of a half-billion dollar industry hugely dependent on tens of thousands of hyperexploited seasonal laborers, nearly half of them women. Women had played a major role in the formation of the Santa María union and had been at the forefront of many struggles by rural poor people throughout the dictatorship. The implications of such female agency for daily gender dynamics was *the* topic of conversation at every union meeting and community dance I attended. Equality between men and women had been formally recognized as central to the union's mission, and men and women heatedly and often humorously debated what this meant for interactions on production lines and in private bedrooms.

I was enthralled. Here were agricultural workers vigorously defending their rights in defiance of stereotypes about rural passivity and the overwhelming force of neoliberal capitalism. Here were poor women articulating a feminist stance, asserting leadership within the labor movement, and engaging with issues of democratization. Here was a story worth telling.

But it was not the story I ended up writing. The heroics I sought to thrust on fruit workers ended up being more complicated and limited than my initial romantic narrative had envisioned. And the working-class radicalism and idealism that I did encounter began to seem, upon closer inspection, less an obvious, automatic response to military dictatorship and proletarianization than a reworking of sensibilities about social justice rooted in an earlier utopian moment: the radical populism of Chile's Agrarian Reform between 1964 and 1973.

I discovered the Agrarian Reform because of workers' memories and despite the conventions of Chilean history's periodization. Most literature sharply differentiates between life before and after the military coup against Popular Unity socialism on September 11, 1973. As the narrative goes, a completely new authoritarian order stopped dead in its tracks the massive land redistribution and widespread peasant mobilization that had been the Agrarian Reform. But in interviews and oral histories with fruit workers and labor activists about life during the dictatorship, men and women repeatedly referenced the Agrarian Reform (as well as the latifundia arrangements preceding it) as a comparative index of their current fortunes. Although opinions about the Agrarian Reform's accomplishments varied widely, there was near unanimity about the fact that it had attempted to politically empower and materially uplift rural poor people in ways utterly unmatched before or since. Whether or not it had succeeded, the Agrarian Reform represented the only rural democratic precedent from which Chilean fruit workers and their advocates could draw for envisioning the post-Pinochet future.

This does not mean that the Agrarian Reform was the only source of reference or inspiration for surviving and critiquing dictatorship. But it was surely one of the most important. In recent years, the role of memory has emerged as a rich and important site of historical investigation. This book, however, is devoted to making arguments about the Agrarian Reform experience itself in order to suggest why its memory matters. It is particularly concerned with questions about gender and the distinct and unequal legacies that the Agrarian Reform bequeathed to women and men. Both the exciting achievements and the sobering limits of present-day Chilean women fruit workers' efforts to advocate equality with men have roots in those years. This book honors and criticizes a utopian project, some of whose goals are still in the making.

acknowledgments

My debts for this book are many. Financial support for initial research was provided by fellowships from the Social Science Research Council and the Inter-American Foundation. Subsequent research was financed by grants from Yale University, the Mellon Foundation, and the University of California at Irvine.

As a graduate student at Yale University, I had the good fortune to work with a number of fine scholars. Emilia Viotti da Costa served as my advisor and provided an extremely smart example of teaching and writing history. Danny James's engagement with feminist labor studies and his pioneering work in oral history were, and continue to be, a source of great inspiration. Nancy Cott's graduate courses and her generous comments on my dissertation helped support this project through various phases. David Montgomery's seminars and comments provided similar continuity. Patricia Pessar kindly served as an additional dissertation reader and offered much helpful guidance.

I am especially grateful to my numerous graduate student comrades, who were always my most direct and rigorous source of intellectual and political orientation and whose friendships I value greatly: Emily Bernard, Lisa Daugaard, Adam Green, Miranda Massie, Gunther Peck, Pam Haag, and Rebecca Weston. Special thanks to Sandhya Shukla for her intelligent feedback on several of my chapters and for her generous commitment to interdisciplinary, transregional collaboration. I owe a truly unpayable debt to Tom Klubock who has read this project in more versions than I can count. His criticism, encouragement, and own wonderful scholarship proved vital to reimagining this project as a book.

I have also benefited from the keen minds and solidarity of numerous other colleagues and friends in the United States. Michael Jiménez provided me with an unmatched example of passion for the historian's craft when I was an undergraduate at Princeton. I join many others in grieving his premature death and feel privileged to have been his student. Peter Winn offered me sage advice on Popular Unity politics and much appreciated faith in my project. I am thankful to John D. French, Gilbert Joseph, and Cristóbal Kay for their suggestions and support. The Duke Labor History Conference provided a particularly rich intellectual space over the years, and I am fortunate to have benefited from its many participants. Temma Kaplan served as a reader for Duke University Press, offering superb and motivating direction on revisions. My editor Valerie Millholland gave excellent, frank advice and helped me steer a straight course.

Since 1996 I have taught at the University of California at Irvine, where my work has benefited greatly from the casual and formal feedback of many intelligent and hardworking colleagues. I particularly thank Marjorie Beal, Sharon Block, Alice Fahs, Jeff Garcilazo, Laura Kang, Lynn Mally, Bob Moeller, Ken Pomeranz, Jaime Rodríguez, Ulrike Strasser, Steven Topik, Anne Walthall, and Jon Wiener. I am also grateful for the rich intellectual environment provided by the UCI Women's Studies Program and the Labor Studies Project. Marc Kanda provided much appreciated expertise on preparing the images for this book.

In Chile, I am very grateful to Gonzalo Falabella, director of the Casa del Temporero, and his staff for welcoming me into the midst of their exciting project and housing me during my fieldwork in Aconcagua. I especially thank Daniel San Martín who served as my informal tutor on multiple aspects of Chilean history and labor movements. His personal kindness and political integrity will always be a model. I am similarly indebted to Erika Muñoz, Olga Gutiérrez, and Raúl Flores for sharing their rich knowledge and filling my nights in Santa María with wry humor and fellowship. Thanks to the leadership of the Santa María Union of Permanent and Temporary Workers for facilitating my interviews, and to the many, many women and men who gave me their time. I am particularly grateful to Miguel Aguilar, Selfa Antimán, María Elena Galdámez, Omar García, Olivia Herrera, Eloi Ibacache, Jaime Muñoz, María Tapia, and Rosa Tolmo.

In Santiago I benefited from a smart and lively community of scholars and friends. Julio Pinto Vallejos and Luís Ortega assisted my affiliation with the Departamento de Historia at the Universidad de Santiago (USACH) and enabled my participation in Chile's first university-based workshop on women's history in 1991. Through this pioneering project at USACH, I deepened relationships with a terrific community of feminist scholars: Teresa Gatica, Lorena Godoy, Elizabeth Hutchison, Karin Rosemblatt, Ericka Verba, and Soledad Zárate. Later, this cohort included Pricilla Archibald, Alejandra Brito, Lisa Baldez, Margaret Power, and Corrine Pernet. These women and their ideas provided, and continue to provide, a source of challenging debate and purposeful solidarity. I am especially grateful for the generosity with which Chilean feminists engaged with those of us coming from the United States. Special thanks to Lorena Godoy and Soledad Zárate for their hard and often solitary labor in promoting the anthology *Disaplina y desacato,* which was the first fruit of that transnational feminist collaboration. I also owe additional gratitude to Liz Hutchison for her insightful comments on my dissertation and manuscript and for her model of professional generosity.

My work in Chile was also aided by the advice and scholarship of Ximena Aranda, Ximena Valdés, and Silvia Venegas. I likewise thank Sergio Gómez, Lovell Jarvis, Ana María Alves, and Wally Goldfrank. I am grateful to the knowledgeable staff at the Biblioteca Nacional for showing me the ropes and facilitating mountains of photocopying. Thanks to Teresa Gatica for transcribing many of the oral histories and to the leaders and staff at Unidad Obrero Campesino for aiding my contacts with labor organizers. Carlos Carrera generously assisted my work at the archive of the ex–Corporación de Reforma Agraria.

Since many of my favorite hours in Chile were admittedly spent not working, no less thanks are due those who buoyed my spirits and provided festive camaraderie: Soledad Falabella, Javier Couso, Alina Polanska, Marek Rekus, Erika Haebrerly, Natalia Valenzuela, Jonnathan Conning, Eduardo Peralta, Claudia Pardov, Francesca Pérez, Regina Manocchio, Cynthia Sanborn, Andrés Barriaga, Micho Seeger, Alejandra Pamjean, Ximena Optiz, and the regulars at the Maestra Vida. I especially thank Miguel Kaiser whose friendship I treasure.

My parents Maggie and Hovey Tinsman are thrilled and relieved by this book's arrival only slightly less than I am. I am grateful for their generosity, patience, and enthusiasm for the different paths my life has taken. My love of politics and community struggles began with them.

Lastly, I thank Erik Kongshaug who contributed to this book in countless ways, not the least of which was editing every word of the manuscript at least twice without complaining. Other debts are more intangible. For his gift of language. For his expansive heart. For making me immensely happy. Fittingly, our son Arlo arrived into the world on the very day the final revisions for this project were put in the mail. Life has been more rewarding ever since.

abbreviations

APROFA Asociación de Protección de la Familia (Association for the Protection of the Family)

CEMA Centro de Madres (Mothers' Center)

CERA Centro de Reforma Agraria (Agrarian Reform Center)

CNPP Consejería Nacional de Promoción Popular (National Council of Popular Promotion)

CORA Corporación de la Reforma Agraria (Corporation for Agrarian Reform)

CUT Central Unica de Trabajadores (United Central of Workers)

IER Instituto de Educación Rural (Rural Education Institute)

INDAP Instituto de Desarrollo Agropecuario (Institute of Agricultural Development)

SNA Sociedad Nacional de Agricultura (National Agricultural Society)

SNS Sociedad Nacional de Salud (National Health Society)

UOC Unidad Obrero Campesino (Worker-Campesino Unity)

UP Unidad Popular (Popular Unity)

Partners in Conflict

Map 1
Chile, provinces and
cities of the central
region.

introduction

Between 1964 and 1973, the Chilean state expropriated almost half the country's agricultural land and began redistributing it to campesino peasants. In nine short years, this policy, known as the Agrarian Reform, virtually dismantled the latifundia system of large estates and semipeon laborers that had dominated Chilean agriculture since the nineteenth century and whose roots were far older. The Agrarian Reform sparked the explosive growth of a militant rural labor movement that, during the same nine years, recruited a quarter-million members and gave the rural poor a meaningful voice in national politics for the first time. It encouraged massive state investments in rural education and health care, including the first national birth control programs, and initiated projects aimed explicitly at mobilizing rural women and young people. These were radical policies with radical goals.

The Agrarian Reform was begun in full by President Eduardo Frei's liberal Christian Democratic government (1964–1970), which aimed to make small peasant farmers the basis for revitalizing capitalist agribusiness. It was accelerated by President Salvador Allende's Popular Unity coalition of Marxist and social democratic parties (1970–1973), which sought to use collective holdings as the basis for creating socialism. Despite profound differences between these administrations, both Catholics and Marxists shared a bold optimism that their version of the Agrarian Reform was revolutionary. Both sought national salvation through restructuring the agrarian economy, the political empowerment of the peasantry, and the moral rehabilitation of rural society. Such zeal reflected both the heady utopianism and the Cold War fears of the 1960s.

PROVINCIA DE ACONCAGUA

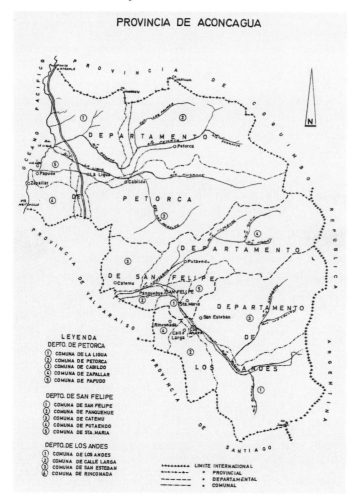

Map 2 Province of Aconcagua, 1970.

It was an era that, particularly in Latin America, reverberated with the aftershocks of the Cuban Revolution and in which numerous countries linked the restructuring of agriculture to modernity. Initial results in Chile were impressive. Until Allende's 1973 overthrow by a bloody military coup, Chile's Agrarian Reform was proportionally the most extensive and least violent land reform project carried out by democratically elected leaders without a prior armed revolution anywhere in Latin America, and arguably the world.

Partners in Conflict tells a story about rural women and men before and during this time of dramatic change. It is a story about the centrality of gender and sexuality to the ways campesino women and men negotiated daily life, participated in, or were marginalized from, political struggle, and benefited from, or were hurt by, the attempt to radically remake rural life. It is, in large part, a success story about the Agrarian Reform's real achievements and the uplift of some of Chile's poorest people. On the eve of the Agrarian Reform's premature end, the lives of most campesino peasants—female and male—had vastly improved. Rural wages had skyrocketed. Tens of thousands of rural families had been guaranteed land; tens of thousands more anticipated such privilege. Literacy rates had risen. Infant mortality and maternal death indices had fallen. Through new unions, men had negotiated better working conditions with employers. Through new community organizations, women had established craft industries and education programs. Together, women and men had fought for faster land expropriations and better housing— and they had won. There was a new emphasis on gender cooperation as men were encouraged to have more respect for wives and women were asked to better inform themselves of husbands' activities. The Agrarian Reform defined spousal partnership as critical to its success and an assurance that both men and women would benefit.

But *Partners in Conflict* is also a story about inequality. Chile's Agrarian Reform empowered men more than it did women. Men, not women, were the direct recipients of land. Men, not women, made up the bulk of rural unions. Men, not women, were defined as principal actors in creating a new world. Most women reaped the fruits of the Agrarian Reform indirectly, as wives and daughters of men who either earned better wages or had access to land. Women's activism largely provided sideline support for men's initiatives. These disparities sprang from the ways that the Agrarian Reform left the principle of men's authority over women fundamentally unchallenged. In particular, a version of patriarchal family remained foundational to the way rural society was rebuilt. This was true for the Christian Democrats' attempt to reform capitalism as well as for Popular Unity's effort to create socialism. Both Catholics and Marxists envisioned the Agrarian Reform as a process in which male citizen-producers would responsibly provide for domesticated, if better educated and more civic-minded, wives and children. Both placed priority on invigorating the confidence of campesino men to achieve the leadership and solidarity necessary for transforming society. The shared rallying cry to "turn the campesino man into his own boss" expressed an emphasis on reconstituting masculinity and defined men as the Agrarian Reform's main protagonists, affirming their ultimate power over women within the supposedly harmonious family.

Yet this is not a simple story about women's exclusion and the triumph of male dominance. Women participated in the creation of the Agrarian Reform, and most rural women benefited greatly from it and applauded its goals. Despite their marginalization within the labor movement, women played significant roles in struggles for housing, land, and higher wages—an activism that opened new spaces for female leadership within rural communities. Although the Agrarian Reform reinforced the principle of men's leadership within the family, its emphasis on mutual support and cooperation between spouses afforded some women the opportunity to challenge male excess and to assert their own needs. At the very least, most rural women enjoyed higher standards of living during the Agrarian Reform, and most understood benefits for men as benefits for themselves.

This book traces the dialectical tensions between women's real uplift within the Agrarian Reform and the gender hierarchies that made such uplift inferior and subordinate to that of men. It recounts the importance of women's labor to Chile's pre–Agrarian Reform world of large estates and subsistence agriculture, and it explores the Agrarian Reform's increasing validation of female domesticity and women's family-based activism. It argues that this contrasted with and complemented the Agrarian Reform's emphasis on transforming men from servile laborers into productive breadwinners and political militants. Finally, it examines the political consequences of gender difference. It challenges longstanding assumptions, still prevalent in scholarly and activist circles alike, that Chilean women were hostile to radical politics in general and opposed to the Popular Unity (UP) project in particular. *Partners in Conflict* argues that most rural women staunchly defended the Agrarian Reform and that the UP had a solid base, if never a majority, of campesina support throughout its tenure. At the same time, this book maintains that men were far better positioned than women to navigate the political turbulence of the Agrarian Reform's later years and enjoyed far greater social freedoms than their female counterparts outside the home. This made women increasingly fearful of the consequences of class struggle and weakened their ability to fully shape the Agrarian Reform as a project.

Chile's Agrarian Reform was unique but not singular. During the twentieth century, a diverse range of political leaderships throughout the world undertook agrarian reforms for the purpose of spurring national development and modernizing supposedly backward rural populations. Agrarian reform was at the heart of all major popular revolutions since 1900, including those of Mexico, Russia, China, Cuba, and Nicaragua. They defined massive land redistribution into communal forms of ownership as key to turning peasants into worker-citizens and to building socialism (or, in the case of Mexico, to protecting peasants and economic sovereignty). The idea that the state could legitimately expropriate land in the name of the social good also gained surprisingly wide acceptance in the capitalist world. Throughout Latin America and Asia—including Venezuela, Peru, Brazil, Indonesia, and the Philippines—numerous agrarian reforms were part of a U.S.-led effort during the Cold War to preempt the attractions of communism by encouraging stable capitalist development. Agrarian reform was meant to break up supposedly feudal land monopolies and to replace them with competitive family farms that would satisfy domestic consumption, encourage industrialization, and spread democratic values.

Chile's Agrarian Reform shared elements of both the capitalist and revolutionary models. It began as an effort to rehabilitate capitalism and became a project for building socialism. Under Frei, it was heavily financed and greatly celebrated by the United States; under Allende, the U.S. government deemed it a communist threat and justification for supporting a military coup. Like agrarian reforms elsewhere, Chile's was heavily directed from above in both phases, reflecting the conviction shared by socialist and capitalist promoters alike that the state had a crucial role to play in transforming society. Yet, as was true for revolutionary projects but less so for capitalist ones, the Chilean Agrarian Reform, both under Frei and Allende, encouraged the mass mobilization of peasants and generated intense class conflict. Similar to that in Mexico in the 1930s and 1940s, China in the 1950s, and Cuba in the 1960s, the explosive growth of Chile's rural labor movement helped peasants successfully challenge, and in many cases displace, their class superiors. Peasant empowerment was extensive even during Frei's Agrarian Reform, an exception among capitalist projects, where governments were generally wary of peasant unions for anything other than consolidating state power. Even under Allende, however, peasant mobilization in Chile unfolded quite differently than in other revolutionary projects. Unlike in Mexico, the USSR, China, or Cuba, Chilean unions were never directly controlled by the state but, instead, composed of multiple, competing tendencies across a broad center-left political spectrum. This made it easier for portions of the labor movement to challenge state power, contest decisions, and shape the course of the Agrarian Reform from below.

It was similarly striking that such a massive mobilization of poor people and redistribution of wealth took place within the context of a capitalist democracy. Chile's Agrarian Reform in both phases was implemented under conditions of political pluralism, through laws and institutions set up to protect private property and without defeating the propertied classes. Land expropriation and redistribution thus rested on laws passed by a congress, and interpreted by courts, in which powerful landowners and other elites continued to serve. Such conditions made Allende's plans for building socialism especially remarkable since, unlike other revolutionary models, the UP set out to dismantle capitalism without full (or even majority) control of state power. Throughout the 1970–1973 period, a diverse coalition of elite and middle-class opponents remained free to openly organize against Allende as well as to control congress, the media, and important sectors of the armed forces. As many would argue in retrospect, this situation surely contributed to the UP's overthrow and cast doubt on the viability of creating socialism without prior revolution. Yet it is perhaps more remarkable that, given the constraints, the UP's Agrarian Reform was as radical and successful as it was.

The exceptionalism of Chile's Agrarian Reform created a flurry of early commentary and scholarship in the 1960s and 1970s. Before the 1973 coup, there was widespread hope that the scale of Chile's land expropriations, combined with extensive social welfare programs and peasant unionization, would provide a model for modernization and democracy elsewhere in the hemisphere. Social scientists and economic development specialists mapped connections between land expropriation and national production, charted the growth of labor organizations and peasants' civic participation, and predicted shifts in rural values and behavior.[1] Most researchers were Chileans based at prestigious universities in Santiago or at nonprofit agencies funded by the United Nations. Others were from abroad, including elsewhere in Latin America and Europe. A large contingent hailed from U.S. government agencies and universities operating in the spirit of, and often with funding from, the Alliance for Progress, a U.S. State Department initiative aimed at encouraging development throughout Latin America.[2] Events in Cuba and debates over modernization keenly shaped the intellectual climate. A largely U.S.-based theory that Keynesian economics and entrepreneurial incentives would spur development stages increasingly knocked heads with a more Latin America–based critique of imperialism and economic dependency. Researchers' political leanings and policy proscriptions varied widely, but all shared a common faith in state-led development and the belief that some version of the Agrarian Reform could succeed.

Following Allende's overthrow, such optimism soured. Discussions about the Agrarian Reform were recast as narratives of failure. The political urgency to explain the reasons behind the coup gave a certain over-determined cast to scholarship (one always knew the story would end badly) and suggested that the Agrarian Reform was partly to blame. But it also produced many superb studies with a critical appreciation of the Agrarian Reform's contradictions. In particular, scholars moved away from the mechanical functionalism of earlier literature on development and emphasized the Agrarian Reform as a process of class conflict and political struggle. Authors such as Solon Barraclough, José Bengoa, José Antonio Fernández, Jorge Echeníque, Sergio Gómez, Cristóbal Kay, Brian Loveman, Ian Roxborough, Peter Winn, and others gave attention to the ways in which land redistribution had intensified social stratification in the countryside by privileging some campesino peasants over others.[3] Although many of these authors were sympathetic to Popular Unity goals, they sharply criticized Allende's government for failing to mobilize migrant workers, a potentially radical base of support, as well as for misunderstanding many peasants' desire for individual, rather than communal, forms of landownership. Scholars placed particular emphasis on the role of the rural labor movement. While viewing unions as a positive sign of campesino empowerment, these writers argued that labor's political polarization had exacerbated divisions among campesinos and encouraged peasants to pursue strikes and land occupations independently of, and often against, the interest of the government in power. Such conflict, it was implied, had undermined the Agrarian Reform's legitimacy and contributed to military takeover.[4]

Women are strikingly absent from these accounts. Most scholarship on Chile's Agrarian Reform tells stories only about men—men's struggle for land, men's empowerment in unions, men's conflicts on the eve of military rule. This tendency partly reflects the Agrarian Reform's actual focus on men: government officials and union leaders rarely mentioned women; documents on strike activities and state-managed farms say little about a female presence. But the omission of women also derives from a certain acceptance by researchers that the Agrarian Reform's focus on men was natural and obvious, undeserving of analytical inquiry. It likewise stems from the generational assumption—shared by scholars across academic disciplines and national borders at the time—that research on women was something separate from the sociology of the agrarian economy and that stories about men could serve as the general history of an era. In most accounts of Chile's Agrarian Reform, the terms *campesino* and *peasant* implicitly designate male characters, but they simultaneously refer to "the rural poor" as a whole. This unwittingly suggests both that women were never actors in the Agrarian Reform and that women's historical experiences were the same as men's.

A few pioneering feminist works on the lives of rural women made important qualifications to this narrative. Patricia Garrett and Ximena Valdés both argued that Chile's Agrarian Reform offered women few benefits and few reasons to support the governments who advocated it.[5] They maintained that the Agrarian Reform's policy of redistributing land to household heads, who were invariably men, prevented women from receiving land and that widespread sexism prevented women's participation in unions. They argued that the minimal organizing of women that did take place served to reinforce women's traditional roles as homemakers and did little to connect women to wider political processes. Research such as Garrett's, which she conducted in the early 1970s, is particularly remarkable since it occurred alongside the more established Agrarian Reform scholarship focusing on men, but was the first to explain and challenge the consequences of men's primacy.[6] She observed, "Symptomatic of [the] problem [in] Chile is that the effective unit of analysis has been the male head of household. The majority of the population—the young, the old, and the female—has no analytical existence. . . . it suggests that something is fundamentally wrong with the model."[7]

Feminist accounts of Chile echo claims by other feminists about agrarian reforms' lackluster benefits for women elsewhere in the world. In their excellent comparative studies of agrarian reforms throughout Latin America, Carmen Diana Deere and Magdalena León also argued that most rural women were excluded from the benefits of agrarian reform because policies focused only on empowering households headed by men.[8] This meant that most agrarian reforms—including those of Peru, Colombia, Venezuela, the Dominican Republic, and Chile—redistributed land and technological support almost exclusively to men. The authors found exceptions only in revolutionary Cuba and Nicaragua, where the state made women's access to land an explicit policy goal and where women's existing domestic responsibilities were addressed through the provision of daycare and other services.

Yet even in the case of socialist agrarian reforms, most feminist evaluations have been pessimistic. Despite initial optimism that revolutions in Russia, China, Cuba, and Nicaragua would have liberating potential for women because all four named gender equality as a primary goal, most feminists concluded that socialist agrarian reforms eventually benefited men far more than women.[9] In cases where land was redistributed to families (the early phases of agrarian reform in the USSR and China, and in specific regions of Nicaragua and Cuba), male household heads still overwhelmingly functioned as the trustees of land.[10] After forced collectivization and the creation of state farms in the USSR and China, women entered the agricultural workforce in droves, far outnumbering male workers by the middle of the twentieth century. Yet men still held more prestigious and better paid jobs, and men comprised the leadership of unions, state-farm assemblies, and advisory bodies to government.[11] Since women's greater agricultural employment in the USSR and China resulted from state efforts to push men into the supposedly more skilled and modern sectors of industry and mining, agrarian reform here replicated gender hierarchies as macroeconomic necessity.

Feminists also challenged socialism's commitment to gender equality in the family. They pointed out that during times of economic and political stress, the USSR, China, Cuba, and Nicaragua all curtailed resources for childcare and other programs aimed at easing women's domestic burdens, while little was done to reeducate men to accept women's new roles or share domestic responsibilities.[12] Judith Stacey's early work on rural China sharpened many of these claims into an explicit argument about patriarchy that deserves special mention.[13] Stacey argued that the extension of patriarchal rights to poor men—something she dubbed "democratic patriarchy"—formed the basis of male peasant loyalty to the Chinese revolution. Stacey maintained that, although the revolution abolished some of the most extreme forms of female subordination (concubinage and footbinding), rural policies enabled peasant men to exercise authority over women in a modern version of the family. Initial radical reforms giving women greater say in marriage and divorce and abortion rights were curtailed to ensure male prerogative.[14] Mary Kay Vaughan's more recent work on Mexico has made similar claims. Echoing Susan Besse's helpful insight into the modern state's role in "modernizing patriarchy," Vaughan compellingly argues that the Mexican agrarian reform affirmed men's political and economic privilege over women while giving women new agency and validation as hygienic housewives.[15]

Feminist scholarship on agrarian reform, together with the broader focus in women's studies on gender and labor, has been crucial to transfiguring old paradigms for understanding work and production. Many feminist contributions have now been incorporated into labor studies and social histories. Feminists have insisted that state policies are not gender neutral, even when they do not specifically address men and women as distinct audiences. They have reiterated Ester Boserup's 1970 seminal claim that economic development projects impact men and women unequally.[16] Most importantly, feminists have placed gender relations within the household at the center of the discussion. They have stressed that women's exclusion from the benefits of agrarian reform derives from their ongoing responsibility for children and housework and from the way men's more privileged positions within the family translate into superior political and economic opportunities outside the home. The analytical focus on patriarchy has underscored how gender inequality results from men's power over women, not merely from differences between what men and women do. In particular, attention to such things as marriage and abortion as sites of subordination has suggested that organizations of sexuality affect who receives land or has political voice.[17]

This book builds on all of these claims, and is particularly concerned with this last issue: the connection between sexuality and how politics is gendered. Sexuality is critical to an understanding of how gender works. Most feminist labor studies have emphasized gender divisions in household labor as the cause of women's marginalization. But little has been said about why women are assigned domestic labor to begin with, why such tasks are devalued in relation to men's, and how such divisions of labor spring from men's authority over women. In other words, what creates gender difference and what structures such difference as male dominance have gone largely unexplored. Put another way, in the case of most agrarian and labor studies, too little has been said about patriarchy and what makes it tick.

Partners in Conflict understands patriarchal power to be about sexuality; particularly, but not exclusively, men's sexual authority over women. Gender—the ideological construction of male and female as different and unequal—is centrally shaped by sexuality. Sexuality refers to wider cultural meanings and practices constructed through and against ideas about the sensual body and, in mid-twentieth-century rural Chile, about heterosexual, procreative sex. Sexuality operates both as ideology and as concrete practice, the parameters of which are generated within the history of class. Sexuality manifests itself in multiple arrangements, including courtship, flirtation, marriage, commercial and informal sexual exchange, human reproduction, bodily displays, and the vast terrain of pleasure, humor, and competition over sexual agency and opportunities. Sexuality is no less social or historically created than gender, but it is distinct and it is fundamental to how gender works, from where gender acquires much of its meaning.

This concept of sexuality brings two broad traditions of feminist thinking into dialogue. It draws on radical and psychoanalytical feminism's longstanding concern with sexuality as the foundation of gender oppression and combines it with Marxist feminism's emphasis on the intersection of gender and class and on the dialectic of patriarchy and capitalism. In reaffirming the importance of sexuality to patriarchy, and in keeping patriarchy connected to the material life of class, it proposes that sexuality should have a centrality to feminist materialist analyses that they have often lacked.[18] This approach adds to the recent and revitalized discussion of patriarchy and political culture in Latin American history, but it refocuses the debate specifically on issues of labor and agrarian reform.[19] In turn, it contributes to a growing and important literature on gender and labor history, as distinct from the study of women's work alone.[20]

Between 1950 and 1973, sexuality was fundamental to the meaning of masculinity and femininity in rural Chile. Sexuality was critical to how women and men were constituted as gendered beings within the latifundia system and, later, within the Agrarian Reform. It underlay women's unequal incorporation into the labor force and political struggle. The assumed naturalness of men's sexual authority over women conditioned gendered divisions of labor and informed the consensus among political parties and rural unions across the political spectrum that female participation in labor struggles should be circumscribed by women's roles as wives and mothers. It underlay the assumption held both by Christian Democrats and Popular Unity leftists that the Agrarian Reform should primarily empower rural men. Sexuality also constituted a central matrix within which campesino men and women embraced and contested the parameters of the Agrarian Reform; they understood social disparities between male and female power in sexual ways and welcomed or resisted land reform and labor mobilization depending on the sexual risks and opportunities they associated with such change.

Patriarchy, and the way it is constructed by sexuality, does not imply women's passivity or necessary exclusion. Women were neither passive nor excluded from Chile's Agrarian Reform. Indeed, much of this book's energy is devoted to recovering just how much women's activities mattered to the Agrarian Reform and how much they benefited from it. In this sense, the book departs significantly from earlier feminist works that showcased how women were left out. This divergence stems from generational shifts in feminist thinking about patriarchy. In earlier scholarship, the term invoked a coherent system of male dominance that functioned to subordinate women throughout society. Given the need to disrupt triumphalist narratives about male progress, as well as to deflect hostility to feminist paradigms, feminists stressed the overarching pervasiveness of patriarchy.[21] More recently, and in response to debates within feminist circles about agency, diversity, and postmodernism, feminists have emphasized patriarchy's heterogeneous and contradictory nature.[22] *Partners in Conflict* does not understand patriarchy as a master grid, but as a multiplicity of arrangements derived from broad principles legitimating men's authority over women. Not automatically linked, these arrangements undergo constant negotiation and change. This more dynamic concept of patriarchy allows for an acknowledgement that, while the Agrarian Reform eroded some forms of male dominance (landowners' sense of entitlement to rural women's bodies), it strengthened others (campesino men's role as breadwinners). It also allows for a consideration of changes in degrees of male dominance and how women's actions affected those changes.

This book rephrases old questions. Earlier scholarship asked whether agrarian reforms treated women and men equally and whether socialism liberated women. Both are important questions, both were largely answered, no. This book asks whether agrarian reform, including a socialist version of it, made patriarchy easier for women to live within and negotiate. It answers that, in many aspects, yes, it did. Patriarchy remained, but the ways it had changed mattered, and they mattered to women.

Partners in Conflict privileges gender and sexuality within a broader narrative about national politics and class conflict. It is a political history and a labor history that is also always about sexuality and gender. It does not merely add women to a story where they were missing.[23] It argues that gender and sexuality involve men and that they constitute key dynamics in implementing and contesting political projects. As a state-led initiative, Chile's Agrarian Reform involved attempts by two governments to refashion gender relations and place them at the service of two distinct models of national development. Yet as numerous scholars, drawing on Gramsci's notion of hegemony, have now noted, states are not closed, coherent apparatuses executing "behavioral revolutions from above."[24] The Chilean state, in both its Christian Democratic and socialist form, was internally divided, and embodied a site of struggle over competing political visions. It attempted to achieve and maintain its various agendas through a multileveled process of refashioning and accommodating existing attitudes and practices about modernity and gender. Not just government agencies effectuated the Agrarian Reform's disciplinary and socializing mission; it also relied on labor unions, oppositional political parties, and the Catholic Church, all of which overlapped or competed with state goals to varying degrees. No less important was the consent and resistance of individual campesino men and women to reformist efforts. While some aspects of the Agrarian Reform's gendered mission were welcomed wholesale, others were only embraced in part or flatly rejected. Men and women, or specific groups of men and women, often took distinct sides.

This book begins in the 1950s with the Chilean latifundia system of great estates and spans the development of the Agrarian Reform throughout the 1960s until its abrupt end with Allende's overthrow in 1973. The first two chapters examine the significance of gender and sexuality in the 1950s and early 1960s to creating divisions of labor within Chile's *inquilino* system of semipeonage and their importance to shoring up landowners' authority over workers and campesino men's authority over women. Chapters 3 through 5 address the Agrarian Reform under the Christian Democrats between 1964 and 1970. Chapter 3 explores the growth of the rural labor movement and the efforts of center and left activists and government functionaries to promote notions of male solidarity, class militancy, and patriarchal responsibility. Chapter 4 examines state-led efforts to appeal to women through a validation of domesticity and a call for gender cooperation in the family. It looks at three programs: Agrarian Reform education projects, all-female organizations called mothers' centers, and Chile's first family planning and birth control programs. Chapter 5 discusses how land expropriations and the creation of state-managed farms produced new divisions within campesino communities, heightening the masculine privilege of some men over others and emphasizing male stewardship of wives and children.

The final two chapters deal with the acceleration of land expropriations and heightened political tensions during the Popular Unity government between 1970 and 1973. Chapter 6 examines the UP's efforts to mobilize rural women by simultaneously continuing the Christian Democratic model of domestic uplift and advocating an expanded economic and political role for women as workers. Chapter 7 explores rural men's and women's very different relationships to the consequences of intensified class conflict. In particular, it discusses how women's inferior incorporation into the Agrarian Reform's most important institutions translated into increased domestic conflicts over sex: the alleged promiscuity of adolescent girls and the supposed infidelity of married men. The epilogue explores the relevance of Chile's Agrarian Reform for understanding the legacy of military dictatorship that followed Allende's overthrow.

This book focuses its story on the Aconcagua Valley, one of Chile's oldest and most productive agricultural centers. Located one hundred kilometers north of Santiago in the province of Aconcagua, the Aconcagua Valley consists of nine counties organized into the two administrative departments of San Felipe and Los Andes.[25] The Aconcagua Valley was one of the first areas where land was expropriated and an early center for labor organizing. Conflicts over land in this area were relatively shorter and less violent than in the Santiago metropolitan area, where urban tensions bled into rural ones, or in the south, where estates were larger and indigenous communities had more immediate claims to land. But although the Agrarian Reform unfolded in regionally specific ways, events in the Aconcagua Valley are broadly representative of dynamics within the Agrarian Reform as a whole. The Agrarian Reform was a national program and, as a social process, it was implemented in ways that frequently shared more than they differed. The inner circles of government and political parties crafted Agrarian Reform policies and rural labor strategies in a highly centralized manner. Although a diverse range of communities embraced and contested them, the pervasiveness of latifundia conditions throughout much of Chile and the national reach of Chile's political parties in rural areas meant that campesinos everywhere struggled within similar structural and ideological parameters.

This book draws on a range of sources cobbled together from what, at the time, proved a difficult and elusive historical record. Most research was carried out between 1991 and 1993, the years immediately following the end of military rule. Due to the Chilean government's lack of resources for maintaining archives and, in particular, the military regime's attempt to control information about the 1964–1973 period, no formal government archive for events after 1960 existed, nor did any formal archives for the labor movement, political parties, or women's organizations.[26] This situation has since changed with the opening of a twentieth-century archive, but in the early 1990s, it was still necessary to visit individual ministries where, although many documents were found, others had been systematically neglected, lost, placed off-limits to researchers, or destroyed. Some ministerial records were technically open to the public, but were warehoused, un-indexed, and in conditions that made their use formidably time-consuming for this study.[27] Whatever the case, some of the more traditional records used for labor and social history were not available or utilized for this study.

But other sources filled in the gaps. The extensive archive of the Agrarian Reform's main government agency, the Corporation for Agrarian Reform (CORA) was invaluable.[28] The Ministry of Health provided records on maternal and infant health, abortion, and birth control; the Ministries of Housing and Agriculture were similarly helpful for information on campesino education and women's groups.[29] Research at the National Institute of Statistics yielded a wealth of economic and demographic information. The Catholic Church and affiliated agencies had the most extensive collection on the labor movement and rural education.[30] Nonprofit research centers and university libraries also had assorted documents on these topics as well as on women.[31] Newspapers and magazines published by the rural labor movement and various political tendencies were one of the most immediate sources on activism in the countryside.[32] Judicial records on domestic violence and municipal registries on marriage and baptism were important to researching gender dynamics in the family.[33]

Lastly, *Partners in Conflict* heavily draws from oral sources, including eighty interviews and oral histories, most of which were conducted with campesino men and women from the Aconcagua Valley, and a few of which with Santiago-based activists and professionals. For reasons of privacy the names of most informants have been altered throughout this text.[34] The oral sources were critical in several ways. Given the difficulty with other sources, they helped establish a basic narrative of events. They also facilitated a certain recovery of rural people's experience not available elsewhere. In the 1960s the majority of Chilean campesinos were illiterate, leaving few written traces of their voices. Middle-class professionals and urban activists authored most records of rural life, including the labor press. This book's focus on gender and sexuality made the issue of recovery still harder. Not only did campesinos not write about their intimate lives, but Agrarian Reform functionaries and political activists—who wrote voluminously—had little to say about the subject. Oral history provided a way to interject questions and elicit responses on themes ignored or suppressed by official records.

This does not mean that oral sources necessarily make for "truer" or more "direct" renditions of events. Like all sources, oral histories are subjective and give only partial windows into the past, not empirical fact. As memories, they are not static recollections, but interpretations filtered through the present and recent past. The oral histories and interviews used in this book were conducted over twenty years after the events they recall and in the aftermath of seventeen years of military rule that aggressively worked to render illegitimate those events. What people were willing to say and how they said it were necessarily qualified by many factors, including fear of retaliation, the military's success at redefining the terms of historical debate, and the interviewer's own position as a North American female professional outsider. Many times oral responses said as much about people's present struggles as they did about the past. At the time the interviews were conducted, much of the Aconcagua Valley's rural poor had lost access to land and relied on temporary wage labor in the highly exploitative fruit export industry developed during the dictatorship. Although civilian rule had just been restored, most of the democratic institutions and cultural radicalism that existed prior to the 1973 coup lay in ruins. The informants' need to reconcile the extreme differences between the 1960s and the 1990s structured their narratives.

Debates about the many ways to use oral sources are rich. As Daniel James and others have shown, oral histories arguably say as much about informants' present-day circumstances, the creation of memory, and interview dynamics as they do about "what happened in the past."[35] But this book assumes that oral histories also tell us about events and attitudes that existed before. Such information is mediated by present circumstances and deciding just what it means is a subjective task, like most tasks of the historian, one of interpretation. In this book, the meaning of oral histories is considered by drawing on techniques of narrative interpretation and by using oral sources to read against the grain of written ones.[36] Often the way people struggled to reconcile inconsistencies in their stories and their silences about particular events were revealing about past conflicts. When compared with government documents, newspapers, and judicial records, oral histories served as counterpoints of clarification, suggesting alternative meanings.

Most significantly, oral histories were revealing in the stark contrast they often painted between the memories of women and the memories of men. Both women and men recalled the Agrarian Reform as a time of heady promise and sometimes painful struggle, but rural men tended to give the Agrarian Reform a far more positive overall assessment than did women. Both men and women recalled the 1960s and early 1970s as a time of vastly improved livelihoods, but men more frequently attributed such material gains to their own political accomplishments. Both men and women equated the Agrarian Reform with campesino empowerment, but women proved far more ambivalent about the costs and consequences of such agency. Explaining these differences lies at the heart of this story.

chapter 1 *Patrón* and *Peón*

Labor and Authority on the Great Estates

In the 1950s, the Aconcagua Valley was one of Chile's most beautiful, wealthy, and productive agricultural areas. Surrounded by the protective and majestic heights of the Andes and bathed by the waters and tributaries of the Aconcagua River, the Aconcagua Valley's 36,600 hectares of cultivated land produced almost 10 percent of Chile's annual agricultural output and boasted a diverse production of wheat, alfalfa, hemp, vegetables, and flowers, as well as some of the country's oldest and fastest growing fruit orchards and vineyards.[1] Such range was rare and fostered by Aconcagua's proximity to the Valparaíso port and its unique temperate climate that allowed multiple growing seasons.[2] Its estates were owned by some of Chile's most prominent families, while its proximity to Santiago and famed natural splendor made it a favorite weekend and summer retreat for the urban elite. Mineral springs in Santa María, renowned wineries in Panquehue, and the luxurious town plazas of San Felipe and Los Andes provided monied travelers with ample comfort and bucolic views of seemingly lush prosperity.

The Aconcagua Valley was also a place of acute inequality and human need. Seventy percent of its 101,763 people resided in rural areas where some one hundred large estates relied on the labor of thousands of impoverished subsistence farmers and landless workers.[3] Spacious colonial houses with patio gardens, servant staff, and imported furniture rose above crumbling adobe peasant huts with no electricity or running water.[4] The Aconcagua Valley's richest landowners reaped per capita in-

Aconcagua Valley.
Below: Santa María county,
Aconcagua Valley. Both
photos courtesy of the
author.

comes over a thousand times that of their laborers, sent their children to be educated in Santiago and abroad, and enjoyed intimate political and familial ties to Chile's financial and industrial elite.[5] Campesinos struggled for the meanest survival. They entered work in early childhood, had an average life expectancy of forty-five, and suffered some of the nation's highest rates of illiteracy, malnutrition, and infant mortality.

As with inequalities throughout rural Chile, disparities in Aconcagua flowed from land monopolies and an oppressive labor system. Although less exacerbated than elsewhere in the country, land in the Aconcagua Valley was solidly concentrated in the hands of a few.[6] In 1955, less than 9 percent of property owners controlled 82 percent of irrigated land, and 3 percent of farm units accounted for 95 percent of all agricultural land.[7] Huge estates—those over two thousand hectares—alone accounted for 60 percent of irrigated land. In contrast, some 900 campesino families owned tiny farms, or minifundia, under five hectares. Another four hundred less impoverished, but still poor, families were small producers with farms between five and twenty hectares. Together, the minifundia and small producer sectors accounted for over 80 percent of all property owners, only 8.3 percent of agricultural land (see Tables 1 and 2).[8]

Reinforcing inequalities in land and wealth was the *inquilinaje* labor arrangement that tied campesinos in semipeonage to estates in return for rights to land. The inquilinaje system dated from Spanish colonial times when royal grants of land and labor consolidated wealth and political power, creating powerful landowners with entitlements to the labor of Indians, mestizos, free blacks, and poor whites who worked in exchange for subsistence rights.[9] Although inquilinaje had changed considerably by the 1950s, it remained foundational to agricultural labor relations throughout Chile. Under this system, the campesino, or inquilino, exchanged labor on an estate for a combination of benefits called *regalías* (from the word *gift*), including access to small plots of land, pasture rights, food, housing, and fuel.[10] Since the eighteenth century, inquilinos had also received small cash payments, but in the 1950s regalías and in-kind goods still comprised 70 percent of an inquilino's compensation.[11] Traditionally, inquilinos resided on the estate, dedicating part of their labor to estate production and part of their labor to their land regalía, which could be farmed for petty commercial as well as subsistence

Table 1 Land Tenure in the Aconcagua Valley, 1955

Farm Size (in hectares)	Percent of Total Farms
Less than 5	56
5–19	26
20–99	10
100–499	5
500–1,999	1
Over 2,000	2

Censo agropecuario: Aconcagua, 1954–1955.

Table 2 Distribution of Agricultural Land by Farm Unit Size, Aconcagua Valley, 1955

Farm Size (in hectares)	Percent of Total Agricultural Land	Percent of Total Irrigated Land
Less than 5	0.4	2.9
5–19	0.8	5.4
20–99	1.5	9.4
100–499	2.3	15.0
500–1,999	3.8	9.8
Over 2,000	91.0	57.5

Censo agropecuario: Aconcagua, 1954–1955.

purposes. Depending on a regalía's size, which in the 1950s ranged from a quarter to ten hectares, inquilinos were required to give a portion of their produce to the landowner.[12] Inquilinos could opt to devote all of their own labor to the regalía instead of to the estate by providing a replacement worker in their stead. However, during harvest and planting seasons, inquilinos were obligated to work on the estate. During these times, they were also required to provide an additional laborer, called an *obligado* (obligated one), whose compensation inquilinos paid themselves. This practice dated from the nineteenth century, when a boom in Chilean wheat exports to California and Australia encouraged landowners to bring more land under cultivation and more firmly wedded inquilinaje to commercial production.[13]

By the mid-twentieth century, inquilinaje reflected a growing crisis in Chilean agriculture as well as government efforts to exercise an expanded regulatory role in the countryside. Beginning in the 1920s and 1930s, attempts to encourage industrialization and assure cheap food for urban workers resulted in government price supports and subsidies for agricultural growers as well as state complicity with landowners in depressing rural wages.[14] Throughout the 1940s and 1950s, the state continued this policy in an unsuccessful move to halt the decline in Chile's agricultural productivity and to reverse a growing balance of trade deficit in agricultural imports that would total 120 million dollars by 1964.[15] Although government assistance to landowners was commonplace throughout most of Chile's history and indicative of the seamless connections between landowning and political power, agrarian policy between the mid-1920s and the 1950s was crafted with an eye toward managing national economic development as a whole and, in particular, toward satisfying the needs of the expanding urban middle and working classes.

Such populist impulse gave rise to the first national labor legislation, including the 1931 Labor Code, which formally defined different categories of agricultural workers and specified their obligations and entitlements. Later legislation in 1948 and 1953 established standards for determining the value of in-kind payments of housing and land, mandated that at least 25 percent of an inquilino's compensation be paid in cash, and entitled agricultural workers to the "family allowance" (*asignación familiar*), a subsidy for children and dependents.[16] Although such laws were unevenly enforced at best, they encouraged landowners to reduce the number of inquilinos on their estates in favor of workers who earned most of their compensation in cash. The mechanization of dairy and grain production after the 1930s further reduced the need for inquilinos by making more forms of work seasonal.

By the early 1960s, inquilinos comprised only a quarter of the paid labor force in the Aconcagua Valley and other parts of central Chile. The majority of estate laborers worked for cash wages, supplemented by in-

Table 3 Paid Agricultural Labor Force by Job Type, Aconcagua Valley, 1964

Total	Inquilino	Permanent	Temporary	Occasional
7,458	1,817	1,212	1,433	2,996
100%	24.3%	16.2%	19.2%	40.1%

Cuadro 6.3, *Censo agropecuario: Aconcagua, 1964–1965.*

kind payments of food, fuel, and sometimes housing, but without rights to land. Out of the Aconcagua Valley's total paid agricultural labor force of 7,458 workers, 24.3 percent were inquilinos, 16.2 percent permanent workers, and 59.3 percent seasonal workers.[17] Of seasonal workers, some worked more than others.[18] Roughly a third were officially classified as "temporary workers" who received a daily wage and labored for between three and six months annually; the remaining two-thirds were "occasional workers" who labored less than three months annually and were paid piecerates for labor-intensive jobs processing fruit, flowers, hemp, garlic, and tobacco. By the mid-1960s, laborers working less than three months a year accounted for almost 40 percent of the Aconcagua Valley's entire paid agricultural labor force (see Table 3).[19]

But if inquilinos did not constitute the numeric majority, the inquilino labor arrangement shaped all labor arrangements on the estate. Inquilinos comprised the core, stable workforce of estates over two hundred hectares, and the contracts of permanent and seasonal laborers evolved as complementary to, rather than competitive with, those of inquilinos. Inquilinaje constituted a coherent labor system that was heterogeneous in form, involving both noncapitalist and capitalist arrangements, both inquilinos and wageworkers.[20] Neither permanent nor seasonal laborers depended on cash wages alone since both received over 20 percent of their compensation in-kind.[21] This practice followed from the inquilino arrangement, which, compounded by the fact that inquilinos received *most* of their compensation in-kind, functioned to depress all agricultural wages. In 1962, the average per capita cash income of campesino families in central Chile was less than fifteen dollars per month.[22]

Permanent and seasonal workers also made up an integral part of the inquilinaje system in that significant numbers of these laborers (as high as one-third in Aconcagua) were the children, spouses, and extended family members of inquilinos on the estates.[23] Others were from households in the minifundia and small producer sectors, which could not absorb all family labor, and which were part of, rather than separate from, latifundia arrangements as a whole. Similarly, as much as half of all occasional laborers were migrants, called *afuerinos* (from the Spanish word *outside*), consisting almost exclusively of men who constantly moved from province to province. The heterogeneous nature of inquilinaje was key to guaranteeing landowners a flexible and cheap labor force. The arrangement of drawing most laborers from subsistence farmers inside or at the edges of the estates allowed landowners to hire or discharge workers on a seasonal basis and to undercompensate them, since it was assumed that substantial parts of their needs would be provided by subsistence agriculture. This latter assumption had a particularly adverse impact on permanent and seasonal workers compensated primarily in cash. A survey of Aconcagua by the National Statistics Institute found that 51 percent of campesino households relying on wage labor earned less than the minimum subsistence salary (*sueldo vital,* calculated as the cost of survival, as opposed to the higher minimum wage), while another 32 percent received only slightly more.[24] This made in-kind payments of food and fuel all the more important. For workers with no access to subsistence cultivation, it made life especially hard. These completely landless campesinos resided in some of the poorest neighborhoods around nearby towns or in shanty settlements on the outskirts of the estates.

Gender, Family, and Division of Labor

Inquilinaje relied heavily on gender hierarchies within campesino families. By the late 1950s, Chile's paid agricultural labor force was overwhelmingly male, and almost all inquilinos were men. According to the census, women comprised only 9 percent of paid agricultural workers in the Aconcagua Valley, only 4 percent of all permanent workers, and less than 1 percent of inquilinos.[25] Of the 664 women who did earn wages for agricultural labor, more than 80 percent were seasonal workers employed less than six months a year, and over half of these worked less than three months.[26] Such paltry employment reflected a dramatic shift from the recent past. As Patricia Garrett and Ximena Valdés have shown, in the late nineteenth and early twentieth centuries, women comprised almost 20 percent of all inquilinos, working primarily as milkmaids, but their numbers plummeted following the mechanization of dairy in the mid-1930s.[27] Indeed, women's loss of work as inquilinas accounts for almost the entire decline in inquilino positions between the 1930s and the 1960s. Whereas the number of inquilinas dropped by 84 percent during this period, the number of male inquilinos declined only by 3 percent.[28] By 1964, a full 99 percent of Chile's 46,961 inquilinos were male.[29] In the Aconcagua Valley, men made up more than 96 percent of inquilinos and permanent workers combined, and more than 87 percent of all seasonal workers (see Tables 4 and 5).[30]

Male inquilinos were usually heads of household, and they depended heavily on the labor of family members. The replacement and obligado workers supplied by an inquilino as mandatory substitutes or supplements to the estate were usually drawn from the ranks of the inquilino's male children and relatives. If such workers received compensation at all, they were paid with food and housing, not cash. The inquilino's family members also carried out subsistence farming on the regalía, and the inquilino's wife usually supervised them during his absence. Regalías grew beans, potatoes, and other vegetables for family consumption, as well as commercial crops such as tobacco. All such cultivation was highly labor intensive, absorbing even the energies of very young children. Adult women, assisted by children, additionally took responsibility for raising the family's chickens, pigs, and goats, and for transforming animals and animal products into cheeses, butter, and *empanadas* (meat pies) for family meals or for sale in nearby towns.

Male permanent and seasonal workers also depended on the labor of female family members, including wives and daughters, mothers, aunts, and sisters. When husbands and other adult men sought work on the estates, women took charge of planting and cultivation. When men were around, women worked by their sides in more gender-specific tasks. Men plowed while women planted beans and potato buds. Women pulled and bound tobacco leaves while men hung the bunches in curing shacks and carted them to town. As in the case of inquilino families, women minifundistas and small producers took primary responsibility for farm animals and the marketing of eggs and milk products.[31] But gender divisions of labor were never rigid, and women frequently performed tradition-

Table 4 Paid Agricultural Labor Force by Gender and Job Type, Aconcagua Valley, 1964

| Inquilino/a | | Permanent | | Temporary | | Occasional | |
male	female	male	Female	male	female	Male	Female
1,816	1	1,100	112	1,268	165	2,610	386
99%	–	91%	9%	88%	12%	87%	13%

Cuadro 6.3, *Censo agropecuario: Aconcagua, 1964–1965.*

Table 5 Percent of Female and Male Paid Agricultural Workers by Job Type, Aconcagua Valley, 1964

| Total Workers | | Inquilino/Permanent | | Temporary/Occasional | |
male	female	male	female	male	female
91.1%	8.9%	96.3%	3.7%	87.6%	12.4%

Cuadro 6.3, *Censo agropecuario: Aconcagua, 1964–1965.*

ally male tasks such as digging irrigation canals and building fences. If a wife fell sick, her husband milked the goats.

Women's unpaid agricultural work was crucial to the maintenance of the inquilinaje labor system as a whole. The flexibility of women's labor allowed male family members to be seasonally available to the estates, providing a place for them to return to during periods of unemployment. Women's meat and dairy products provided a significant part of the family diet as well as supplemental cash income. Campesina women were exclusively responsible for preparing the family's food, delivering meals to male family members working on the estates, sewing and laundering the family's clothes, hauling water, cleaning, and raising children. As Florencia Mallon and Carmen Diana Deere have each argued in different Peruvian contexts, campesina household labor was vital both to campesino survival and capitalist profitability.[32] Campesina women's labor not only reproduced the agricultural labor force, it generated productive value. It produced goods and services for family members that did not have to be purchased, allowing landowners to pay less than the full cost of getting an able-bodied worker into the field.

Women's household labors were arduous and could consume between twelve and fourteen hours daily.[33] Such work began as early as 4:00 A.M. when a woman rose to rekindle the wood or charcoal fire and warm bread and *máte* (a strong tea) for her husband's breakfast. Thereafter she roused and fed her children, swept the dirt floors of the house's one or two rooms and outside patio, tossed leftover food and vegetable skins to pigs and chickens, gathered eggs, and squatted to milk any goats and sheep the family might possess. She spent two or three hours kneading dough for the day's bread and cooking the midday meal so that, if her husband was working for the patrón, it would be ready to place in a bucket and deliver to the estate after noon. Clothes were washed on a daily basis—a process that involved up to four hours of hauling and boiling water for the laundry tubs in the back of the house, double or triple washing and individually scrubbing specific items, rinsing, wringing, hanging, and, later, ironing. After the midday dinner was served and cleared, early afternoons were spent making cheeses and empanadas, while the cooler hours of the late afternoon found her in the family garden or regalía—weeding, irrigating, and pulling onions and potatoes. Afterwards, she hauled more water from irrigation ditches or wells and, if necessary, replenished stocks of firewood. Around 7:00 P.M. a light supper of leftovers from the midday meal or bread, cheese, and tea was prepared, after which a woman might hand-sew a pair of pants from a flour sack for her adolescent son or finish knitting a tunic for her husband. In between and during all of these tasks, women nursed infants, watched over toddlers and small children, supervised the labor of older children who could work, and cared for invalid family members who could not. Children, especially daughters, shared or sometimes fully assumed their mothers' responsibilities for certain tasks. But adult women held primary responsibility for housework. Even if they leaned heavily on the labors of children, they still had the longest workday of anyone in the family.

Women also provided labor directly on the estates. Although their significance as inquilinas had evaporated, their employment as paid seasonal workers expanded by almost 30 percent between 1935 and 1955.[34] This increase reflected the growing commercial cultivation of labor-intensive

fruit and vegetable crops. In the Aconcagua Valley, women were employed on estates for an average of two to four months a year, picking beans and tomatoes, sewing and curing tobacco leaves, bagging garlic and onions, sorting dried raisins, and harvesting grapes and peaches.
Such tasks were closely supervised. Women worked in teams and under
the direction of a male administrator or other employee who monitored
the pace of women's work and who took responsibility for ensuring the
quality of produce.

Men's estate work was far more varied and less task-specific than
women's. Men worked in mixed teams of inquilinos, permanent
workers, and seasonal laborers and could be directed to do any of numerous different tasks within a given month, week, or day. Men were
also employed as seasonal laborers in fruit and vegetable cultivation and
at times worked side by side with women. But men's seasonal tasks differed from women's, involving what were considered the heavier and
less detail-specific responsibilities such as pruning fruit trees, pulling tobacco, hauling bags and crates filled with produce, and plowing under
dead plants and shrubs. Male seasonal workers were also employed for
longer periods of time than their female counterparts. Prior to and after
the fruit and vegetable harvest, they were shifted to other parts of the
estate where they joined male permanent and inquilino workers in the
cultivation of wheat and hemp and the care of livestock.

Cultivating and harvesting grain and hemp and raising livestock were
exclusively male affairs and absorbed the majority of male labor throughout the year. Men also had sole responsibility for digging, cleaning, and
managing the estate's irrigation canals, repairing and erecting fences,
and constructing and maintaining estate buildings. Although both men's
and women's work was supervised—either directly by the landowner or,
more often, by an employed administrator—men were less closely regu-
lated than women. When a group of male workers was sent out to dig
a ditch or plant a particular field, they were often left to complete the
task with no more than an occasional progress check by the landowner
or administrator making rounds.[35]

The gender division of labor on estates and women's inferior positions
within the paid agricultural workforce had social and ideological foundations, rather than resulting from any natural production requirements
or real differences between men's and women's work abilities. Despite

the fact that some aspects of men's estate work demanded considerable strength (such as hauling grain bags and digging ditches), it was the *idea* that women were unsuited for such labor that precluded women's employment in more permanent and better paid tasks. On the small plots and family farms of the minifundia and small producer sector, women frequently joined male family members in, or had primary responsibility for, tasks labeled "men's work" and "heavy tasks" on the estates. In this unpaid agricultural sector, women, not men, were in charge of livestock, and women frequently dug irrigation canals, repaired fences, and pruned grapevines.

Divisions of labor flowed from assumptions about gender authority and responsibility within the campesino household. "Household" included the human relationships of family kin as well as the material relationships of subsistence and petty commercial farming, the life within the four walls of campesino homes and the life on the land families cultivated. As a system, inquilinaje assumed an abundance of family labor in which married men headed families and directed wives' and children's labor. Both landowners and campesinos themselves assumed that an adult married woman was her husband's dependent and subordinated to his authority. Although both campesino men and women viewed marriage as a partnership in the struggle for survival, the ethos of collaboration usually reinforced, rather than challenged, male prerogative. A wife's work responsibilities were defined in terms of direct labor and service to her husband, children, and extended family members. This entailed raising children and caring for elderly parents as well as household maintenance and production, work that itself included both domestic housework and farmwork in family gardens and subsistence plots. Work beyond the household realm of family land and house was considered supplemental to a wife's primary responsibility for husband and children, even if such work was also recognized as vital to family survival.[36]

By the late 1950s, rural households in Aconcagua contained an average of six persons.[37] Although campesina women bore an average of eight children, many infants died within their first year, and adolescent and young adult offspring frequently left the parental home for considerable periods to seek work.[38] Almost half of rural households were nuclear families, while the rest included grandparents, unmarried siblings, cousins, in-laws, and nonkin such as afuerinos who boarded or worked for the family as obligados.[39] The relation between nuclear and extended family forms was fluid, shifting with the changing needs of the household's members. Recently married couples often lived for a few years with one of their parents, usually the young man's, until they could set up their own home. In the event that a marriage ended because of separation, abandonment, or death, adult children might return to live with their parents or be taken in by married siblings.

Marriage was of vital importance to campesina women and most were wives at some point in their lives. By 1960, a full 73 percent of women in rural Aconcagua between the ages of twenty-five and sixty were married, while another 4 percent cohabitated with men in common-law marriages.[40] Seven percent were widowed or separated; only 15 percent were single.[41] For most campesinas, survival required marriage to a wage-earning man and/or to a man with access to land. Agricultural work on estates was usually too short-term and badly paid to allow a woman to support herself. Although some women held land titles in the minifundia and small producer sector, men more often held land, and all inquilino land regalías were entrusted to men.[42] Rural women worked as domestic servants, laundresses, and vendors in proportions more than double that of their employment on estates, but they still comprised only 8 percent of the paid rural labor force.[43] In a study of campesina households in the 1960s, over 70 percent of women reported that they had never held formal employment at any time during their life.[44] Most rural women who did not eventually marry migrated to towns or cities, accounting for the fact that, by 1960, men significantly outnumbered women throughout the Chilean countryside. In Aconcagua, men comprised 54 percent of the rural population, in contrast to women's 46 percent.[45]

The minority of unmarried women who stayed in the countryside, or who later lost their husbands to death or separation, led an extremely precarious life. The widows of inquilinos were sometimes ejected from estates, while widows of minifundistas could lose land access to male relatives.[46] Poorly paid and scarce, domestic service and seasonal agricultural work became unmarried women's primary employment options. Other single women might survive by taking in outside laundry or boarders and by combining such income with the wages of older children. The majority subsisted as members of extended families in the households of kin. By 1960, women headed only 2 percent of Aconcagua households listed in the census as dependent on agricultural labor.[47] Although rural women headed 8 percent of all rural households, the majority did so by means other than agricultural labor, usually domestic service.[48] Whatever solution single women cobbled together, it was invariably more materially impoverished and vulnerable than that of women with husbands.

Marriage was also important to men, but men could, and did, survive more easily without it. An inquilino or permanent worker who lost his wife did not lose access to land or employment. For men without access to land, having a family could mean a hardship, since it entailed supporting dependents not engaged in subsistence production. As a result, men usually delayed marriage well into their late twenties and early thirties. In 1960, almost 70 percent of men in rural Aconcagua under age thirty were unmarried.[49] Seasonal workers, especially afuerino migrants, were particularly hard-pressed to support families because of inadequate employment and the need to move from region to region. These laborers' tendency to remain single probably accounts for the almost one third of men between the ages of twenty-five and sixty who never married.[50] As did single women, single men usually resided in extended campesino families. But almost always men, usually married, headed these extended families. In rarer cases, single men assumed the role of household head in their capacity as uncle, cousin, or in-law. That campesino family arrangements were diverse did not make marriage and married men's authority any less central to campesino gender arrangements as a whole.

As was true for wives, husbands worked for the greater good of their families. For small farmers and inquilinos with sizeable land regalías, the family plot was usually seen as the preferred place of work while wage labor assumed secondary importance. But married men's relationship to household-based work differed significantly from that of married women. Although subsistence farming was considered a family effort, a clear hierarchy gave men, not women, ultimate managerial authority. Husbands could command the labor of wives, rather than the other way around. Husbands, not wives, made decisions about when they and their male children would seek paid work on estates and when they would farm their family plots, as well as when and whether wives and female children would work for wages beyond the household.[51] Similar to what

Christine Delphy has argued about French peasants, campesino house-holds were, regardless of their impoverishment, economic arrangements in which men extracted labor from women, children, and other relatives, male and female.[52]

Patriarchal marriage principles governed the logic of men's authority over women even in households with single heads. Where uncles or brothers served as household heads, men's expectations that nieces and sisters would haul water and prepare meals were based on ideas about what women naturally did in their capacity as wives. This even held true in relationships between fathers and daughters. Fathers expected daughters to wash clothes and prepare meals not simply, or even primarily, because of their parental rights to make claims on children but, more fundamentally, because daughters were females whose natural responsibilities to men were defined by marriage. To a more limited extent, women heads of household also enjoyed a measure of patriarchal authority in their ability to direct the labor of working children, adult female dependents, and elderly or invalid men. But a crucial difference was that female household heads never had wives.[53]

Campesino men's authority over women sprang from an intricate web of institutional and cultural factors that privileged husbands over wives in Chilean society generally. Various legal codes enshrined a husband's control over his wife's material goods and physical person. The Labor Code required a woman to have her husband's permission to work in paid employment.[54] The Marriage Code stipulated that matrimony involved a woman's agreement to obey her husband and to live with him in order to procreate and assist.[55] A married woman was legally represented by her husband and prohibited from selling commonly held property, even if she had bought it with her own earnings.[56] She could not acquire debt or credit, nor could she leave the country without her husband's permission. The Criminal Code made it a petty crime for a married woman to have sex outside of marriage, but it did not similarly criminalize like actions of men. Such laws reflected the broader society's cultural assumptions about gender rights and established legitimate boundaries of male behavior toward women. If the specific details of these codes were not readily available to most campesino men, their logic was nonetheless absorbed through the osmosis of legal ideology into "natural" facts of life.

Catholic influences worked in a similar way. In the mid-twentieth

Inquilino couple
and their home.
UP pamphlet series,
NOSOTROS LOS
CHILENOS, courtesy of
the University of
Wisconsin Land Tenure
Center.

century, Catholic doctrine held that the fundamental purpose of marriage was procreation and that a wife's primary duty was to bear children
and support and obey her husband. A husband's, on the other hand, consisted of heading, protecting, and providing for the family. Most campesinos in Aconcagua did not have consistent exposure to formal catechism, but they still received regular exposure to Catholic sensibilities.[57]
They only infrequently attended church services. Priests were chronically lacking and, because most clergy were hired with the blessings of
local landowners, many campesinos saw church services, and especially
the sacrament of confession, as instruments of social control. But popular rituals that took place outside church walls, particularly processions
for local saints and the festivals of Christmas, Easter, Lent, and Pentecost, relayed Catholic gender ideals nonetheless. Despite their skepticism
of priests, campesinos did highly value Catholic marriage and baptism,
rituals that required at least an occasional venture to mass.[58]

Landowners and urban-based educators also promoted Catholic attitudes toward marriage. Both landowners and Catholic social reformers encouraged religious evangelism and rural marriage throughout the 1940s and 1950s as a means of ameliorating class conflict and establishing social peace.[59] Both were concerned with the rise of leftist labor organizing among campesinos since the 1930s. Under the institutional umbrellas of the lay organizations Catholic Action and the Rural Education Institute (IER), middle-class Catholics ventured into the countryside to ease rural poverty through basic education and vocational instruction, which they combined with catechism. They advocated marriage and conjugal reciprocity as the basis of social improvement. Despite the fact that many of these reformers also advocated campesino labor unions, many landowners applauded Catholic efforts as a way to inoculate campesinos against radicalism and stabilize the labor force. Landowners built and repaired chapels and schoolrooms on estate property, sponsoring religious missions and, occasionally, a teacher's salary.[60] According to oral histories, campesinos were encouraged and sometimes coerced to establish formal marriages in order to keep their jobs.[61] Under the logic that workers with families were more loyal and manageable, employers gave preference to married men with children, especially in the position of inquilino.

Inquilinaje in the 1950s assumed the existence of campesino patriarchy, including women's dependence on men and primary responsibilities for children and housework. Short-term jobs in fruit and vegetable production were seen as appropriate for women because they conflicted less with women's household responsibilities.[62] This hierarchy complemented landowners' needs for temporary labor during seasonal intervals. Women who resided in the local area were seen as a more reliable source of seasonal labor than male migrant afuerinos. Because they were women—presumably wives and female dependents—they could justifiably receive less pay. Meanings attributed to male and female bodies further naturalized these gender divisions. The seasonal fruit and vegetable work of women was coded as less demanding than men's full-time, presumably more physically taxing, labor, such as plowing and hauling. Binding tobacco leaves and braiding garlic required the same attention to detail that enabled women's expertise in sewing and cooking; digging ditches and erecting fences demanded the brawn and endurance embodied by farm animals and poor men.

Inquilino family.
UP pamphlet series,
NOSOTROS LOS
CHILENOS, courtesy of
the University of
Wisconsin Land Tenure
Center.

Gender divisions of labor in the unpaid minifundia and small producer sectors seemingly challenged these understandings since, there,
men sewed tobacco leaves, women occasionally plowed, and both men
and women's work had an ongoing permanence. But ultimately they
did not. Women's unpaid tasks in the family plot (bean picking or digging ditches) and work in the family house (preparing dinner) were seen
as seamlessly and constantly combined. In contrast, women's paid seasonal work (sorting raisins for an employer) was seen as a temporary

infringement on women's family responsibilities (preparing dinner and bean picking), while the prospect of women being paid to dig ditches was nonexistent. The reality that campesino houses were usually physically located on, or close to, regalías and gardens, making it easier for women to combine farm work and housework, enabled such distinctions. But more fundamentally, the difference arose from the fact that women's work on family subsistence plots was understood as labor performed for husbands and families, whereas work on estates served an employer. Despite the fact that women's estate labor was inferior to men's in pay and length of employment, it potentially raised questions about campesino men's authority over women in ways women's subsistence agriculture did not. The coexistence and intimate connection between paid and unpaid agricultural sectors intensified the valuation of men's labor over that of women's. Paid compensation on estates (either in cash or in-kind) compelled a distinction between different types of work and forced decisions about who should receive wages for which types of labor. The translation of family gender arrangements into work organizations, which mobilized assumptions about men's primary economic responsibilities and women's obligations to the household, not only justified men's higher pay and more steady work, it also associated both paid work and estate work with men.[63] Given the social and political, if not always economic importance of large estates to Chilean agriculture, labor at the heart of Chile's agrarian economy was defined as work done by men.

Meanings of Power

Relationships between the landowning patrón and the campesino worker were cast in racial terms.[64] Inquilinaje was closely associated with the indigenous and African servitude of colonial times, an era when Europeans and Creoles dominated non-European and mixed *castas* (castes). Although far removed from the Spanish legal codes and social boundaries enforcing such hierarchy, inquilino labor on estates in mid-twentieth century Aconcagua was still construed as service owed in return for subsistence, and employers regularly referred to inquilinos as *indios* (Indians). The use of the term *indio* is especially significant given that campesinos staunchly rejected it, considering themselves neither *indios* (colloquially a pejorative reference) nor *pueblo indígena* (a more dignified reference to indigenous people). By the 1950s, most campesinos in Aconcagua and elsewhere in central Chile shared a mestizoized culture and identity that referenced a combined European and indigenous ancestral heritage.[65] They firmly placed "real" Indians as living further to the south and north, literally and figuratively on the edges of Chile, and not where they themselves resided; they were not Indians. The memory of African ancestry, small but significant in colonial times, had been erased all together. Instead, campesinos referred to themselves as *pueblo chilena* (Chilean people) or *raza chilena* (Chilean race), mestizo formulations with origins in nineteenth-century ideas about whitening. These terms acquired more populist and sometimes antiracist meanings during the 1930s and 1940s when, as historians Thomas Klubock and Karin Rosemblatt have argued, *raza* and *pueblo* were promoted by Popular Front governments as an assertion of cross-class national unity and a counterforce to North Atlantic inferences of Latin American inferiority.[66] Although more research is needed on the subject, Chile seems to have undergone a process not unlike the one historian Jeffrey Gould has identified in the case of Nicaragua, where the myth of European-Indian *mestizaje* proposed a racial homogeneity (however mixed in origin) as the basis of the nation. This resulted in the invention of new national races (Nicaraguans, Chileans) and the systematic suppression, if not cultural loss, of indigenous and African practices and memories.[67]

Whatever the origin of raza chilena and pueblo as mestizaje myths, the fact that Aconcagua campesinos embraced such notions while their employers reserved the right to call them indios suggests, above all, that race functioned as a sign delineating codes of class privilege and domination. Landowning elites also claimed to be raza chilena, yet vigorously sought to distinguish themselves from the masses of rural poor. Landowners were, themselves, a heterogeneous group, insecure about maintaining status. They included a minority of very wealthy and powerful families who owned Aconcagua's largest estates and who had connections and investments in Chile's banking and industrial sectors. They also included families who had lost their fortunes and who clung to land for purely social and political reasons. Some claimed ancestry in Spanish colonial families; others traced lineage to Italian, British, and German immigrants from the nineteenth century. Since 1900, many of Aconcagua's medium-sized estates had been acquired by investment-seeking entrepreneurs. At least a half dozen families had Arab surnames, reflecting the impact of a wave of Palestinian immigration in the mid-twentieth century.[68]

Landowners boasted of their Chileanness, trumpeting their national mission of providing the country's food and their historic role in settling national territory.[69] While the first claim stressed landowners' authentic commitment to the Chilean nation, the latter claim invoked Europeans' original conquest of Indians and suggested that landowners played an ongoing civilizing role.[70] Landowners embraced Chilean mestizaje, but more heavily emphasized the European quotient of the mix. Recent Arab influences were ignored or ostracized. Elite-run newspapers in Los Andes and San Felipe proclaimed Aconcagua's Spanish colonial architecture the finest in all of Chile and attributed the region's agricultural prowess to the ingenuity of Italian winemakers and English businessmen. On the Edwards estate in Santa María county—a property owned by Chileans with British ancestry and powerful banking interests—tea was held ritually at the traditional Anglo-hour of four o'clock, in pointed contrast to the more common Chilean practice of observing the colloquial *once* (eleventh hour) tea in the evening.[71] On Sundays, gentlemen rodeo associations known as *clubs de huasos* assembled propertied men with wide-brim black hats and embroidered capes, mounted on neatly groomed horses with Chilean flags in their manes, for parades and competitions that referenced Spanish festivals in nationalist terms. Although these Sunday rodeos had a populist edge and included as participants many small farmers and inquilinos with horses, elites sponsored and led them. They confirmed class hierarchies in racial ways, representing the privilege of owning a sizeable estate, or the proximity to such privilege, as Chileanness with cosmopolitan and European accents.

Above all, racialized symbols categorized relationships to service, distinguishing those with the power to demand service from those obliged to provide it. The landowning elite saw campesinos as indios (or associated them with what Indians presumably had been) since, by definition, inquilinos served and were subservient. This notion was extended to all campesinos, even those without formal inquilino obligations. Not only were all campesinos potential inquilinos, but other rural arrangements were formed within the logic of inquilinaje. Integral to notions of service and servitude, campesinos were racialized as inferior because of poverty, illiteracy, supposed squalor and superstition, all markers that distanced them from the modern refinement of their social superiors. To paraphrase from anthropologist Roger Lancaster's discussion of mestizaje in Central America, it was not that European landowners dominated Indian campesinos in Aconcagua, but that "Europeanness" dominated "Indianness."[72] If both aspects were integral to notions of raza chilena, landowners were clearly more associated with the former and campesinos with the latter. Moreover, since raza chilena was important to notions of citizenship, elite predilections of seeing campesinos as indios suggested that they saw the rural poor as less than full members of the nation—lying closer to barbarism than civilization.

Race also functioned as a sign of hierarchy among campesinos. If they rejected the term *indio* for themselves, refuting employer inferences of campesino racial inferiority by insisting on their own Chilean pedigree, they accepted the equation of Indianness with servility and regularly tossed indio around as an insult toward other campesinos. Given the disparities between rural workers within inquilinaje—inquilinos' relative security versus the vagaries of wage work; small farmers with sizeable farms versus minifundistas—the word *indio* could be hurled at other campesinos for diverse reasons of jealousy or conceit, but always as a signal of disdain that underscored competitions between campesinos and the limits of class solidarity. In oral histories, former inquilinos, minifundistas, and permanent workers all derisively referred to afuerino migrants as *sureños* (southerners) and *rotos* (broken ones). The first term references the Chilean south, a region with significant indigenous Mapuche communities, while the second term connotes social dysfunction, violence, and recklessness. Aconcagua's more permanent campesino population also described afuerinos as "untrustworthy" and "living like animals" in the patrón's barn or corral, perpetually drunk and accepting compensation largely in alcohol.[73] Here indio meant debauched outsider, miserable wanderer, and cause of wage depression.

But inquilinos were also called indios, mostly by minifundistas and small farmers who saw inquilinos as beholden to landowners and lacking independence. Permanent and seasonal wageworkers sometimes called inquilinos *indios apatronados* (the patrón's Indians) in reference to the loyalty inquilinos presumably gave employers in return for security. The meaning of *indio* slipped back and forth between accusation of inferiority and threat, and defensive affirmation of the accuser's own self-worth. In this sense, *indio* also questioned a worker's manliness: if indios were those who did not know the worth of their own labor or those who slavishly submitted to the boss, not being an Indian was measured by one's capacity for dignity and independence.

If campesinos accepted the pejorative meaning of Indianness, they were more equivocal about the superiority of Europeanness. Money, sophistication, and power were associated with a type of whiteness linked to cosmopolitan leisure and urban life, in contrast to the rural isolation and hard labor of campesinos. But they also regarded such refinement as problematic. In an oral history, Miguel Acevedo, a former seasonal worker from San Esteben county, lamented that campesina girls who left the countryside to work as domestics in Santiago and Valparaíso returned home feeling "too good" for fellow campesinos: "They came back with pretty clothes—no flour sacks for them! Only factory clothes, fancy and with makeup. They came back whiter (*más blanquita*) and didn't want anything to do with country boys. Only city boys would do for them!"[74]

Offering women's sexual rejection of men as a trope for community disintegration, Acevedo warned of the threat posed by a whiter, urban world. At the same time, his implied longing for citified girls to show affection for country boys evoked a desire for that world. Emilio Ibáñez, a former seasonal worker from Santa María county, remembered his first venture to Valparaíso with similar ambivalence and misogynist edge. On one hand, the trip landed him six weeks work in construction for better wages than anything offered back home as well as the opportunity to "see many beautiful, blonde and redheaded women" in the bars around the port. But as a campesino marked by a country way of speaking and patched clothing, he was jeered by those same women as an indio and asked whether or not he knew how to eat with a fork.[75]

Inside the estates, campesinos more regularly associated elite pretensions of racial superiority as markers of employer illegitimacy. Campesina women who worked as domestics in patrón households often experienced the modern conveniences of fine living as abuse. Refrigerators were regularly padlocked to prevent servants' access and domestics were sometimes prohibited from using hot water faucets under the pretense that they would waste it since maids preferred bathing with cold water.[76]

Domestics ate inferior food than their employers and were forbidden from using the china or silver. If the domestic lived at the residence, she usually slept in a tiny room without furniture or a source of heat. Such gross material distinctions served elite efforts to position themselves above campesinos, but campesina servant women termed such practices as evidence of employer inhumanity, not superiority. As one campesina woman recalled her experience in an oral history, "What kind of person treats another person like that? Their fancy things made them the real animals."[77]

Campesinos also challenged the racial legitimacy of their employers by questioning their Chileanness. Inverting the positive meaning that landowning elites associated with European heritage, campesinos often described the Aconcagua Valley as a place controlled by "foreigners" and referred to their patrón as a *gringo* (a reference to wealthy North Americans and Europeans).[78] If such allegations were uttered only outside the patrón's earshot, they served as an important way for campesinos to counter elite racism. Giving their own populist spin to the nationalist terms *pueblo* and *raza chilena,* campesinos linked rural land monopolies with foreigners, suggesting that Europeanness (or too much of it) disqualified landowners from being real Chileans. Instead, real Chileans were, by inference, campesinos. Strikingly, campesinos placed landowners of Palestinian or Arab descent completely outside the nationalist mestizaje spectrum, commonly referring to them as "Turks," and occasionally as "Jews."[79] While in the case of a patrón with Italian, Spanish, or English heritage campesinos alleged that it was Europeanness that marked their employer as an outsider, in the case of Arab heritage, campesinos employed a European-derived racism and anti-Semitism to signal illegitimacy.

Racialized relationships between patrón and worker were also patriarchal. Both male and female campesinos encountered the male patrón as the most validated and overarching source of power in rural society. Although some landowners were women, either because of inheritance or elite desire to legally subdivide property, managerial authority usually remained a masculine privilege.[80] This legitimated male dominance generally and represented class authority on the estates in gendered terms. The reality and acceptance of male authority naturalized class hierarchies into commonsense daily interactions of benevolence and deference, control and dependence. One of the most immediate models was the patrón's authority within his own household. The families of large landowners, as well as those of surrogate administrators who ran estates in the case of absentee landowners (relatively rare in Aconcagua), were almost always headed by men who made decisions regarding production, administration, and sale of the family's estate.[81] The patrón assigned sons and hired employees to the various daily supervisory tasks. He usually oversaw operations himself from a privileged perch on horseback or the seat of his truck. Inquilinos and hired workers alike tipped their hat to the patrón and stepped off to the side of the road as he passed. Campesina women instructed daughters who worked as servants in the patrón household to never look their male employer in the eye.[82]

Inquilinaje centrally involved relationships between men. Masculine domination of men was integral to class exploitation. The patrón provided work upon which the survival of other men depended, and he commanded the bodies and evaluated the labor of his male social inferiors. The highly personal and arbitrary nature of labor contracts particularly emphasized vertical ties between male employer and worker. Landowners approved of, and promoted, patriarchal arrangements in campesino households, including the idea that male household heads provided a family's primary economic sustenance. However, they reserved the right to give and take this ability away. Decisions about who qualified for the relatively more secure position of inquilino were based on a patrón's personal evaluation of a campesino's performance, loyalty, disposition, and years of service. Despite legal requirements to the contrary, inquilino contracts were usually verbal and easily terminated if a worker proved unsatisfactory. Inquilinos could be, and were, evicted from their homes and land regalías at any time.

Permanent and seasonal workers faced an even more tenuous situation. Employers offered verbal contracts on an annual or biannual basis and denied them to workers who had proven troublesome the previous year. Since, unlike industrial employers, agricultural employers had no legal obligation to compensate workers who were released or fired before the expiration of a contract, such workers held no guarantee that the patrón would honor the full length of these short contracts. Although a landowner had an incentive to maintain the size and composition of his labor force during the growing season, the high levels of rural unemployment and underemployment facilitated the replacement of undesirable workers at all times.

Campesino men's vulnerability to the patrón's goodwill was especially reflected in the practice of paying estate workers in-kind. As agricultural wages fell in real value by some 40 percent throughout the 1950s, the quality and quantity of compensation in fuel, housing, and firewood made the difference between miserable and manageable poverty and distinguished between a "good" patrón and a "bad" one.[83] Despite laws regulating in-kind payments, landowners exercised almost unilateral authority in determining their content and worth, and tended to grossly overestimate their value.[84] Nonetheless, because in-kind payments were crucial to campesino survival, they marked men's ability to provide for families. The patrón's arbitrary allotment of such payment reinforced the idea that such ability hinged on employer benevolence rather than contractual obligation.

Paternalist rites of generosity reinforced the capriciousness of patrón authority. Landowners and administrators routinely donated liquor and meat to workers for national and religious holidays, paid for wedding and baptism parties, and provided pigs and cattle for communal meals during harvest festivals.[85] Such gifts suggested a kinder, even fatherly stance of employers toward workers. They also made the patrón central to campesino sociability and reminded campesino men of the fragility of their place as household heads since, as recipients, they figured as dependents. When Anita Hernández, the daughter of an inquilino, was married on Casa Quilpúe estate in San Felipe county in 1952, it was the patrón, not her father or family, who sponsored the festivities. The wedding feast lasted several days and included all workers from the estate, with the landowner providing the *chicha* (a strong wine) and *aguardiente* (grape spirits).[86] During the late summer, wheat-threshing activities known as the *trilla* were transformed into estatewide festivities lasting up to two weeks.[87] In the morning men brought wagonloads of cut wheat to be fed into a thresher powered by circling horses; women set boiling pots of water on open fires in preparation for a meal of *cazuela* (chicken or beef stew) to be accompanied at midday by liquor and additional meat delivered by the patrón. Music, dancing, and other socializing took place intermittently until after sunset.[88] At Christmas, and during Chile's Independence celebration on September 18, landowners gave workers individual bonus gifts of food and clothing. Employers extended charitable acts to all agricultural workers, not just inquilinos, but they reserved special treatment, such as paying for medical expenses or supporting a widow, for the families of a favored few. As with payments in-kind, patrón generosity obscured the value of labor and promoted the idea that campesino livelihood was contingent on the landowner's personal magnanimity rather than on the worth of work.

The patrón's wife, or *patrona*, often played a key role in paternalist rites. At Christmas on the Piguchén estate in Putaendo county, the patrona visited each inquilino family individually, delivering candy in return for children singing Christmas carols instead of throwing the customary party for estate workers.[89] The patrona also often ran a small store (*pulpería*) on the estate that sold things such as blankets, cooking oil, kerosene, alcohol, and secondhand pants and boots from the army. These items were usually dispensed on credit and deducted from weekly wages. On payday the patrona would sit at a table next to her husband and itemize for each worker what had been purchased and, not infrequently, what debt was owed the store. Occasionally small debts were "forgiven" in return for a campesino family providing the labor of a daughter or son for the patrona's needs. During a particularly rainy winter, the patrona might dispense extra blankets free of charge or, more commonly, free of charge until the spring planting season provided campesinos with more regular employment.[90] The patrona could be as capricious and authoritarian as her husband, but her acts of charity were meant to soften the more severe aspects of inquilinaje. Functioning as her husband's wife, and often dealing directly with campesina women, the patrona's activities emphasized a maternal caring for workers and strove to cast class inequalities as the more natural hierarchies of family.

When benevolence and paternalism no longer secured control over workers, direct force took their place. Landowners and their surrogate administrators physically disciplined workers and regularly intimidated them with the threat of violence. Inquilinos on San José estate in Putaendo county complained to sociologist Sergio Gómez that their patrón hit workers for no other reason than having a hot temper and that he constantly swore as he roamed the estate in surveillance.[91] Miguel Acevedo and Raúl Fuentes, former workers in San Esteben and Santa María counties, recalled in oral histories that workers were regularly beaten for showing up late or failing to complete tasks to satisfaction.[92] Some employers carried rifles or revolvers as they supervised estate work and poked workers with gunpoints.[93] When María Galdámez's father, an inquilino, was kicked off an estate in Santa María county "because of the pure spite of the patrón," the employer sent his two sons and one administrator to the family's house. The men broke down the door and dragged Galdámez's father out by his shirt, "kicking him like an animal."[94] The San Felipe and Los Andes newspapers intermittently reported more extreme incidences of such violence, including a 1958 case in which an unnamed landowner shot the agricultural worker, Tomás Quiroga Báez, in the stomach for disputing the worth of his housing regalía.[95]

But direct force was never the primary means of coercion. Instead, hierarchies of masculine authority were reproduced through daily rituals of humiliation and humility. When inquilinos and other laborers reported to work on San Miguel estate in San Esteben county early in the morning, they stood barefoot in front of the patrón, hat in hand and eyes lowered, as their employer gave them instructions from horseback.[96] They were required to walk single file behind the horse as the patrón led them out into the field.[97] Workers who arrived late to the Miraflores estate in Santa María county were deprived of the mid-morning ration of bread and had to make do with water until the noon meal.[98] The most troublesome workers—including those who started fights with other workers or who showed up drunk or hungover to work—were assigned undesirable tasks such as digging irrigation ditches and shoveling animal manure.[99] The patrón penalized inquilinos by decreasing the number of animals his workers could keep on their regalías or by forcing them to give up one of their sheep or chickens.

Employers and administrators also directly infringed on campesino men's patriarchal authority within their own households. Inquilinos were frequently told which son or male family member should serve as the supplemental obligado worker and were requested to provide female family members for seasonal work during the harvest or for domestic service in the patrón's household. Employer requests for women's labor constituted a particular affront to campesino men's authority since, in addition to circumventing their right as household heads to allocate family labor, it challenged their rights as husbands to control the whereabouts of women. Widespread fears among campesinos that employers sexually

preyed on campesina women who worked beyond their households concretized the insult. The rape of a man's wife or daughter by the patrón
dually symbolized a campesino man's subordination: it stripped him of
exclusive sexual dominion over his womenfolk and rendered him powerless to prevent it.

It is difficult to know the exact extent of employer rape of campesina women since most rapes went unreported either to officials or to
a woman's family. In oral histories, both campesino men and women recalled rapes of women by employers as a common feature of life on the
great estates; yet they usually referred to such violence in general terms as
"something that happened a lot," rather than in specific details that befell
particular individuals. Rape was clearly a trope that powerfully symbolized, for both campesina men and women, the disempowerment of campesinos as a whole. The violated woman represented class vulnerability
as the sabotage of campesino patriarchy—poor men's inability either to
protect women or to exercise real control over their households. But rape
also happened, and it happened to women. Rape not only represented
social control, it was one of its most overt forms. If rape functioned as a
sign of elite men's domination over poor men, it was always first about
men's domination of women. Employers and administrators felt entitled
to the bodies and labor of all campesinos, male and female, but elite men's
sense of sexual entitlement seems to have been largely reserved for campesina women; and heterosexual sexual violence had a very specific role
in the broader mechanics of social control.[100]

Employer rapes of campesina women not only terrorized, hurt, and
humiliated a woman, but they potentially alienated her from her community. Although rape victims were not usually expelled from their
households, it was difficult for them to marry, less because of taboos
surrounding virginity (which seem to have been relaxed in rural Aconcagua), than because the woman was associated with patrón violation.
The familial shame surrounding rape usually militated against women
divulging rapes even to other family members and, when they did, campesino households closed ranks to conceal the information. The enforced
silence upheld the patriarchal authority of both the employer and campesino household. The threat and possibility of rape disciplined women
as workers in relation to male supervisors and landowners, and as members of campesino households. Spaces beyond the campesino household

were defined as hazardous for women—places that merited extra caution and deference. Rape delineated between optimal sites of male and female work, posed women's bodies as potential threats to the masculine integrity of rural households, and emphasized campesino patriarchy as a bulwark against such incursions.

Rape posed a particular danger for female domestic servants. Not only was such work highly isolated but, more fundamentally, it was construed as personal service. By definition, domestic servants tended the intimate needs of household members, a formulation that, within the patriarchal logic of a patrón's household, was easily extended to mean meeting, or being forced to meet, men's sexual demands. Sex was presumably part of what employers bought when they paid or obliged a campesina woman to perform housework—a labor associated with wives, even if a patrón's wife, by definition, was exempt from waxing floors and changing sheets.

Sexual access to female domestic servants was also understood as a racialized privilege. The servant-employing elite referred to female domestics as *chinitas* or *indias* (literally "Chinese girls," connoting female Indians), terms that invoked the racial hierarchies of the colonial past and connoted sexual accessibility. The terms *india* and *china* indicated women of low and mixed caste, by definition women of little sexual virtue; *china,* in particular, was associated with sexual flirtation and concubinage. Patrón authority to thrust the markers of colonial castes onto mid-twentieth-century campesina women with largely mestiza identities and cultures worked to naturalize the sexual nature of labor relations in the 1950s as well as to sublimate their coercive character. The idea was that the relation between landowner and india or chinita was a timeless aspect of life in the Chilean countryside—a consensual, if unequal, arrangement between man and woman, patrón and peón.

Contested Survival

The arbitrariness of landowner authority did not go unchallenged. Throughout the middle of the twentieth century, reform-minded populist governments, both civilian and military, increasingly subjected rural labor relations to regulation by law and state bureaucracies. The 1931 Labor Code extended to agricultural workers the same entitlements afforded industrial workers in the 1920s, including rights to written contracts, Sunday pay, severance compensation, and the ability to petition employers with grievances. It also specified arrangements pertaining specifically to agricultural workers, such as the quality of housing and land regalías and the number of days inquilinos were required to provide obligados. As historian Brian Loveman has shown in his pioneering study of the early rural labor movement, campesinos persistently used this legislation to give legitimacy to longstanding grievances and to contest the practical terms of their employment. They annually filed thousands of formal complaints to the Labor Department, regularly petitioned local labor tribunals, and often appealed directly to government authorities, including Chilean presidents.[101] They denounced abusive bosses, cited labor code violations, and demanded higher wages and expanded land entitlements.

Campesinos also challenged landowner authority through rural unions. Formal organizing efforts in the countryside date from the first part of the century and began in Aconcagua. In 1919, the urban-based Federation of Chilean Workers (FOCH), led by the eventual founder of the Chilean Communist party, Luis Emilio Recabarren, formed a short-lived union of inquilinos and miners in Catemu county.[102] The 1931 Labor Code formally recognized the right of agricultural workers to form unions, collectively bargain, and strike. Throughout the 1930s, the Communists and Socialists organized a handful of unions in the Aconcagua Valley and dozens elsewhere in central Chile.[103] Sometimes organized labor had upper-class messengers on the inside: a union formed in 1937 on the Santa Rosa estate in San Felipe county evolved from a series of study sessions on the labor code held for campesinos by the patrón's son, a law student in Santiago and member of the Socialist party.[104]

But, ironically, leftist organizing efforts were abruptly cut short by the complicity of the very leftleaning populist leadership that initiated them. Between 1938 and 1952, three consecutive Popular Front governments—which included coalitions of the Radical, Socialist, and Communist parties—gradually rescinded the 1931 Labor Code's guarantee of campesino organizing rights. In a dramatic capitulation to powerful landowning interests and pressure, which Brian Loveman has compellingly argued was a concession exchanged for landowner acquiescence to populist social welfare and industrialization policies in urban areas, President Pedro Aguirre Cerda suspended agricultural workers' rights to collectively bargain and strike in 1939.[105] In 1948, President Gabriel González Videla enacted the Law for the Permanent Defense of Democracy outlawing the Communist party, a move that eliminated the most aggressive organizer of campesinos and cast suspicion on all rural labor activists. Most devastatingly, a year prior to the ban on the Communists, González Videla signed a new rural labor law that stripped campesino unions of any real power and effectively made most forms of organizing illegal. The 1947 legislation, Law 8.881, required that half of a union's membership, and all of its elected leadership, be literate. It offered no protections for organizers or redress for workers fired for suspected union activity. Labor petitions could be presented only once a year and never during a harvest or planting season. It essentially eliminated the right to strike. The 1947 labor law had dramatic consequences: between 1947 and 1964, Chile had only fourteen legal rural labor unions nationwide, with a paltry total membership of 1,647 workers.[106]

Labor organizing and campesino education did, however, continue. The Socialist party, and some communists working clandestinely, began to focus on southern estates and indigenous areas. Ironically, those communists internally exiled to remote parts of Chile became positioned to inform campesinos about basic legal entitlements and to serve as catalysts for drafting labor petitions.[107] Throughout the 1940s and 1950s, progressive Catholic clergy and laity also reached out to rural workers. They were inspired by Catholic social reform doctrine, which urged an easing of extreme poverty and the harmonizing of class relations throughout the twentieth century. Catholics were also eager to make organizing inroads against the Left in its hour of persecution. In 1947, the year that the draconian Law 8.881 went into effect, the activist priests Father Alberto Hurtado and Bishop Manuel Larrain founded the educational organization Chilean Union Action (ASICH) to inform campesinos about their remaining labor rights and strategize about union organizing. The organization had one of its seven national bases in the city of San Felipe, where Catholic activists helped estate workers draft petitions and sponsored education and cultural events.[108]

Despite these efforts, rural labor as a movement in no way constituted a powerful force. Labor tribunals were chronically understaffed and labor laws were rarely regularly enforced. The byzantine requirements for submitting labor petitions frequently served to disqualify formal complaints. Local inspectors and government functionaries from Santiago often identified more with landowners than workers. Labor organizers and educators, including both leftists and Catholics, regularly faced harassment; workers who dared to become involved with them were often fired. Landowners also created their own "unions" in attempts to quash independent organizing efforts. When Don Alegría, the owner of Piguchén estate in Putaendo county, discovered a labor activist organizing on his property, he forced all of his workers and the organizer to assemble in front of his house for a mock union meeting in which he bated them, saying, "Children, if you have any questions of this gentlemen [the organizer], ask them now, because the Señor Diplomat doesn't have much time and will be leaving soon."[109] Don Alegría then proceeded to have himself "elected" president of the new union and the organizer kicked off his premises.

Ultimately it was not within the rural labor movement that most campesinos forged an understanding of class exploitation or challenged landowner authority. Certainly the efforts of labor activists to promote ideas about campesinos' legal rights informed workers' concepts of justice and possible action. One did not have to attend formal meetings or sign a petition to know what activists were advocating. But on a daily basis, campesino identities and actions evolved more spontaneously as practical responses to, and reinterpretations of, the paternalist and coercive arrangements of everyday existence; they constituted what James Scott first termed "everyday forms of resistance" that develop within peasants' own moral economy of subsistence rights and patrón obligations.[110] To campesinos, liquor and food provided by their bosses for weddings or harvest festivals were not gifts but deserved compensation for services rendered. If campesinos saw their fate as wedded to the personal beneficence of an individual patrón, they also saw allotments of firewood, repairs to their houses, expansions of their land regalías, and shares of produce as rightful entitlements that they had earned. Rural men and women grumbled among themselves when the number of goats or kegs of wine provided on Easter or Independence Day were inadequate, and they widely viewed estate stores as places of theft and abuse. Campesinos on Piguchén estate in Putaendo county told sociologist Sergio Gómez that one winter a charitable institution donated bundles of sweaters for campesinos' use, but that, instead of distributing them, the patrona put them up for sale in the estate store.[111] Although there is little reason to doubt the story, its veracity is less important than its expressed outrage at employer greed and its allegation that the patróna had stolen and profited from goods originally freely given to campesinos.

Workers also openly complained about insufficient rations of fuel and food. Grievances to social superiors usually took the form of individual supplications for understanding and generosity. But beyond a boss's gaze, campesinos often took measures into their own hands. Landowners accused their workers of breaking into their storage facilities and stealing their livestock during holidays.[112] They maintained that the theft of tools and grain was routine throughout the year and that when workers were left unsupervised on a job they destroyed fences, broke farm equipment, and labored at a snail's pace.[113]

Afuerinos were seen as a particular problem. As workers who often hailed from the more indigenous Chilean south or other perimeters of the country, afuerinos were community outsiders with seasonal contracts and no entitlements to land. They appeared to gain the least from paternalist arrangements and, in turn, seemed to owe the least deference to social superiors. As single men accustomed to moving from job to job, afuerinos presumably proved less vulnerable to the possibility of being fired than inquilinos or permanent workers did. From an employer perspective, afuerinos' very lack of power within the inquilinaje system made them threateningly independent, a condition that reinforced the tendency to label afuerinos unruly Indians. Landowners complained that afuerinos habitually arrived drunk to work, provoked physical fights with supervisors or other workers, and vandalized the barns and sheds where they lodged.[114] Afuerinos were blamed for the disappearance of tools and livestock and for abandoning their jobs on an estate before its completion. Lastly, they were accused of being political agitators. When a warehouse filled with hay went up in flames in Panquehue county in 1958, the owner attributed it to "malevolent outsiders and communists [who] masquerade as workers [and] attempt to promote discontent and ill will."[115]

It is doubtful that afuerinos posed the organized threat that landowners supposed. As migrants constantly on the move, afuerinos rarely would have had the opportunity to build the enduring relationships necessary for politicizing others. Moreover, despite leftist organizing efforts among indigenous communities in the south, the efforts of all labor activists focused overwhelmingly on inquilinos and permanent workers, not afuerinos. But if afuerinos' disregard for employer property was more spontaneous than planned, acts of sabotage and arson nonetheless constituted displays of defiance. Regardless of their effectiveness, they arose out of concrete grievances usually shared by other workers.

Inquilinos usually disputed landowner authority in less overt ways than burning down buildings or abandoning their jobs. Although they also engaged in petty thievery and sabotage, it was their own labor rather than the patrón's property that most often became the site of resistance. Inquilinos markedly preferred working their own land regalías to working on the larger estate. A study conducted by Chilean sociologists Rafael Baraona and Ximena Aranda in the late 1950s found that over 50 percent of inquilinos in Putaendo county sent a replacement worker to fulfill their labor obligation in the hacienda fields in order to dedicate themselves full-time to their own cultivation.[116] Likewise, in the minifundia sector, when family members sought employment as wage laborers on estates, it was most often older male children (and occasionally women) who did so.[117] The choice to reserve the energies of a household's primary worker and authority figure for a family's own immediate needs carved out an important space of at least symbolic autonomy. It emphasized the value of laboring for one's own family over that of working for the patrón.

However, the preference of inquilinos and minifundistas for laboring on their own plots never posed a real threat to the latifundia system. Some landowners objected to the practice and complained that the replacement workers were too young or unskilled. Still, such protests resulted mostly from landowner irritation at inquilino interference with estate labor decisions. Despite the oppositional meaning inquilinos attached to it, the regalía arrangement benefited landowners more than it did inquilinos. The inquilino's obligation to provide replacement workers and additional laborers throughout the growing season more than made up for an inquilino's personal withdrawal of labor. The regalía belonged to the patrón and could be taken away at any time; it kept workers resident on the estates, provided landowners with a flexible labor pool, and reinforced workers' dependence on landowners.

In the end, the lives of campesinos in the Aconcagua Valley and much of the rest of Chile were circumscribed by landowner authority and the requirements of latifundia in ways extremely difficult to challenge successfully. Acts of withholding labor, destroying fences, or stealing pigs and chickens certainly demonstrated campesinos' unwillingness to passively accept unjust arrangements, but such resistance ultimately failed to substantially change the concrete structures and power relations that made campesino livelihood so vulnerable. On a daily basis, the landowner or his surrogate held the only authority on an estate. It was the landowner's near monopoly on power that held the latifundia economy together. The concentration of land in a few hands and the state's unwillingness to assertively intervene in rural affairs reinforced and created such authority.

chapter 2 Binding Ties

Campesino Sexuality and Family Negotiations

In 1965, the sociologist Laura Collantes conducted an unusual and widely read study on campesino sexuality in the Aconcagua Valley county of Santa María. In it she described relationships between rural men and women as a "pre-human world of frustration and ignorance."[1] Giving particular attention to adolescent girls, Collantes argued that the moral backwardness and lack of human affection in the campesino household "deformed more than formed rural women" and caused daughters to grow up "without moral or intellectual guidance from anyone."[2] Collantes claimed that female children were seen only "as another mouth to feed" and that the brutish machismo of rural men made women's eventual entrance into marriage unbearable. She tallied a litany of horrors common to campesino households, including incest, rape, adolescent pregnancy, child marriages, alcoholism, and wife beating. Reporting on one campesina's reaction to a daughter's decision to marry, Collantes quoted the woman as saying, "Stupid girl, you want to marry but that is because you don't know what it is to suffer. . . . When you marry, you must put up with so many humiliations. . . . [Men] are like animals and worse when they arrive home drunk."[3]

Collantes's assessment of campesino gender relations as deeply warped reflected mid-twentieth-century attitudes held by most sectors of Chile's upper and middle classes that the rural poor comprised a primitive, racially inferior class whose moral and rational faculties placed them at the margins of civilized society. Although reform-minded commentators such as Collantes connected campesinos' inadequacy to poverty, they tended to imply that it was the rural poor's already existing degeneracy that perpetuated their misery. If the squalor of campesino dwellings facilitated sexual promiscuity as Collantes alleged, she saw ignorance and, in particular, rural men's animal-like lasciviousness as enabling depravity in the first place. If campesinos' work schedules and lack of recreational facilities made rural homes caldrons of frustration, she most blamed family dysfunction on a tendency of uneducated people toward violence. She ignored any serious consideration of how latifundia shaped the campesino household or of how the forms of male domination she encountered were rural variants of, rather than "pre-human" exceptions to, the validation of male authority over women in Chile generally.

But if Collantes pathologized the rural poor, she offered a unique view of campesino lives through her attention to gender relations and sexual practice. In the 1950s and early 1960s, urban-based intellectuals wrote voluminously on the inequalities generated by Chile's agrarian economy, but Collantes was almost singular in her focus on exploitative dynamics between rural men and women. Bolder still, she implicitly proposed that rural women experienced poverty in ways fundamentally mediated by their sexual subordination to men. If Collantes saw this as a primary cause of rural backwardness, she nonetheless suggested that sexuality and sexualized forms of oppression were central to the experience of gender and class.

Sex and Authority in Marriage

The campesino family was one of the sites where the structures of authority underlying latifundia and inquilinaje were most intimately produced and contested. The rural poor experienced and reacted to the demands on their lives and labor in family ways that flowed from their unequal positions as women and men. Men's relative economic privilege resulted from the complex forms of social and, in particular, sexual power that they wielded over women within the family; this in turn buttressed women's economic dependence on, and social subordination to, men. It was within a family context that a majority of campesinos most immediately experienced, acted out, and explained to themselves the meaning and justification of contrasts between men's and women's lives. It was in terms of marriage and courtship that notions about sexual rights and duties—and closely related to this, gender difference—evolved. It was in terms of struggles for the survival of an entire household that definitions of men's and women's different obligations and authority materialized. If the family was not the only place where such meanings were generated, it was the place they were most acutely felt, embraced, and challenged.

Sex lay at the heart of a campesino husband's assumed right to command authority over other aspects of a woman's labor and person. A campesina woman's first pregnancy often predated, and served as a precursor to, a woman's entry into marriage with the involved male party. Thereafter, sexual relations and childbearing became a women's principal marital obligations, intimately tied to the rationale for why wives provided husbands with household labor. When a woman laundered clothes and cooked, raised children and cleaned, managed the family garden or sold homemade goods, she did so not only for her own family, but also for a family headed by her husband. Husbands expected these services from women because they were wives, and they presumed to assign and regulate wives' activities because they understood male entitlement to female labor as an extension of the sexual authority guaranteed men over women by marriage. To paraphrase the works of Carol Pateman and Christine Delphy, wives' sexual obligations to husbands provided the contractual logic for men's sense of entitlement to women's bodily labor in a much wider range of activities.[4]

In oral histories, many women recalled having little control over when they would have sex or the number of children they bore. Anita Hernández, the child of inquilinos and a lifetime agricultural worker in San Felipe county, remembered overt coercion as characterizing her married life with Manuel Rojas, a seasonal worker whom she married in 1951 at age fourteen. Hernández bore ten children in her first eleven years as a wife and recalled sex as involving little consensual agreement and even less affection. She characterized it as a marital right unilaterally and abusively asserted by her husband and closely tied to notions of possession: "He would force me to have [sexual] relations with him whenever he wanted, even when I was indisposed [menstruating] or recovering from childbirth. You can't imagine how much that hurt! But he didn't care, he only thought of his pleasure and said that's what a wife was for. If he didn't do it, someone else would."[5]

Other women's experiences were far less grim. Most saw sex and childbearing as matter-of-fact duties of marriage. Sex could be agreeable, a terrain of both pleasure and affirmation. Children provided emotional satisfaction and a crucial source of family labor; they also constituted a tangible symbol of a wife's fulfillment of the marriage bargain. María Galdámez, a former seasonal worker from San Felipe county, recalled that "as long as [she] wasn't too tired, a little caressing was a sweet thing on a Saturday night."[6] Other women reported that on evenings following paydays, when spirits were high, husbands "could count on their wives [to be interested in sex.]"[7] But even congenial arrangements usually took shape within the parameters of wifely obligation and men's greater authority. As Olivia Torres, the wife of a permanent worker in Panquehue county, described this situation, "Men expected they could have [sexual] relations with their wives when they wanted, and it was easier to give in than put up a fight since [objection] would put him in a bad state of mind, and he might be drunk. [Sex] is part of what a wife owes her husband even if it was something he enjoys much more than she."[8]

The ambivalence of many rural women toward sex as a duty they performed more for men's satisfaction than their own was intimately connected to women's lack of control over reproduction. For most women, sex always involved the high probability of pregnancy and attempts to prevent or subsequently deal with unwanted pregnancy could be painful and life-threatening. If most rural women welcomed a certain number of children, most also desired to limit pregnancy for health and economic reasons.[9] Medical birth control methods had been available in Chile since the early twentieth century, but campesinas had almost no access to them during the 1950s.[10] Women attempted to control their reproduction through a variety of homespun and practical remedies that they passed along through all-female networks and that varied widely in effectiveness. Women drank bitter herbal teas at different times during their menstrual cycles, inserted slivers of soap as uterine barriers, douched with vinegar and boric acid solutions, urinated after intercourse, and entreated God not to send more children.[11] The more fortunate women enlisted their male partners' cooperation in sexual abstinence. To terminate unwanted pregnancies, women ate mixtures of straw and borage or consumed special drinks that produced abdominal convulsions. Failing that, they sought the services of midwives or knowledgeable neighbors to have externally provoked or surgical abortions. In rarer cases, women committed infanticide.[12]

Women took high risks in attempting to control their fertility. Many oral remedies for preventing pregnancy or inducing abortion were toxic, provoking violent side effects and occasional death. Home-fashioned soap barrier methods and acid douches produced inflammation and infection. Abortion was illegal and dangerous. Midwives in the Aconcagua Valley were occasionally arrested for performing abortions and denounced as monsters in the local press.[13] Although criminal status was generally reserved for the practitioners rather than the recipients of abortion, women who sought to terminate their pregnancies placed themselves in physical peril.[14] Unlike the relatively safe abortion procedures of elite clinics in Santiago, rural abortion techniques were usually unsanitary and medically unsound. Abortion was induced by physical blows to the abdomen, the insertion of wooden sticks into the cervix, or the scraping of the uterine wall with sharp household objects.[15] Resulting complications were multiple and frequently fatal. In 1964, over 1,200 women were admitted to San Felipe and Los Andes hospitals for abortion-related hemorrhage and infection.[16] In the same year, the Chilean affiliate of International Planned Parenthood estimated that 11.7 of every 1,000 women of fertile age in Chile died from abortion each year.[17]

Beyond the physical risks women faced in avoiding or terminating a pregnancy, they also had to deal with possible male opposition. Some women reported having husbands who openly approved of their birth control efforts, usually because spouses agreed on the optimal family size. Most men considered reproductive matters, beyond their entitlement to have sex with their wives, to be "female matters" shrouded in the gender-specific secrecy of women's knowledge of, and responsibility for, childbirth. They professed to understand and interfere little with the measures women used to regulate fertility. But male claims to ignorance also indicated that women intentionally hid from men their use of contraceptive and abortive remedies for fear of husbands' retaliation. Norma Cárdanes, the wife of a permanent worker in Santa María county, told her husband that the herbal anticontraceptive teas she drank made her womb more fertile because he had once hit her for using a soap barrier method.[18] To avoid a similar reaction from her husband, Violeta Ramírez, the wife of an inquilino in San Esteben county, told her spouse that abstention from sex during the first two weeks following her period would make it easier for her to conceive during the last two.[19] Although both husbands likely understood their spouses' intentions, it is significant that both men felt the need to explicitly prohibit contraception.

Men's objections to wives' use of birth control or recourse to abortion varied in reason. Most campesino men closely associated their virility with the number of children they fathered. As one former inquilino enviously remarked in an oral history about a neighbor, "He was really manly (*muy hombre*) to have so many children."[20] Some men connected women's efforts to avoid pregnancy with challenges to their authority generally or with enabling wives to have affairs. Others disagreed with wives over the desirable family size. Above all, men understood childbearing as a natural responsibility of women, and of their wives in particular. As one man stated simply in an oral history, "[Women's ability to bear children] is the reason why men take wives."[21] Children stood as one of the few tangible material and emotional resources available to the rural poor. This fact, compounded by the Catholic-inspired, societal disapproval of birth control and criminalization of abortion, made men feel that opposition to wives' contraceptive efforts was moral and just.

Most campesina women shared men's view of childbearing as a natural wifely duty, of children as valuable, and of abortion as immoral. But, as women, they were positioned quite differently. Often overwhelmed by existing childrearing obligations or bodily wearied from former pregnancies, women sought to manage their fertility as a basic check on life's circumstances. Such action did not challenge either the expectation that a woman would bear multiple children or that a husband should have sexual access to his wife. But it did indicate women's determination to affect the parameters in which they lived as wives and mothers. Women's solidarity with one another in sharing information, keeping secrets, and assisting pregnancies and births enabled such agency. Although their actions did not question women's basic sexual obligations to husbands, they designated reproduction as a zone of female rather than male authority and, in doing so, contested the boundaries of men's prerogative over female sexuality.

Campesina women's recollection in oral histories that sex was something that wives "owed" their husbands emphasized marriage as an exchange. A woman performed sex and childbearing as duties in return for something—namely men's material obligation to wives and family. Such obligation assumed men would contribute their monetary and in-kind compensation to the campesino household as well as labor on any family-farmed subsistence plot or parcel. Women, in turn, owed men sex and household labor, including both domestic housework and subsistence farming. Such arrangements bolstered both men's and women's understanding of marriage as a partnership, while still affirming male authority over women.

Campesino marriages formed intricate webs of mutually reinforcing, but unequal, gender obligations and rights—resembling arrangements that historian Steve Stern has helpfully termed "patriarchal pacts."[22] Women owed men an exclusive sexual loyalty and all of their household labor. Campesina wives felt husbands also owed them a basic sexual loyalty, particularly as a sign of economic commitment, but women were rarely positioned to demand total fidelity. Within the parameters of patrón control, men made the ultimate decisions about the allocation of their own labor as well as of women's, and they reserved the right to keep part of their meager cash incomes for their own use. Likewise, although men vehemently insisted on female sexual fidelity (and availability) within marriage, they reserved the right to extramarital flirtations, affairs, and sometimes additional marriages. These were not mere double standards; they constituted the basis of male authority over women. Sex governed the logic of men's appropriation of women's labor as well as men's general sense of access to women. Sex, in essence, rendered the "patriarchal pact" of campesino marriage "patriarchal."

But if marriage was a pact of right and obligation underwritten by sex, men and women often disagreed sharply over the precise meaning of those arrangements. Daily quarrels could and did sometimes end in violence. Although both women and men initiated frays and dealt blows, husbands far more often than wives seriously harmed their partners. According to oral histories, wife beating was extremely widespread in campesino households and considered a commonsense result of what men and marriage were naturally about. Husbands' right to discipline wives constituted part of the hegemonic framework of conjugal living. In oral histories, most women attributed wife beating to men's essential nature:

"men are like that, period" (*el hombre es así, no más*), "especially when drunk" (*más cuando curado*). Yet if women took husbands' violence as a fact of life, they did not necessarily accept such violence as just or inevitable. The very assessment that men were particularly volatile when drunk suggested an indictment of male excess and irrationality and implied that men who did not drink made for preferable partners. Likewise, although campesina women less consciously acknowledged this, the frequency of wife beating suggested not only that men felt entitled to discipline wives, but that wives frequently challenged men's interpretations of conjugal duties—leading to the very situations that provoked violence. In both instances, wife beating revealed the boundaries and tensions of campesino marriage arrangements.[23]

Between 1958 and 1965, rural women in the five counties of San Felipe department filed an annual average of ten assault charges (*lesiones*) at the Juzgado de Crimen against husbands and common-law spouses (*convivientes*).[24] The legal cases were unique, not in their violent character, but in the extent of the violence involved and the exceptionalism of the women's willingness to take judicial action.[25] In a majority of cases, women cited male sexual jealousy as the "cause" of male aggression. They stressed the severity of physical injury they suffered and the repetitive nature of such violence. The women complained that men used force as a means of policing their interactions with other men and of insisting that a wife's primary obligation was to serve her husband in the home. Men, in turn, justified violence as appropriate punishment for their wives' transgression from the duties circumscribed by marriage and cohabitation.[26]

Typical of these cases was that of Isabel Quiróz, who, on September 25, 1958, denounced her common-law husband, Manuel Báez, an agricultural laborer in Putaendo county, for slashing her face with a knife in a jealous rage provoked by her dancing with another man when the couple dined at a neighbor's home.[27] Quiróz insisted that she had only danced with her husband, but that Manuel Baéz had been drunk "as usual" and, therefore, had imagined her misconduct. She testified that her husband habitually beat her after consuming alcohol and accused her of "not keeping house properly." Such cases underscore men's understanding of sexual access to women both as a general male right and as a specific feature of marriage. That many men interpreted women's flirtation, conversations, informal meetings, and dancing with other men as infidelity suggests that men presumed total and unrivaled access.

Many women understood male jealousy as closely linked to a woman's ability to have sex and bear children. In an oral history, Marta Ramírez complained that her husband often became violent during the last months of her pregnancies or the first months following a birth because she would refuse to have intercourse with him and was often unable to maintain the household at previous standards.[28] For infertile women, husbands sometimes employed violence to control their wives' supposed capacity to become sexually involved with other men. Hernández recalled that her husband's aggression toward her escalated dramatically when, after the birth of her tenth child, a doctor insisted that she get a hysterectomy against the protests of her spouse: "After the operation he really began to beat me badly. He was furious, said I had gotten sterilized so that I could run around with other men and that now I didn't serve for anything as a wife or as a woman. He refused to have [sexual] relations with me, started seeing other women and staying out for months. When he came back, he'd be drunk and he'd beat me. He split my head open several times."[29]

Tellingly, cases involving male jealousy often included accusations of women's inadequacy as housewives. Men cited housekeeping failure as further proof of a woman's sexual transgression. Some men felt that a woman's inability to have sex or to procreate made her less useful as a housewife. The connection suggests that men saw female sexual and domestic services as inseparable duties of a proper wife. Sexual performance and, specifically, a reproductive capacity were understood as part of a wife's household obligations. And the worth of a wife's housekeeping chores was measured in sexual terms. When a pregnant woman could no longer have sex or a sterilized woman could no longer bear children, her husband might cease to value her domestic labor.

A second common reason for conjugal violence cited in both oral histories and court records involved quarrels over women's opposition to male authority in the household. While childrearing and household management were considered female responsibilities, men often insisted on their right to override wives' decisions. Women objected to this infringement on their authority, particularly when it came to the care of children. Ensuing conflicts could prove volatile. In 1965, María Guerra was hospitalized with severe cuts on her abdomen and buttocks inflicted by her common-law husband, Hernán López, an agricultural laborer from San Felipe county. Guerra testified that López had turned on her because she had tried to prevent him from disciplining her sixteen-year-old son with a knife: "I told him to hit him with a clean hand and not the knife, so he stabbed me, saying that even though he is not the boy's father, he is the man in the house."[30] In an oral history, Sonia Cárdanes complained of similar conflicts with her husband, Jorge León, an agricultural laborer in Santa María county: "When he was around, it was the worst. I'd have my way of disciplining my girls, but when he got home, everything was his way. He'd hit them and me for not having the house exactly as he wanted; if they had forgotten to sweep the floor he'd hit them, and if I intervened he always set on me."[31]

In oral histories, campesino men and women alike summarized the domestic balance of power in the 1950s and early 1960s as "the man runs the home" (*el hombre manda en la casa*).[32] Unlike the situation of the mythic urban woman, who was colloquially referenced as *la reina del hogar* (queen of the home), the campesino household did not provide rural women with a distinct terrain of jurisdiction. In cities, residential neighborhoods tended to be separated from places of work. Although poor urban women's domestic authority may have been exaggerated, latifundia more fully blurred distinctions between the household and agricultural labor. Campesino men labored both in the patrón's fields and on their subsistence regalías near the family's home inside the estate. This meant that while women worked at home, men were often around.

The especially servile nature of men's estate work, under the close surveillance of an overseer or patrón, emphasized the rural household as one of the few places where poor men could exercise the autonomy and authority theoretically guaranteed them as men in a patriarchal culture but largely denied them by class. Campesino men regularly monitored the behavior of wives and children and were heavily involved in household decisions.[33] Men decided at what age a child would be withdrawn from school to enter work as well as whether or not a wife would labor as a domestic or laundress. Men often made the family's few purchases at the estate store and took charge of marketing female handicrafts and foodstuffs in nearby urban areas. Husbands often felt their sexual prerogatives threatened by allowing a woman to go into town and possibly come into contact with other men.[34]

A third factor cited by women in cases of conjugal violence involved women's opposition to a husband's sexual liaisons outside the home. If men demanded sexual faithfulness from wives, they jealously guarded their own sexual freedom outside marriage. Although most women found themselves obliged to comply with such arrangements, they frequently condemned men's sexual libertinage as unjust and argued that marriage should involve greater (even if not complete) mutual fidelity. In 1959, Orfelina Vargas, a twenty-nine–year-old housewife, legally denounced her common-law husband, Luís Aguirre, an agricultural worker from San Felipe county, for beating her during a fight over his habit of frequenting local brothels. Aguirre insisted that it was none of Vargas's business if he went to brothels and that she "had an obligation to stick with him through the good and the bad."[35] Elena Vergara received a similar message from her husband, Armando Gómez, an agricultural worker in Putaendo county, when he began physically retaliating against her for complaining about his affairs with other women. As she recalled in an oral history, "When I complained about the other women, he would beat me, or if everything wasn't as he liked when he returned, he would beat me, or if I wouldn't have sex, he would beat me. I felt such shame to walk in the streets with him, because everyone knew he abused me and saw other women. Once, when I asked him why he felt he had the right to be a womanizer when I fulfilled my obligation as a wife, he said because I'm a man, and I have nothing to lose. You are a woman and can lose everything.'"[36] Whereas the sexual lives of married women were confined to the boundaries of marriage, men's were not. Men insisted on their right to extra-conjugal sexual relations and to a wife's sexual fidelity. This reflected not male hypocrisy but a logical extension of the entitlements of rural manhood, conceived of centrally in terms of male sexual privilege. For many men, "being a man" meant access, at least in principle, to multiple women, including exclusive rights over at least one woman who served him at home.

Poor rural men referred to themselves as *huasos,* a term roughly translated as "country men," but with a highly elastic meaning. When employed by urban classes, usually in reference to campesino migrants to the city, *huaso* was a derogatory and racialized reference to rural primitivism. In contrast, *clubs de huasos,* the equestrian and rodeo associations favored by landowning elites, used the term to connote *gentleman* or *esquire.* When used by campesinos, *huaso* implied male virility, combative-

ness, and freedom—a sharp counter to both urban and rural elite prejudice. As many campesinos explained in oral histories, a huaso was so
strong, independent, and irreverent that no man had a hold on him,
not even the patrón.[37] Or, as one popular campesino melody playfully
boasted, "A huaso works like a bull, drinks like a horse, fights like a
rooster, and conquers women like a man."[38] Campesino huasos also provided for families, but above all being a huaso meant being one's own
boss and having a certain facility with women.[39]

In the 1950s and 1960s, few working-class men could have overtly
challenged patrón authority or exercised freedom over the terms of employment. This made drinking, camaraderie with other male workers,
and sexual prowess all the more central to defining masculinity. Armando
Gómez's response to his wife—that he could do what he wanted because he had nothing to lose, whereas she couldn't because she would lose
everything—was a precise, if cruel, analysis. Extraconjugal affairs could
enhance Gómez's status as a man—as a huaso—but Vergara's status as a
woman—defined chiefly as a sexually loyal wife and mother—would be
jeopardized by affairs and give Gómez a just reason for leaving her. Significantly, contemporary rural folk idioms designated the huaso's appropriate female companion not as a señora, or wife, but as the china, a coy
and sexually available young woman, implicitly of indigenous descent.

All legal cases on wife beating filed between 1958 and 1965 that were
available for examination involved the denunciations of common-law
partners (*convivientes*) rather than legal spouses. Apparently married
women did not feel it effective to denounce violence by men to whom
they were legally bound. In part, married women were constrained by
Chilean law, which required a married woman to live with her husband
and made few exceptions for extenuating circumstances.[40] A judge could
imprison an abusive husband for assault, but he could not order a husband to move out while continuing to provide materially for his family.
Moreover, because divorce was illegal, if a husband abandoned his wife,
she would be unable to form a similar legal union. Although many separated women entered informal marriages as convivientes, they had no
legal entitlement to a man's property or earnings, nor were they guaranteed that a male conviviente would recognize their children. Single or
separated women who lived as convivientes were relatively more able
than married women to leave a union or risk its termination as a result

of legal denunciations. A common-law husband usually had more insecure economic obligations, especially if he had a legal wife elsewhere.
Moreover, if a woman was single, she could risk a conjugal rupture in
the hope that she could find a more suitable partner, even a marriage.

The vast majority of women never reported or left violent partners.
The dramatic lack of employment options for women, coupled with
their responsibility for children and the desire to have their offspring recognized and provided for by fathers, militated heavily against leaving a
relationship, no matter how physically abusive. Anita Hernández recalled
that on the one occasion she fled to her mother's house to escape Manuel
Rojas, her mother sent her back the next morning saying, "Well, he's
your husband now, he owns you. There's nothing to be done." Hernández
spoke to women neighbors, drawing solace from their similar experiences. One friend encouraged her to abandon Rojas and seek work as a
domestic servant in town, but Hernández dismissed the advice immediately: "What was I to do with seven kids at home? They needed their
father, and I needed a man." She coped by minimizing contact with her
husband, putting herself and the children to bed before he arrived home.

Years later, in the mid-1970s and during the beginning phases of
a military dictatorship, Manuel Rojas finally left Anita Hernández for
good. Strikingly, she placed an enlarged picture of him, in military uni-
form from his service during the 1950s, in the center of her living room,
where it remained in the 1990s when interviews for this book took place.
This portrait seemed less an act of homage than an act of defiance: a refusal to let her husband leave and an insistence that he had responsibility
to the household. In the context of military rule, it also seemed an ironic
comment on the regime's strident promotion of patriarchal duty. But
such firmness was shot through with betrayal and rage. During one interview, Hernández displayed several old photos of the couple in which she
had cut out her own face with a pair of scissors—a gesture suggestive
of both her symbolic power to leave him and of a painful self-loathing.
She lamented bitterly, "I put up with so much, but I never abandoned
him, never thought of it. I'm not like the women of today [in the 1990s]
who—one fight, one slap and puff! they leave. No, I worked hard to keep
the family together."[41]

If women felt unable to leave abusive situations, they were not acqui-
escent. By confronting husbands directly or complaining in solidarity to

each other, women contested their men's view of marriage and sexual entitlement, even if they were unable to change it substantially. Hernández's self-perception as a martyr for the family assumes that a good marriage should have consisted of male, as well as female, fidelity and male reliability in providing for the household. Such women embraced the ideal of a workable male-headed household because they understood it to be their best survival option: Given women's acute economic vulnerability and sole responsibility for childrearing, a male worker who contributed regular income to the household offered greater material security than trying to support children on one's own. Women articulated objections to wife beating more on the grounds that it threatened family well-being than because it violated their integrity as individuals. But it was precisely accusations of male failure to families that challenged male privilege as husbands defined and understood it.

Not all husbands beat their wives. And when they did, they did not necessarily always do so regularly or extensively. This mattered. Marriage and cohabitation involved high degrees of cooperation and consent between spouses. Agreement could outweigh disagreement, and not all dissent ended in violence. Wives exacted commitments from husbands and enjoyed some direct authority over their daily household routines and the raising of children. But the existence of female agency and spousal collaboration did not undermine the fundamental patriarchal character of campesino marriage and husbands' particular sexual control of their wives. The principle of male authority was understood by both men and women as natural and commonsensical. Women's authority over very specific household-based tasks did not threaten this, and wives' cooperation with husbands actually helped sustain it. Even if a husband did not have to resort to violence, marriage positioned him to secure specific emotional, reproductive, and material resources that were understood in sexual terms.

Adolescent Daughters and Parental Authority

Parents' control of children also sustained male authority in the campesino household. Determining when and in what capacity a son or daughter would begin working as well as the use of any earnings resulting from such labor was the domain of parents and, in the last instance, usually of fathers. Such questions were decided in accordance with the family's survival needs and the male household head's obligations to the patrón. The economic precariousness of campesino livelihood, together with the dependence of the latifundia and minifundia economies on family labor, abetted the subordination of individual desire to collective need within the rural family and reinforced the authority of men to establish priorities.

In oral histories, both men and women recalled childhood in the 1950s and 1960s as a time of minimal leisure and extensive work obligations. They remembered family life as collaborative and united, but also as one in which solidarity was forged chiefly through strict obedience to parental and, in particular, paternal authority. Both boys and girls labored in the family's garden or plot from as early as age five. If fortunate, they might attend a local school for a few years, combining it with their continued productive responsibilities. By age twelve most children had full-time work responsibilities either at home, on a family parcel, or as seasonal workers on an estate. Within the household, women most regularly assigned and monitored children's work: cleaning, weeding, chopping, or taking care of siblings. But ultimate decision-making power over whether a child would work on the estate or for the household usually resided with fathers. Couples jointly discussed options, and women's household needs were accommodated, but wives did not assign work to children over the opposition of husbands.[42] Women possessed authority within the household on the basis of their status as mothers — or, in the case of in-laws, grandmothers, and aunts, as generational elders. This specifically female authority, not to be confused with a watered-down version of male dominance, developed and was exercised within the logic of patriarchal hierarchies. Women's authority as parents, aunts, or grandmothers was never independent of male control and its legitimacy was in part shaped by the idea that fathers and male household heads were an ultimate source of authority within campesino communities.

Children complied with parental demands out of a shared sense of familial solidarity and a desire to earn parental respect. A mother's insistence that a daughter wash the family's laundry or a father's assignment of his son to specific tasks on the estate had a logic for parents and children alike. But force also ensured children's compliance to parental authority. As Patricia Carreras, a resident of San Esteben county, re-called of her childhood, "Back then children respected their parents. Re-spect, respect. But oh, the poor one who dared otherwise! They'd be humiliated with the stick!"[43] Physical beatings administered by both fathers and mothers were common experiences for most children. Cas-tigation ranged from soft slaps with the hand to harsh whippings with a stick. Force was employed mainly as a means of punishment for tasks left unfinished or poorly executed, sullen or rude responses, and unac-counted absences from home. In other cases, parental violence against children flowed from more general family tensions, such as fights be-tween spouses or loss of employment. In most instances, parents under-stood force as a natural extension of their obligation to discipline and shape children's behavior. But it was also a means of reinforcing authority within the household. Similar to the way husbands understood violence (or its threat) as an acceptable way of controlling the sexual loyalty and economic energy of wives, parents saw force as a legitimate means of exacting labor and obedience from children.

Daughters were of particular concern for campesino parents. Not only did daughters have less economic value than sons given latifundia's pref-erence for male workers, but their ability to bear children posed a poten-tial strain on a household's already scarce resources. The likelihood that a sexually active daughter would become pregnant, coupled with the economic dependence of women on unions with men, emphasized the parental need to monitor a daughter's sexuality until securing a proper marriage arrangement. Parents negotiated a delicate balance between heavily restricting a daughter's interaction with men and insisting that, once a daughter had become pregnant, the responsible male party had an irrefutable obligation to marry and support her.

In contrast to the case with sons, daughters' positions in the family were mediated chiefly by their sexual relations to men. From infancy, a girl's sexuality represented a source of familial concern. Both cam-pesino men and women widely believed infant girls to be a source of envy and desire, and, therefore, especially vulnerable to the malevolent intents of neighbors and outsiders who might cast the evil eye (*mal ojo*) on their daughter, causing her sickness or death.[44] Beliefs about the evil eye were widespread throughout rural Chile as well as in many urban areas. They encompassed a wide range of ideas about the power of other members of the community, especially those with fewer resources, to injuriously or fatally curse their neighbors out of jealousy or hate. Such ideas dated from colonial times and had diverse social origins and meanings, but by the 1950s, beliefs about the evil eye seem to have most commonly related to infants and children who died, fell sick, or developed debilitating illnesses. Although boys were also vulnerable, girls were thought to be especially at risk. Parents protected daughters by tying religious amulets around their necks, dressing them as boys or with clothes worn backwards, or by withdrawing affection from them. Commenting on the impact of such practices in the early 1970s, Patricia Garrett likened campesino treatment of girls to a "kind of child abuse."[45] Yet rural strategies to ward off the evil eye toward girls might be more appropriately understood as an effort to protect girls from predators, especially sexual ones.

Whatever the case, as a girl matured, the family rigidly monitored her interactions with boys and men. After the age of ten, boys and girls in the same family, or cluster of houses on an estate or rural neighborhood, were commonly forbidden to play together; their tasks on land parcels were spatially separated. Daughters were prohibited from leaving home unless accompanied by an adult or sibling. Even when girls worked as seasonal wage laborers on the estates during harvests, they did so alongside a parent, older brother, or married sister.[46] Elena Vergara, the daughter of inquilinos, recalled that after she reached puberty, her grandmother made her dress in boys' clothing whenever she ventured to other parts of an estate or into town.[47]

Of course, it was impossible to completely limit a daughter's contact with male company. In the neighborhoods in town or on the outskirts of estates, houses stood close together, making relations between neighbors fluid and heterosexual interaction frequent. For families who lived within the estates or on isolated parcels, the labor-intensive needs of household survival often militated against desires to monitor a daughter's behavior. Girls had to fetch water, gather firewood, and sell homemade cheeses. If it was preferable that such girls have chaperons, an extra body could not always be spared. During community festivities such as wakes, weddings, and harvests, keeping watch on daughters proved even more difficult. Amid the dancing, drinking, and singing, opportunities for heterosexual interaction abounded, ranging from awkward flirting and touching during a traditional *cueca* (folkdance) to slipping behind a shed or into a field for more intimate contact.

Daughters could pay a high price for such pleasures. In oral histories, many women maintained that, as girls, they received intense interrogations and frequent beatings if they tarried in returning home from household errands. Many claimed they were forbidden from attending community festivals or, if they did attend, were not permitted to dance. Even seemingly innocent exchanges between boys and girls could cause parental concern and castigation. Angelica Saéz's mother slapped her for talking to boys who worked in the same vineyard.[48] Victoria Ibacache's father hit her for allowing a young man to accompany her and her younger siblings home from school.[49] The suspicion or discovery that a daughter had engaged in sexual intercourse provoked the most severe parental recrimination. As one woman recalled, "If your parents caught you sneaking out of the ravine with a boy, or if your mother found a mess in your clothes, that was it! The punches and shouting would never end!"[50]

Parental anger flowed less from the fact of a daughter's sexual activity itself than from fears about a possible pregnancy and the availability of a marriage partner. In the event that the responsible male party could not or would not marry her, she would become a material burden on her parents. Her future prospects of marriage decreased not so much by loss of virginity as by the reticence of prospective suitors to support another man's children. Despite campesinos' identification with Catholicism, the moral significance that the church accorded premarital female virginity was not of overarching importance. Most campesina women had sex and many were pregnant prior to marriage; both cases usually facilitated betrothal and a subsequent wedding. For women of various social classes throughout Latin America, female sexual activity and men's marriage promises historically had been closely linked in concepts about honor.[51] But ties between mid-twentieth-century Chilean campesino notions of virtue and virginity were less intertwined than they were in discussions about honor elsewhere.

Parents also worried about protecting their daughters from rape.[52] Beyond concern for young women who worked as domestic servants in the landowner's household or for social superiors in town, campesinos worried about their daughters' sexual vulnerability to rural men from their own communities. In the almost three dozen rape cases involving rural poor people formally reported to the San Felipe Juzado de Crimen between 1950 and 1964, all of the accused perpetrators were listed as agricultural workers, neighbors, or boarders in the family home.[53] In all but a few cases, the reported victims were adolescents and almost half were pre-pubescent girls. The parents who filed the charges stressed their daughters' total sexual innocence, virginity, and—in at least four cases —alleged their daughter's mental disability. This reflected campesinos' familiarity with the broader social and historical equation of virginity with female innocence as well as an effort to argue that their daughter had been completely incapable of consent.[54] According to oral histories, rapes affected a wide age spectrum of young, unmarried women. However, the importance of ruling out consensual sex probably accounts for why older adolescent girls and adult women did not see the courts as viable places for pressing rape charges.[55] Post-pubescent girls and young women were thought capable of consenting to sex, therefore making rape difficult to "prove" in court, even if they claimed to have previously been virgins. This made married women's ability to pursue rape charges all but impossible, and it bolstered notions about the need to tightly regulate adolescent daughters' heterosexual interactions.

In cases of consensual sexual unions that resulted in a daughter's pregnancy, parents made every effort to ensure an ensuing marriage. Concerns about a girl's young age or her material contributions to the family became secondary to the need to secure a permanent union that would support the daughter and expected child. Parents' energies shifted from preventing a daughter's contact with men to widely publicizing their daughter's obvious sexual relationship to a particular man. They stressed the already existing conjugal relation between the pair—the fact that the couple had had sex and were procreating—as evidence of the young man's obligation to marry. Even in the event that the implicated male was unable to economically provide for a wife and child because he was too young or erratically employed, the girl's parents often continued to insist on marriage and ended up supporting the couple themselves or obliging the young man's parents to do so.

In most cases, the pregnant young woman's parents succeeded in expediting their daughter's marriage with little difficulty. The young men involved often lived on the same estate or in the same neighborhood.

Networks of reciprocity, shared assumptions about a man's obligation to provide for his offspring, and the expressed need from both sets of parents for their children to ultimately form families all combined to pressure a young man to marry a woman with whom he had conceived. But there were many exceptions. If a young woman became pregnant by an afuerino or other community outsider, local pressure for the man to marry became less effective. If the man was married or a member of an elite family, marriage ceased to be a solution at all. According to municipal birth records from the five counties in the San Felipe department, unmarried women gave birth to roughly 20 percent of all children born between 1951 and 1965.[56] Although nearly a quarter of these single mothers subsequently married their child's father, the percentage of childbearing women who never married, or who spent a significant portion of their adult lives as single mothers before marrying, was significant.[57]

In rare instances, it might have behooved a woman with children not to marry or otherwise form a permanent union with a man. If she had a stable job as a domestic in town or was one of the few women with permanent agricultural employment as a dairy worker, she might adequately support her children while avoiding the difficulties associated with marriage or cohabitation. Lilia Muñoz, a permanent worker from Catemu county, had four children by two different men and never married. Although the option of marriage to either man had never been Lilia's to decide since both men already had wives, she insisted in an oral history that she chose not to have a husband because her life was better without one: "Why have a husband? I fed my own children. I didn't need a man telling me what to do, how to raise my children, how to serve him. Husbands are abusive, they take advantage, make you a servant. I didn't want it. Thank you, no. I run my life myself. [*Yo me mando sola.*]"[58] Other single mothers probably shared Lilia's feelings, and married women may have envied her independence. But Lilia was an exception. The dearth of economic opportunities for women made marriage women's best survival option, and remaining single hardly guaranteed autonomy from male authority. Most single mothers survived by staying in their parents' household, where they were subject to the dictates of fathers or male relatives.

As a rule, young women sought husbands, and their parents strongly urged their daughters to marry. But parental and filial interests in marriage did not always coincide. In contrast to their parents' wishes, daughters frequently pursued intimate relations with men and sought pregnancy and a subsequent marriage as a means of escaping the parental household. Where parents endeavored to postpone their daughter's sexual activities, both out of fear of the inadequacy of the girl's potential sexual partner and out of material need for her labor, daughters often used sex as leverage against parental authority.

Elena Vergara began "to go with" (*andar con*) her future husband, Armando Gómez, at age fourteen. Vergara maintained that she purposely got pregnant in order to "get out of [her parents'] house."[59] She complained that her father regularly hit her and that her mother was an alcoholic. She was strictly prohibited from seeing boys and suffered frequent beatings from her father as a result of her relationship with Gómez. Vergara's mother also castigated her, pulling her daughter's hair and withholding meals. Vergara claimed that her parents opposed her relationship to Gómez both because they said he was a womanizer and because they counted on her wages as a housecleaner at a local hospital. Nonetheless, Vergara's pregnancy abruptly changed the situation. Within a month of announcing her condition, Vergara was married to Gómez and had left her parents' home with their consent to live with her in-laws. She recalled, "My mother was so angry. [But] she told me, 'Well, you've done it. You have to go and be his wife now.' I was happy to go."[60]

Unfortunately for Elena Vergara, her gamble that life with Armando Gómez would be less abusive backfired. Her mother-in-law frequently yelled at her and hit her for being incompetent at domestic chores, and her new husband soon began seeing another woman. When Gómez also began hitting Vergara and forbade her to leave the home unaccompanied by his mother, Vergara remembered that she recanted the wisdom of her decision: "My mother was right, really. I suffered more as a wife than as a daughter. But I saw things differently when I was a girl."[61]

So did many other young women. Even in situations less abusive than that of Vergara's family, daughters frequently understood life with a husband as preferable to one with their parents. For some, this assessment came simply from a desire for the adult status accorded the acts of childbearing and household establishment. For others, the advantages of marriage were measured directly against the degree of misery in the parental home. Whatever the case, many rural young women did not become sexually involved with men or got pregnant accidentally or through acts of coercion; pregnancies often constituted careful wagers, calculated in terms of other options.[62]

This balance was negotiated in a variety of ways. Not every young woman eagerly desired to leave her parents, and most waited to marry until they were far into their twenties, doing so with partners of whom their parents approved. Despite contemporary urban images of campesina childbrides, rural women married relatively later than city women (on average at age twenty-four in contrast to the urban average of twenty-two) and had the majority of their children in their late twenties and thirties.[63] Similarly at odds with urban stereotypes of rural familial disorder, adolescent pregnancies among rural girls were less common than among urban girls.[64] Still, many young campesina women did pursue early permanent relationships with men and had secret sexual encounters, enabled by their occasional employment or other responsibilities outside parental households. In the event that such women became pregnant, parents' consent to their daughter's marriage was often matter-of-fact.

For other women, an unbearable home situation in combination with parents' strict control over their lives compelled more drastic responses. Many simply ran away from home. A few ventured to Santiago or Valparaíso in search of work, but most stayed in their native county, forming unions with men in open challenge to their parents' authority. Outraged and fearful parents employed multiple strategies to secure their daughters' return. They appealed directly to the family or man harboring their daughter, threatening that they, or he, would be responsible for anything that happened to their daughters. Others followed their daughters' movements, waiting for an opportunity to physically force them back home. In one instance, a father took a shotgun to the house where his runaway daughter was staying with her boyfriend and fired shots in the air until she came out and agreed to return home with him.[65]

Still other parents sought legal solutions from the provincial courts. In cases where the daughter was a legal minor (under age twenty-one), parents could bring criminal charges of "home abandonment" (*abandono de hogar*) or "inducement to abandon home" against daughters and/or their male partners. These charges requested that a judge force a daughter to return home and that the law penalize the involved male with a fine or a short jail term. The rural poor regularly appealed to the courts to assist them in the control of their daughters. In the five counties of San Felipe department, rural families filed an annual average of fifteen home abandonment cases at the Juzgado de Crimen throughout the 1950s and 1960s.[66] In a majority of cases, an adolescent girl's parents accused a man of encouraging or forcing their daughter to leave home. In fewer cases, the young woman's parents charged their daughter with willfully leaving home. In both instances, the plaintiffs demanded their daughter's return and, in some instances, the man's punishment.

The testimonies given in home abandonment cases illustrate conflict between parents' assumed prerogative to regulate the sexual lives of daughters and young women's efforts to use sexual unions with men to escape parental authority.[67] Parents generally argued that a judge should force their daughter to return home in order to protect her from a coerced and dangerous sexual relationship. In contrast, young women stressed the consensual nature of their relationships and, in particular, their sexual character as evidence that they had entered into conjugal partnerships that superseded parents' rights.

In 1963, an inquilino couple from the Casas Quilpué estate in San Felipe county filed charges against their nineteen-year-old daughter, Julia Fuentes, for running away to Santiago to live with her boyfriend, Juan Flores.[68] The couple complained that their daughter had left her position of employment as a domestic servant on the estate and that she had placed herself in "disgrace" by going to live openly with a man, a thing the boyfriend may have forced her to do. They asked the judge to demand their daughter's return home. In contrast, Julia Fuentes testified that she had gone to Santiago only for a short trip and that she had been given permission to do so by her employer. She also stated that she intended to marry her boyfriend over the wishes of her parents. Beseeching the judge not to return her to her parents' home and to allow her to marry, Fuentes emphasized the long-term and sexual nature of her relationship with Flores and stressed that she had received an offer of matrimony: "I have had a friendship with Juan Flores for many years. I have had sexual relations with him many times, and during [these past days] I had [sex] with him again voluntarily. Juan Flores is single and has promised to marry me."[69] Julia Fuentes's will ultimately prevailed. Her parents dropped the charges, and she married Juan Flores the following week.

There were many such cases. Young women enjoyed frequent success in overcoming parental objections to their unions with men by stressing the relationship's already sexual nature. If the young woman was pregnant, the likelihood that she would successfully prevail against her parents increased even more. While judges had no legal authority to force parents to allow a daughter to marry, they could decide that the charges of home abandonment were invalid and permit the couple to continue cohabitating if they felt sympathetic to the young woman's cause. In such cases, most parents resigned themselves to a marriage since this was preferable to their daughter becoming a single mother.

In addition to stressing the sexual nature of their relationships with men, young women frequently testified that they suffered extensive physical abuse in their parents' home. When fourteen-year-old Raquel Rubilár was brought before the court in 1957 on home abandonment charges, she told the judge that she not only had "been having intimate relations with [the man with whom she fled] for a very long time now," but that both her mother and father were drunkards who frequently beat her.[70] Similarly, when the mother of María Elena Saavedra accused her daughter of abandoning home to have a sexual relation with her boyfriend, Saavedra defended her action by testifying that her mother sometimes beat her so badly that she "couldn't get out of bed in the morning."[71] Young women's allegations of abuse at home were intended to discredit their parents and to justify their sexual behavior. They demonstrated both the willingness of young women to use sex to flee oppressive family conditions and such women's gamble that a husband's authority would be more bearable than that of parents.

However, not abuse, but the longstanding nature of a young woman's sexual relation with a man and the couple's professed desire to marry, ultimately persuaded a judge to pressure in a young woman's favor. When fifteen-year-old Eugenia Gómez ran away from home in 1962 because her mother's beatings had allegedly resulted in a miscarriage, the judge upheld the request of Gómez's mother that her daughter return home.[72] Significantly, where her mother maintained that her daughter had left home "to have sexual relations with her boyfriend," Eugenia Gómez claimed that she had fled to a girlfriend's house to escape her mother's blows and that she had not had sexual contact with any man during that time. In Gómez's case, the judge upheld parental rights to guard their daughter's sexuality over the young woman's claims that her household was unbearable. Parents countered their daughter's complaints of abuse with accusations of the daughter's sexual misconduct. What worked against Gómez and made this case unusual was her denial that she had a permanent sexual union with a man. Ironically, this left her vulnerable to charges of sexual promiscuity and compromised her ability to show she had an acceptable alternative to her parents' guardianship.

Settlements of home abandonment cases through marriage were contingent on two factors: a sexual relationship between the couple (preferably a longstanding one or one that had resulted in pregnancy) and the willingness or ability of the young man involved to wed. At times, parents brought charges against men not to secure their daughter's return, but to pressure a man to marry. However, the fact that a couple did not engage in a sexual relationship or that the man could not support a wife considerably weakened arguments for marriage. When an inquilino couple in San Felipe demanded that a judge pressure Juan Tobar to marry their daughter Lucía Tapia after "she [ran away] from home and had sex with him," the magistrate initially agreed to perform the ceremony (which both Juan Tobar and Lucía Tapia apparently wanted), but stopped when Juan Tobar's father appeared in court to protest that his son did not have a job and that he would be unwilling to support the couple.[73]

Home abandonment cases underscore how young women negotiated their position in rural society in sexual ways. Whether or not a woman was sexually active, and with whom, was central to the meaning of being a daughter as well as to that of becoming a wife. Getting pregnant or forming a stable sexual union with a man constituted a young woman's surest way out of the parental home, while to establish a marriage almost meant entering into arrangements that affirmed a husband's sexual authority over a wife. Young women actively influenced and challenged the terms of their positions within families by trading or withholding sex, but they ultimately bargained between two options that both presupposed their subordination in sexual terms.

Sex, Gender, and Authority

In the 1950s and early 1960s, life in Aconcagua and elsewhere in rural Chile meant a struggle for all campesinos, women and men alike. But campesina women suffered campesino men's authority in addition to that of the patrón. Gender inequality sprang from the interface between latifundia's specific requirements for labor and contemporary patriarchal notions, embraced throughout Chilean society, about men's entitlement to women's bodies and labor. Relations within the campesino household, in both their collaborative and coercive forms, developed as practical and rational responses to an oppressive labor system spawned by a society that already assumed the appropriateness of women's sexual subordination to men. Men wielded authority over women's domestic and productive labor because the energies of wives and daughters were presumed to belong to husbands and fathers in their capacity as household heads and men. This sense of entitlement was understood and reinforced sexually. A woman's sexual fidelity and accessibility to a particular man was central to being a wife as well as to a daughter's ability to leave the parental household. In contrast, men's license to multiple sexual relationships and their relative freedom from the scrutiny and control exercised over women's sexual lives constituted one of the main bases of men's assumed right to exercise authority over women in other realms.

Women's exchange of sex for material security, which entailed men's stewardship of women's sexuality and labor, made common sense to most campesinos, male and female. It was understood as mutually beneficial. But if marriage and family arrangements seemed natural, they were negotiated on a daily basis and frequently maintained through force. Women contested men's degree of control over their lives and challenged men's vision of marriage by insisting on greater sexual reciprocity. Men strove to ensure no undue challenge to their authority and women's assumption of wifely demeanors and responsibilities.

The economic and social relations of latifundia shaped and exacerbated forms of male dominance within the campesino household. The lack of permanent employment opportunities for women fueled women's material dependence on men. In addition, the importance of family labor to estate production and subsistence cultivation compelled men to exact underpaid work from wives and children in the patrón's fields and to rely heavily upon women's unpaid housework in the home and on family land. Yet the very privileging of male over female labor and the specific organization of gender hierarchies within rural families presupposed women's already existing subordination to men on sexual grounds. The idea that men were more practically suited to most work

on the estates and that women were naturally responsible for childrearing and dependent on employed males underlay women's exclusion from
most forms of employment and consequently reinforced the importance
of marriage and family to female survival. The notion that masculinity
derived its meaning from a man's ability to be independent and to command authority over his social dependents emphasized relations with
female family members as one of the few realms where poor men could
exercise male prerogative. Latifundia conditioned the day-to-day reality
of rural men's social dominance over women, but men's relative privilege
was sanctioned by notions and practices of sexual hierarchy that existed
independently of latifundia and that could prove stubbornly persistent
even in its absence.

chapter 3   Making Men

Labor Mobilization and Agrarian Reform

On June 19, 1965, a thousand campesinos from Aconcagua rallied in front
of the National Palace in Santiago, waving Chilean flags and handpainted
banners proclaiming, "Give land to the man who works it!"[1] The men
and women in attendance had arrived early in the morning after several
hours of cramped travel in old buses and open trucks. They came in their
best clothes, toting gifts of chicha and empanadas. A group of dancers
clad in colored smocks and aprons was prepared to give a performance
of the traditional cueca. The campesinos gathered to celebrate Chile's
new president, Eduardo Frei Montalva, who had been elected just the
previous year on promises to undertake an agrarian reform that would
"turn the campesino into his own patrón." They also assembled to ask
the chief executive to move faster in fulfilling his pledge. At the day's
end, a delegation submitted a petition, signed with thumbprints and signatures, calling for accelerated land expropriations and the inclusion of
campesinos in decision-making processes.[2]

   The crowd from Aconcagua constituted one of few gatherings of
organized rural poor people in Chile's capital in modern times. It signaled
the birth of a new, ideologically diverse labor movement that would pro-
pel rural workers to the center of national politics over the next decade.
Following the 1964 election of a Christian Democratic administration
committed to significant land reform, campesino unions throughout
Chile transformed from small, clandestine cells into huge working-class
organizations with material backing from the state. Between 1964 and

1970, the number of rural workers belonging to unions leapt from under 2,000 to over 140,000, and would reach almost a quarter million by 1972.[3]

Unions became the single most important conduit connecting the rural poor to what became the Agrarian Reform process. They fostered a new sense of citizenship among a historically disenfranchised population and nurtured campesinos' confidence that poor people were taken seriously by the state and political parties. They generated intense debates within rural communities over the relationship between private property and social justice, between landownership and wage labor, between the state and peasant movements. Rural unions also served as the vehicles through which campesinos contested the particular form of land expropriation and redistribution, as well as who benefited and on what terms. By the late 1960s, unions would stand at the forefront of volatile and often violent confrontations between workers and landowners, unions and the government, and among different groups of campesinos.

At the June rally in front of the National Palace, however, overtures to the patriotic and conciliatory nature of the Agrarian Reform muted fears about social conflict. The pro-government daily, *La Nación,* gushed that the "humble visitors" had demonstrated their confidence that the Frei administration "would realize their hopes for a better life and the certain progress of the nation."[4] Ignoring the presence of communist and socialist unions in the crowd, as well as the petition admonishing the president to move faster, the newspaper praised the rally's sponsor, the Catholic Union of Christian Campesinos (UCC), for seeking a harmonious road to social improvement. As proof of such amicability, the paper stressed the hardworking and family-oriented character of the crowd, and, in particular, the presence of women. It described rally participants as "workers with farm tools in their hands and wives at their sides," and it applauded the dance performance of campesino couples whose female members wore sashes "printed with their hopes and dreams."[5] When President Frei emerged on the palace balcony to greet the multitude, he also emphasized the importance of family to a successful Agrarian Reform:

> *Compañeros,* you will have a Reform that will lift up your family and the entire nation. We will not merely give you a handful of dirt on which to starve, but family parcels on which a man can become an agriculturalist

who provides for his family and produces for the Nation. . . . We will make this Reform firmly, without anger. We will do it with people with clean hearts, not those boiling with hate. . . . We will construct organizations controlled neither by the state nor by political parties. . . . It will be a Reform without [partisan] flag-waving or political agitation, but that of an organized people creating a new nation.[6]

The President's words reflected both the lofty aspirations and the blatant contradictions of the Christian Democratic Agrarian Reform. Between 1964 and 1970, the Frei administration initiated the most significant redistribution of private wealth in Chilean history—expropriating almost 20 percent of all agricultural land—while attempting to avoid class conflict. It facilitated an unprecedented surge in popular mobilization—unionizing almost half of the nation's rural laborers—while discouraging the politicization of working-class organizations. It promised the creation of a new society—decreeing a "Revolution in Liberty"— while remaining committed to existing social structures.

Notions about family and gender played a crucial role in reconciling these paradoxes and promoting the Agrarian Reform. Frei repeatedly invoked the male-headed family as a metaphor for national progress and political peace. He insinuated that, just as wives and children collaborated with a husband or father in sacrifice for a family's welfare, so, too, would willing cooperation by all social classes benefit Chile as a whole. The ideal of a national family was meant to have particular appeal to Chile's landowning and financial elite, whose support for a prudent and efficient Agrarian Reform the Christian Democrats saw as crucial to avoiding political upheaval and violence. Prominent landowners belonging to the National Agricultural Society (SNA) already sat on the boards of Chile's major financial policy-making institutes, including the Central Bank and the Corporation for Development (CORFO).[7] Frei expanded this role by including SNA members on Agrarian Reform councils and in bureaucracies, stressing landowners' tradition of national leadership and paternalist responsibility for campesino dependents. The rural poor figured within the national family as junior partners—most frequently as children whom the Agrarian Reform would help mature into men. Campesino participation was welcomed within a context of natural deference to state benevolence.

The male-headed family also became the object of concrete policies. As Frei told his visitors from Aconcagua in 1965, the Agrarian Reform would permit campesino men to provide for wives and children in order that productive families, in turn, could feed the nation. Although this goal implied a concern for women as well as men, male heads of household were seen as the immediate subjects of the Agrarian Reform. Frei had campaigned throughout 1964 on a promise to create 100,000 new campesino proprietors, a pledge that envisioned the transformation of male inquilinos into yeoman farmers who produced adequate surpluses for the domestic market. The addition of a new class of male producers to Chile's tiny landowning elite would symbolize the country's transition from underdevelopment to modernity.

The Frei administration deemed reconstituting and invigorating campesino masculinity crucial to this process, and it saw unions as the primary vehicles of male transformation. The Christian Democrats, together with labor activists of both Catholic and Marxist orientation, understood unions as vital to educating campesino men for their class mission within the Agrarian Reform. For government officials and labor activists alike, the goal of creating a new class of small producers principally implied men, already understood as the primary workers and heads of family. Unions would prepare men for the job. They would break the oppressive and paternalistic cycles of latifundia culture, often blamed for keeping campesinos in a perpetual childhood. They would provide the adolescent rites of passage that prepared campesinos for adult roles by showing men the value of class solidarity, democratic procedure, and efficient cultivation.

This mission of class uplift and masculine rehabilitation also had racial implications. Elite and middle-class tendencies to blur categories of inquilinaje and Indianness, and to associate all rural poor people with primitivism and irrationality, were commonplace among Agrarian Reform government functionaries as well as labor leaders. Understanding race as almost indistinguishable from rural culture and class, both groups entrusted unions with a certain civilizing mission. Unions would replace depraved practices with moral behavior, barbarity with citizenship. They would turn submissive inquilino peons into proactive, self-reliant, and productive members of the nation. Under Agrarian Reform everyone would benefit, but able men first needed to be created to lead the way.

Christian Democracy and the Origins of the Agrarian Reform

Eduardo Frei's 1964 election and the launching of the Agrarian Reform resulted from an uneasy marriage between sincere progressive impulse and conservative realpolitik. Frei's Christian Democrats constituted one of Chile's youngest and most heterogeneous parties. Formally established only in 1957, Chile's Christian Democratic party drew its support and leadership primarily from the middle-class ranks of teachers, lawyers, doctors, white-collar employees, and small business owners, but it had solid ties to elite industrial and financial circles as well as a growing base among urban and rural workers.[8] Such diversity reflected the multiclass alliances spawned by Chile's rapid urbanization as well as the Christian Democrats' specific success at promoting class cooperation as an ideal. Throughout the 1964 campaign, Frei touted his "Revolution in Liberty" motto to promise that his party would harmonize the interests of labor and capital, empowering the poor without engendering class conflict. While firmly rejecting socialism, Christian Democrats condemned monopoly capitalism and imperialism and defined a central role for the state in managing the economy and providing social welfare. Dramatic progress was promised in the hyperbole of "revolution," while the modifier "in liberty" assured social peace and rejected leftist goals of toppling the propertied elite.

The Christian Democratic vision of social uplift drew on a decades-long effort by Catholic reformers to denounce social injustice while providing ideological and institutional alternatives to Marxism. The papal encyclicals, *Rerum Novarum* (1891) and *Quadragesimo Anno* (1931), which both had declared excessive capitalist greed and international socialism Christianity's greatest threats, inspired waves of reformist efforts by progressive clergy and devote laity. Chilean Catholics had been organizing schools, unions, and youth programs in poor neighborhoods since the 1910s. In the 1930s, the writings of French philosopher Jacques Maritain inspired a generation of Jesuit-educated students at Santiago's elite Catholic University (including Eduardo Frei and many of his future ministers) to criticize latifundia as the basis of Chile's underdevelopment. In 1938, these youths broke away from the Conservative Party to form Christian Democracy's direct predecessor, Falange Nacional, which worked closely with progressive Catholic institutions in promoting land reform, labor rights, and state-provided welfare.

As was true elsewhere in the world, Catholic reformism in Chile was deeply influenced by the growing success of the Marxist Left. The first systemic critiques of latifundia and demands for massive land redistribution were made in the 1910s by the Socialist Workers Party and the Chilean Workers Federation (FOCH), both led by the eventual founder of the Chilean Communist Party, Luís Emilio Recabarren. The Left also initiated the first efforts to unionize rural workers in the early 1900s; either Communists or members of the Trotskyist National Poor Peasant League led the most militant inquilino land occupations and strikes of the 1930s and 1940s. After 1930 the Communist Party dominated Chile's growing trade union movement in cities and mines. Between 1938 and 1952, the Communist and Socialist parties were elected to national leadership as part of successive Popular Front coalition governments.[9] These administrations championed a version of state-led development and cross-class alliance between workers and industry which Christian Democratic ideals would later echo. Although Popular Front governments suppressed rural organizing in a concession to landowners, they simultaneously oversaw the creation of labor tribunals that formally recognized the principle of campesino labor rights and the state's prerogative to enforce them.[10]

By the late 1950s, popular support for the Left and for land reform reached a new high. Electoral politics had become more participatory and democratic: Women were granted full suffrage in 1949 and legislation in 1958 made voting compulsory and introduced the Australian ballot (a single official ballot), which allowed voters to conceal their party preferences for the first time in Chilean history.[11] Electoral reform dealt a significant blow to landowners' political power by disallowing the tradition of distributing only specific party ballots to campesinos. With patrón control over rural votes no longer a given, Marxist, Christian Democratic, and small social democratic parties launched organizing efforts in the countryside. These changes especially benefited the Left. In the 1958 presidential race, Salvador Allende's People's Action Front (FRAP), a coalition uniting Socialists and Communists, came within three percentage points of victory on a platform that called for campesino unionization and the end of latifundia.

The near win by the Left, quickly tailed by news of the Cuban Revolution the following January, profoundly influenced Christian Democracy's 1964 political platform and helped ensure its electoral success. It tipped the balance of power within Christian Democratic circles leftward, toward reform-minded professionals critical of capitalism and who argued that reducing social inequalities and mobilizing the poor should be given priority. Although the Christian Democratic Party continued to reflect its significant business constituencies' concern about economic growth and modernization, it turned decidedly more populist and focused on the working classes. Eduardo Frei belonged to the more elite and pro-business faction of the party, but he received the party's nomination due to his stature as a veteran statesman and because of his willingness to preside over a platform more radical than anything he had advocated previously. Meanwhile, the prospect of a possible victory by Allende (whose Left-coalition was now emboldened by popular enthusiasm for Cuba) pushed Chile's wealthiest families and right-wing political parties to reluctantly join forces with the Christian Democrats and accept Frei as a candidate. This ensured an electoral majority for Frei who decisively beat Allende; but it gave a misleading sense of elite support for Christian Democratic reformism.

The United States aggressively supported this center-right alliance. Cold War politics played a major role in the first years of the Agrarian Reform. Amid its panic over the Cuban Revolution, the United States targeted Chile as a critical danger zone in its hemispheric war on Communism, singling out the anti-Marxist, but reform-minded, Christian Democrats as its front-line soldiers. In 1963, the United States channeled millions of dollars and the energies of scores of economists, political advisors, and campaign strategists into the Christian Democratic Party. Following Frei's election, Chile became the largest per capita recipient of U.S. foreign aid in Latin America, obtaining over a quarter billion dollars in grants and loans between 1965 and 1966. It then restructured its enormous foreign debt on extremely favorable terms.[12] The United States also looked on Chile as a showcase for its new Latin American development and security program, the Alliance for Progress.[13] Begun in 1961 under President John F. Kennedy and continued by President Lyndon Johnson and President Richard Nixon, the Alliance for Progress aimed to diffuse support for Marxism. It encouraged Latin American governments to undertake economic development projects and structural reforms (including the modernization and expansion of the military), which Washington would help design and finance. At its inception, Kennedy pledged that the program would pump ten billion dollars into Latin America over the ensuing ten years and declared that agricultural reform would be one of the most important structural adjustments. The architects of the Alliance for Progress—mostly Harvard-trained development specialists—viewed latifundia as an incubator of revolution and argued that land reform would create Midwestern-style family farms as the foundation of healthy capitalist development and lasting social peace.

Important groups of Chileans agreed with the basic premise of the Alliance for Progress, but with a different twist. Since World War II, Chilean intellectuals had led vibrant debates in Latin America over national development and modernization. In the mid-1950s, Chile joined the United Nations Economic Commission on Latin America (ECLA) that, under the initial leadership of Argentine economist Raúl Prebisch, argued that Latin America needed a unique path to development that imitated neither the North Atlantic capitalist model nor that of the Communist Eastern Block. ECLA blamed Latin America's economic woes on imperialist relationships with the United States and Europe and, specifically, on Latin America's historical dependence on importing industrial goods in return for exporting primary products. Importantly, ECLA did not reject capitalist economics and clearly defined itself as a political and commercial partner of the Western NATO alliance. However, ECLA posited that, given the inequalities of the current world market and the structural legacy of colonialism, Latin American development would require aggressive state planning, economic protectionism, and generous credit from North Atlantic governments and lending institutions.

Within Chile, ECLA's ideas were widely disseminated by members of the pro–Christian Democracy DESAL (Center for Economic and Social Development for Latin America) and by social scientists at the Catholic University.[14] These Catholic reformers embodied the ascendancy of nationalist technocrats who, although mostly self-defined as anti-Marxist, shared the Left's view of the state as the engine of modernization as well as the premise that economic development and social justice required a significant structural overhaul, including land reform. They also agreed with the Left's view of latifundia as a feudal institution and a source of national underdevelopment. Both Catholics and leftists decried Chile's inability to feed its population and the consequent agricultural trade imbalances, which rose from $77 million to $124 million between 1954 and 1963.[15] Both also blamed chronic underutilization of land and deteriorating rural wages for the massive rural migration to Chile's already overburdened city slums. In short, by the early 1960s, there was broad agreement across the center-left political spectrum on the need for some type of agrarian reform. Only its nature and extent were contested.

Ironically, responsibility for enacting Chile's first Agrarian Reform legislation fell to President Jorge Alessandri's rightist coalition government of the Conservative and Liberal parties. Alessandri had narrowly defeated Allende in the polarized elections of 1958 and firmly represented the interests of the landowning elite. But congress remained in the control of center and left opposition parties that favored agrarian reform and, joined by heavy pressure from the United States, forced Alessandri's signature on Agrarian Reform Law 15.020 in 1962. This first Agrarian Reform law established the basic institutions and legal guidelines for land redistribution. It reiterated the principle, enshrined in Chile's 1925 Constitution, that private property was of public interest, and it defined the terms under which property could be expropriated, the most important of which constituted abandonment or poor exploitation.[16] The law also instituted a mechanism for reimbursing landowners for expropriated terrain and a special court for processing landowner appeals. It curtailed landowner authority over workers by providing campesinos with new wage and job protections.[17] Lastly, this Agrarian Reform law created three state agencies to execute policy: the Corporation of Agrarian Reform (CORA), with the power to expropriate land and reorganize it into vaguely defined "centers of agricultural production"; the Institute for the Development of Agriculture and Livestock (INDAP), to lend technical and financial assistance to small producers and campesinos; and the Superior Council of Agricultural Production (CONSFA), to coordinate regional and national agricultural planning.[18]

Despite the boldness of this first legislation, the Agrarian Reform did not start in earnest until after Frei's 1964 election. Alessandri openly opposed expropriations and was loath to alienate his elite base of support. He followed the lead of Chile's powerful landowner associations in redefining the Agrarian Reform's goals strictly in terms of increasing productivity. Both the SNA and a smaller group of landowners, the Southern Agricultural Consortium (CAS), responded shrewdly to what, in the early 1960s, seemed the Agrarian Reform's inevitability. For decades landowners had vociferously denounced all mention of agrarian reform as antipatriotic and communist; but following the 1962 passage of the first Agrarian Reform Law, both the SNA and CAS began alternating such warnings with tempered endorsements of a limited agrarian reform that would focus on modernizing agriculture and improving efficiency.[19] The SNA, in particular, promoted the idea that agrarian reform should create incentives for growers to expand cultivation and increase yields through subsidized technology, better seeds, and improved credit and prices. Land expropriation and redistribution should be limited to abjectly abandoned land and property already controlled by the state. Alessandri's policy closely mirrored this philosophy, and during the course of his tenure, he only expropriated sixty thousand hectares, two thirds of which pertained to a single publicly owned estate.[20] Critics from both the political center and the Left derisively labeled his effort the "Flowerpot Reform."

The Christian Democrats promised to undertake a real Agrarian Reform that would prove nothing short of revolutionary. They would pursue both economic modernization and social justice. The Agrarian Reform would redistribute land to campesinos and raise productivity on farms of all sizes. Agricultural self-sufficiency would erode external debts and enable more robust industrialization. When combined with other Christian Democratic goals, such as purchasing a controlling interest in Chile's copper mines (something Frei called the "Chileanization" of copper), it would help shore up economic sovereignty. At the same time, the Agrarian Reform would uplift the poor. The state would sponsor improved education, health care, and housing. New civic organizations would integrate campesinos into national political life. Lastly, the Agrarian Reform would legalize and support the rights of rural workers to unionize and fight for better economic conditions.

The Christian Democrats' dual priority flowed from divisions within the party between Catholic social reformers, who argued that class harmony required redistributing property and educating the poor, and Catholic businessmen and technocrats who emphasized modernizing commercial markets and increasing productivity on existing estates. But it also reflected a shared belief that capitalism could simultaneously be made more efficient and more democratic, and that the right policies could achieve this goal without class conflict. Campesinos were to organize, receive land, and enjoy better standards of living without jeopardizing agricultural production or penalizing large landowners who farmed efficiently. While Frei condemned the underutilization and mismanagement of agricultural land, he carefully praised the initiative of entrepreneurial growers and assured them the retention of their property. Likewise, while sternly warning landowners of vigorous prosecution in case of any violation of workers' rights, he lectured rural labor leaders that the purpose of unions was to protect campesino interests within the boundaries of the law and that illegal activity would not be tolerated.

Mobilizing Men: The Early Efforts

Rural labor organizing began to regain a cautious force in the late 1950s and early 1960s, just prior to Eduardo Frei's election. It was spearheaded not by the Christian Democrats but by the Communist and Socialist parties and by Catholics acting independently of party affiliation. Despite the Alessandri administration's antipathy toward worker mobilization, the anticipation of some type of agrarian reform legislation galvanized political activists and encouraged more flexible interpretations of existing labor codes. Following the 1952 relegalization of the Communist Party by the populist administration of military strongman Carlos Ibáñez, leftists resumed their decades-old organizing activities in the countryside. In a renewed spirit of unity, born partly of Allende's attempt to forge a populist alliance for the 1958 elections, communists and socialists collaborated in 1956—breaching differences that had often bitterly divided them in the 1930s and 1940s—to create the National Federation of Campesinos and Indians (FCI). As its name implied, the FCI emphasized the need to organize the indigenous communities concentrated in the south as well as the workers on Chile's large estates in the central valley. In Aconcagua, the FCI had strongholds in the counties of Catemu, San Esteben, and Rinconada; by 1964, it had organized unions in each of these areas.[21]

Despite the Left's longstanding presence in rural areas, independent Catholics were also growing into a stronger force in many parts of the central valley by the early 1960s, especially Aconcagua. The Catholic worker advocacy group, ASICH (Chilean Union Action), had been running leadership training programs for campesinos from its regional headquarters in San Felipe since the late 1940s. Capitalizing on the five-year ban on the Communist Party, ASICH had made Catholic unionism a compelling alternative. In 1953, Emilio Lorenzini, a leader in ASICH as well as in Falange Nacional, helped mobilize rural workers in the southern county of Molina for a massive labor strike and march on Santiago.[22] Events in Molina firmly established Catholic progressives as a significant voice for social justice in the countryside. After 1960, ASICH's major union offshoot, Christian Campesino Unity (UCC), continued the group's work. Until 1967 the UCC constituted the dominant rural labor federation in the Aconcagua Valley, establishing unions in all nine counties and claiming a membership of several thousand.[23]

Catholic and leftist labor organizations competed for constituencies and clashed ideologically. The UCC was avidly anti-Marxist and promoted unions as *gremios* (vocational associations) aimed at reconciling patrón-worker tensions by representing campesino interests and improving rural living standards. It also staunchly eschewed all political party affiliations. Although most UCC activists were sympathetic to, if not members of, the Christian Democratic Party, they argued that the Catholic ideal of a nonpartisan labor movement could be achieved only by organizing independently of party leadership. In contrast, FCI activists saw unions as vehicles for politicizing workers, intensifying class conflict, and challenging landed authority; they understood the Communist and Socialist parties as essential to the process. Lastly, Catholics and leftists disagreed on the goal of land reform. While the UCC embraced the Catholic insistence on the subordination of private property to the social good, they called for the redistribution of land to individuals organized into cooperatives of small farmers. In contrast, FCI placed greater emphasis on farming land collectively or in permanent cooperatives, although it accepted small individual holdings as a possible form of land tenure.

For all their differences, Catholic and leftist demands showed significant ideological overlap and, in practice, their organizing strategies proved quite similar. By calling for an "end to man's exploitation of man" and for the "subordination of the private good to the social good," the UCC echoed the Marxist idea that socializing the means of production was crucial to creating a just society. Both the UCC and the FCI demanded the abolition of the restrictive 1948 rural labor code and advocated the creation of rural unions on the basis of counties rather than individual estates. Both condemned latifundia as inefficient and socially unjust and demanded the redistribution of land "to the man who works it." Both focused organizing efforts around petitions for higher wages, weekly bonuses, rain-day pay, family allowance payments, and adequate housing.

Catholics and leftists also agreed on the primary target of their organizing efforts — male inquilinos. Both attributed the evils of latifundia to the inquilino labor system and gross concentrations of land. While the Left blamed this situation on capitalism and Catholics blamed it on greed, both aimed their reformist zeal at the large estate and the inquilino worker. For both, the inquilino most fully embodied campesino oppression, despite the fact that, by the 1960s, inquilinos comprised only a minority of estate workers and usually suffered less impoverishment than minifundista farmers and seasonal workers. Rooted in peonage and colloquially referred to as a type of slavery, inquilino labor arrangements powerfully symbolized both the historic injustices and the current backwardness of Chilean agriculture. In practice, labor organizers also targeted permanent workers who comprised a significant portion of the labor force and who lived and worked under conditions similar to those of inquilinos. The Communists differed slightly by also stressing the importance of organizing seasonal workers, especially migrants. But all labor activists, whether they saw their ultimate goal as creating a socialist society or as healing divisions within a Christian community, defined their primary mission as empowering inquilinos.

The focus on inquilinos made unions masculine affairs. Both during the labor movement's early resurgence and throughout its rapid acceleration after 1964, men comprised 94 percent of rural union memberships in the Aconcagua Valley and in the rest of Chile.[24] On one hand, this figure's remainder correlated to women's presence in the paid labor force, where they comprised less than 1 percent of inquilinos and 5 percent of permanent workers.[25] But the very fact that inquilinos were overwhelmingly male to begin with, and that the labor movement chose them as a focus, resulted from already existing assumptions about gender and family inseparable from how labor markets and union strategies developed. The inquilino symbolized campesino oppression and potential militancy precisely because most inquilinos were male. Both Catholic and Leftist labor organizers assumed inquilinos to be men with families, naturally male heads of household. Inquilinos represented the totality of injustice because of latifundia's two-pronged insult to them as men: they were never simply workers laboring under exploitative conditions, but also husbands and fathers unable to adequately provide for dependent women and children. They were also men whose humiliation (and, labor activists hoped, rage) was caused by the coercion of another man, the landowner. Rural women and male seasonal and migrant workers also endured exploitation (often more extensive), but neither could represent latifundia's injustices in the same way. Women were already considered naturally subordinated to men, both within and across class. Male migrant and seasonal workers potentially shared with inquilinos the masculine indignity of bowing to the patrón, but as often single men, they lacked responsibility for, and authority over, a family. With married inquilino men the labor movement's principal targeted audience, reconstituting men's authority within the campesino family became integral to broader calls for workers to stand up to the boss. In 1962, the UCC's monthly paper, *Tierra y Libertad,* ran a front-page article about a campesina woman whose husband beat her for associating with union activists.[26] Frightened of patrón retaliation, the husband had refused to respond to UCC invitations to join his brothers in struggle. Bravely, the battered wife had continued gathering information and finally convinced her wayward husband to join the union. Together with fellow workers, the man soon won a salary raise and was reunited with his wife in conjugal bliss. The paper praised the heroic wife as "a quiet, valiant woman who saved her husband by teaching him the pride of winning a better life for his children."[27]

Although this tale of female sacrifice acknowledged women's political savvy, its main theme stressed the connection between union membership and appropriate manliness. Real men liberated themselves from the emasculating fear of the patrón by collectively struggling to provide for their dependents. Valiant women nurtured this manhood, even at the cost of physical abuse. The story affirmed the principle of male dominance over women within projects of class uplift. While not actually condoning wife beating, it took such behavior to be a natural reaction to female assertiveness. Wife beating served as a narrative device for emphasizing the masculine inadequacy of men who did not join unions, suggesting that union men did not have to resort to force to maintain authority at home. Only campesino men who assumed manly responsibilities could achieve working-class victories and conjugal harmony.

Cultivating campesino assertiveness toward male bosses represented a particular concern in the labor movement's quest to reconstitute rural manhood. Both leftists and Catholics blamed the presumably feudal culture of inquilinaje for turning campesino men into children unable to challenge patriarchal authority, and both urged emboldened displays of manliness as a remedy. The Communist daily, *El Siglo,* and the Catholic monthly, *Tierra y Libertád,* as well as other labor periodicals featured illustrations of diminutively figured campesino men—eyes lowered, hats in hand—cowering beneath the oversized image of a great landowner, accompanied by articles discussing how unions and the Agrarian Reform would end unmanly domination and make campesinos truly free men.[28] As an ASICH pamphlet written in 1961 asked rhetorically beneath the illustration of a giant patrón and his miniature workers, "Are you free when you have to sign your name [to vote] according to the Boss's dictates? Are you free when you are malnourished and without hope? No, you are not free, you are a slave! . . . Only an agrarian reform will set free men's initiative!"

Both the practice and culture of rural unions were explicitly masculinist. Until well after Frei's election, the need to hold union meetings clandestinely shrouded union activity in an air of danger that precluded most women's participation and lent a tough heroism to that of men. In the Aconcagua Valley, labor activists from the UCC and FCI gathered handfuls of men under bridges or in remote shacks, relaying information about labor laws and drafting petitions for raises, housing repairs, and better regalías.[29] Afterwards, the men would visit other houses on the estate, recounting the meeting's content and collecting thumbprints and signatures. In the event that a suspicious landowner or administrator passed by, campesinos would pretend they had gathered to drink aguardiente and gamble. Since discovery might end in the loss of a job, secrecy from the patrón and trust between fellow workers was paramount. Risk bound workers in collective responsibility and fostered a sense of rebellious agency. In an oral history, Armando Gómez, a former permanent worker and early union leader on the Lo Vicuna hacienda in Putaendo county, recalled the first unionizing efforts as tests of masculine bravery and daring: "We had to be so careful. . . . If the patrón found out, the next day you'd be out in the street with your family. Only the real tough guys would dare, only those with courage or who were crazy. It was crazy, but I did it because I had had enough of the patrón's abuse, of the rich squashing the poor, of being treated like an animal rather than a man. The unions made campesinos men."[30]

According to Gómez, union activism required the essentially masculine traits of toughness, courage, and risk taking. Such activism presupposed a worker's recognition that the patrón compromised his dignity as a man. Union men refused the racialized humiliation of being treated "like an animal," insisting that they were men. It was asserting one's manhood, not the mere fact of joining a union, that constituted what Antonio Gramsci called counter-hegemonic action—conscious acts that contest the logic of domination even without overturning it.[31] Armando Gómez's admission that such "craziness" could cost a campesino his job acknowledged the limits of unions, but stressed their very existence as heroic feats by campesino men against rich men.

Not all campesinos were up to the challenge. Armando Gómez's declaration that "the unions made campesinos men" implied that campesinos who shied away from unions lacked adequate manliness. Workers who refused to sign petitions were ridiculed as *amarillo* (yellow), *maricones* (faggots), and *mujeres* and *niñas* (women and girls). Such sexualized derision defined appropriate working-class militancy in terms of a male persona willing to take risks. Union machismo differentiated acceptable from unacceptable manly behavior within a bipolar sexual economy of dominance and submission in which adequate masculinity was positively associated with exerting power over someone else. Union men "gave it to the patrón," instead of "taking it." Women, girls, yellows, and faggots specified cowardice, *not* true manliness—in effect, the opposite of union machos. More specifically, to be like a woman or girl was to be a *maricón*—understood in 1960s rural Chile as a man who sexually received from another man rather than as a homosexual identity. To lack the courage to join a union was to be like a woman, timid and dominated by other men (the patrón), just as a wife was sexually dominated by her husband. It was not that union members saw men who shied away from unions as the same *as* women. Women, by definition, could not become union men, whereas men who refused to join unions refused to assume masculine responsibilities.[32] They were less than full men; they continued to "take it from the boss."

The tremendous price many men paid for participating in unions informed and reinforced union machismo. Class conflict over unions involved (lost) battles of manliness in which bosses asserted patriarchal authority and reminded workers of their vulnerability and dependence. Throughout the 1950s and early 1960s, the rural labor press complained that hundreds of workers were fired annually for union activism on trumped-up charges of absenteeism and alcoholism.[33] Landowners and supervisors threatened workers with force, brandishing rifles during the workday and paying personal visits to workers' homes.[34] Landowners expelled union organizers from estates at gunpoint and sometimes beat them with shovels, knives, and revolvers.[35] Retaliation also took more everyday forms of pressure such as assigning known activists to the most undesirable tasks, illegally forcing inquilinos to labor on Sundays (the only day available for union meetings), and selling campesinos' sheep and pigs on the pretense that the animals had wandered out of their pens.[36]

If such intimidation strained relations between campesino men who did and who did not bear the risks of labor activism, it heightened the masculine purpose of those who did join unions. Accusations by union members that men who shunned labor organizing were unmanly aimed both to humiliate a reticent man in front of his peers and to bolster union members' own sense of masculine purpose. Precisely because of the danger, union activities defined a brave and confrontational masculine stance in opposition to employer attempts to discipline workers as dependents.[37] Signing a petition made one's sympathies public and required face-to-face interaction with the patrón since, according to law, copies of petitions had to be personally submitted by delegations of workers to both the employer and the local labor tribunal. Such actions demanded more than courage; they required commitment to defend working-class male honor—the resolve to stand behind one's name and word in confrontation with social superiors. In an oral history, Emilio Ibáñez, a former permanent worker and FCI union member on an estate in Santa María county, recalled his first experience signing a petition as a sudden and irreversible moment of masculine self-affirmation: "There was no going back. That was it. My name was on the paper for all to see. I was frightened, but I knew I had to be a man now or never. The patrón only understands force, and by joining with my compañeros, I knew we would be strong enough. Enough! I told the patrón 'enough!' to his face. We stood up and said, 'We may work for you, but we deserve respect as workers and as men.' Yes, after that day, I stopped taking my hat off to the patrón."[38]

Ibáñez's insistence that campesinos demanded respect both as workers and as men underscores the duality that made union masculinity specifically working-class. The demand for respect invoked the principle of equality between men at the same time it recognized and qualified an unequal relationship between campesino and boss. To the extent that Ibáñez and his compañeros worked for the patrón under highly unequal terms, they insisted on recognition and compensation for their value as laborers. To the extent that both the patrón and campesinos were men, they insisted on equal treatment on the basis of gender. Emilio Ibáñez understood that both types of respect were won, first, through masculine self-esteem ("I was frightened, but I had to be a man") and second, through men's collective action ("by joining together, we would be strong enough").

The importance of personal risk and rebellion to rural masculinity did not originate with the Agrarian Reform. Belligerent displays toward the boss had long characterized campesino resistance; but, for the first time, the unionizing efforts of the 1960s gave male outrage and struggle a sustained, collective shape with political representation at the national level. Estate visits by UCC or FCI organizers from Santiago and the pressure on labor tribunals to meet at least some campesino demands gave workers a sense of support from urban allies. This legitimated rural men's efforts to challenge employer authority and enabled campesinos to build formal political alliances with other social actors.

Union Power, Class Conflict, and Male Militancy

Frei's 1964 election particularly emboldened campesino men's sense of support from more powerful allies—quite suddenly the state threw its political and financial weight behind the cause of rural labor rights. The Christian Democrats joined forces with left opposition parties in congress to overhaul the existing rural labor code. The resulting Law of Campesino Unionization, Law 16.250, ignited a virtual explosion in rural organizing even before its official enactment in 1967. It legalized new types of campesino unions and actively facilitated their creation. It established the county, rather than the individual estate, as the basis of union organization, loosened the criteria for joining and holding elected positions in unions, allowed migrant and seasonal workers to form unions, and prohibited employers from firing unionized workers or barring labor activists' access to estates. Lastly and crucially, the law created a state-administered mechanism for financing unions through joint contributions of employers and workers.[39]

The new law had immediate and spectacular results. In just one year, between 1967 and 1968, the number of unionized campesinos in Chile leapt from less than 10,000 to 76,356, and climbed to 140,293 by 1970 (see Table 6).[40] The law also explicitly encouraged the labor movement to take national institutional forms. It permitted unions to form nationwide confederations and allowed these to bargain on behalf of regional unions throughout the country. Both of these measures spurred the consolidation of distinct political tendencies. In 1968, the UCC joined with two smaller Catholic federations, the Independent Campesino Movement (MCI) and the National Association of Campesino Organizations (ANOC) to form the Libertád (liberty) confederation.[41] That same year, the FCI merged with the Socialist Party–affiliated National Workers' Front to create Ranquíl confederation, named after the site of a violently suppressed mobilization of campesinos in the 1930s.

Meanwhile, the Frei administration launched its own aggressive campaign to create rural unions loyal to the Christian Democrats. The most pro-reform wing of the Christian Democratic Party, which soon dominated the main Agrarian Reform agencies, urged the use of rural unions for the democratization of the countryside by involving campesinos in organizations that would pressure and represent for their interests. This echoed the ideological bent of independent Catholic unions, but, in practice, Christian Democrats advocated unions for partisan purposes.

State-led efforts to create unions were spearheaded by INDAP, responsible for campesino education and technical support.[42] Under Frei, INDAP was first led by Jacques Chonchol, a visionary advocate of using unions to break down the walls of latifundia and to make campesinos agents of their own destiny. In contrast to the independent Catholics, who wanted unions to foster employer-worker harmony, Chonchol accepted a certain amount of class conflict as inevitable to creating a true revolution

President Frei signing the second Agrarian Reform Law, 1967. CORA promotional literature, courtesy of the University of Wisconsin Land Tenure Center.

in liberty. He also advocated land redistribution into cooperatives and other communal holdings, in addition to individual parcels. These views overlapped with those of the Left and were rejected by many others in the Christian Democratic leadership. They did achieve popularity with the youthful and more reform-minded generation that sought employment as civil servants in INDAP and CORA. Well before the 1967 passage of the Law of Campesino Unionization, INDAP and CORA functionaries descended into the countryside, armed with state legitimacy, financial backing, and a missionary zeal to inform campesinos of the impending labor code and assist in establishing new unions.

Unions sponsored by INDAP were grouped into the national Triunfo Campesino (campesino triumph) confederation, which, despite its technical designation as a "nonpartisan" entity, received explicit backing from the Christian Democratic Party and Frei's administration. INDAP's organizing efforts spurred the growth of the rural labor movement across the political spectrum but secured a disproportional role for Christian Democratic unions. The creation of the Triunfo confederation symbolized the state's support for all rural unions, but implicitly promised addi-

Table 6 Campesino Union Membership by
Confederation, Chile, 1968–1970

Confederation	1968	1969	1970
Libertád	17,421	23,204	29,132
Ranquíl	18,253	30,912	43,867
Triunfo	39,288	47,510	64,003
Sargento Candelaria	1,394	1,743	1,605
Provincias Ag.	n/a	355	1,686
TOTAL	76,356	103,724	140,293

Salinas, *Trayectoria.*

tional benefits to unions belonging to the Christian Democratic camp. As the rural labor movement raced to include almost half of all rural workers in the country by 1970, the number of unions affiliated with Triunfo quickly surpassed that affiliated with either the Left or the independent Catholics.[43] By 1970, Triunfo accounted for 46 percent of the entire unionized rural labor force, while the Ranquíl confederation affiliated with the Communist and Socialist parties claimed 31 percent, and the independent Catholic Libertád confederation accounted for 21 percent (see Table 6).[44]

The Aconcagua Valley proved a particular stronghold for INDAP— where Triunfo accounted for 73 percent of the region's 4,476 unionized workers in 1969.[45] Although these numbers dropped significantly in 1970, Triunfo's stiffest competition in the region—unlike the case nationally—came from the independent Catholics rather than from the Left.[46] While Ranquíl accounted for a respectable 17 percent of Aconcagua's 6,213 union members in 1970 (up from a mere 4 percent the year before), their numbers in Aconcagua remained well below the Left's national average.[47] The political alliances in Aconcagua reflected the immediate legacy of Catholic activism by the UCC. Since Christian Democracy formally shared the confessional and anti-Marxist orientation of the independent Catholics, INDAP organizers found Aconcagua campesinos already familiar with their message, even if they never quite succeeded in entirely replacing the independent Catholics (see Table 7).

The emergence of Christian Democratic unions as a dominant force

Table 7   Number of Unionized Campesinos by Confederation,
Aconcagua Valley* and Aconcagua Province**

Confederation	1968*	1969*	1970**
Libertád	739	1,007	2,462
Triunfo	1,657	3,273	2,700
Ranquíl/FCI	260	196	1,051
TOTAL	2,656	4,476	6,213

*Includes the departments of San Felipe and Los Andes only.
**Includes the entire Aconcagua Province, including the department
of Petorca.
Fondo de Educación y Extensión Sindical, *Descripción numerica de la
organización sindical campesina chilena 1968–1969* (Santiago de Chile:
Ministerio de Trabajo, 1969); Salinas, *Trayectoria.*

in the rural labor movement neither fundamentally altered the substance
of local union activism nor did it balance their ideological focus on men.
Like unions affiliated with the independent Catholics and the Left, the
Triunfo unions called for sweeping land reform but focused their immediate energies on submitting petitions and conducting strikes aimed
at improving working conditions on existing estates. Like their competition, their membership consisted almost completely of male inquilinos
and permanent workers. The Christian Democrats also believed in the
necessity of transforming campesino peons into able producers and providers; it became official state policy following Frei's election. Men who
could support their families and efficiently cultivate the land were to be
the basis of a reinvigorated rural citizenry, and INDAP saw male labor
activism as the means for achieving this end.

The volume and intensity of labor actions increased enormously after
1964 and brought campesinos substantial material gains. Rural workers
in Chile submitted more than two thousand petitions to the Ministry of Labor between 1964 and 1967, and nearly the same number in
1968 alone.[48] In Aconcagua, campesinos submitted more than one hundred petitions by 1967, with the majority of grievances involving accusations of landowner default on wage and social welfare obligations.[49]
Some petitions and organizing efforts met with immediate concessions.

In 1965, a UCC union on the Bellavista estate in Putaendo county won increases in firewood and food allotments, a guaranteed eight-hour workday, and a pledge to bring electricity to campesino homes.[50] Elsewhere in Putaendo, UCC unions on the Lo Vicuña and El Tártaro estates wrested promises from landowners to build four new schools and forty-one new housing units.[51] All labor petitions involved requests for higher pay, which, combined with state-decreed hikes of the minimum wage, raised campesino incomes dramatically. Between 1964 and 1967, real wages in rural Chile rose almost fivefold, from annual rates of 269 escudos to 1,350 escudos. By 1967 employers were legally obliged to pay all wages in cash rather than partially in-kind.[52]

Such gains involved constant negotiation and frequent conflict. Often landowner concessions were exacted at a price. In one petition brokered by the UCC in Putaendo county, workers won a pledge from employers to provide them with transportation to and from work, eliminating an onerous three-hour walk. But the arrangement required that the inquilinos work on the estates themselves, a provision that eliminated the cherished practice of sending an obligado to work in one's stead.[53] In another highly publicized case in San Esteben county, a landowner agreed to share an unspecified percent of his annual profits with workers in return for workers' agreement to provide additional labor on the estate and to generally "cooperate with the administration."[54] Often such trade-offs were not even possible since landowners and managers routinely refused to answer petitions or to comply with pledges made on paper. The SNA's monthly magazine, *El Campesino,* denounced labor activists as Marxist agitators fomenting class hatred, and local chapters counseled members on evading petitions. The SNA cautiously expressed a willingness to work with the Frei administration to promote an agrarian reform geared toward modernization and efficiency, but it remained openly hostile to rural unionization.

Campesinos responded forcefully to landowner recalcitrance. Whereas half a generation earlier rural workers had felt largely powerless to directly confront employers in an organized fashion, the regular presence of labor activists, including openly pro-union government functionaries, encouraged a more aggressive, collective stance. Campesinos repeatedly went on strike. Whereas rural strikes had numbered fewer than a dozen in the early 1960s nationally, almost six hundred strikes took

Campesino demonstrations for land. UP pamphlet series, NOSOTROS
LOS CHILENOS, courtesy of the University of Wisconsin Land Tenure
Center.

place in 1966 alone.[55] The province of Aconcagua recorded no strikes in
the early 1960s but forty-four between 1964 and 1967.[56] Although most
strikes lasted less than a week and usually did not overtly interfere with
production, they often served as the catalyst for government intercession
on workers' behalf.

Before 1967 most rural strikes were technically illegal, but campesinos acted in confidence that the state would recognize the justice of
their cause. They were often able to take advantage of divisions within
the Christian Democratic government and Christian Democracy's populist stance to expand the law's application. The Ministry of Labor and
provincial labor tribunals complained that INDAP and CORA personnel
openly advocated and helped organize strikes as a way of provoking

government intervention in the resolution of a petition.[57] Campesino unions submitted supplemental petitions and letters that carefully invoked the Christian Democratic promises to create a new and improved agrarian economy, nurture the poor's civic participation, and deal sternly with irresponsible, unproductive landowners. A 1965 letter to CORA from striking workers on Bellavista estate in Putaendo county defended the strike by condemning patrón intransigence as immoral and an obstacle to progress. The letter elided the issue of campesinos' own agency and, in a gesture that revealed the extent to which campesinos understood both their need for a powerful state ally and their own legal transgression, emphasized the government's paternalist role in protecting the poor from injustice: "This gentleman [manager] has no human sentiment whatsoever. You [the functionaries of CORA] hold in your hand the power to protect us. . . . We ask that it be you who takes on this case to ensure that there is a real Agrarian Reform on this hacienda where for years they have exploited the inquilinos and where we are still being exploited as much as ever."[58]

Such humble overtures to state benevolence coexisted with more aggressive demands that the Agrarian Reform be swiftly put into action—particularly the goal of redistributing land. Although most initial labor organizing focused on improving wages and living conditions, campesino unions began making explicit demands for estate expropriations immediately following Frei's election. In June 1965, the UCC in Aconcagua wrote Eduardo Frei to insist that a second Agrarian Reform Law being drafted allow estates to be expropriated on the basis of excessive size, regardless of productivity.[59] The Communist and Socialist parties had long supported this demand, and in the mid-1960s it became a rallying point for the entire rural labor movement.

Between 1965 and 1966 alone, rural workers filed over two hundred petitions with CORA, including twenty-eight from Aconcagua, demanding the expropriation of specific estates.[60] Hundreds more requests were made verbally.[61] The Agrarian Reform law required CORA to respond to such petitions with a survey of the estate and an evaluation of its qualification for expropriation. The agency's slowness in conducting surveys, a tardiness caused more by its excessive workload than lack of will, often frustrated campesinos. They were particularly impatient with the infamously long delays between CORA's official decision to expropriate

"All abandoned or badly cultivated land can be expropriated." Popular Promotion pamphlet, courtesy of the University of Wisconsin Land Tenure Center.

and the actual date the agency took possession of the land. In the case of the Bellavista estate in Putaendo county, CORA made a decision to expropriate in 1965, but did not assume charge of the estate until three years later.[62] Routine throughout Chile, such delays were caused by land-owners' legal right to appeal CORA decisions and the Frei administration's general tolerance for lengthy hearings. On Bellavista, campesinos attempted to expedite the process by flooding the local tribunal and CORA office with petitions and by carrying out several short strikes in 1965 and 1966.[63] Lacking results as the case dragged into its third year, they finally escalated pressure by physically taking over the estate in a brief land occupation.[64]

Land occupations, called *tomas de tierra,* became a major campesino strategy for protesting perceived violations of labor agreements and delays in land expropriation; they would continue throughout the Agrarian Reform. A toma usually involved campesinos blocking the main entrance to an estate, impeding flows of farm equipment, produce, and workers. Workers brandished shovels and pitchforks and carried Chilean flags and banners painted with demands. In a number of cases, landowners, supervisors, and their family members were held captive in their houses. Land occupations lasted anywhere from a few days to several months, and they varied widely in their leadership and militancy.[65] In Triunfo-dominated counties such as Santa María and San Felipe, petitions for expropriation and subsequent land occupations were often initiated with the participation of INDAP functionaries in conjunction with the local CORA office. In such cases, tomas served a largely symbolic function, with workers occupying an estate on the day the landowner relinquished the property deed to the government. In other cases, such as a one-day land occupation of the El Cobre estate in San Esteben county in 1966, INDAP functionaries helped organize tomas in order to provoke (or to enable) CORA authorities to intervene against a recalcitrant patrón who had refused to negotiate with unions and suspended production.[66]

Land occupations in leftist or independent Catholic strongholds evolved more independently of government design and frequently involved confrontation with local authorities as well as landowners. The UCC-organized toma of the Bellavista estate in 1966 aimed to shame the government into moving faster on an expropriation decision it had already made. The occupation ended peacefully but with the threat of force when several dozen local police arrived.[67] Tomas organized by Communists and Socialists in Catemu and San Esteben counties in 1968 sought to force CORA to survey and expropriate estates that the agency had not yet considered.[68] Large-scale police actions involving tear gas and gunshots ultimately terminated both occupations, but, in a lesson not lost on campesinos, both estates were expropriated the following year. Land occupations became increasingly confrontational during the late 1960s as land reform accelerated. They often involved significant conflicts between union leaderships and their working-class constituents as well as among campesinos themselves. However, even in their most collaborative and strictly symbolic forms, tomas were a crucial means through which campesinos participated in and influenced the Agrarian Reform as a whole.

Labor mobilization and its tangible victories bolstered connections between class militancy and campesino manliness. Strikes and land occu-

Campesino men
at a toma.

Sign reads,
"Workers' Property."
Both photos from the
UP pamphlet series,
NOSOTROS LOS
CHILENOS, courtesy
of the University of
Wisconsin Land
Tenure Center.

pations overwhelmingly involved men who served petitions on bosses, negotiated with government authorities, and physically occupied estate property. The implicit danger of nighttime vigils and prolonged tomas led many workers to carry weapons, ranging from sticks and shovels to shotguns.[69] Overt violence in rural Chile remained comparatively minimal given the magnitude of labor mobilization and land expropriations; it was even more rare in Aconcagua than around Santiago and in the south. Nonetheless, campesinos' armed style symbolically underscored the militancy of workers' solidarity and their readiness as men to defend class interests.

The issue of brandishing weapons had particular significance for campesino men's relationship to male bosses who had long used arms to intimidate workers. Weapons signified which men had the power to require other men to tip their hat and lower their eyes. Pascual Muñoz, a former inquilino in Santa María county, recounted that even when campesinos did not carry shovels or shotguns, the very existence of the labor movement and the promise of the Agrarian Reform gave campesino men a sense of resistance toward employer humiliation. Class solidarity and the assertion of male dignity could also serve as weapons for facing down the boss: "I was not afraid of the rich! One day, to set an example, Don Gernardo [the patrón] came on horseback and stopped right in front of me and took out his pistol, a big pistol, and he said, 'Maybe I'll just fire a shot at you!' I crossed my arms and just stood there in front of him. 'Look,' I said, 'I'm not afraid of you or your gun. I am not afraid of you because I'm not an ignorant fool, and I'm not a monkey.' . . . And he was afraid of me!"[70]

The story's precise veracity is less important than the sense of courage and manly pride its author attributes to working-class mobilization during the 1960s. The labor movement encouraged a confident defense of male honor. Workers did not believe themselves equal to the patrón or that they had neutralized his social power. Rather, they asserted a specifically working-class masculinity that historian David Montgomery first termed "a manly bearing toward the boss" and that Thomas Klubock and Steve Stern have more recently discussed as poor men's powerful counterpoints to elite humiliation.[71] The goal was not so much to be able to behave exactly like the boss. Sticks were not the same as pistols and, more often than not, campesinos' main defense was only their moral authority. What was important was not to behave like the patrón, but to show the boss one's willingness to stand up to abuse rather than tremble before it. Pascual Muñoz's emphasis on Don Gernardo riding horseback and carrying "a big pistol" dramatized the patrón's masculine social (and probably sexual) power and therefore also the courage of campesino men who stayed planted "right in front" of their superiors, not off to the side of the road with hat in hand. Likewise, Muñoz's story glorified campesino men's ability to force the patrón to see their humanity and intelligence. The declaration that campesinos were not "ignorant fools or monkeys" challenged the racialized imagery of inquilinos as primitive and animal-like. And if the campesino could not yet structurally depose the boss, he could psychologically reverse masculinist class and race hierarchies. In the triumphant end to Muñoz's story, the patrón became afraid of his worker.

Not all landowner response to unionization amounted to overt intransigence. Paternalist efforts to neutralize labor movement radicalism abounded. According to surveys conducted by CORA, many employers initially met, or even anticipated, demands for higher wages and improved housing in an effort to head off attention from Agrarian Reform agencies and to qualify as responsible landowners who would be spared expropriation.[72] In the mid-1960s the SNA aggressively promoted an image of landowners leading the crusade for rural improvement. *El Campesino* featured regular articles on landowners who built state-of-the-art housing and schools for their workers as well as editorials that soberly reminded the readership of the social as well as economic responsibilities of being a good businessman. The SNA also promoted organizational alternatives to unions, creating the vocational association Provincias Agrarias Unidas (united agrarian provinces) to unite small farmers and inquilinos and to advocate the ideals of private property.

But such efforts patently failed to stem the tide of unionization. Membership in Provincias Agrarias Unidas was never more than a few thousand nationally; strikes and land occupations continued to escalate. A sense of betrayal and threat pushed even the most conciliatory landowners into alliances with the majority who had always vociferously opposed accommodating labor's demands. The SNA published monthly tallies of strikes and union membership, while their local chapter in Aconcagua called on landowners to unite and join ranks to protect private property and prevent labor organizers from entering estates.[73] Landowners also used mass communication such as radio to misinform and intimidate workers. As Armando Gómez recalled in an oral history of programs broadcast from San Felipe, "[They] threw pure garbage at CORA, warning [campesinos] that [CORA] would take away their children, take away their chickens, their animals. Later, after CORA announced the Agrarian Reform, the bosses would talk about there having been massacres, so that inquilinos [wouldn't] want anything to do with it."[74]

At the daily and most intimate level, conflict took place in the constant negotiations between workers and bosses over authority on the estate. Campesinos reported that employers beat labor activists, terminated inquilino entitlements, and, in some cases, suspended production altogether.[75] Administrators complained that workers arrived late to work, refused to complete assigned tasks, drank on the job, vandalized property, and stole animals.[76] Although not new, such behavior took on an overt political character in the context of massive unionization and the Agrarian Reform. In 1966, twenty male workers from the El Maitén estate in Santa María county halted their labor digging an irrigation canal at 4 P.M. and went to a local party to drink and roast meat from a cow they had slaughtered. When they were fired for drunkeness and theft of the cow, the men (all members of an INDAP-created union) collectively confronted their employer and successfully negotiated a reinstatement of their jobs: they succeeded in establishing that the cow belonged to one of the workers and had insinuated that the remaining workers on the estate would go on strike if the patrón did not meet their demands.[77] Importantly, the workers reportedly explained to the patrón that "we helped you [the patrón]. . . . we'd built your canal, and now we deserved to serve ourselves."[78]

Workers' sense of a right to set boundaries on employer authority in the workplace was enabled by the labor movement's growing power and intimately tied to the issue of manly respect. In the story about El Maitén, campesinos challenged the boss's right to discipline workers and to unilaterally decide work tasks. Moreover, they insisted that the patrón recognize their labor building the canal as a type of help (*apoyo*), implying that they worked by their free will, even out of generosity, rather than because the patrón had the right to force or demand their labor. They went on to claim entitlement to reward themselves with abundant quantities of alcohol and meat, a sensual overindulgence typically reserved for men in general and the upper classes in particular. Yet, crucially, issues of worker agency and manly respect were both contingent on the collective action of union members in a political climate of credible strike threats.

The various leaderships within the rural labor movement—including leftists, Christian Democrats, and independent Catholics—all worked to buttress campesino men's sense that masculine agency depended on collective action. An INDAP training manual for Triunfo unions instructed local leaders on how to use the pedagogical techniques of the Brazilian literacy teacher Paulo Freire to help campesinos "emerge from passivity and isolation" into "critical awareness and solidarity."[79] Training also sought to encourage the men to discuss their problems and brainstorm solutions with one another. Union education was to be about agency through collective self-reflection, not rote memorization by individuals. In a training pamphlet for the Communist and Socialist unions of Ranquíl, a cartoon illustration of a lone campesino looking miserably through a window at his patrón's wealthy home decried the isolation and impotence of inquilinos before union mobilization. This image was paired with a contrasting drawing of a group of smiling, well-dressed campesinos representing the confidence and prosperity that men achieved through solidarity with fellow workers.[80] Union educators urged campesinos to see the social nature of knowledge and to understand that social agency depended on first sharing a common analysis and mission with other men. As Ossa Pretot, a spokesperson for rural projects run out of the Office of the Presidency, explained the purpose of campesino education, "Man will never be free until he knows what he is worth. . . . [He] needs this to become [part of] a people conscious of its responsibility. . . . You don't win liberty with laws, but by transforming men's minds."[81]

INDAP functionaries and national labor leaders often explicitly cast campesino unionization as a rite of passage to manhood. They explained and understood the political logic of the labor movement in terms of gender and family. They denounced landowners for failing their paternal obligations and celebrated state education programs and unions as schools that would enable campesinos to pass from infancy into full adulthood. At an education workshop in 1966, the president of the independent Catholic MCI, Ulises Díaz, made this comparison explicit: "We campesinos are passing from the childhood that has dominated us through an adolescence. We had bad parents who gave us things without teaching us. And now we are realizing through courses like today how to confront life. . . . [But] we need to mature more. . . . We need committed actions so that nobody will stick our thumb back in our mouth!"[82]

Although the Left would have disputed Díaz's reference to latifundista parents "giving things" to their campesino charges, Socialists and Communists also deployed gendered notions of family and generation as analogies for class domination and worker solidarity. They agreed with the depiction of latifundia as a dysfunctional family that turned working-class men into suckling infants as well as with the prescription that bold action toward self-liberation was analogous to men "growing up." Individual campesinos also echoed this sensibility. As one worker gratefully told INDAP educators at a 1966 training session for campesino leaders held in Santiago, "You have treated us like men, not children, and we have eagerly taken advantage of the opportunity to begin conquering more and more."[83] Although national labor leaderships usually stressed the incomplete and ongoing nature of campesino maturation, they took all sizeable forms of collective action as markers of an already achieved adulthood. Following a mass meeting of some 3,500 campesinos at the Aconcagua Campesino Congress in 1967, the independent Catholic monthly *Campo Nuevo* exclaimed with bravado, "Now Aconcagua has begun to roar, compañeros! Now things have gotten serious! . . . We have become a mature political force!"[84]

The political cleavages and rivalries unionization created complicated the goal of male unification on a practical level. The tri-partisan division of the labor movement established institutional and ideological competition among Christian Democratic, leftist, and independent Catholic organizations and caused factional infighting among workers on estates with more than one confederation present. Triunfo's explicit ties to the Christian Democratic government fostered a less aggressive strategy than that of Ranquíl and Libertád unions. Some campesino men never joined unions, while those who did, did not always agree on the degree of union militancy. Inquilinos with entitlements to land tended to be less enthusiastic about collective or cooperative forms of landholding than did campesinos without access to any land. Workers on well-managed estates frequently opposed expropriation, and they saw the main purpose of unions in the negotiation of fair wages and working conditions.

Such rifts in the movement developed into volatile conflicts in later years, but throughout the first half of the Agrarian Reform, campesino men's sense of being drawn together in unprecedented and powerful ways outstripped fears about dissension. The vast majority of rural men —as high as 90 percent—who lived and worked on estates in central Chile joined a union if one existed in their area.[85] Organizing experiences and the emergence of a union culture forged close links of male camaraderie. Submitting petitions and executing strikes required coordinated and unified efforts, while daily confrontations with the patrón encouraged workers' sense of a shared burden and collective potential.

Above: Voting for union leaders. *Left:* Newly literate campesino practices signature. Both from CORA promotional literature, courtesy of the University of Wisconsin Land Tenure Center.

Despite their differences, Ranquíl, Triunfo, and Libertád cooperated with each other on a regular, institutional basis. During land occupations or ceremonies commemorating an expropriation, men from different unions on other estates and neighboring counties would come to lend strategic solidarity. The leadership training workshops held in Santiago or other cities offered many campesino men the first opportunity they had ever had to travel outside their home province and to meet men from other parts of the country.

Paradoxically, the partisan and personal rivalries among campesinos could add to men's sense of unity with one another. As Thomas Klubock has argued, workers' combative competitions with one another can prefigure the militancy of their challenges to employer authority.[86] In fighting man-to-man among one's peers, poor men confirmed the masculine bravery necessary to confront the boss. When thousands of campesinos gathered at provincial and national campesino congresses after 1967, workers sat segregated by confederation and often engaged in raucous clapping and foot stomping when members of rival camps attempted to speak.[87] Such fractiousness served more as displays of bravado and power (to indicate which confederation held control) than as challenges to working-class unity. Competitive rituals of drinking and gambling usually followed union meetings. Although such activities occasionally led to threats and punches between adversaries, they also signified men's solidarity. Fistfighting could serve as an arena in which union men established credibility in others' eyes. After 1967, most unions formed soccer teams that regularly competed in leagues at the county, provincial, and national levels.[88] Soccer enabled men from different *comunas* and confederations to meet and transpose political conflicts onto the physical arena of sport. Although animosities could run high following a particularly grueling match, players usually shook hands after the game and shared alcoholic drinks.[89]

Union culture also forged bridges across generations. Older men shared cautionary tales (and the occasional heroic story) about thwarted union efforts and repression in past decades. In contrast, many of the younger men who dominated local union leaderships held bolder and more optimistic attitudes. Many of them had entered the labor movement in the 1960s with the Agrarian Reform in full swing, and several men could look back on previous, successful union experiences in sporadic jobs as miners and construction workers.[90] At least a few years of primary school also created a higher rate of literacy among the younger men, which facilitated their knowledge of labor codes and national organizing strategies and often placed sons in the position of teaching their fathers. According to Armando Gómez, who was elected as a union leader in his mid-twenties, campesino men would gather on a weekly basis and choose one literate worker to read aloud the labor press, legal documents, political pamphlets, and stories. Gómez recalled with great tenderness that these rituals—strongly reminiscent of anarchist practices earlier in the century—involved younger men giving older men a rudimentary grasp of the alphabet. As he exclaimed in an oral history, "How excited and proud I was to do that work, and how proud those old guys felt when they could finally sign their own name!"[91]

Older men may have felt more ambivalent about learning from younger men, and as later conflicts would show, many fathers did not relish following the lead of their sons. Still, the circumstances of mass labor organizing tempered the rigid deference campesino fathers historically demanded from sons, even as they afforded poor rural men of all generations an unprecedented access to educational resources. Older men shared with younger men a commitment to campesino solidarity and a sense that the labor movement enabled them to better defend their interests and dignity as men.

Manliness and a Woman's Place

If the labor movement brought men together, men's sense that unions did not, and should not, directly include women also keenly shaped its fraternity. Working-class codes of manliness took their daily meanings from men's interactions with other men and, at times, seemed to have been directed only at men. But they were also always about women. The construction of campesino masculinities relied fundamentally on women, even in their apparent absence from the scene.

A small number of women achieved formal union member status on the basis of laboring as permanent wageworkers, but they participated in union meetings only occasionally.[92] In some instances, nonmember women accompanied their husbands to union meetings, but they rarely spoke, did not vote, and could cause their spouses embarrassment. Pedro Reyes, a former inquilino and member of a Ranquíl-affiliated union in San Esteben county, recalled in an oral history that, when his wife Isabél insisted on going with him to a meeting regarding a possible strike, other workers ridiculed him as henpecked: "She was the only woman out of ten people. They just stared at me, looked evilly at each other and asked if I always needed my señora to put my pants on."[93]

The charge that Pedro lacked adequate manliness because his wife accompanied him reflects the degree to which campesino men not only understood unions as appropriate only for men, but also as associations actually threatened by the presence of women. Confronting the patrón with petitions, strikes, shovels, and surly behavior were acts of masculine, working-class challenge to male social superiors. The direct involvement of women questioned the exclusivity of male heroism. Given the centrality that the restoration of campesino masculinity had to unionization, the exclusion of women from membership was implicitly necessary, and the broader culture of the labor movement worked to enforce this.

Whether in the potential danger of nighttime vigils on occupied haciendas or in the jocular rivalry of a soccer match, the all-male character of unions preserved them as communities of peers and political weapons for vindicating campesino manhood. Not coincidentally, labor organizers and educators often contrasted the transformation of campesinos into union men with domesticity. As a training manual for Triunfo explained, "We are subjects conscious of our worth, dedicated to fighting to build a more humane world, rationally and through critical consciousness. Otherwise we are domesticated, permitting others to decide things for us, always at the orders of others."[94] Although the word *domesticate (domesticar)* implied a broad range of relationships of containment and subordination in rural Chile, including the submission of animals to masters, it was most closely associated with women, particularly with female domestic servants. Women and servants naturally took orders from others but unions allowed men to decide things for themselves, to be critically conscious and proactive: to not be domesticated, to not be women.

Beyond unions' exclusion of women, their affirmation of men's dominion over women and, in particular, men's sexual access to female bodies, defined their masculine integrity. Men were presumed to enjoy this authority primarily in relation to wives, but aspects of union culture celebrated a more general principle of male power over and sexual assertiveness toward women that implied a man's sexual style, as distinct from sexual activity. Such style could be asserted well beyond the four walls of a man's own household. Many of the most important union cultural spaces were constructed around activities reserved exclusively for men— ritualized excessive drinking, smoking, gambling, and sports. Such diversions affirmed the principle that men, not women, had the authority to spend time and resources for personal pleasure and relationships beyond those of the household. They also implied that men had the power to forbid women access to such privileges. All-male drinking sessions marked men's freedom to bodily indulge (and spend money) outside the parameters of their homes and the gaze of female family members. Men acknowledged their exclusive gender right to such gratification and its close linkage to male sexual entitlement. Not accidentally, drinking and sporting events involving union men became times for sharing lewd jokes and fantastical sexual stories about women, not just for arguing over politics and fumbled goals. As Emilio Toledo, a former member of the Triunfo-affiliated union in Santa María, fondly recalled such leisure in an oral history, sex, rather than the Agrarian Reform, usually constituted the preferred topic of conversation: "When the serious stuff was over, men talked about women. Oh, we were without shame! Each recounting his conquests—none of which were usually true—and bragging about the girls he would snag next—none of which were possible. . . . In the end, everyone would be so drunk and silly, they'd really think they were going to take advantage of being out of the house to have an affair [*aventura*] . . . but, of course, almost everyone went home with his hat in his hand!"[95]

In sharing accounts of their sexual exploits of women—however fictitious or unrealized—union men competed with and challenged each other's virility, confirming each other's membership in a common fellowship partially defined by men's sexual access to women. Certainly rural labor unions did not invent the idea that manly men exercised sexual prowess, but the concept of male sexual freedom and access to women proved integral to how the practice and culture of the rural labor movement developed.

National labor leaderships stressed the importance of men's responsibility to families and upstanding behavior as the basis of class solidarity, but the rural labor movement also encouraged the idea of male sexual privilege as a natural part of union manhood. Weekend training sessions for campesino leaders in Santiago often included entertainment featuring female dance troupes and skits that humorously and ironically dramatized men's perpetual vulnerability to the charms of women.[96] In one skit, recounted in an oral history, two successive women turned down the advances of a married campesino man: the first because she was middle-class and prejudiced against campesinos, and the second because she was married. The third woman accepted but, as it turned out, was pregnant by another man.[97] Similarly, the labor press across the political spectrum devoted special comic pages to working-class humor.[98] Cartoons and jokes poked fun either at men's thwarted attempts to seduce sexually voluptuous, often half-naked, women; or at men who were henpecked or sexually denied by their wives.

The playful banter about sexuality affirmed men's right to sexually pursue multiple women and insinuated that this was an inherent component of working-class masculinity. However, it also belied a certain apprehension about female sexuality and men's ability to dominate it. As historian Christine Stansell has argued, male jests about men who cannot successfully capture the women they chase and empty boasts about unconsummated sexual exploits underscore the insecurity of male sexual privilege: women's power to deny men their manhood and the gap between men's desires and what was possible.[99] In the labor movement, the ridicule of men who could not control their wives or successfully execute an affair flowed from a misogynist acknowledgment of women's authority within marriage. Yet such anxiety reinforced rather than undermined the principle of male sexual dominance. It suggested that men needed to avoid humiliation by women's hands by being more sexually confident and aggressive. It also underscored the need to preserve unions and certain key union activities as all-male safe havens for a certain performance of masculinity.

Fears that women opposed the Agrarian Reform informed and exacerbated anxieties about women's capacity to thwart men. In the 1958 presidential elections, twice as many women nationally had voted for the Right's candidate, Jorge Alessandri, as for either Frei or Allende.[100] This fact had provoked a frenzy of campaign appeals to women (mainly in urban areas) by Christian Democrats and Allende's FRAP during the 1964 elections. But despite the apparent success of such efforts (in 1964 a solid majority of women voted for Frei, and a strong minority for Allende), apprehension endured that women were politically reactionary. Campesino men complained that wives objected to their clandestine labor activities, were ignorant of class politics, and could not be trusted with sensitive information. Acknowledgments that women's structural isolation in the household impeded their engagement with wider political processes coexisted with beliefs that innate female traits of religiosity and simplicity made women inherently more conservative than men. In both scenarios, female ignorance had the potential to destabilize the class solidarity necessary for progressive change.

In 1969, the Communist daily, *El Siglo,* noted with nervous relief that rural women were gradually acquiring proper class consciousness and supporting male family members in revolutionary struggle:

> It is important to emphasize that the participation of [rural] women has always lagged behind that of men. . . . this can be explained by woman's dependence on man, which has impeded her ability to acquire a consciousness of class. . . . The passive position of rural women toward the struggle for [campesino] rights and the [dignification] of the family has often served as a break on the combativeness of their husbands, brothers, and fathers, and as a way for the patrón to use women to stop campesino liberation. . . . fortunately more women are coming to understand that the problems of their children, the unemployment of their husbands, the conditions of housing, etc., require the transformation of society and the struggle for rights.[101]

The article remarkably blamed female conservativism on women's dependence on men, but it did not call for structural changes in household divisions of labor. Rather, it called for women's heightened identification with men's unemployment and family poverty, the causes of which women presumably misunderstood. The image of women as easily manipulated by landowners implicated women as unwitting sexual agents of class betrayal. First, it implied that a woman's bond to the (male) patrón could be stronger than that to her husband or father. Second, it suggested that women could use their persuasive powers over male family members to weaken men's labor militancy. In short, the possibility of female disloyalty threatened the virility of the male labor movement. This was expressed in the saying, reportedly common among labor organizers and rank-and-file campesinos alike that, "the only thing worse than a reactionary landowner is a wife who does not support you."[102]

The labor movement rushed to assuage its anxiety about female loyalty with vigorous overtures to the importance of the family. If women were unwelcome as union members in practice, they were assured that unions first and foremost concerned themselves with the uplift of campesino families, whose interests they assumed to be synonymous with women's. The rural labor press and union training pamphlets from all political camps solemnly pledged that the main objective of unions was to assist men in becoming able providers for their dependents. The discourse of INDAP and other aspects of the Christian Democratic agenda echoed these proclamations, promising that the Agrarian Reform would make campesinos productive farmers and able heads of household. Women, the activists assumed, would applaud the empowering of their family's breadwinner.

All factions of the labor movement encouraged women to show their support by providing unions with assistance in their capacities as wives, daughters, and mothers. Women were asked to understand men's union obligations, including late-night meetings and absences from home. They were also requested to join some union events in auxiliary or symbolic capacities. The labor press enthusiastically reported that wives marched side by side with husbands in public demonstrations demanding that petitions be honored or land expropriated. Women performed folkloric dances at ceremonies legalizing unions, attended special INDAP workshops on the goals of the Agrarian Reform, cleaned union meeting facilities, organized union festivities at Christmas and on Independence Day, and provided food for workers on strike or at tomas.[103] Independent Catholic unions hosted beauty pageants to select young women to figuratively represent them as "campesina queens."[104]

The rural labor movement celebrated women's activities to stress the level of campesino solidarity for the Agrarian Reform and to legitimate the nature of working-class demands in the public eye. The presence of women symbolized union members' status as family men engaged in a noble project of community uplift on behalf of dependents. It also implied that women understood and supported the activities of male family members, while men were eager to alleviate the plight of wives. Noting the participation of women in a march following the 1964 UCC Congress in San Felipe, the Catholic monthly, *Campo Nuevo,* commented, "The rural woman showed, in [an] extraordinary capacity, her firm resolve to parade with her brother, husband, and boyfriend who attended the Congress. . . . The fairer sex is interested in unionization because of its importance to achieving family stability and to ending injustices so that all can live with dignity."[105]

Although various groups across the political spectrum shared perceptions about the proper place of women in the labor movement, important differences existed. Independent Catholics and Christian Democrats placed particular emphasis on the family as the basis of society and articulated Agrarian Reform goals in terms of uplifting the rural household as a unit.[106] Although men were to form unions as workers, their goal was to dignify the family and, by extension, the campesino community.[107] Well-organized families and communities, in turn, would help unions achieve their goals. This discursive emphasis on family and community downplayed the need to organize campesinos as a class, and minimized the corresponding connotation of class conflict. It also implied a need to organize all family and community members, including wives, mothers, and daughters.

The independent Catholic MCI listed "the incorporation of women into the process of social mobilization" as one of its institutional goals, and INDAP called for the creation of women's organizations affiliated with male unions as a way to unite the family and represent its interests.[108] INDAP ran occasional informational workshops for campesina women, and the MCI sponsored the first national conferences of rural women in Valparaíso and Aconcagua in 1964 and 1965.[109] Although both INDAP and the MCI encouraged female wage earners to join unions, they focused largely on helping women to better understand the union activities of their male family members and the importance of the Agrarian Reform as a whole.[110] The 1965 rural women's conference in Aconcagua ended with a general vote to collaborate with "men's organizations, unions, and neighborhood societies."[111] Nonetheless, the very fact that these meetings brought together several hundred women from across the country (including a delegation from Santa María county) demonstrated a serious effort to mobilize women.[112] The conferences also addressed some issues specific to women, such as female education and health care.[113] The goal, MCI organizers maintained, was to break women's isolation in the home and help housewives see that only a well-organized community could help them achieve their family interests. Boasting its success toward this end, an MCI general assembly in 1965 concluded that "until recently, campesinas were considered passive, caged within the family circle, but times are showing that this lack of consciousness [is waning] as women participate in organizational movements."[114]

The Left also stressed the importance of united families and wifely support but placed more emphasis on organizing women as workers. Both the Communist and Socialist parties, together with their affiliated rural labor movements, advocated women workers' incorporation into unions and the equalization of women's and men's working conditions. In the 1964 presidential elections, FRAP had countered the Christian Democratic strategy of promoting the defense of motherhood with its own claims that the Left defended women workers as well as mothers. Allende campaigned on an extensive platform of women's labor rights, including equal pay, day care, maternity leave, unrestricted access to all types of work, and the right to join unions without male consent.[115] Although the Christian Democrats also endorsed these measures, the Left had initiated most of them, and Socialists and Communists rhetorically addressed women as workers on a much more consistent basis. The Left had proclaimed women's inclusion in the labor movement a formal goal since the turn of the century, and they applied it with renewed momentum in the 1960s.[116] At its 1962 congress, the Communist Party declared that "national liberation" would entail the promotion of women's work "in all aspects, as factory workers, campesinas, and professionals."[117] The same year, the FCI committed to fighting for "campesina women's complete equality with men" in unions, the improvement of women's lives, "be they salaried workers or housewives," and the promotion of female sports.[118]

A political commitment to organizing the entire rural labor force propelled the Left's acknowledgment of women as workers. The Communist Party, in particular, consistently argued for the unionization of seasonal and migrant workers to prevent landowners from undermining the labor movement's gains with temporary labor.[119] With almost 20 percent of seasonal laborers female, women were of special concern. Women also became an important organizing target because of the Left's focus on indigenous communities. Since as early as the 1930s, the Communist Party had singled out the Mapuche in southern Chile as one of the country's most disenfranchised and potentially revolutionary rural populations. The creation of the FCI in the 1950s was meant to unite Indian and non-Indian peasants; it denounced Chile's historic discrimination against native peoples and praised Mapuche communal landholding practices and militant solidarity. Mapuche women's importance derived from the fact that they often performed the bulk of the subsistence cultivation on community lands and played key political roles as shamans. The FCI listed the protection of indigenous women's entitlement to participate in cooperatives as one of its early organizing goals.[120]

Despite this assertive agenda for women, however, the Left's effort to expand female membership in rural unions during the Agrarian Reform had only very minor practical success. Throughout the 1960s, women leaders within the Left-dominated United Workers' Central (CUT), the labor movement's national umbrella organization, bemoaned the low campesina union membership and complained about the failure to recruit female organizers.[121] Although indigenous women may have participated in unions to a somewhat larger extent than the rest of the country, female membership in Left-affiliated unions did not exceed the tiny national average of 4 to 6 percent in the primary agricultural sector of central Chile (including Aconcagua).[122] Despite the Left's exceptional recognition of women workers, the majority of FCI and Ranquíl "women's issues" were defined as the nonworkplace-based concerns of education, health care, and culture.[123] In contrast to their approach to organizing men, neither Communists nor Socialists regularly urged the creation of more permanent employment for women.[124]

In many ways the Left ended up, in practice, paying less attention to women than did its competitors. Relative to the independent Catholics and Christian Democrats, the traditional Marxist emphasis on the workplace as the primary site of class struggle downplayed the need to mobilize the family. Although the Left stressed themes of family solidarity, it more overtly privileged the role of proletarianized workers. The Left labor press frequently praised the importance of women's labor in subsistence farming, but such work placed women outside the sphere of commercial production—seen from a traditional Marxist perspective as taking place on the large estates—and therefore outside the immediate target of the Left's organizing efforts.

Given its focus on the commercial workplace, together with its practical failure to organize seasonal and women wage-workers, the Left ended up giving women a very limited role in transforming society. Whereas the independent Catholic and Christian Democratic labor movements called on women to join (albeit from the sidelines) in a collective project aimed at family uplift, the Left's equation of class struggle with union activity down-played the need for female participation beyond women's moral support for men's cause. Unlike the Catholic and Christian Democratic unions, neither FCI nor early Ranquíl-affiliated unions appear to have had women's departments in the Aconcagua Valley until the early 1970s. Leftist labor education centered more exclusively around the labor code and land reform, defined as primarily male concerns, and it rarely offered parallel "feminine instruction" on home economy.[125]

The Left tended to stress that the successful struggle of men would ultimately aid in meeting women's needs. Although the leftist labor press praised women for their solidarity and political savvy, it more often represented them as victims of class oppression. Stories of women beaten callously by police, evicted from estates, left crippled by farm work, or weeping over starving infants peppered issues of *El Siglo* and *Unidad Campesina*. While such reports featured female experiences, they emphasized men's, not women's, disempowerment within the existing system. The tales lamented men's impotence to provide for and protect families and called on male workers to collectively struggle to save women and children.[126] Whereas the independent Catholic and Christian Democrats boasted about female participation in marches and public ceremonies to emphasize the absence of class hatred, the Left more often employed women's suffering as a symbol of existing class exploitation and as a call for men's confrontational militancy.

As a whole, however, political tendencies within the rural labor movement and in the Frei administration shared a basic philosophy about the kind of men unions should create and about the place of women in labor mobilization. Unions were vehicles for transforming campesino peons into men conscious of their worth as human beings, men who were capable of taking responsibility for changing their circumstances. Women were to support men and provide symbolic heft to manifestations of class solidarity and community uplift. The differences between Catholics and Marxists mattered, and they mattered more as the Agrarian Reform progressed. But the position of different political factions, and the level of confrontation they encouraged and against whom, shifted depending on the government in power. Catholics and Marxists had shared common strategies prior to Frei's election; after 1970 they would switch places in their relationship to the state. In the end, they agreed on the essence of what constituted desirable masculine characteristics in union members, even as they offered different visions of the future.

Campesino men responded eagerly to the labor movement's call to manly action. The mandate that workers stand up to the patrón resonated deeply with campesino anger at gross exploitation and ritual humiliation. It gave a collective political punch to the everyday belligerence and disobedience that campesinos had long displayed as a way of mediating the terms of subservience. The labor movement's appeal to rural masculinity made sense to campesino men, and they willingly participated in crafting the codes of union manliness. Although the risks involved in union organizing prohibited some men's participation in unions, they bound men together in new forms of community and added to the workers' sense of masculine purpose. Solidarity emerged from men's competitive displays of worthiness to one another and their collaborative and individual demonstrations of strength to the boss. As powerful allies materialized within the Chilean state and congress, the element of danger lessened (but never disappeared) and was increasingly replaced by bravado and a confidence that working-class men could be agents of their destiny.

This sense of agency was inseparable from the all-male nature of unions and the labor movement's affirmation of men's dominion over women. Male authority over women within the campesino household pre-dated the labor organizing efforts of the 1960s and had been one of the few ways in which poor rural men exercised authority within latifundia society. The labor movement buttressed this by ennobling it within a project of turning campesino men into able heads of household who protected and provided for female dependents. It also urged rural working-class men to flex their masculine powers beyond the confines of the household, to expand their sense of manly jurisdiction to include making demands on employers and the state. This brand of masculinity presumed a certain confluence of gender and class antagonisms: militancy toward the boss, the exclusion of women from most union spaces, and a public style of sexual prowess intertwined to shape union manhood. Although the labor movement courted women's sympathy and stressed family uplift and conjugal harmony as the object of mobilization, it kept women at a careful distance.

chapter 4 Promoting Gender Mutualism

Rural Education, Mothers' Centers, and Family Planning

The male bravado of the rural labor movement was tempered by repeated celebrations of the Agrarian Reform's family-centered goals and
an appeal to partnership within the domestic unit. State functionaries,
labor activists, Catholic progressives, and other social reformers stressed
the campesino household as the bedrock of rural community and the
crucible for forging a modern agrarian culture. If campesinos required
lessons in farm management, democratic procedure, and personal hygiene, proper values would first be nurtured at home. Within the home,
each family member would contribute to the building of a new society
through gender- and generation-specific roles. Adult responsibilities
were distinguished from those of youth and, in particular, male from
female; each would contribute to the whole. With the family serving as
the model for social peace in turbulent times, campesinos were called
on to collaborate within natural differences as they pressed forward in
creating a more egalitarian world. Bracing against the conflict that such
change implied, reformers promoted an ideal of gender mutualism—the
harmonious cooperation between men and women—as the glue to hold
rural families and campesino society together.

Ideas about gender mutualism centrally shaped the Agrarian Reform's
education and organizing projects. Although campesino labor unions received the bulk of resources and attention (and often themselves served
as the site of broader education efforts), other programs specifically targeted women, youth, and the family. These included adult literacy classes,

special agricultural schools, mothers' centers, youth clubs, parents' centers, neighbors' councils, and Chile's first national family planning initiative. Sponsored largely by the state and independent Catholic organizations, these projects aimed to modernize family relations and place them at the service of national development.[1] Specifically, they aspired to effect a three-pronged cultural transformation: enhancing men's productive and bread-winning capacities; rationalizing and validating women's domestic work; and promoting campesino youth's civic responsibility and peer camaraderie.

Cultural transformation was key. As a modernization project, the Agrarian Reform was rooted in a nineteenth century liberalism that juxtaposed barbarism with civilization and equated campesinos, in particular, with subordination and Indianness. One of its chief goals was to turn campesinos into Chilean citizens—autonomous, educated, and fully integrated into the political and economic fabric of national life. This sense of cultural dichotomy and the primacy of gender to its conceptualization was precisely illustrated in an organizing pamphlet distributed by the Catholic labor organization ASICH in the early 1960s. Above a caption reading, "The Agrarian Reform will elevate the culture and capabilities of campesinos," the picture of a patrón glowering down at a barefoot man holding his hat in hand was contrasted with a separate picture of domestic bliss in which a campesino man stood reading the newspaper while his wife, seated in a chair by his side, listened to the radio and read a book; two maps—one of Chile and the other of the world—hung in the background.[2] The Agrarian Reform, the message implied, would replace servility, ignorance, and primitiveness with independence, literacy, and connection to national and international concerns. Men and women would both benefit, but their participation would be gender-specific. Other cartoons in the same pamphlet featured pictures of smiling men tilling the soil and women purchasing textiles in local shops. The Agrarian Reform thus promised to help men become productive farmers and able providers while enabling campesina women to be efficient housewives and savvy consumers.

The view of modernization as a process of inclusion that fostered productivity, consumerism, and citizenship was shared across the center-left political spectrum, but the Christian Democrats championed it especially. As INDAP leader Jacques Chonchol described the purpose of

"Agrarian Reform is necessary so that campesinos can conquer their freedom and become involved in the civic, cultural, and economic life of the Nation, solidly contributing to the country's progress and the well-being of all." Illustration from ASICH pamphlet. UP pamphlet series, NOSOTROS LOS CHILENOS, courtesy of the University of Wisconsin Land Tenure Center.

Agrarian Reform education programs: "The goal is to make the campesino population emerge from its traditional mentality in the shortest time possible . . . to help the campesino develop the resourcefulness to make the most out of his income and to take advantage of the many small [opportunities] available which, until this time, he has ignored out of ignorance. . . . And finally, the goal of education is to incorporate the campesino masses into the national community: into the political community, the cultural community, the economic community, and the social community."[3] The theme of incorporation was particularly important to Christian Democrats since many held that the much desired cultural transformation would first require mass mobilization and participation by the poor in civic life. This thinking, elements of which the Left shared, was shaped by the theory of marginality promoted by DESAL and the Sociology Department at the Catholic University.[4] Marginality theory attributed Chile's underdevelopment to the fact that only a minority of people participated in the country's major economic, social, and political institutions; more participation by more people would hence promote modernization. Expanding on this idea, and in contrast to the Left's emphasis on class exploitation, Christian Democrats and other Catholics defined social injustice primarily as a problem of insufficient liberal democracy—the inadequate representation of different social groups in public institutions. The answer to inequality lay in promoting education and civic participation through associations of social peers.

In 1965, Frei created the National Council for Popular Promotion (Consejería Nacional de Promoción Popular), dependent on the Office of the Presidency, to create community organizations that would "encourage different marginalized groups to participate toward mutual goals" and to "open the possibility that the people of Chile, in very conscious, thoughtful, insightful, and imaginative ways [will] go on to define a new society."[5] Working closely with INDAP, Popular Promotion was charged with assisting the formation of organizations that would represent poor people's interests: unions to defend men's interests as workers, mothers' centers to promote housewives' concerns, youth clubs to address the interests of adolescents, neighbors' councils to advocate families' housing needs. As Patricia Garrett has noted, Christian Democrats saw such mobilization as having transcendental importance.[6] An internal document from Popular Promotion gushed that the 1968 legislation granting legal recognition to new community organizations was nothing less than revolutionary:

> First, because it will organize the entire community from the base to the highest national level. . . . Second, because the new society will organize itself and become conscious of the value of self-expression for the first time in history. . . . Third, because through these organizations the

community will participate at all levels of decision making. . . . Fourth, because the community thus organized will [become] a mobilized and mobilizing force for the new community. . . . [The community] having power, knowing how to use it, prepared to exercise it, will put pressure on different levels in such a way that it is difficult to imagine the consequences.[7]

Popular Promotion's model of organizing reflected not only a liberal concern with interest representation, but Catholicism's more corporate vision of vertically ordered social groups, with an emphasis on family. In contrast to the Left's goal of revolutionary mass mobilization through class solidarity, the Christian Democratic philosophy envisioned joining persons of similar economic status to represent occupational and familial interests within existing, albeit reformed, structures.

Women were important targets of Christian Democratic education and organizing efforts. Although the Agrarian Reform always primarily targeted campesino men as subjects, the Christian Democratic and broader Catholic emphasis on family uplift stressed an individuation of family members' roles and needs. During the 1964 presidential race, the Christian Democratic party had made a special point of appealing to women of all classes, organizing hundreds of women's committees nationwide and emphasizing that it alone truly defended Chilean mothers and housewives. Once elected, Frei continued to address women as a distinct constituency. He introduced legislation to eliminate women's unequal status in the Chilean marriage code; he expanded milk programs for infants; his administration drafted the first national plans for day care services; and major investments were made in prenatal and maternal health care. Although such measures received heavy political backing (and in many cases original sponsorship) by the Left, the Frei administration succeeded in taking credit for them, validating the Christian Democrats self-portrait as the party for Chilean mothers.[8]

The Christian Democrats also specifically emphasized organizing women for civic and political purposes. In 1964, Frei initiated plans for a Feminine Service, a program through which adolescent girls and young adult women would perform short-term teaching and social work for the public good.[9] The administration also urged the creation of special women's departments in all existing organizations such as political parties and unions. In 1967, Chile hosted the first Congress of Latin American Christian Democratic Women to promote increased female leadership and participation in Christian Democratic parties throughout the hemisphere.[10] In 1969, the National Office of Women was established to coordinate programs and legislative efforts that "promote women's full participation in all aspects of social life."[11]

While the Christian Democrats celebrated women's capacity to contribute to social change, they carefully stressed that such energies would complement rather than compete with those of men. When announcing the Feminine Service program, Frei compared women's nurturing labors in hospitals and schools to men's sacrifice in military service.[12] At the Congress of Latin American Christian Democratic Women, First Lady María Ruíz-Tagle urged women to "work hand in hand with men in uplifting [the continent.]"[13] Although the National Office on Women sponsored conferences on such topics as "women and work" and "female community leadership," the bulk of its activities addressed infant-maternal issues; it was implicitly hostile to feminism.[14] As the Office's director, Gabriela Merino, cautioned sternly, women's advancement would never come through reversed gender roles or female gains at male expense: "The attitude of women shouldn't be about establishing an absurd matriarchy in the country through feminist demands but, on the contrary, a total respect for ourselves, looking together with men for happiness [and] a just society."[15]

But the Christian Democrats viewed women as more than strictly wives and mothers. Much fanfare was made of middle-class women's continually growing presence in the professions, and there was recognition that working-class women labored outside the home by necessity.[16] The push for women to become integrated into national and community organizations itself defined a realm of appropriate female activity beyond the domestic. Nonetheless, if the Christian Democrats acknowledged that women were not exclusively wives and mothers, all women were nonetheless also seen as wives and mothers—some of whom had additional responsibilities. Domestic obligations, particularly for children, were defined as the primary concern of all women. As a result, the party construed women's civic participation in terms of female caregiving: women contributed to the public good through empathy, patience, cooperation, and resourcefulness.

Within the logic of gender mutualism, feminine traits tempered the rough edges of men, helping men harness their energies for familial and national ends. In an implicit criticism of unbridled male dominance, the Frei administration urged men to appreciate wives' talents and to welcome women's involvement in community organizations as offering a unique and necessary female perspective. As Karin Rosemblatt has shown, state efforts to tame Chilean men and foster national development by promoting domesticity date back from the urban reform and industrialization initiatives of the 1930s and 1940s.[17] The 1960s differed in the state's effort to systematically promote domesticity in rural areas and its more explicit call for women's participation in civic political life and men's acceptance of female agency. As a representative from the National Office on Women explained during a United Nations seminar on development, it was up to Chilean women to be more assertive in public life and incumbent on men to transcend longstanding gender prejudices that depreciated women's perspective: "The human family lives in a moment of accelerated change with profound transformations. . . . If women adopt marginal roles . . . we fear repeating men's old errors of, many times, not allotting due importance to the feminine values [that women] are so ready and capable of contributing: love, a sense of family, devotion to peace—which is not, as women know, simply the absence of war, but the presence of fraternity and justice. These worthy contributions must be allowed to be adopted in the concrete and put into practice."[18]

The Frei administration's education and organizing efforts also specifically targeted youth. They recognized young people in their teens and early twenties as a distinct constituency whose formation was vital to Chile's future, but whose current status as single dependents living with parents made their interests and needs distinct from those of adults. Government and nongovernment youth programs alike focused on vocational training, civic education, and cultural recreation. Young people were urged to acquire modern skills for their future roles in the nation's workforce as well as a patriotic interest in and knowledge of Chilean politics and current affairs. The programs also explicitly encouraged youths to socialize and identify with their peers and to see themselves as a culturally and politically distinct group. Despite the gender-specificity of many vocational programs, youth programs as a whole were coed and promoted new models of heterosexual organizing.

The impulse to create distinct social and political organizations for young people had urban origins, but it expanded to rural areas after 1964. Since the 1940s, Catholic Action had sponsored recreational and educational youth programs in Santiago aimed at offering working-class adolescents ideological alternatives to Marxism. The Socialists and Communists concentrated their efforts on high school students and, after 1960, on the University of Chile, whose student body included a growing minority of lower–middle- and working-class youth. The Christian Democratic and National parties competed for young followings at the elite Catholic University. Although young people could not vote until age twenty-one, the increasing numbers of urban youth who delayed entrance into the labor force to pursue education compelled political parties to reach beyond the workplace to cultivate future memberships.[19]

With the Agrarian Reform, youth organizing spread to the countryside. In the Aconcagua Valley, most political parties operated separate youth branches by the late 1960s. Open to young men and women under age twenty-one, these political youth clubs urged adolescents to make their own demands for better schools, university scholarships, vocational training, and cultural resources. Youth political clubs elected their own leaders and sponsored an array of cultural activities such as dances and music festivals.

The emphasis on youth organizing also encouraged student volunteerism and unique opportunities for youth encounters across class. University students from Santiago and other urban areas spent school vacations repairing housing and distributing government health care brochures in working-class neighborhoods. With the initiation of the Agrarian Reform, middle-class youths flooded the countryside each summer to dig irrigation canals, build union meeting halls, and teach literacy classes.[20] Such labor was inspired by the Cuban Revolution's youth brigades that provided armies of middle-class teachers for literacy and health campaigns; it was also motivated by the example and financial backing of the U.S. Peace Corps program that sent recent U.S. college graduates abroad to assist development projects in poorer countries. Campesino youths joined their city-dwelling counterparts in a variety of projects, creating rare moments of cross-class interaction and occasional solidarity. The paternalist logic of volunteerism was easily disrupted. While literacy projects involved urban youths teaching rural youths, cultivation and irrigation tasks more often implied the reverse. Rural young people also undertook their own volunteer efforts, planting experimental plots of fruit trees and making costumes for local dance contests. The Frei administration heralded all of these activities as examples of young people's civic spirit—evidence that Chile's youth was lending its unique skill and energy to national benefit.

The idea of the family conceptually fused the different impulses and constituencies of Christian Democratic education and organizing projects. If men, women, and adolescents each had distinct needs and talents and were encouraged to organize as interest-specific groups, all interests were meant to contribute to the greater good of the family and, by extension, society. Mutual collaboration between husbands and wives and parents and children would reconcile internal differences. As a 1964 edition of the Rural Education Institute's monthly publication for campesinos, *Sucro y Semilla,* preached, "In order to live happily, we all must be able to count on others to fulfill their obligations. None of us can be independent from the rest. The housewife needs her husband to work and to give her money, he needs her to make the evening meal, and she needs their son to cut the firewood. We need each other mutually."[21]

The Catholic Christian Family Movement, which regularly published essays on family and marriage in local and national newspapers, stated the case for family unity more bluntly. A 1967 editorial in the San Felipe daily *El Trabajo* discouraged any blurring of gender roles and advised parents to exercise responsible authority over children, even while allowing their offspring the freedom for self-expression:

> Family Unity does not mean family uniformity. . . . We are not saying that all elements of the family should be equal. Family Unity needs variety. This unity is achieved when husbands, like wives, maintain their own personalit[ies] and direct their energies toward family ends, mutually helping one another, educating the children well, and making sure that the children are not simple reproductions of themselves. Children are not pieces of mud that one shoves into the same mold. The greatness and strength of family unity resides precisely in that it is formed by persons who are different from one another, be they of one sex or the other, or be they of certain physical and intellectual capabilities. Regardless, they complement one another.[22]

The ultimate goal was not to eliminate gender and generational differences, but to mobilize within them in the faith that Chilean society would march forward toward a modern future with each family member contributing his or her utmost.

Rural Education

The attempt to educate campesinos along gendered and familial lines was not new. Throughout the first half of the century, Catholic reformers and modernizing landowners sought to promote campesino domesticity as a means of easing class conflict and rationalizing labor relations.[23] As historians Elizabeth Hutchison and Soledad Zárate have shown, a supposed connection between stable gender roles and social peace had proven central to reformist efforts to quell class conflict during early industrialization.[24] Its centrality continued throughout the creation of an urban-focused welfare state after 1930.[25] But the Agrarian Reform's educational programs differed. Whereas earlier Catholic and landowner initiatives to address campesinos were sporadic and, in most parts of Chile, nonexistent, the Agrarian Reform marked the first systematic attempt by the state to address rural gender roles throughout the countryside. The Frei administration particularly soft-pedaled the theme of social order in order to more commonly emphasize domestic harmony as a basis for campesino empowerment.

Education programs sponsored by progressive Catholics in the 1950s and early 1960s provided a model for later Christian Democratic projects. Throughout the central valley and in Aconcagua, IER and ASICH ran leadership training and vocational classes that promoted binary, complementary gender roles. An agricultural school for women sponsored by IER in Rinconada county trained women "to integrally assume their religious, family, civil, and social responsibilities by dignifying the home."[26] The school offered women courses in home economy, folkloric dance, and moral-religious values to complement UCC seminars for men (also held in the school) on land reform, social legislation, and union formation. IER's weekly radio program, "Sucro y Semilla," was divided into gender-specific sessions—one for women, entitled "Family and Morality," and one for men, entitled "Agrarian Reform and Social Change."[27] Women's social responsibility was defined as residing in the spiritual and ethical domain of the home, in contrast to the male terrain of politics and social change. Vocational programs particularly targeted youths. In San Esteben and San Felipe counties, local parishes used church lands to instruct boys in grape and peach production while, inside the church, girls took classes in sewing and weaving.[28] IER ran programs for young women in canning and family gardening while instructing boys in mechanics, cattle raising, and dairy farming.[29] Although such instruction offered both girls and boys skills for earning income, female contributions were to be made from within the household, while male contributions connected more clearly to commercial production.[30]

After 1964, the Frei administration expanded on these Catholic models and absorbed them into a comprehensive plan for reforming education nationally. Given the links Christian Democrats made between education, civic participation, and social transformation, the Frei administration stressed the creation of educational opportunities for adults as well as the improvement of programs for children and youth. Between 1964 and 1970, almost three thousand new schools were built, almost half in rural areas, and accelerated training programs licensed as many teachers in 1966 alone.[31] The Frei administration streamlined Chile's existing system of multiple education routes to emphasize a foundational basic education for all students. It was followed by a two-tract higher education system of either university or vocational school. Multiple state agencies, including CORA, INDAP, Popular Promotion, and the National Institute for Professional Education (INACAP), made available adult education programs that stressed basic literacy and technical knowledge. Efforts to eradicate adult illiteracy were highly successful. Whereas 48 percent of rural men and women were reported as illiterate in the 1960 census, this figure had plummeted to 20 percent by 1970.[32]

INDAP played a particularly important role in rural education. It heavily stressed the importance of distinct, collaborative gender roles within the household so that, as one manual read, "the family unit [can] convert itself into the protagonist of its own progress."[33] The agency recognized women as crucial actors within the family and INDAP literature listed "women's incorporation into economic development" as a policy goal.[34] Although INDAP distributed basic information on labor rights to wage-earning women, it viewed women's economic involvement largely in terms of female household management and female understanding of the labor issues faced by male family members.[35] The agency primarily addressed women through its Department of Education and Home Economy whose mission was to "foment the organization of campesina women and train them in improved techniques and arts of homemaking."[36] Since the Agrarian Reform aimed to uplift rural families, facilitating women's responsibilities as wives and mothers was integral to a successful policy. As a 1965 policy statement read:

> In all programs aimed at elevating the general productivity of [rural] areas, training for the rural woman is vital since, as a mother, it is she who affects the spiritual development of the family and, as a housewife, it is she who determines a family's standard of living by transforming new income into concrete benefits. . . . [INDAP's] programs aim to give the rural woman new skills and attitudes that allow her to [better] execute the role that corresponds to her as a member in the family nucleus. The programs propose to elevate women to a legitimate and just position [within] a society that is democratic and progressive.[37]

Women played a twofold role: as mothers, they held responsibility for the family's spiritual education; as housewives, they controlled the family's budget and consumption. Accordingly, INDAP offered women classes on hygiene, nutrition, child development, first aid, and household budgeting. It also sponsored small, income-generating projects such as cheese and conserve manufacturing, which women could undertake from home.[38]

In contrast, INDAP programs for men focused on creating competent producers and responsible household heads. In collaboration with the Ministry of Education and INACAP, the agency held seminars on credit, farm management, tractor maintenance, irrigation, and fruit cultivation. On private estates, INDAP offered men instruction on union formation, social legislation, the history of the Chilean labor movement, and collective bargaining.[39] Such programs aimed to prepare at least some men as independent agriculturalists and the rest as technically adept and socially informed farmworkers. Entrepreneurial know-how and worker efficiency were to be the foundations of a new rural manhood. The President of CORA, Rafael Moreno, explained the purpose of education programs for members of Agrarian Reform units and private estate workers in 1967: "We aim to convert the modest campesino into a small businessman, to eliminate his diminutive status and to elevate him to the consciousness of knowing his worth as a human being."[40] The director of INACAP, Agustín Albert, echoed Moreno's vision when he, following an agreement with CORA to train 4,770 campesinos throughout the country, proclaimed, "The Agrarian Reform must be efficient, and in order that it be efficient, men must be trained on two planes: technical and entrepreneurial. For it is the campesino who will decide the success of the Reform; thus, he must be given the knowledge that permits him to plan, administrate, and elevate production."[41]

Education programs for men placed particular emphasis on teaching them problem-solving and responsibility. Instructors drew heavily on the techniques advocated by Brazilian literacy teacher Paulo Freire whose ideas Popular Promotion officially adopted as formal guidelines in 1965.[42] Following Freire, education facilitators eschewed top-down teaching methods in favor of open-ended styles that emphasized constant participation by students. Campesinos were asked to brainstorm about the nature and causes of the problems they faced and to collectively enumerate and select strategies for solving those problems. As one manual prepared by INDAP advised instructors, "Individuals need to determine what are realistic goals for themselves. The facilitator should help the campesino focus on the need to search for his own solutions. . . . It is fundamental to achieve active participation by students instead of the passive receipt of knowledge."[43] The emphasis on campesinos taking initiative flowed from the importance that INDAP personnel (and social reformers across the center-left political spectrum) attached to men's personal transformation. To break with campesinos' presumed entrenched culture of servility and dependence, rural men would first have to awaken to their human potential and be afforded the opportunity to actualize it. When combined with the Frei administration's more specific productivity goals, this philosophy championed a masculine ideal of proactive citizenship and entrepreneurialism.

Agrarian Reform youth programs stressed personal growth and transformation as well. Popular Promotion and INDAP closely collaborated in establishing youth clubs (*clubs juveniles*) to promote the political, vocational, and cultural development of adolescents so that "the new generation would be prepared to assume their future responsibilities."[44] Youth clubs included both boys and girls and hosted a variety of activities, including educational forums on labor rights and the Agrarian Reform, volunteer projects for building community centers, and cultural festivals with competitive dances and singing.[45] Youth clubs encouraged ado-

Popular Promotion and INDAP folk music and dance project for
rural youth. Popular Promotion pamphlet, courtesy of the
University of Wisconsin Land Tenure Center.

lescents to take seriously their future contributions as adult citizens.
They stressed that, while young peoples' current obligations within their
parental family provided training for these responsibilities, youths also
needed to acquire skills beyond what parents could give. Likewise, the
cultural and political emphasis of youth clubs suggested that adolescents
had interests distinct from those of adults and that they should create
social spaces free from immediate adult control.

To train rural young people in new cultivation techniques, INDAP also
established special youth agricultural schools, often coordinated with
vocational programs offered by IER.[46] Vocational training was usually
gender-specific (mechanics and fruit cultivation lessons for boys, handi-
craft and animal husbandry lessons for girls), but some classes were coed,
giving small numbers of young women an opportunity to discuss vegetable hybrids and drive tractors alongside young men. Although girls certainly received the message that their future lay in modern homemaking,
youth programs explicitly encouraged girls' participation in activities
outside the household and viewed their paid agricultural work as a positive (if temporary) good. In contrast to INDAP's approach to adult men
and women, the coed nature of youth programs suggested large amounts
of overlap between girls' and boys' interests as adolescents. Youth pro-

grams looked upon heterosexual socializing as healthy preparation for spousal roles within the family. Radio programs and youth magazines associated with IER humorously advised adolescents about dating and marriage.[47] Although counselors firmly warned against premarital sex, they looked approvingly on coed gatherings as a good way for adolescents to mature emotionally and eventually find permanent mates.[48]

Beyond helping campesinos and campesinas to realize their potential, Agrarian Reform education programs aimed to foster greater communication and harmony between men and women. Gender mutualism was envisioned simultaneously as an ultimate result of family uplift programs and as a necessary starting point for implementing such strategies. Parables of cheerful campesino marriages in which husbands ably provided for women and children and wives skillfully maintained their households appeared repetitively in the rural labor press of all political tendencies as well as in the educational pamphlets of IER, INACAP, and INDAP. Both Popular Promotion and INDAP offered specific family education minicourses for women that included descriptions of men's work responsibilities and union activism in order that, as one INDAP manual explained, "wives can appreciate their spouses' daily routines."[49] Instructors of men's courses were urged to impress on their male students the vital importance of "the roles that women play[ed] as home managers and educators of children."[50]

The mutualist ethos offered a subtle critique of the most overt forms of campesino male dominance, providing a competing definition of masculinity that stressed male responsibility, moderation, and parity. Men were exhorted to accord greater respect to women's domestic and childrearing responsibilities and to remember that family solidarity was critical to working-class progress. Toward this end, men were urged to participate more in family life and to share information with their wives. INDAP manuals for rural labor unions outlined discussions for teaching men how to educate their families about the Agrarian Reform and, in particular, stressed the need for men to keep wives informed about their activities.[51] Emphasizing breadwinning as a crucial component of masculinity, rural educators preached that truly capable men worked together with their wives and paid attention to family needs. Many local labor leaders echoed this philosophy. In a 1970 government study on union organizing, one union official voiced the sentiment, common to many

Illustration from CORA union organizing pamphlet, ca. 1968, courtesy of the University of Wisconsin Land Tenure Center.

of the sixty informants in the survey, that the purpose of literacy and education classes was to "change the campesino man's mentality to be more responsible with his children [and wife]."[52]

Campesina women's willingness to be more assertive and involved in the lives of their husbands and the broader community was to match such male responsibility. As one evaluation of INDAP's activities reported, this was to entail the acquisition of "new values," such as an appreciation for Agrarian Reform objectives, as well as "women's emergence from under their submission to men."[53] In a remarkably frank acknowledgement of sexism, a 1969 INDAP project outline for women specified that the "social prejudices of campesino men and men in general" constituted major obstacles to women's inclusion in community organizations. But it also cited women's acceptance of such prejudice as compounding the situation.[54] In remedy, INDAP called for educating both men and women "to achieve consciousness" about the value of women in community organizations. It also promoted the creation of women's departments in all existing unions and cooperatives, so that women could provide "community work, be it in the area of service, recreation, or culture."[55]

Most campesinos, male and female, agreed with the educational focus on men's and women's different, but reciprocal, responsibilities. Women welcomed the public validation of existing household tasks and found particular gratification in the call for husbands to show wives more respect. Men were enthusiastic about being taken seriously as economic producers and flattered by the constant reference to their roles as heads of household. Dramatic improvements in campesino earnings strengthened support for the model and made the Agrarian Reform's goal of male breadwinning a concrete possibility in ways it never before had been.[56] In an oral history, María Ibacache, the wife of a former permanent worker on an estate in Los Andes county, recalled the first years of the Agrarian Reform in extravagant terms, perfectly mimicking the official ideal: "My husband was so proud to be taking care of his family! He would come home for lunch every day beaming. He complimented my cooking and would always bring a little gift. . . . We consulted each other about everything, we were a unit . . . and because he was proud, I was also proud and happy."[57]

But gender mutualism also created new conflicts. Improved material welfare did not, in itself, ensure happy marriages. Wives interpreted the ethos of spousal cooperation to mean that husbands should give them more respect and autonomy. Men often interpreted it to mean that women should support and obey their husbands. Men showed particular skepticism about INDAP's official push to involve women more in their decisions. When an INDAP functionary encouraged men to speak more frequently with their wives about union activities, did this mean that a man was supposed to seek his spouse's permission to participate in a strike or share a drink with fellow comrades? At the very least, the edict that men should keep wives informed about their activities opened space for female criticism.

There was also discord over money. Married men did not readily hand wages over to wives, despite the official celebration of women as budget managers. Men saw their much improved incomes as reward for hard labor and political work and understood control over money as part of being a household head. However, as wages replaced payments in-kind, women increasingly depended on cash to provide meals and clothing to families. Men's decisions over how much money women needed and who would make cash purchases clashed with women's growing sense of entitlement to men's earning power. As Anita Hernández explained in an oral history, "I thought, well, [my husband is] making more money now, so he should give me more for the children. Of course, he always said that he would buy what we needed, but he never did, and he would leave me with only a few bits of change to buy bread. . . . it was difficult to confront him, you see, he was hard . . . it made me so mad!"[58] In some cases, women abandoned all hope of partnership with their spouses. Sonia Araya, a campesina from Los Andes county, became so frustrated that she asked her husband's employer to give her a portion of his wages each month, "seeing that my own husband couldn't be counted on."[59]

Campesino men were particularly wary that Agrarian Reform education programs required women to leave home. Although such initiatives predominantly aimed to assist wives in becoming better homemakers, campesina women regularly complained that husbands forbade their participation in INDAP workshops and literacy classes.[60] Men's anxiety about women's extra-household activities was closely wedded to their sense of entitlement to women's labor and sexuality. Women's participation in education forums detracted from the time that a wife spent cooking, laundering, or weeding the family garden; simultaneously, it permitted women's interaction with men who were not family members.[61] Men made special requests to INDAP, IER, and Popular Promotion functionaries that literacy classes and seminars be gender-segregated.[62] Marta Castro, the wife of a permanent worker in Putaendo county, recalled in an oral history that her husband would only allow her to attend coed literacy classes in the company of the couple's fourteen-year-old son.[63]

Perhaps men needn't have worried so much. The Agrarian Reform's gender mutualism did not question the notion that, in the end, women were naturally more dependent on men than the reverse. If INDAP gently criticized male prejudice against women, it did not challenge men's general social privilege or husbands' ultimate authority over wives. Lest there be any doubt about this issue, INDAP purposely consoled men that its outreach to women was not meant for "a woman to compete with her husband, but to work together with him in constructing a new society."[64] A training manual for union organizers distributed by INDAP outlined the logic of male prerogative within conjugal partnership even more clearly. Discussing the merits of each family member doing his or her duty, the manual rhetorically questioned, "Does everyone have equal power and responsibility in your family?" It went on to discuss the importance of each member accepting authority from the household head in the name of family unity.[65] Perfectly illustrating this ideal, IER's offi-

Insignia of the Instituto
de Educación Rural
(IER)

cial insignia featured the silhouette of a campesino couple in which the
husband's and wife's arms were linked in evidence of a shared commitment to a common project; but the man's figure towered over that of the
woman, and the man held a shovel in one fist (symbolic of men's primary
relationship to the means of production), while the wife's hand held only
that of her husband (see above).

Yet despite its maintenance of hierarchy, the Agrarian Reform's brand
of gender mutualism did, as campesino men sensed, signal a meaningful change. Although it built on longstanding practices of reciprocity, it
defined more concrete limits to male authority and positively affirmed
women's agency. Even as the Agrarian Reform more clearly distinguished
between productive and domestic spaces, it advocated a role for women
in men's affairs as well as in the newly emerging realms of campesino
political and civic life. Within the campesino household, overt forms of
male dominance were frowned on, and female activities received primary validation. Men could still be patriarchs, but they were supposed
to be modern and benevolent patriarchs. However unequally, they were
supposed to share the stage with women.

Mothers' Centers and Civic Domesticity

In the spirit of gender mutualism, the Agrarian Reform encouraged campesina women to create their own organizations. Women's most direct
form of civic participation in the 1960s came through entities called
mothers' centers (*centros de madres* or CEMAS), associations of mothers and

housewives. Created for both rural and urban women, CEMAs were sponsored by the state as well as by independent political organizations to provide a gender-specific basis for integrating poor women into processes of popular mobilization. According to the law that formally constituted them, CEMAs had a twofold mission. First, they were to function as schools where "women who [had] common interests and shared as a principal goal the solution of problems specific to their [economic] condition and sex within a neighborhood context" could acquire skills "appropriate to their sex." [66] Second, they were to constitute the means for women's collective representation in community activities.[67] As Teresa Valdés, Edda Gaviola, and others have shown, CEMAs aimed to harness women's energies to the state project of Agrarian Reform, not to foster a woman-centered project with gender-based claims.[68] Nonetheless, CEMAs constituted a massive and unprecedented mobilization of working-class and poor women. By 1970, nine thousand CEMAs existed nationwide, with a total CEMA membership of 450,000 women. By 1973, CEMAs would number twenty thousand and claim a membership of almost one million.[69]

CEMAs dated from the 1930s and had various ideological and political roots. During the Popular Front, the Socialist and Communist parties collaborated with the feminist Movement for the Emancipation of Chilean Women (MUCECH) to create mothers' and housewives' associations that provided solidarity for working-class struggles.[70] In competition with these associations, Catholic activists formed housewives' committees that discussed religious values and warned against the evils of Marxism. State involvement began in the 1950s under Carlos Ibáñez (1952–1958) whose People's Clothing Foundation organized mothers' centers to distribute basic household necessities.[71] But only after Frei's election in 1964 did mothers' centers become a massive, national phenomenon that extended to rural areas. In the early 1960s, the Women's Department of the Christian Democratic Party organized CEMAs to galvanize women's electoral support for Frei; after the election, CEMAs became central to the Christian Democratic policy goal of fostering peer associations.[72]

Despite the fact that CEMAs came to be associated almost exclusively with Christian Democracy and the Frei administration, labor activists of various political colors formed the first such centers in rural areas.[73] In the early 1960s, the independent Catholic UCC established a CEMA each time it created a union.[74] By 1965, the women's department of the independent Catholic MCI claimed to have CEMAs throughout the Aconcagua Valley with a total membership of seven hundred women.[75] Communist and Socialist activists also formed CEMAs parallel to their unions in San Esteben and Catemu counties.[76] Only after the 1967 enactment of the Law of Campesino Unionization and the creation of Popular Promotion did the Christian Democratic government surpass the labor movement in organizing rural women. Like labor leaders before them, INDAP and Popular Promotion officials coordinated the formation of CEMAs with that of unions, a symbiotic relationship that facilitated the creation of women's organizations in even the most isolated rural areas.[77] By the late 1960s, the predominance of government-initiated CEMAs reflected INDAP's dominance in the process of rural unionization generally, but at no point did the state act alone.

A CEMA consisted of thirty to fifty campesina women who met weekly at a church, municipal building, or, in some cases, its own meeting hall. Mothers' centers grouped women of diverse occupational backgrounds, including seasonal wage laborers, small farmers and minifundistas, and wives of inquilinos and estate workers. While rural CEMAs were working-class in character and elected their own leaders from the membership, they had frequent visits from urban middle-class representatives of political parties, government agencies, and the Catholic Church. Despite their diverse origins, the activities of all CEMAs shared a focus on domestic education, economic self-help, and community volunteerism. Mothers' centers regularly hosted talks on hygiene, nutrition, prenatal care, first aid, and parenting. They also offered minicourses in crochet, embroidery, and weaving, and organized exhibitions for the sale of members' handicrafts.[78] Members made toys for neighborhood children at Christmas and collected relief for families affected by drought and earthquakes.

Although Catholic and Christian Democratic organizers envisioned CEMAs, like unions, as nonpolitical associations, the centers became a battleground for competing political agendas in the rural labor movement and served as vehicles for linking women, however tangentially, to wider political processes.[79] All CEMA organizers, including representatives of the Frei administration, agreed that education about the Agrarian

Reform should take center stage within the organization. This invariably raised issues about the competing goals of different political factions in the rural labor movement. In oral histories, several women recalled CEMA meetings as generating intense arguments over Agrarian Reform politics. Silvia Herrera, the former president of a predominantly Socialist CEMA in San Esteben county, remembered that she often acted as peacemaker between feuding members: "The women were very opinionated . . . there was a lot of disagreement. One member would say that she liked Frei and another woman would say that that was easy for her to say since her husband was [an Agrarian Reform land recipient], but that her husband was still exploited by the patrón. . . . Then everyone would start having their say."[80] In 1966, attempts by Popular Promotion to unify Aconcagua Valley mothers' centers in a single CEMA federation ended in bickering and division. Accusing the state agency of using CEMAs for partisan (i.e., Christian Democratic) ends, mothers' centers formed by Socialists in San Esteben county and independent Catholic CEMAs in Putaendo county each broke away to form separate federations.[81]

The various political camps within the rural labor movement had subtle but important differences in their approaches to CEMAs, which reflected their competing views of women's place in the Agrarian Reform as a whole. Catholic labor organizations envisioned mothers' centers as primarily helping women to become better housewives and to support male activism. As an MCI pamphlet stated:

> The Mothers' Center teaches us how to make use of available resources in order to create a happy domestic life. The Center is the social place where campesina women get to know each other, pass moments of joy, and learn to live as sisters. The Center should be a place where we learn to prepare and apply ourselves in the role that corresponds to us as women, to live with dignity and to find happiness in our homes and communities. It is where we learn to help collaborate in the success of the Agrarian Reform, in its unions, cooperatives, etc., because it is women who have for so long felt the problems of our times.[82]

Independent Catholics defined mothering and homemaking as women's natural calling—"the role that corresponds to women"—but sought to endow these tasks with civic meaning and a sense of female solidarity. "Learning to live as sisters," CEMA members would contribute to the social good by collectively learning how to better attend to their individual families. Likewise, CEMAS would teach women about the Agrarian Reform so that wives might better understand and support husbands.

The Frei administration shared the independent Catholic vision of civic domesticity but placed more emphasis on CEMAS as vehicles of social mobilization and democratic participation. Mothers' centers would unite women around their common interests as mothers and housewives, provide for women's collective contributions in public forums, and facilitate women's community volunteer work. When the Aconcagua Valley offices of INDAP and CORA held town meetings, they issued special invitations to CEMAS along with those to unions, neighbors' councils, sports clubs, and associations of small property holders.[83] The Frei administration also saw CEMAS as having a limited economic function. The centers would assist the sale of female handicrafts and garden production so that women could make cash contributions to the household. INDAP sponsored minicourses for women on horticulture and animal husbandry and offered small credits for raising rabbits and pigs. During the 1964 presidential campaign, Frei promised to supply every Chilean homemaker with a sewing machine. While this ambitious target was never met, the government claimed to have distributed some nine hundred sewing machines in the Aconcagua Valley between 1968 and 1970.[84] The goal of enabling homemakers to generate additional income was distinct from that of incorporating women into wage labor. Women's economic contributions would be made from within the household in ways presumably more compatible with their responsibilities as wives and mothers. This validated the material importance of women's activities while emphasizing a gender division of labor in which men remained the principal producers and providers.

The Socialists and Communists also used CEMAS to organize women as wives and mothers. But the Left saw civic domesticity as a means of incorporating women into class struggle. In contrast to the independent Catholic and Christian Democratic insistence that CEMAS remain nonpolitical, the Left openly acknowledged that mothers' centers should be instruments for political education and partisan mobilization. The centers would not only help create better mothers, but militant mothers at that, who understood the need for radical change. Mothers' centers would generate female support for communist and socialist positions on the Agrarian Reform as well as for the Left's call to nationalize banking and copper. In Catemu county, the president of the FCI-affiliated union paid monthly visits to CEMAS to inform women about possible labor conflicts and to encourage their solidarity.[85] During the 1964 and 1970 presidential campaigns, representatives from the women's departments of the Communist and Socialist parties traveled from Santiago to San Esteben county to hold seminars on leftist platforms.[86] The Left also envisioned CEMAS as an organizational basis for making material demands on the state. It encouraged the centers to apply for sewing machines and rural housing subsidies as part of its larger call for the redistribution of wealth.

Mothers' centers enjoyed popularity among rural women and as much as 30 percent of adult campesinas in central Chile belonged to or casually participated in one.[87] By 1970 Aconcagua province had 246 registered rural CEMAS with an estimated total membership over seven thousand.[88] The centers brought together women of different generations and varying economic situations. Many younger and a few older women worked seasonally as agricultural laborers or domestic servants. The vast majority of women worked within the household, and it was to this membership that CEMAS primarily catered. Many working women found their needs only partially met. Katarina Antimán, the wife of a former afuerino in Santa María county, worked year-round in different temporary agricultural jobs. She recalled in an oral history that while she benefited from CEMA literacy classes, she saw sewing and craft activities as irrelevant luxury: "I didn't have time to sit around knitting sweaters or cutting out ornaments. I had to be in the estate at seven in the morning and didn't get home until seven that evening. CEMAS were really for the more fortunate women who were housewives. They could go to all those meetings, sewing and gossiping. I was poor and had to be both a housewife and a worker."[89]

Other female wageworkers expressed similar frustrations. Because men often objected to wives' and daughters' nighttime absences from home, most CEMAS met during the day when men were working. This restricted the participation of wage-earning women to Sundays or months when they were not employed, which resulted in a predominance of non–wage-earning, older women in memberships and leadership positions. Mothers' centers offered no specific advice about women's employment conditions outside the home, a silence resulting in part from

Mothers' center craft display cosponsored by Popular Promotion. Popular Promotion pamphlet, courtesy of the University of Wisconsin Land Tenure Center.

the assumption that unions would address such issues and that women's wage work remained secondary to their roles as wives and mothers. It was not that CEMAs disapproved of women's employment outside the home; most campesinas worked for wages at some point in their lives, and the centers acknowledged this as both natural and necessary. However, their inattention to female employment reinforced household-based work as the behavioral norm for campesina women and contributed to the invisibility of women wage earners as socially significant.

The centers' disinterest in addressing women as workers contrasted sharply with the active role they encouraged women to take in other extra-household activities. Indeed, their very focus on women's roles within the family frequently served as a catalyst for rural women's participation in organizing activities outside their homes. Calling on rural housewives to collectively defend and improve the lot of their families, CEMAs promoted an explicitly public role for women. They hosted dances and community dinners to raise funds for sewing machines or to contribute to a school or neighbors' council. They sponsored children's games on holidays and took collections of food and clothing for families affected by floods and earthquakes. Such activities extended definitions of "family" and, hence, "women's," issues to broader community situations and institutions.[90] Although community solidarity was hardly new, the political context of the Agrarian Reform emphasized CEMAs as spaces of campesino empowerment, not just survival.

CEMAs were the primary vehicles by which rural women participated in the rural labor movement. If mothers' centers failed to champion the cause of women workers, they actively urged campesinas to help defend the economic interests of campesino men. Men's fights for better wages and access to land were viewed as critical to ameliorating the material misery of rural households. Rural unions of all political colors solicited CEMAs to lend auxiliary support to labor struggles, and women vigorously responded. The centers sent female delegations to join men in union marches and official ceremonies in town plazas. They held dances and community dinners to raise money for unions, sewed union banners, and furnished innumerable meals for union meetings. Most significantly perhaps, CEMAs had an institutionalized presence during strikes and other labor actions by organizing "common pots" (*ollas comunes,* rough equivalents of soup kitchens) to provide on-site meals during prolonged labor conflicts.[91] The common pots allowed women to collectively pool resources while symbolically demonstrating family unity and class solidarity.

Mothers' centers allowed women only supporting roles in union dramas. They challenged neither the overwhelmingly male nature of the rural labor movement nor the primacy of men's roles as economic providers. Their elevation of domesticity to the exclusion of other female roles obscured women's existing needs as wage earners. It defined their productive, if unpaid, subsistence and petty commercial work as "domestic" (household-related) and, therefore, as lying outside the Agrarian Reform's primary policy focus on large estates and commercial production. Despite the fact that, for the most part, women continued to perform the same types of labor that they had before the Agrarian Reform, CEMAs increasingly defined this labor as either nonproductive or of secondary productive importance (to that of men). This, in turn, implied that women's political and civic roles within a national project charged with transforming productive relations necessarily remained secondary and supportive to those of men, the primary workers.

But CEMAs gave women an independent and institutional presence *as women* in Agrarian Reform politics. Increasingly defining campesina women as housewives, they promoted an ideal of housewife activism in which women worked not for individual families, but for the entire community. When CEMAS offered solidarity with striking men or organized community social events for unions, they did so as formal organizations of women, not as individual wives and daughters of male workers. When CORA initiated the first state-managed estate (*asentamiento*) in Putaendo county in 1967, a CEMA incorporating the wives of the new members presented the CORA official with a formal letter, signed by the membership and emblazoned with the CEMA's official stamp.[92] The letter praised the government for its commitment to the Agrarian Reform and affirmed women's commitment to working for the prosperity of the unit. Such gestures illustrated that women not only saw themselves as having a role in the Agrarian Reform, but that they perceived this role as requiring gender-specific representation, parallel to and mutually supportive of men. Following the creation of the MCI Aconcagua Federation of Mothers' Centers in 1968, a delegate from Santa María county proudly responded to a reporter's inquiry about the purpose of CEMAS, "We are showing that, like men, [women] can work for the benefit of the country."[93]

Beyond providing support to male unions, CEMAS enabled women to carve out a realm of community struggle with women, not men, as the primary protagonists. Throughout the Agrarian Reform, mothers' centers played major roles in the fight for better housing. They competed with, and often surpassed, the efforts of the male-headed neighbors' councils officially responsible for representing the rural poor on this issue. They assisted families in applying for rural housing subsidies, petitioned sub–ministries of housing for electricity and potable water, and wrote letters to municipal politicians requesting more frequent bus service or the construction of roads to isolated areas.[94]

Mothers' centers also directly participated in overt confrontations with government housing authorities. In February 1965, the CEMA and neighbors' council of the rural San Felipe neighborhood Aguirre Cerda organized a suspension of residents' monthly payments to the state Rural Housing Corporation (CORVI) in protest of the agency's failure to repair buildings damaged by a January earthquake.[95] According to newspaper accounts, the standoff involved 1,400 households and lasted over a year,

compelling over fifty visits by various national and provincial government officials to the housing development. In addition to the insistence
on repairs, organizers demanded the inclusion of the neighbors' council
on local government housing committees, the increase of rural housing
subsidies, and the construction of children's playgrounds. They issued letters, signed by both the CEMA and the neighbors' council, to CORVI, the
Aconcagua Intendancy, and President Frei condemning the poor quality
of construction and complaining that the lack of government coordina-
tion caused particular anxiety to housewives who were being forced to
interrupt their work to constantly move their families from one site to
another.[96] Although lack of documentation makes it difficult to assess
the dynamics of state reaction to such protest, *El Trabajo* reported that
most of the protesters' demands had been met by July 1966.[97]

Women played a critical role in such struggles. While housing was
never an exclusively female issue and the male leadership of neighbors'
councils tended to overshadow that of CEMAs in official meetings and on
state-appointed commissions, women's involvement moved beyond the
symbolic. According to one government study, women submitted over
90 percent of the applications and petitions to the government for access
to housing and better living conditions between 1966 and 1970.[98] Women
invoked a moral authority as housewives to insist on the state's obligation to provide material assistance to poor families and to establish the
right to influence government policy. In May 1966, the CEMA of a rural
San Felipe neighborhood called Esperanza organized a demonstration to
protest the eviction of twelve mentally ill residents by a CORVI social
worker.[99] Community leaders from five other neighborhoods joined the
women in issuing a public statement condemning the evictions as "in-
tolerable and inhumane" and calling on the Intendancy to reinstate the
persons and to provide adequate medical assistance. In 1967, San Felipe
women formed part of a delegation that met with CORVI officials in Santiago to complain that high unemployment in Aconcagua made it impossible for residents to make payments on their housing debts.[100] The
delegation warned that women would be forced to start a "massive common pot for urban workers and campesinos" if quota payments were not
suspended.

Mothers' centers expanded, rather than constricted, the social meaning and practice of rural women's household labors. If they were in-

strumental in transforming campesinas into housewives through their redefinition of all household-based work as domestic, they were not simple instruments of social control by the Christian Democratic government or any other CEMA sponsor. While contributing to the invisibility of women wageworkers and bolstering the ideal of male breadwinning, CEMAs' emphasis on domesticity offered assistance and validation to some of campesina women's most taxing and already existing responsibilities for children and household-based production. They provided concrete material and educational benefits, allowing women to acquire new skills and to generate income. Combined with the Agrarian Reform's broader philosophy of gender mutualism and its push to get men to accord greater respect to wives, CEMAs more concretely defined the household as a place of female jurisdiction and authority. Lastly, the centers broke the monotony and isolation of rural household routines and created an exclusively feminine space outside the family in which women could socialize and participate in political life. If most CEMAs (excluding those dominated by the Left) urged women to think of themselves as outside partisan politics, they paradoxically established channels through which women in fact received political education and became socially active. Mothers' centers' structural parallelism to unions created vehicles for women's semi-independent, if never equal, contributions to the Agrarian Reform.

Birth Control and Family Planning

The promotion of gender mutualism proved especially promising for campesina women in matters of sex. In the name of improving family welfare, the Frei administration launched Chile's first nationwide birth control programs.[101] Beginning in 1965, the National Health Service (SNS) joined with APROFA (the Association for Family Promotion, a private affiliate of International Planned Parenthood) to promote family planning as a central part of public health policies. Family planning efforts included the creation of prenatal and postnatal health and nutrition programs, instruction on reproductive health and parenting, and the dissemination of, and education about, medical birth control. In rural areas, these initiatives developed parallel to the Agrarian Reform's broader education and mobilization projects. They had radical implications for rural women's ability to control fertility and negotiate with men. Family planning programs made contraceptives and reproductive health care accessible to marginalized populations for the first time in Chilean history and lent official sanction to the idea that family size should be limited and consciously planned. Simultaneously, they established guidelines as to who should determine and have access to the means for controlling family size. Just as CEMAS, unions, and education projects did, birth control and maternal health programs generated normative ideas about the rural family and appropriate relations between campesino men and women.

Family planning emerged as a public policy priority in Chile during the mid-1960s as domestic alarm over the increasingly miserable status of maternal-infant health dovetailed with an international effort led by the U.S. Alliance for Progress to strengthen Latin American development efforts through population control. In 1965, APROFA shocked Chilean policy-making circles with the publication of a study claiming that over 140,000 abortions—or one abortion for every two live births—were performed in Chile annually.[102] The study also estimated that one in every five abortions resulted in death, a number that accounted for nearly 40 percent of the nation's extremely high maternal death index (28.3 deaths for every 1,000 fertile women).[103] The bad news about abortion and maternal death combined with existing concerns that infant mortality rates had risen throughout the 1950s. Despite a significant reduction in the early 1960s, by the middle of the decade Chile reportedly still ranked second only to Haiti in having the highest proportion of infant deaths in the hemisphere: 95.4 deaths for every 1,000 live births.[104] Although such low world standing was likely an exaggeration (Chile kept far more reliable health statistics than most other parts of Latin America), health officials believed Chile to be worse off than its neighbors and, in any case, Chilean mothers and infants were dying at unacceptable rates.

APROFA blamed infant and maternal death on poverty and lack of birth control and maternal health programs. It urged the Frei administration to actively promote sex education, reproductive health, and birth control in impoverished neighborhoods.[105] Throughout the 1960s, APROFA principally shaped national birth control and family planning policies and incorporated reproductive health strategies into the agenda of state agencies working with popular organizations. Representatives from APROFA served as advisors to Popular Promotion, the National Central Coordinator for Mothers' Centers, and the SNS Department of Family Planning (established after 1966). The association signed formal contracts with each of these government agencies and, after 1970, created provincial offices throughout the country, including one in the Aconcagua Valley, physically located within the SNS building in San Felipe.

The cost of maternal health and birth control programs during the Frei administration was underwritten by the United States government and private U.S. foundations. Between 1964 and 1970, Chile received over five million dollars for family planning initiatives from the combined contributions of USAID, International Planned Parenthood, the Pathfinder Fund, the Ford Foundation and, in particular, the Rockefeller Foundation.[106] APROFA estimated that 50 percent of all birth control methods disseminated during Frei's tenure were funded by the Rockefeller Foundation alone.[107] USAID provided funds for the expansion of Santiago's principle obstetrics and gynecology clinic at Barros Luco Hospital and for the establishment of new obstetrical-gynecological schools and midwife training programs in provincial universities. Although the various U.S. government agencies and foundations differed in their tactical approach and understanding of the broader social implications of birth control, they shared a belief that population control constituted a fundamental prerequisite for development. The Alliance for Progress had established the reduction of Latin America's population growth rate to 2.5 percent as a major policy goal. It linked large family sizes both to poverty and to political instability. The Malthusian underpinnings of this perspective were never far from the surface: a hearty fear of poor people fed the belief that progress was impossible without birth reductions in the most disenfranchised (and politically volatile) sector of the population. It implied that the poor's reproductive capacity was itself responsible for mass misery and at times emphasized population control, rather than structural reform, as a strategic priority. World Bank President Robert MacNamara most cynically expressed this sentiment when he, in 1964, reportedly claimed that, "[It is] better to spend one dollar on family planning in the Third World than ten on development."[108]

Chilean officials also connected reduced population growth with economic development and modernization. However, in the 1960s, Chile's population expanded at an annual rate of 2.7 percent, only slightly higher than the goal set by Alliance for Progress. Reducing the alarming abortion and infant-maternal mortality rates was of far greater concern to Chilean policy makers than curbing population growth. Birth control programs emerged as part of a more comprehensive effort to improve reproductive health care for women and children as a whole. Education campaigns encouraging couples to limit family size in accordance with their resources were promoted in conjunction with expanded prenatal and postpartum services. When the SNS announced the first national health program to include family planning in 1965, it carefully named it "Family Health and Birth Regulation" and conveniently abbreviated and most commonly referred to it only as "Family Health."[109] In addition to providing free consultations on contraceptives and educational seminars, the SNS guaranteed free hospital care for deliveries and abortion-related complications. It expanded training programs for midwives and increased staff in small urban and rural clinics where all pregnant women and new mothers were encouraged to go for pre- and postnatal exams.[110] The Family Health program was further complemented by legislation providing other benefits to mothers and children, including the provision of prenatal cash allowances for pregnant women (1964), the extension of maternal leave for working women (1970), and the expansion of milk and nutritional supplement programs for poor mothers (1970).

The infant-maternal health component of Family Health efforts enjoyed immediate success. Prenatal and postpartum consultations became available to rural women in even some of the most remote parts of Aconcagua through the creation of Rural Health Posts and mobile health units in vans. Ambulance transportation was provided for women in labor as part of a concerted effort by the SNS to encourage all women to give birth in the hospital. UNICEF and USAID funded extensive immunization campaigns against polio, measles, diphtheria, and tetanus. By 1969, SNS claimed that 90 percent of all births in the Aconcagua Valley took place in provincial hospitals, dramatically up from 36 percent in 1960.[111] Infant mortality in the region reportedly declined by nearly 25 percent between 1965 and 1970, and the number of maternal deaths almost halved.[112]

Predictably, the birth control component of Family Health programs proved more controversial, and including it under a wider policy umbrella aimed at improving infant-maternal health had several advan-

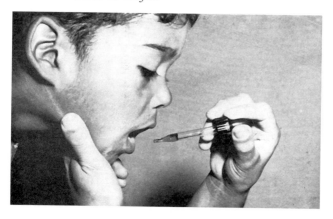

"Accessible medicine is one of the goals of the Revolution in
Liberty." Popular Promotion pamphlet, courtesy of the University
of Wisconsin Land Tenure Center.

tages for a Christian Democratic administration. First, the term invoked
the Christian Democratic emphasis on family improvement and gender mutualism. It celebrated mothers and children, while urging greater
cooperation between husbands and wives. If the desire to reduce abortion and infant-maternal mortality compelled the Christian Democrats
to sanction the use of contraceptives, the concept of Family Health
allowed the government to continue championing the importance of
motherhood and the sanctity of the family. Closely related to this, Family
Health enabled the government to defend itself against criticism that
proclaimed the dissemination of birth control as immoral. Practicing
Catholics and more socially conservative Christian Democrats, including Eduardo Frei, professed to personally oppose medical contraceptives
and avoided public endorsements of this part of the program. Instead, the
government highlighted maternal-infant services and described family
counseling programs in vague terms, suggesting to advocate only the
rhythm method. This practice acknowledged the Catholic Church's official condemnation of birth control while simultaneously circumventing it.

But the Chilean Church was itself split over the issue. Most of the
Church hierarchy formally supported Pope Paul VI's 1968 assertion in
the *Enciclica Humanae Vitae* that both education about and use of contra-

ceptives violated divine law. But a few prominent clergy, including Cardinal Raúl Silva Henríquez in Santiago, accepted family planning education and medical contraceptives as crucial to fighting poverty. While sharing the pope's objections to birth control on theological grounds, such leaders argued that the use of contraceptives ultimately represented an individual's moral choice. In 1968, Silva Henríquez publicly likened the denial of information about contraceptives to couples to the denial of information about vaccines to children.[113] Many Catholic organizations and priests who worked in poor communities shared the cardinal's view. In rural areas, IER and other Catholic reform groups pursued a double strategy of informing women about the existence of medical contraceptives while encouraging periodic abstinence.

Couching birth control in terms of Family Health also helped quell criticism from the Left. Both the Communist and the Socialist parties had called for accessible birth control and family planning programs for Chile's poor for decades, and both continued championing this cause throughout the 1960s. But the Left loudly objected to U.S. involvement in birth control programs because of the authority it gave an antisocialist government in determining policies concerning the working class. Denouncing U.S. participation as a breech of sovereignty and an effort to control the poor, the Left challenged the Christian Democrats to find (unspecified) alternative sources of funding. But Socialists and Communists also had difficulties consistently opposing the Christian Democratic initiative since Family Health programs promised to promote better health for working-class mothers and children and were, in the end, Chile's very first state-sanctioned and nationally promoted project for placing free contraceptives in the hands of the poor.

In the Aconcagua Valley, APROFA sponsored the first family planning programs for campesinos. Beginning with a 1966 conference on sex education for SNS workers and teachers in Los Andes, the agency went on to develop informational programs in hospitals, schools, CEMAS, and parents' centers throughout Aconcagua.[114] The association distributed comic books (*cartillas*) on sexual hygiene and family planning to popular organizations as well as medical bulletins on contraception and childbirth to medical professionals.[115] The agency's various educational seminars for health workers and community leaders constituted its most important labor. Seminars varied in content and pedagogy depending on the audience, but all shared the dual emphasis of strengthening communication between campesino spouses and encouraging birth control practices. Seminars began with discussions of conjugal communication and the importance of family planning to economic welfare and marital harmony. These were followed by a more technical section on how to obtain, use, and monitor different contraceptive methods. Colored charts and plastic models of the human body as well as U.S.-donated Walt Disney interpretations of family planning in Spanish translation enhanced talks to rural men and women. Seminars for SNS staff, health workers, and teachers were more technical, including reviews of national health and reproductive statistics and film presentations on IUD insertion, sterilization, and vasectomy.

In 1969, APROFA began soliciting the cooperation of the labor movement. In July of that year, it coauthored a public statement with the United Workers Central (CUT) demanding free and accessible birth control for all working-class women, and it held several national conferences and regional seminars on family planning for urban and rural labor organizers.[116] Despite APROFA's obvious concern with improving women's health, the agency's overture to organized labor was explicitly designed to appeal to working-class men. When APROFA held a four-day seminar for campesino union leaders and SNS workers in San Felipe in July 1969, it invited primarily men and entitled the seminar "The Worker and His Responsibilities as a Household Head."[117] Sessions on such themes as "The Family as a Social System" and "Family Planning and Family Well-Being" encouraged the male attendees to understand birth control as facilitating working men's duties as family providers. This strategic choice flowed from APROFA's assumption that working-class men in general, and campesino men in particular, objected to birth control because it threatened their sense of virility and because they feared contraceptives would allow wives to become sexually promiscuous. The agency attempted to diffuse such opposition by stressing male authority within family planning decisions as an extension of men's responsibilities as household heads. The agency's seminars for union men emphasized the economic benefits of limiting family size and called for "responsible sexuality" as opposed to "sexual freedom." Educational efforts for female audiences also underscored men's role in family planning. APROFA workshops at CEMAS encouraged greater communication between spouses over matters of reproduction and offered advice to women on how to gently win over reluctant husbands.[118]

The promotion of birth control as a family matter necessarily involving men was a pragmatic response to the social reality of male dominance. Given men's existing authority, conjugal couples, not individual women, seemed the logical target of a successful family planning campaign. But the proposal that female reproduction should involve male consent bolstered the principle of husbands' control of wives' bodies. Women who requested IUDs or prescriptions for birth control pills at SNS clinics and hospitals were routinely asked if they were married and if their husbands approved of their use of contraceptives.[119] Many doctors and midwives insisted that women's husbands accompany them to medical appointments involving birth control.[120] Married women who desired sterilizations were required to present a husband's written consent to such operations and to confirm that they had already given birth to at least two live children.[121] All of this marked a substantial change from the all-female world in which women had exchanged knowledge about and used homemade and herbal contraceptives, whatever their effectiveness. Although women also encountered male opposition to these more traditional methods, clandestine action and female networks had allowed women to more easily circumvent men then. In contrast, Family Health programs defined birth control as the expertise of medical professionals and as a prerogative of husbands as well as wives.

For adolescent girls, access to medical contraceptives was stricter still. The SNS prohibited birth control prescriptions to unmarried women under the age of twenty-one without the written permission of both parents. Although parental control of unmarried daughters' sexuality was commonplace before the 1960s, it had most directly involved mothers' vigilance. With the promotion of medical birth control, fathers also received official license to control daughters' fertility. Moreover, the promotion of birth control as a family issue emphasized marriage as the only appropriate site of sexual activity, overtly discouraging it for the young and unmarried. Although this had long been an ideal throughout Chile, it had coexisted with widespread premarital sex and significant numbers of children born out of wedlock in rural areas. Family Health programs permitted single women over age twenty-one to obtain contraceptives on their own, but they did not address these women as a constituency in public education campaigns or promotional literature. Marriage and the nuclear family were the clearly preferred and officially sanctioned norms.

But within marriage, Family Health programs promoted a positive image of both sexuality and birth control. If they affirmed the principle of husbands' control over wives, it never remained the only message nor necessarily the practical result. Family planning efforts encouraged less coercive and less unequal sexual expectations, including concrete limits to men's sexual privilege. APROFA and SNS seminars defined limiting family size and joint decision making by husbands and wives as modern behavior and equated modernity with the desirable and respectable. They labeled parenthood a mutual responsibility, but cartoon education pamphlets especially warned campesino men against the foolishness of equating virility with the number of children one fathered, and argued that modern men had manageably sized families they could adequately support. Campesina women were urged to become more knowledgeable about their bodies and to see female reproductive cycles as natural and healthy. Seminars also encouraged them to expect their husbands' collaboration in discussing whether smaller families would be achieved by using contraceptives or by practicing periodic abstinence. Despite the fact that family planning projects took for granted and reinforced existing principles of female sexual fidelity, they strongly suggested that men should also show more fidelity to wives. They likewise insisted that adult women should have a say over how and when a couple had sex and that women, rather than men, should take charge of enforcing codes of female sexual responsibility. Despite the restrictions placed on adolescent girls' and single women's access to birth control, reproductive education and expanded gynecological services potentially offered women of all ages and marital statuses more knowledge about their bodies.

Family planning efforts achieved significant results. APROFA reported that the total percentage of fertile-age women using medical birth control methods throughout Chile almost tripled between 1965 and 1970, jumping from 5.1 percent to 14 percent.[122] During this same period in the Aconcagua Valley, over 1,500 women annually scheduled birth control consultations at SNS facilities, nearly double the quantity of women who had inquired yearly about contraceptives immediately prior to 1964.[123] A 1968 study by sociologists Armand and Michèle Mattelart estimated that fully 14 percent of campesinas in central Chile used medical birth control, while over 65 percent said that they would use contraceptives if they were available.[124] Most impressively, the National Statistics Institute (INE) reported that Chile's fertility rates (measured in terms of the average number of children a women had in a lifetime) fell by an astounding 24 percent between 1965 and 1970.[125] Whereas the Chilean woman bore 4.9 children in 1965, the number had fallen to 3.86 by 1970; for poor rural women, the average fell from 8.07 children to 6.09 children.[126] As hoped for, family planning efforts also lowered rates of abortion and maternal death. Between 1964 and 1970, Chile's estimated abortion rate fell over 30 percent and the rate of maternal death (including abortion-related causes) dropped by almost 40 percent.[127] In the Aconcagua Valley, the number of annual abortion-related hospitalizations declined by 24 percent.[128]

But there were limits to such success, and urban and middle-class women generally benefited more than their campesina counterparts. In contrast to the Mattelart study, APROFA reported that less than 6 percent of rural women used contraceptives in 1970.[129] The Mattelarts themselves claimed that some 40 percent of campesinas knew nothing about birth control and that of those who did, a majority did not have access to a facility that dispensed it.[130] Multiple factors conspired, including transportation expense and distance from clinics, requirements that women on birth control have regular checkups, and the irregularity and often inadequately advertised nature of APROFA and SNS educational events. In oral histories, campesina women recalled thinking they would have to pay for contraceptives; others feared that birth control pills and IUDs entailed permanent sterilization.[131]

But by far the most commonly cited reason for rural women's inability to access contraceptives was male opposition. APROFA repeatedly cited men's objections to family planning as the agency's primary obstacle in working-class and rural neighborhoods. Rural women interviewed in the late 1960s and early 1970s by the Mattelarts and Patricia Garrett reported that husbands regularly forbade them even to investigate the use of contraceptives.[132] Oral histories conducted for this book told similar stories. Victoria Antimán, the wife of a former permanent worker in Panquehue county, eagerly approached her husband in the late 1960s about the possibility of getting an IUD since the couple already had four children. While her husband agreed that further children were undesirable, he forbade her to go to the SNS because of his fear that "[she] wished to be sterilized and become an 'unnatural woman.'"[133] Norma Reyes's husband, an inquilino in San Esteben county, prohibited his wife from using contraceptives because they would presumably allow her to be unfaithful.[134] Other women reported that their husbands opposed medical birth control because they disagreed with their wives over the optimal number of children. Anita Hernández was told by her husband that she should have "the number of children that God sends."[135]

Whatever a man's formal reason for objecting, many seem to have agreed with Victoria Antimán's husband that medical birth control made women "unnatural." Emilio Ibáñez recalled in an oral history that men forbade wives to use contraceptives because childbearing represented the essence of being a woman and a wife: "Women were of the house. They [were supposed to have] the children that God sent and to take care of them. If not, why have a wife?"[136] Husbands' concern with preserving wives' childbearing nature intimately involved their own self-understandings as men. If the answer to Ibáñez's rhetorical question, "Why have a wife?" was "So that she can bear the children God sends," the answer to the corollary question, "What is a husband?" was, in part, "A man who fathers as many children as possible."

The fact that the state sponsored Family Health initiatives and that they offered services within health care facilities staffed by professionals, posed a challenge both to men's sense of authority over wives and to their notions of masculinity. The possibility that women could limit pregnancies (and men's demonstrable virility) through visits to hospitals and clinics removed the practice of birth control from the premises of the male-headed household (even if women more than men had always controlled homemade remedies). Despite the routine practice of requesting women to obtain husbands' consent to use contraceptives, many campesino men saw doctors and midwives as usurping sexual jurisdiction over wives. APROFA's educational campaign added to this anxiety. Public discussions about birth control and family planning promoted the idea that reproduction was a social, not just a family or individual, concern and that men should voluntarily consent to the state's effort to help women limit pregnancy. Although APROFA carefully stressed men's interest and responsibility in birth control, many men continued to see family planning as a threat to traditional markers of authority and sexual prowess.

But the idea linking masculine virility to a procreative capacity existed in tension with the value men attached to being successful providers and responsible household heads. Like women, men had an interest in limiting family size in accordance to their resources, and many husbands cooperated, either directly or indirectly, with their spouses' use of homemade remedies and requests for abstinence. Others openly supported wives' recourse to the more effective medical contraceptives provided by sns. Raúl Ahumada and Sergio Contreras, former inquilinos from Catemu county, reported in an oral history that they encouraged their spouses to take birth control pills and accompanied their wives to San Felipe Hospital to provide appropriate consent.[137] Walter García, a former permanent worker in Los Andes county, claimed that he saw nothing unnatural about his wife, Selfa, using birth control since "God had sent me enough children."[138] The fact that rural fertility rates reportedly fell by almost a quarter of their original level between 1964 and 1970—despite the small numbers of campesina women apparently using medical contraceptives—suggests that the educational mission of Family Health campaigns to promote gender mutualism in reproduction was highly successful. Men were, indeed, cooperating with wives in preventing pregnancy.

But women also challenged men's notions about sexual obligation and entitlement within marriage. Family planning's emphasis on cooperation between spouses in sexual matters and basic male fidelity combined with the Agrarian Reform's broader message of gender mutualism and male respect for wives to give some campesina women a stronger sense of entitlement to limit conjugal sex and demand husbands' reciprocity. Paradoxically, the extent of this challenge most readily surfaces in complaints of wife beating filed by women at local courts.[139] As was true prior to the Agrarian Reform, wife-beating cases during the 1960s overwhelmingly involved men's insistence that wives, by definition, owed husbands exclusive sexual and domestic services on demand.[140] But what was new in the 1960s was a greater willingness by women to claim they had the right to deny husbands sex because men had failed to fulfill their roles as breadwinners and respectful partners.

In October 1969, Eugenia Puebla filed charges against Onofre Poza, her husband and an agricultural worker, for splitting her lip open because his lunch was not ready when he came home at noon and because she refused to have sex with him.[141] Eugenia Puebla testified that she purposely had not prepared her husband's lunch because that morning "he [had] left [her] at home with all the work [and] had come home drunk."[142] She maintained that Poza became enraged about the lunch and "grabbed [her] by the shoulders so that [she would] sleep with him." Puebla told the judge that, when she resisted, her husband started "beating and kicking her."[143] Onofre Poza's testimony differed markedly. While admitting that he had hit his wife, he said nothing (either in defense or in denial) about trying to sexually force himself on her. Instead, he maintained that his wife had also been physically violent to him, that she was responsible for her own injuries, and that he had actually received his lunch after all: "My wife served me lunch, and it was cold. . . . I complained and she screamed [at me]. This made me mad, so I gave her a little slap on the face. She then took a jar and threw it at my head. Then she ran into the street and fell down, which is why her face is like it is."[144]

Prior to the Agrarian Reform, men had also beaten their wives for failing to serve meals and refusing to have sex. But what makes cases like Eugenia Puebla's interesting is the explicit reference to wifely obligations (whether sex or dinner) as something that women owed on the condition that husbands fulfilled their roles as good spouses. Puebla intentionally denied her husband his lunch (or served him a cold one) because, in her opinion, Onofre Poza had failed to properly work that morning and because he had arrived drunk. She insisted that there were limits to her sexual obligations and that she had the right to refuse angry and drunken advances. Of course campesina women expected things from husbands and set limits even prior to the Agrarian Reform. But the official promotion of gender mutualism, including new definitions of sex as involving responsibility and consent, more sharply defined marriage arrangements and gave women reason to demand more cooperative behavior from men. Significantly, Poza did not defend his actions, as was common in the 1950s, in terms of an openended marital right to physically discipline his wife.[145] Rather, he implied that he had acted responsibly as a husband (he had given her a little slap when she screamed at him) and blamed his wife's own failure to exercise similar restraint (her recourse to jar throwing and hysterics) for the resulting bloody lip.

Some women went so far as to interpret gender mutualism to mean the entitlement to break off sexual relationships and pursue new ones when a partner failed to uphold his end of the bargain. In 1970, Sonia Bruna told the court that her common-law husband, José Muñoz, an agricultural worker, had beaten her in the face after she "decided [that she] wanted nothing more to do with him and was seeking other company."[146] José Muñoz admitted to his actions, but defended them on grounds of his marital right to castigate his partner for infidelity. As he stated in his testimony, "We were making a married life together, and I surprised her talking with another man. I asked her for an explanation, and since I had already pardoned her for a similar situation, I hit her in the face."[147] Sonia Bruna's boldness reflected the particular assertiveness of the small proportion of campesina women who cohabitated with their partners, as opposed to being legally married. Sonia Bruna deemed José Muñoz an incompetent husband (for reasons not apparent in her testimony) and attempted to leave her spouse rather than continue enduring his unacceptable behavior. Whether or not she was actually seeking the sexual company of the man with whom Muñoz caught her talking, she clearly felt she had a right to do so. She did not see herself as being obliged to honor wifely duties (including sexual loyalty) under any and all circumstances; and she saw it as her prerogative, not Muñoz's, to determine when affection and loyalty would be transferred to another man.

As with the effort of CEMAS and Agrarian Reform education projects, family planning initiatives offered campesina women new agency and resources while suggesting at least some basic limits to unbridled male authority over women. Infant-maternal health and birth control programs meaningfully improved campesina women's lives, both in terms of women's physical well-being and control over reproduction and in terms of less coercive normative definitions of sexuality within marriage. Yet as was true of other state efforts to address the needs of campesina women and to incorporate them into processes of social uplift alongside men, the Christian Democrats' Family Health initiatives bolstered an ideal of family in which husbands had stewardship and prerogative (albeit benevolent and more limited) over wives. Family planning programs, like CEMAS, reached out primarily to married women, stressing matrimony and family as the only appropriate sites of sexual activity. Ironically, this ensured that the very women the state seemed to most disapprove of as mothers—adolescent girls and single women—had the most difficulty preventing pregnancy. Family planning programs encouraged women to exercise control over their bodies and to communicate more openly with husbands, but they confirmed men's right to determine the limits of that agency. This complemented the Christian Democrats' larger effort to promote family uplift and gender cooperation while preserving male authority within conjugal structures of mutualism.

chapter 5 Struggling for Land

Worker Bosses and Campesina Militants

For most rural poor people, the Agrarian Reform was synonymous with land redistribution. The labor movement's unanimous cry to "Give the land to the man who works it!" resonated deeply with seasonal wage laborers and inquilinos alike. Eduardo Frei's pledge to create 100,000 new campesino farmers generated enormous hope. Land redistribution was both a symbol and a concrete measure of the Christian Democratic commitment to social justice. It constituted the scale by which campesinos, male and female, weighed the government's success and legitimacy. As such, land reform was as problematic as it was exhilarating. The Frei administration undertook expropriations unprecedented in Chile's history, but it fell far short of its projected goals. It reorganized huge sectors of the agrarian economy in ways that improved campesino access to land, but it failed to create even one fifth of the promised number of small farmers. The gap between official bravado and concrete delivery generated considerable impatience and heightened worker militancy against the very government campesinos looked to for support.

Land reform also created new divisions among campesinos. The expropriation and reorganization of land included only a minority of the rural poor, almost exclusively men. This produced a male working-class elite whose new access to land and ability to "be their own bosses" became the masculine standard to which landless men aspired. Campesina women benefited from land reform almost exclusively through their family relationships to recipient men—as wives and daughters. This strengthened existing gender hierarchies, reinforcing married women's economic dependence on men and bolstering husbands' sense of authority over wives. Women challenged the latter, pushing the Agrarian Reform's ideal of gender mutualism as a counterforce to excessive male control, but most accepted men's exclusive entitlement to redistributed land. Overall, most women vigorously supported land reform. Expanding on notions of civic domesticity, women made militant demands for faster expropriations, and as the Agrarian Reform became more conflictive and volatile, they joined men in mass takeovers of private property.

In the Aconcagua Valley, the process of land reform under the Christian Democrats mirrored that in Chile as a whole but was relatively swifter and more extensive. Between 1964 and July 1970, the state expropriated thirty-seven estates, including 28 percent of all irrigated farmland in the department of San Felipe and 32 percent of all irrigated land in the department of Los Andes.[1] Total expropriations throughout the Aconcagua Valley amounted to 12,044 hectares of irrigated land and 32,046 hectares of nonirrigated land (see Tables 8 and 9).[2] By the time Eduardo Frei left power, almost 90 percent of this land was organized into 22 joint government-worker administrated production units called *asentamientos* (settlements) and included an estimated 1,500 campesino families.[3] In Chile as a whole, the Christian Democrats expropriated 20 percent of all irrigated farmland, organized roughly 60 percent into asentamientos, and incorporated a total of 18,000 campesino families into the Reform sector.[4]

Land reform was relatively swifter in the Aconcagua Valley than elsewhere for several reasons. Since Aconcagua contained some of the country's richest agricultural property, CORA and the Ministry of Agriculture saw it as an obvious showcase for demonstrating that the Agrarian Reform could increase production. The region's proximity to Santiago facilitated the state's ability to oversee expropriations and redistribution. No less importantly, the rural labor movement in Aconcagua was highly organized and dominated by independent Catholics and Christian Democrats. Eager to maintain the allegiance of its partisan allies, the Frei administration concentrated its first reform efforts in UCC and Triunfo strongholds.

Three of the first expropriations anywhere in Chile took place in the Aconcagua Valley. They lent a testament to the Frei administration's

Table 8 Agricultural Land Expropriated under Frei, Aconcagua Valley and Chile, 1965 to July of 1970 (in hectares)

Region	No. Estates	Irrigated Land	Non-Irrig. Land	Dry Land	Total Land
San Felipe department	18	6,752	30,531	105,850	143,133
Los Andes department	19	5,292	1,515	94,043	100,850
Aconcagua Valley	37	12,004	32,046	199,893	243,943
Chile	1,412	290,601	602,065	3,200,673	4,093,339

Figures for Aconcagua Valley calculated from fichas de expropriación, CORA. Figures for Chile qtd. in Barraclough and Fernández, *Diagnóstico*, 71.

Table 9 Irrigated Agricultural Land Expropriated under Frei, Aconcagua Valley and Chile, 1964 to July of 1970 (in percentages of total irrigated agricultural land)

Region	Total Irrigated Land Expropriated
San Felipe department	28%
Los Andes department	32%
Aconcagua Valley	30%
Chile	20%

Figures for Aconcagua Valley calculated from fichas de expropriación, CORA. Data on total agricultural land listed in the *Censo agropecuario: Aconcagua, 1964–1965*. Figure for Chile qtd. in Barraclough and Fernández, *Diagnóstico*, 71.

cautiousness as well as to the political nature of land reform decisions. In 1965, CORA expropriated two properties in Putaendo county: Bellavista estate, a 2,800 hectare property owned by the Catholic Church, and a smaller, individually owned estate, Rabuco Pachama. In San Esteben county, the agency expropriated a 170-hectare estate called El Cobre.[5] All three properties underwent expropriation for poor exploitation, and all three owners legally appealed the decision. Negotiations were particularly prolonged in the case of the Church-owned Bellavista estate.

Although the Church's formal support for the Agrarian Reform made an outright rejection of the government's action difficult (and three strikes by frustrated workers in 1966 an embarrassment), Bellavista's owners played on the Christian Democrats' unwillingness to directly antagonize the Church in order to negotiate a generous reserve and to delay CORA's possession of the land until 1968.[6] In contrast, the government employed a jingoist nationalism to expedite its will on the Rabuco Pachama estate owned by a Palestinian immigrant. When the owner appealed CORA's decision to expropriate, the government had him expelled from the country on the spurious grounds that, as a "foreigner," he was not allowed to "impede government policy" or "exploit Chilean workers."[7]

Most expropriations occurred when outside pressure compelled the Frei administration to act. Fully two-thirds of land expropriated in the Aconcagua Valley between 1964 and 1970 was taken away in the last two years of Frei's tenure. This was a direct result of campesino labor organizing in the aftermath of the 1967 Law of Campesino Unionization and the passage of a second, more extensive Agrarian Reform Law in 1967.[8] The Communist and Socialist parties pushed the second Agrarian Reform Law (Law 16.640) through congress in alliance with leftleaning Christian Democrats. It legalized expropriations on the basis of size (estates over eighty hectares of basic irrigated land) and on the basis of landowner failure to comply with social legislation. Reaching far beyond the provisions of the first Agrarian Reform Law's allowance for expropriation in cases of abandoned or poorly exploited land, the new legislation empowered the state to target even efficient producers and to directly attack the twin pillars of latifundia: land monopolies and oppressive labor conditions.

But as a rule, the Frei administration hesitated to flex its new legal muscle unless so obliged. Over 85 percent of all land it expropriated was targeted under earlier legislation's criteria of abandonment and undercultivation.[9] The reluctance to fully utilize the second Agrarian Reform Law reflected a standoff between two increasingly polarized camps within the Christian Democratic Party and a resulting stalemate over the pace and purpose of the Agrarian Reform. The more conservative faction, including Eduardo Frei and CORA president Rafael Moreno, continued to champion the importance of agricultural efficiency, be it by large or small producers, and was eager to maintain strong alliances with large landowner associations like the SNA, which denounced the 1967 law as legalized theft. On the other side stood INDAP leader Jacques Chonchol and most of the Catholic and Christian Democratic rural labor movement who insisted that the Agrarian Reform's priority should lie in dismantling latifundia through a massive transfer of land to campesinos. Chonchol openly criticized the subdivision of estate land into many individual farms, warning that this would perpetuate a peasant economy and undermine productivity. By the late 1960s, this more radical contingent of the Christian Democratic Party sounded increasingly like their Marxist competition, calling for an end to capitalist exploitation and the creation of at least some collective forms of property. But despite this leftward push from within, the Frei administration as a whole fortified the more conservative perspective of CORA's leadership. Chonchol was eventually ousted and expropriation policies remained cautious.

Divisions within the Christian Democratic Party also manifested themselves in the particular kind of reorganization the expropriated land underwent, namely the ambiguous nature of the asentamiento. Asentamientos were established by the second Agrarian Reform Law on the basis of an expropriated estate, or the combination of several estates; their size varied widely, from a few hundred to several thousand hectares. Legally, asentamiento land pertained to the state but was farmed and coadministrated by former inquilinos and other workers whom CORA selected to be asentamiento members (*asentados*). Asentamientos were designed to last four to six years, at which point asentados would vote on whether to continue farming the unit collectively, divide the land into fully individual farms, or form cooperatives. The provision for campesino voting resulted less from the Christian Democratic emphasis on popular participation than from disagreement within the party as well as with the Left over the ultimate form of land tenure. More conservative Christian Democrats maintained that asentamientos should be divided into private individual family farms. The Catholic labor movement looked more favorably on cooperatives. Chonchol and others in INDAP agreed with the Socialists and Communists that individual titles should be combined with collective forms of proprietorship. Rather than resolve these tensions, the law kept the asentamiento's legal status purposely vague. It legitimated three types of possible proprietorship—individual, cooperative, and permanent asentamiento—and left the issue of final tenure to a later decision.

Bossing and Being Bossed

Asentamientos had a lofty, transformative mission. They were imagined as providing former inquilinos and other rural workers with new management and technical skills as well as with an appreciation for democratic process, knowledge that would presumably turn campesinos into able producers and good citizens. Responsibility and initiative would replace fatalism and passivity; individual aspirations would receive nurturing alongside more communal commitments. Accordingly, each asentamiento member was allotted an individual land plot that could be farmed for subsistence as well as commercial purposes. Individual plots were meant to foster personal investment in the Agrarian Reform while preparing asentados to become family farmers. Each asentado was also required to regularly work on the larger, undivided portion of the asentamiento in return for a monthly, government-advanced portion of the asentamiento's estimated annual proceeds called *antícipos* (advanced earnings).

As contemporary and later critics of the Agrarian Reform noted, asentamiento arrangements resembled those of inquilinaje and led to accusations that the state had merely replaced private latifundia with state latifundia. But the asentamiento differed meaningfully from the private estate. First and foremost, the asentamiento embodied the state promise that campesinos would soon own their own land. Within the Agrarian Reform's broader development goals, asentamientos defined their worker-members, not elite landowners, as the key to national productivity and modernization. Consequently, asentamientos stressed campesino self-management and civic participation in contrast to the supposed servility of traditional inquilinos. General assemblies that included all asentados as members and elected officers from the membership internally governed the asentamientos. General assemblies met monthly to assign members to administrative committees that oversaw the asentamiento's daily affairs, including construction, tractor maintenance, irrigation, cultivation, harvesting, and accounting. General assemblies also directly connected asentados to Agrarian Reform agencies and regional governments by relaying requests and grievances to local INDAP and CORA offices and by electing five representatives to serve with

Asentamiento member receives
news of future land rights.
Popular Promotion official
pamphlet, courtesy of the
University of Wisconsin Land
Tenure Center.

CORA functionaries on the regional "asentamiento council," a government body that made production and investment decisions.[10]

In practice, government officials exercised disproportional authority over the asentamiento. INDAP functionaries regularly oversaw asentamiento committees and regional CORA offices established production targets, determined levels of capital and technical investment, set payment schedules, introduced new crops and technologies, and controlled product commercialization.[11] But if the government heavily managed the asentamiento, it was not the same as the patrón. Asentados did not lower their eyes or tip hats to CORA officials, and the change was more than symbolic. General assemblies and asentamiento councils kept asentados informed of policy changes and gave workers regular, direct access to state agencies. Daily authority over work schedules made asentados "their own bosses," at least in the field. As one asentado from Putaendo county recalled in an interview with researchers in the 1980s, whatever the constraints of government, it was liberating to sense that government officials finally paid attention to campesino concerns. Asentados felt a collective and individual responsibility for their own performance:

"There were a million problems [with CORA], but at least you had the guarantee of going freely to discuss the problems that arose [with the authorities]. . . . There were interviews with the Ministry of Agriculture, they listened to us. . . . And the best was that we began to work for ourselves. Now, nobody bossed us, only the will of each man himself. We worked harder because we worked for ourselves, and we looked out for one another."[12]

Asentamientos, like rural unions, were almost exclusively masculine. But unlike unions, which included the vast majority of campesino men, asentamientos included only a small minority of already relatively privileged rural men. The second Agrarian Reform Law specified that land recipients be "household heads" (*jefes de hogar*) with considerable prior agricultural experience.[13] Asentados were selected through an elaborate point system that weighed such factors as marital status, number of dependents, occupation (with preference given to inquilinos and permanent workers), and specific skills in mechanics, tractor driving, fruit cultivation, and irrigation. Although regulations did not explicitly prohibit women's asentamiento membership, married women were automatically classified as dependents rather than household heads. Single and widowed women who headed their own households were usually excluded due to "lack of sufficient agricultural experience," a designation resulting from gendered definitions of women's temporary wage labor as less skilled than men's permanent employment, and of women's unpaid subsistence farming as secondary in importance to men's commercial cultivation. But if virtually all women found themselves excluded from asentamientos, a majority of men were also left out. The preference for inquilinos and permanent workers with large numbers of dependents weakened the applications of single or recently married men and/or of seasonal laborers and afuerinos. Minifundistas or men working on small or medium estates faced further disadvantages. By 1970, asentamientos included only an estimated 10 to 15 percent of male agricultural workers in the Aconcagua Valley and Chile as a whole.[14]

But for those men lucky enough to be included, the asentamiento nurtured a bold sense of masculine independence and accomplishment. The asentado's feeling that each man "commanded himself" and looked out for fellow workers fulfilled the labor movement's vision of a union manhood in which male workers stood on equal footing with the patrón

Left: Asentamiento general assembly meeting. *Below:* Asentamiento members discuss production plans. Both from CORA promotional literature, courtesy of the University of Wisconsin Land Tenure Center.

and in fraternal solidarity with each other. Asentados boasted of their access to circles of political power and of the self-sufficiency that flowed from (at least the perception of) being self-employed and self-managed. Referring to themselves as "owners" and "bosses," they christened asentamientos with heady names such as "The Triumph" and "United Victors" and converted old estate buildings into community recreation halls decorated with posters advertising literacy campaigns and campesino cultural festivals.[15] Following the 1968 creation of "The Sunflower" asentamiento in Santa María county, the new members strung a banner from an exterior adobe wall proclaiming, "On this estate each man is his own patrón!"[16] If the watchful presence of CORA and INDAP made this less than fully the case, the announcement expressed workers' jubilance at the old boss's absence and their own greater control over their lives.

Asentamientos placed new material resources into members' hands. Asentados received priority in state-sponsored housing programs and over 80 percent had their houses repaired or newly built in the first few years of the asentamiento.[17] Pasture land was cultivated with new crops, cattle and goat herds were expanded, trucks and tractors were purchased, barns and storage bodegas were repaired, new schools and community buildings were constructed, and, in some cases, televisions and phones were made available for communal use.[18] On individual plots, asentados were allowed to raise larger numbers of farm animals than were inquilinos and to keep all profits from any commercial sale of crops. In addition, asentados obtained immediate guarantee of the benefits of Agrarian Reform social welfare and labor legislation: they worked eight-hour days, enjoyed a Sunday rest, received pay on rain days, and earned annual vacations. As recalled in an oral history by Emilio Ibáñez, who became an asentado in Santa María county, the spectacular improvement in living standards boosted male confidence: With the asentamiento, "a man didn't depend on a little salary that he might have the luck to get paid. . . . We paid ourselves a good salary because the asentamiento allowed us to. [It] also [allowed] us to equip the place with machinery without debt, to have all we needed."[19]

Beyond claims to a newfound financial power, emerging notions of asentado manhood took meaning from new hierarchies between working-class men. Asentamientos, like private estates, hired large numbers of seasonal workers, mostly men, to labor during planting and harvest cycles. Within the logic of the asentamiento, this technically made asentados employers of other men. In structurally replacing the patrón, the asentado inherited parts of his former boss's social and emotional power based on the ability to exert control over other men's labor and

Left: Asentamiento member demonstrates new dairy machinery. *Below:* Asentamiento members astride new thresher. Both from CORA promotional literature, courtesy of the University of Wisconsin Land Tenure Center.

persons. Asentados assigned tasks to hired male workers and supervised their work. They also directed the labor of the smaller, but significant, numbers of women who worked as hired seasonal laborers on asentamientos, but dominion over women had greater continuity with the past. The ability of asentados to direct the labor of other male campesinos meant something different. Certainly the latifundia system had regularly placed some rural men in charge of others, when, for example, campesinos served as supervisors and inquilinos contracted obligados. But the asentamiento created a new class of worker-bosses with future ownership rights to the means of production. It made asentados the employers of men formerly their social peers or, at the very least, their seasonal workmates.

But relations between asentados and hired male workers hardly replicated those between patrón and inquilino. Asentamientos paid hired workers far superior wages to what inquilinos had earned in the late 1950s and early 1960s; weekly income for hired workers often surpassed that paid to asentados through government advances.[20] Moreover, the Agrarian Reform's language of class solidarity and appeals to the shared experience of campesino life maintained horizontal bonds between asentamiento members and nonmembers. Still, the relationship created considerable conflict and resentment. In oral histories, men who worked seasonal jobs on asentamientos in the Aconcagua Valley complained that asentados thought they were "better than everyone else" and that they routinely assigned hired workers the most taxing jobs.[21] Miguel Acevedo, a former temporary laborer in San Esteben county, claimed that asentados "thought they were kings" on the asentamiento where he worked, often refusing to work themselves and preferring to supervise their help in a pale imitation of the onetime patrón.[22]

Tellingly, countercomplaints that it was the hired workers, not the asentados, who lagged on the job surfaced in oral histories with asentamiento members. Jacobo Fernández, a former asentado from Santa María county, alleged that because hired workers knew that CORA would pay them their wages regardless of their output, "they didn't work, out of pure laziness," a situation related to the more fundamental problem of hired workers refusing to recognize asentados' authority.[23] According to Fernández, "they didn't respect us. They would do whatever they wanted. Come [to work] when they wanted, leave when they wanted. There was no one to make them behave."[24] Such lament betrayed a desire by at least some asentados to receive the same respect as the former patrón. It also suggested asentados' investment in an image of themselves as unjustly wronged employers. Jacobo Fernández's very description of hired workers as lazy and unmanageable echoed traditional landowner attitudes toward inquilinos.

Some of the hardest feelings between those who did and those who did not belong to asentamientos were generated by the fact that asentados often stopped participating in the rural labor movement.[25] Following the creation of an asentamiento, members usually left off union meetings, resigned from elected union positions, and showed up more rarely at support actions for strikes and land takeovers elsewhere. In part this reflected asentados' changed relationship to unions: technically self-managed, asentados employed others. Since they had already acquired much of what the labor movement defined as its goals, it was not always clear what the objective of continued mobilization within a union would be. But for campesinos who were not asentamiento members, asentados' withdrawal from unions constituted a class betrayal of both worker solidarity and popular egalitarianism. Asentados appeared disinterested in helping former comrades achieve the same privileges they had and seemed to increasingly identify with an employer sensibility. Miguel Merino, an organizer for the Triunfo confederation, summarized this sentiment in an interview: "There was a lot of bitterness about asentados leaving [the unions]. . . . Asentados felt different, better. . . . They developed a businessman's attitude, saw themselves as small producers and small employers, even big landowners, not workers."[26]

But resentment toward asentados was often the flip side of envy and admiration. Most campesino men who complained about asentado arrogance simultaneously aspired to what asentados had: the markers of self-determination and a guarantee of future property ownership. The Christian Democratic government and Catholic labor movement aggressively equated campesino masculine self-realization with family farming and entrepreneurial spirit. Asentados even represented the fulfillment of some of the Left's collectivist aims. Despite the asentamiento's cultivation of individualism (through allotments and the possibility of future individual land titles), the asentamiento had replaced private property with a state enterprise purportedly owned by workers and geared toward large-scale production. Thus asentamiento members embodied the Agrarian Reform's success across a wide political spectrum. Asentados were objects of official celebration and featured prominently at government ceremonies marking the Agrarian Reform's advance as well as in countless newspaper and other media reports about the transformation of the countryside. Despite their relatively small numbers, they received a disproportional share of state resources. Most importantly, asentados' access to land became a model to which landless workers aspired. As Miguel Acevedo, the hired worker who grumbled about asentado bosses, also confessed, "What I really wanted was to be part of the game."[27]

If asentamientos created new hierarchies between men, they concretized existing ones between men and women. Asentados proved particularly eager to display a reinvigorated masculinity by more strictly bossing the parameters of female domesticity. In oral histories, several wives of asentados recalled their lives as becoming more isolated after the creation of the asentamiento.[28] Men's higher earnings lessened the need for married women to seek seasonal agricultural jobs or domestic service positions. In some cases, men actively prohibited such work.[29] On El Tártaro–Lo Vicuña asentamiento in Putaendo county, asentados withdrew their wives and daughters from their former jobs of caring for the estate's cows and goats and replaced them with hired male workers.[30] As one former asentado, Pedro Alvarez, explained in an oral history, men saw such restrictions as a benevolent paternalism: "As asentados, we made enough money to finally support our wives and allow them to raise the children. On the asentamiento, our wives lived more easily. . . . Their only relationship to the fields was to bring their husbands a bucket of food at noon. . . . They were happy to have more time for the home where they worked hard enough."[31]

Women's involvement in community activism also greatly lessened. In oral histories, wives of asentados complained that following the creation of the asentamiento, their husbands insisted that they cease, or greatly reduce, their involvement in CEMAs and INDAP workshops.[32] Meanwhile, asentados' own withdrawal from the labor movement ended wives' participation (however marginal to begin with) in support activities for unions.[33] Almost no women participated in the asentamiento's general assembly meetings or served on administrative committees.[34]

Left: Asentamiento worker
harvesting grapes.
Below: Campesino tending a
new vineyard on an asentamiento.
Both photos from CORA promotional literature, courtesy of
the University of Wisconsin Land
Tenure Center.

The logic was that, since the political and economic goals of the Agrarian Reform had now been achieved (through the formation of the asentamiento), the need for women's civic activism on behalf of men's struggles no longer existed. Men could assume responsibility for the daily administration and production, freeing women to devote themselves to children and home.[35]

Asentados' enthusiasm for female domesticity and confidence that such arrangements benefited wives was symbolically and materially reinforced by CORA's provision of new housing on asentamientos. Crumbling one- or two-room adobe structures that had originally served as living and sleeping quarters for entire families were replaced or rehabilitated into homes with two or more separate bedrooms, a living space, and a small kitchen separated from the living room, usually connected to electricity and, occasionally, running water. These spatial arrangements refashioned campesino family relationships as hygienic and modern, as opposed to promiscuous and irrational, stressing the individuated activities of sleeping, eating, and meal preparation, in contrast to a more seamless communal living. As Ximena Valdés and Kathya Araujo have noted, this arrangement had particular ramifications for women.[36] The creation of small kitchens, distinct from the main living space and often of a size that accommodated only one person, emphasized cooking as a solitary activity. If feeding families had long been women's responsibility, houses built by CORA suggested that cooking was something a woman did by herself, apart from the activities of the rest of the household.

Of course women enthusiastically welcomed expanded and better-quality accommodations, especially access to electricity and greater privacy. Yet the asentamiento's higher living standards came with new types of work and heightened certain forms of isolation. In addition, asentado men's efforts to exercise tighter reign over wives often conflicted with women's notion that they should enjoy a relative autonomy. Rosa Saá, the wife of an asentado in Santa María county, complained in an oral history that despite the benefits of the asentamiento, her chores became more burdensome and her husband more demanding after the couple moved from a neighborhood on the outskirts of town to a new house inside the asentamiento:

> Of course it was very nice to have the house and to have more money, lots of money! But really, I tell you, life for me got harder, not easier. Before,

I was closer to the [water] well, to [provision] stores, and I had neighbors. [On the asentamiento] everything was so much harder. . . . I had to walk longer for water and had to make all our food even though now we had money to buy bread . . . and [my husband] wanted me to bring him his lunch every day even though [the asentamiento] provided a meal. . . . I could have taken [the bus] to town, but my husband wouldn't hear about it. He wanted me in the house. He didn't care if I had more work to do, he seemed to think I could be a million persons. . . . Sometimes I would get so mad I would just leave. "To do my job I must go to town," I would say . . . but that always started a fight.[37]

Rosa Saá's husband, Pascual Muñoz, recalled his wife's reaction quite differently: "She complains now. Well, she complained then . . . and I scolded her. . . . Yes, it took her a long time to accustom herself to living on the asentamiento, but I always thought that life was easier for her too. As I saw it, I made enough money to put shoes on the children and to buy her cloth [for sewing]. She didn't need to go into town. . . . See, she had enough to do just keeping the house and back then, it was felt that the woman should be in the house. . . . In town, there is too much danger of [a man] having the cap pulled over his eyes [being sexually deceived]."[38]

The discord between these two accounts is telling. While Rosa Saá welcomed an improved standard of living, she objected to what she felt was a more lonely existence and onerous workload and resented her husband's insensitivity and efforts to control her. Pascual Muñoz, on the other hand, felt certain that his increased economic power eased his wife's load; her "difficulty adjusting" was a small price to pay for shod children and sewing materials. Mostly, Rosa Saá and Pascual Muñoz disagreed about what it meant for a wife to leave home and venture into town. Whereas Muñoz objected to Saá's spontaneous trips to Santa María on the grounds that they might allow her to be sexually unfaithful (or at least encourage gossip that she was), Saá saw them as necessary to performing her job as a housewife. If the asentamiento was going to burden her with additional domestic responsibilities, her husband would have to accept that fulfilling such obligations would necessitate her greater mobility.

If some women challenged asentados' sense of entitlement to boss wives, most did not object to women's exclusion from asentamiento membership.[39] In the Aconcagua Valley, women seem not to have initiated a formal, collective protest to the legal provision that asentados be household heads. For married women, this silence reflected existing gender divisions of labor and the realities of dependence. Married women saw the asentamiento as providing greater material security to the entire family, not just to men. Married women's enormous responsibilities for childrearing and household production usually overshadowed seasonal participation in wage labor, both in terms of the gross time that women dedicated to such activities and in terms of what women considered their primary role. At no point during the Agrarian Reform did either the state or the labor movement challenge women's exclusive responsibility for children and household. Given this silence, married women saw efforts to strengthen men's ability to provide for families as benefiting them as well.

The position of single women differed. For that minority of unmarried, widowed, or separated campesina women who provided the majority of financial support for their families, women's exclusion from asentamiento membership constituted a barrier to material advancement and greater independence. Lack of documentation makes it difficult to determine to what extent, and in what forms, single women contested their situation.[40] But according to oral sources, female heads of household did apply for asentamiento membership and petition for greater access to employment in the Reform sector.[41] Such actions rejected the official notion that women's access to Agrarian Reform benefits be contingent on relationships with men and insisted that the state consider the economic marginality of women who headed families. Single women's seeming inability to effectively press these points reflected their organizational weakness and inferior positions within the waged labor force. The labor movement did not champion the needs of female heads of household nor did it challenge the unequal categorization of men's and women's agricultural experience (i.e., distinctions between permanent and temporary, paid and unpaid work). Mothers' centers assumed that all rural women were married or would marry. Likewise, the Christian Democratic government presumed men to head all campesino families. Together with the focus on empowering putatively more experienced inquilinos and permanent workers, this attitude meant the state could not address single women without fundamentally redrafting the Agrarian Reform's design.

But single women were not without benefit. Paradoxically, given its celebration of female domesticity, the Agrarian Reform generated substantial increases in women's paid agricultural employment. Chile's national agricultural productivity expanded at an annual rate of 4.6 percent between 1965 and 1968, the result and cause of a growing rural workforce.[42] Despite the widespread notion in existing scholarship that rural women lost agricultural jobs and became housewives during the Agrarian Reform, the number of women earning wages in agriculture in the Aconcagua Valley more than tripled between the mid-1960s and early 1970s.[43] The 1964–65 Agricultural Census for the Aconcagua Valley listed 664 women as wage-earning agricultural workers; by 1975, this number had jumped to 2,122.[44] Moreover, women's representation in the entire paid agricultural labor force rose from 11 percent to 16 percent during this period, while the proportion of female seasonal workers leapt from 12 percent to 25 percent (see Tables 10 and 12).[45] The vast majority of new jobs (at least 64 percent) went to single and widowed women, approximately half of whom were under age 30.[46] Increases in female employment were regionally specific, rather than national, and concentrated in central Chile where the Agrarian Reform was most extensive.[47]

In the Aconcagua Valley, the rapid expansion of fruit cultivation provided many of these new jobs. Beginning in 1962, and accelerating quickly after Frei's election, the Chilean Development Corporation (CORFO) pursued an aggressive plan to increase the value of agricultural crops by developing fruit exports.[48] A technology exchange program between the University of Chile and the University of California aspired to remodel Chile's central valley on that of California's profitable San Joaquín region. On asentamientos, CORA converted land formerly devoted to wheat and hemp into peach orchards and vineyards. Small and medium growers received special credits from INDAP to undertake fruit cultivation in the private sector; large growers secured similar financing directly through CORFO. Despite the fact that years later, in the 1980s, Chile's military regime would claim (and receive) credit for nurturing a spectacularly profitable fruit export industry as part of its neoliberal "economic miracle," it was Chile's state-led Agrarian Reform that first wedded commercial fruit exports to national development and provided them with sustained support.[49] In the Aconcagua Valley, the number of hectares devoted to fruit increased by 30 percent between 1965 and 1975.[50] Nationally, earnings from fruit exports more than doubled from 10 million dollars to 25 million dollars between 1962 and 1970.[51]

Fruit production was labor-intensive and generated an abundance of seasonal jobs in staking, pruning, picking, sorting, and packing. Latifundia arrangements had long concentrated women in fruit and vegetable work, but demand for female laborers also grew as the Agrarian Reform expanded grape, apple, and peach cultivation. Women found seasonal work on asentamientos, but had far greater employment opportunities on small and medium-sized farms in the private sector where more modest landholdings, combined with generous government incentives, made fruit cultivation especially attractive. By the early 1970s, fully three quarters of Aconcagua's fruit production were concentrated on properties under one hundred hectares. Although there were a few asentamientos this size, most such farms were in private hands.[52]

Despite the expansion of women's employment, the idea that the Agrarian Reform provided jobs only for men and allowed (or obliged) women to dedicate themselves more fully to their households continued to prevail as common knowledge. In oral histories conducted both during and after the 1960s, rural men and women of all marital statuses and ages recalled the Agrarian Reform as a time when campesino men worked and campesina women were housewives.[53] The triumph of this domestic ideal, despite the large numbers of women entering wage work, is telling of the Agrarian Reform's ideological success and the hegemony of its particular version of the male-headed family. Its policy focus and discursive emphasis on men as producers and workers dovetailed with the push by organizations such as INDAP, IER, and CEMAS to ennoble women's work by simultaneously distinguishing it from that of men's and locating it more solidly within the household. Together they overwhelmed the alternative meanings posed by the effective increase in women's paid employment. Ironically, women were defined more exclusively as housewives at the very moment many more of them actually worked outside the campesino household.

This situation marked a meaningful shift from the recent past. Prior to the Agrarian Reform, men's work had received greater validation than women's, and household responsibilities had heavily defined female roles. But women's subsistence farming and seasonal paid work had also been recognized as vital to the latifundia economy, leaving distinctions between household and non-household female labor more blurred. As the Agrarian Reform gained momentum, the value attached to women's non-household work diminished, while the campesino household increasingly came to be defined as existing outside the sphere of agricultural production and, hence, as marginal to the most pressing political concerns.

The far more substantial increases in the quality and quantity of paid agricultural employment for men further reinforced the invisibility of female wage employment and its increase. In the Aconcagua Valley, *all* new jobs for women in agriculture were seasonal, usually lasting an average of three months or less; the number of permanent paid jobs for women actually decreased slightly.[54] In contrast, permanent agricultural employment for men in the Aconcagua Valley almost doubled, from 2,916 permanent and inquilino workers in 1964 to 4,751 permanent workers in 1974.[55] In addition, there were 2,234 new seasonal jobs for men.[56] As the total number of paid agricultural positions expanded by an impressive 43 percent between 1964 and 1974, most employment, and all permanent jobs, went to men. Whereas the 1,500 new agricultural jobs for women were all seasonal, almost half of the over 4,000 new positions for men were permanent. Although the Agrarian Reform significantly increased women's paid agricultural employment, men had vastly more and more secure agricultural jobs (see Tables 10, 11, and 12).

Lastly, the invisibility of women's new work opportunities was shaped by the fact that such jobs went overwhelmingly (but never exclusively) to single and widowed women, and disproportionally to women in their twenties or younger. The Agrarian Reform's insistence on addressing all adult campesina women as married and its definition of adolescent girls as a distinct group of "youth," itself a temporary condition, defined female agricultural employment as an exception or, at most, as a generational rather than a normative condition. Not that increased female employment remained without impact. On the contrary, more agricultural jobs and much better wages enabled female household heads to more easily support families and allowed adolescent girls to make monetary contributions to their families while living at home. According to economist David Hojoman, such opportunities practically halted rural women's migration to urban areas in search of employment as domestic servants.[57] Wage-earning opportunities also introduced new family dynamics. Although most daughters still turned wages over to parents, usually to mothers, there was greater possibility that a daughter might keep a small bit of cash for herself. This heightened generational ten-

Table 10 Number of Women in Paid Agricultural
Employment, Aconcagua Valley, 1964–1975

Year	Permanent Workers	Seasonal Workers
1964	113	551
1975	111	2,011

*Censo agropecuario: Aconcagua, 1964–1965; Censo agropecuario:
Aconcagua, 1975–1976.*

Table 11 Number of Men in Paid Agricultural
Employment, Aconcagua Valley, 1964–1975

Year	Permanent Workers	Seasonal Workers
1964	2,916	3,876
1975	4,751	6,110

*Censo agropecuario: Aconcagua, 1964–1965; Censo agropecu-
ario: Aconcagua, 1975–1976.*

Table 12 Percentage of Men and Women Comprising the Paid
Agricultural Workforce, Aconcagua Valley, 1964–1975

Year	Total Workers		Permanent Workers		Seasonal Workers	
	Men	Women	Men	Women	Men	Women
1964	89%	11%	96%	4%	88%	12%
1975	84%	16%	98%	2%	75%	25%

Censo agropecuario: Aconcagua, 1964–1965; Censo agropecuario: Aconcagua, 1975–1976.

sions since campesino mothers in particular presumed the right to benefit from and direct daughters' labor. Fights over daughters' wages usually revolved around the girl's right to take such action, rather than whether her keeping a few pesos to herself would impoverish the family.[58] Even as small an indulgence as a daughter spending money on a hair comb for herself symbolized an independence outside the principle of female sacrifice for the family.

But the changing lives of daughters and the improved conditions for other single women did not fundamentally disrupt the Agrarian Reform ideal of female domesticity. If more available and better-paid agricultural jobs made survival easier for the small numbers of female heads of household, the highly seasonal nature of such work did not afford anything resembling economic independence for most women. The vast majority of campesina women, including most female wage-earners, continued living in households that accorded men's earning power and authority ultimate importance. Moreover, within the Agrarian Reform's logic of men becoming able household heads, the meaning of a daughter working for wages differed quite significantly from that of a wife doing so. Asentamiento members might have insisted or preferred that their spouses withdraw from paid jobs as displays of their own manly ability to provide, but they had less problems hiring single women and adolescent girls from outside the asentamiento or even letting their own daughters take temporary jobs on private estates. Authority over wives mattered most. If marriage was not a reality for all women (or men), the Agrarian Reform's ideal of marital relations cast a long shadow over all gender definitions, creating normative expectations for women and men regardless of their specific situation.

Gender and the Struggle for Land

Asentamientos generated a strong sense of entitlement both inside and outside of the Reform sector. With land expropriations gaining momentum and the labor movement growing exponentially after 1967, the rural poor pressured the Christian Democratic government to redistribute land and resources more quickly. Workers on private estates continued pushing for wage hikes and new housing, playing to landowner fears of the second Agrarian Reform Law's expanded expropria-

tion provisions. For many workers, improved compensation and working conditions were an end in themselves. For others, the enviable lives
of asentados energized fantasies of CORA converting their own places of
employment into asentamientos. The rural labor movement's unanimous
belief across the political spectrum that the Frei administration was pro-
ceeding too slowly with land reform emflamed these hopes. Unions continued to concentrate organizing energies on wages and entitlements,
but they often strategically linked these campaigns to quests for expropriation. Labor disputes over working conditions regularly escalated into
demands for land. It was an open secret that the fastest way to gain CORA's
attention and force its overly cautious hand in favor of expropriation
was through a prolonged labor conflict in which the government became obliged to intervene. Delays in government action fueled frustration, and the gap between promise and delivery increasingly provoked
clashes between rural workers, landowners, and the government. Between 1967 and 1970, the number of rural labor conflicts rose dramatically, totaling more than 4,000 strikes and 639 land occupations in four
years (see Table 13).[59] In 1970, the Ranquíl, Triunfo, and Libertad confederations joined hands to create a multipartisan committee for coordi-
nating labor actions throughout the country, including several one-day
national strikes to protest government failure to enforce existing labor
legislation and adequately pursue land reform.[60]

In Aconcagua, as in much of Chile, campesino efforts to speed government action made labor conflicts not only more numerous, but also
more physically confrontational. In 1967, workers in Putaendo county
held landowners captive in their homes during a joint occupation of the
neighboring El Tártaro and Lo Vicuña estates, forcing CORA to bring in
the police and local governor as mediators. The action eventually resulted
in a formal decision to expropriate and create an asentamiento.[61] Following the seizure of the nearby El Piguchén estate, workers employed
less aggressive tactics but similarly focused on using the landowner for
maximum political leverage. In negotiations with CORA, they insisted
on the expropriation of the entire estate without a reserve; but in an explicit role reversal of paternalist magnanimity, they requested that their
former patrón be allowed to remain in his home until his death.[62] In both
cases, land occupations occurred on the heels of prolonged and unresolved strikes over wages and inquilino land use. Worker demands for ex-

Table 13 Labor Action and Agrarian Reform in Rural Chile, 1964–1970
(Petitions, Strikes, Occupations, Expropriations, and Union Membership)

Year	No. Labor Petitions	No. Strikes	No. Land Occupations	No. Estates Expropriated	No. Unionized Campesinos
1964	31	39	2	n/a	1,658
1965	395	142	13	99	2,118
1966	526	586	18	264	10,647
1967	1,167	693	9	217	54,418
1968	1,852	684	26	220	76,356
1969	n.i.	1,127	148	315	103,635
1970	n.i.	1,580	456	293	140,293

Figures from Cuadros 1–3, Appendix, qtd. Academia de Humanismo Cristiano, in
Historia del movimiento campesino.

propriation had evolved—whether spontaneously or through conscious
anticipation—from landowner failure to negotiate in good faith. And
worker militancy had hastened, if not initiated, CORA's move to expropriate.

Beginning in April 1968, Aconcagua province occupied the national
spotlight for months when a strike and subsequent land occupation
in Longotoma county (just north of the Aconcagua Valley) escalated
into violence.[63] Following CORA's formal expropriation of the enormous
20,000-hectare estate, Santa Marta, the landowners blockaded themselves inside the estate's main building with a small minority of some two
dozen inquilinos who sided with their employers against expropriation.
According to pro-government and leftist newspaper accounts, the bar-
ricaded rebels threatened to dynamite other estate buildings, randomly
shot rifles out of windows, and made nighttime attacks against campesinos who supported the expropriation. Police were called to forcefully
dislodge the protesters and over four hundred unionized workers and
asentamiento members from throughout central Chile, including a large
delegation from the Aconcagua Valley, who had traveled to Longotoma
to lend support to the government action.[64] However, with the opponents of expropriation removed, the campesinos who had supported the

government's action refused, in a quick turn of events, to return home. Instead they turned their focus on CORA, demanding the immediate creation of an asentamiento and the inclusion of all former Santa Marta workers as asentado members.[65] Conflict over these requests prolonged the estate occupation, as well as police vigilance, for another two months. Although the attempt to force an inclusive asentamiento membership policy on CORA remained largely unsuccessful (only 103 of the original 180 workers became asentados), campesino pressure succeeded in getting the asentamiento established in record time, by July of that same year.[66]

As the Longatoma conflict vividly illustrated, not all campesinos supported expropriations. Most land occupations that escalated into demands for expropriation deeply divided estate workers. During the 1967 toma of the Lo Vicuña and El Tártaro estates in Putaendo county, at least a third of the two estates' more than two hundred workers opposed expropriation and continued working in violation of a concurrent strike.[67] Primarily older and better-positioned inquilinos who feared losing existing rights voiced opposition to expropriation.[68] For example, land regalías on El Tártaro estate averaged between two and three hectares, whereas land allotments on asentamientos were usually under one hectare.[69] Thus, incorporation into the Reform sector could likely decrease the amount of land inquilinos individually farmed. Even many inquilinos with regalías smaller than asentamiento allotments saw expropriations as an unacceptable risk. Suspicion abounded about the government's ability to protect workers from patrón retaliation and to make good on promises to grant land titles. Minifundistas who eked out livings on subsistence farms often felt, at best, ambivalently toward expropriations. They usually could not qualify for asentamiento membership and feared that the elimination of private estates would curtail seasonal employment opportunities. Campesina women's marital status and the occupational positions of male family members conditioned female attitudes. Women who opposed expropriations were usually the wives or dependents of inquilinos and minifundistas. Female heads of household may also have lacked enthusiasm about expropriations given their relatively greater employment opportunities in the private sector.

But opposition to expropriation did not mean opposition to the Agrarian Reform as a whole. Although fear of patrón reprisal often factored in the former, it was never the only, or even the most important reason. As numerous scholars have noted, Agrarian Reform meant different things to different campesinos, depending on a worker's position within the latifundia economy and the conditions on individual estates.[70] Opposition to expropriation was specific rather than general—a judgement about the particular estate where a worker lived and labored, not about the Agrarian Reform's broader mandate to reorganize property relations. Men who opposed expropriations were usually union members enthusiastic about the Agrarian Reform's push for higher wages and improved living conditions; some were veterans of militant strikes to achieve these ends. They often supported land expropriations elsewhere, but deemed such action inappropriate or disadvantageous for their own place of work. Given the labor movement's success at wresting concessions from employers, some workers argued that expropriation was most powerful as an unrealized threat. As one inquilino who had opposed the expropriation of El Tártaro estate explained this logic in an oral history: "When [the patrón] felt the pressure, he treated us well. He accepted all of our demands because he knew what would happen if he didn't. . . . Each year we put forth a petition, and he accepted everything."[71]

But others did not deem such reaction sufficient. Entitlement to own land and manage oneself constituted the fundamental meaning of the Agrarian Reform. If inquilinos figured prominently in the ranks of those who opposed expropriations, they were also among land reform's greatest advocates. Even for those inquilinos with relatively sizeable land regalías, the promise of personal ownership sounded compelling. For other inquilinos with inadequate land access, and for permanent and seasonal workers with no access to land, expropriations held greater potential still. The labor movement staunchly supported faster land reform. Despite partisan differences, independent Catholic, Christian Democratic, and leftist activists all urged rural unions to make expropriation demands.

Union militancy increasingly became defined in terms of supporting expropriations, sharpening moral and masculine distinctions between those who did and those who did not endorse such action. While female opposition to expropriations was dismissed as womanly ignorance, male opposition was more overtly disdained as unmanly cowardice and a betrayal of class solidarity. In polarized situations such as strikes and land occupations, inquilinos and other workers who opposed expropriations quickly saw themselves identified as subservient to the patrón, whether or not they had supported other labor actions against their employer. In a gesture that reworked latifundia's hierarchies of privilege, the inquilino's relatively better status was denounced as a source of dependence on class superiors and a barrier to achieving manly independence through risk taking and militancy with other men. As Armando Gómez, a former member of Putaendo county's Triunfo-affiliated union, complained in an oral history about men who opposed the expropriation of Lo Vicuña estate, "They didn't want [expropriations] because they were accommodated [*acomodos*], taken care of by the patrón, and felt their situation was just a little bit better than everybody else's. They wouldn't risk anything."[72] Accusations of inadequate manliness also involved notions of racial worthiness that juxtaposed true masculine independence with Indian subservience and slavery. Jacobo Fernández, formerly of the Libertad-affiliated union in Santa María county, blamed opposition to expropriations on the degeneracy of Chilean mestizaje and campesinos' inability to transcend a racially inscribed servitude: "They were so patrón-identified [*apatronado*]. Because of their Chilean blood, they thought of themselves like the boss's own Indians!"[73]

Both men and women joined struggles for faster access to land and resources. Although strikes and land occupations overwhelmingly involved men, women participated in support roles as wives and daughters, and occasionally as workers. While women rarely challenged men's more privileged positions within the Agrarian Reform overtly, their actions often juxtaposed masculinist paradigms for social change with more gender-inclusive visions. When CORA expanded its expropriation targets in the late 1960s, Susana López, a forty-five–year-old dairy worker and single head of household, began regularly attending union meetings in Panquehue county along with two female coworkers married to invalid husbands. López argued that women in their positions needed firsthand knowledge of changes. As she recalled later in an oral history, "Since we were responsible for our families and were workers, we had to be informed. We also wanted those old guys [*viejos*] to know that women were for the Agrarian Reform and would not run from confrontation."[74] López refuted the labor movement's stereotype of rural women as disinterested and fearful of Agrarian Reform politics. Claiming structural parity with men, she explained her growing interest in union meetings both in terms of her position as a head of household and as a worker. She also called male militancy into question by labeling union men *viejos* ("old men," "old farts"), inferring that women might hold up better under fire.

Other oral histories echoed the prospect that women could prove more radical than men. María García, the granddaughter of inquilinos in Santa María county, recalled heated arguments in which her grandmother, a communist, would chide her grandfather, a member of a Christian Democratic union, for insufficient militancy: "Grandma liked Allende and Grandpa was for Frei. . . . [She] was always telling him to switch unions, switch parties, because only the Left would really help the poor. . . . She was the one who made him go to meetings, and she would always go along."[75] In a similar tale of female agency, Jorge Tejedo, the former president of the Triunfo-affiliated union in San Felipe county, recalled that during a four-day strike in 1967 on the Santa Rosa vineyard, women workers not only joined with men in a work stoppage, but voiced more militant demands than men: "The women were stronger than the men. They were the first ones to support a strike, and they insisted that we not give up until the patrón had given in to all of our demands. Oh, they were great ones for solidarity! They [told] men, 'Don't be hens, be men and stand up for your rights, for your family, like we are.'"[76]

Accounts of women shaming men into bolder action were consistent with the labor movement's focus on grooming men to defend campesino interests. As in recurrent stories in the labor press, Jorge Tejedo's tale of women's greater militancy functioned as an implicit rebuke of male workers' inadequacy; female assertiveness was meant to inspire men to action, but men, not women, were ultimately supposed to lead. Still, the remarkable image of women cajoling male workers to be "men and not hens" suggests a certain acknowledgement by Tejedo that women could appropriate union machismo. Encouraging men to be like women in their level of worker militancy, women presented female toughness as an example of proper masculine behavior. Likewise, they defended their resolution to "stand up for their rights and families" as appropriate female activism in contrast to the behavior of other women/men/hens. While such action did not articulate women's concerns in terms of "women's issues," women's insistence on their right to participate in a strike and their level of commitment did not merely function to push men to lead. It urged men to see (and Jorge Tejedo to narrate) labor struggles in heterosexual terms.

One of the most dramatic instances of campesina women's participation in Agrarian Reform labor struggles anywhere in Chile occurred during a 1968 strike and estate occupation in San Esteben county. On June 14, three hundred workers on eleven estates jointly struck in protest over landowner refusals to respond to petitions. The local union, an affiliate of the Ranquíl confederation, demanded a 150-percent salary raise, larger land regalías, and expanded provisions of food, firewood, and housing.[77] The strike lasted forty-six days and ended in a violent confrontation between workers and the Christian Democratic government. Despite considerable efforts by INDAP and the Ministry of Labor to reach a settlement during June and July, landowners continued to reject the petition demands as grossly inflated. The union condemned patrón intransigence as a sabotage of Agrarian Reform labor policy and, in late July, called on Eduardo Frei to expropriate the eleven estates and establish new asentamientos.[78] On July 28, one hundred campesinos and a dozen university students occupied the most prominent estate, San Miguel, and held its owner, Ruperto Toro Bayles, and his family captive in their home.[79] The government immediately condemned workers' actions as illegal and suspended all negotiations. Following a four-day standoff and fruitless attempts by Communist and Socialist legislators to intercede on the workers' behalf, the government responded with force. On August 1, three hundred police, six minitanks, and eight trucks descended on San Miguel to dislodge the protesters. As the police fired tear gas and machine guns into the air, several campesinos occupying the main house returned fire with old shotguns and crudely fashioned Molotov cocktails. At the conflict's end, two policemen and several dozen campesinos were wounded, one five-year-old girl dead, and all one hundred protesters arrested and imprisoned in Valparaíso.[80]

At the beginning of the conflict, both the San Esteben strike and the San Miguel occupation most directly involved only men. Since it occurred during the Chilean winter month of July, few women were employed on the estates, and, according to oral sources, women do not seem to have participated in union meetings about either action.[81] On the day the police arrived with tanks, union officers ordered women to stay in their homes for protection.[82] But women did play important parts mobilizing support for the labor actions. They set up common pots to provide men and their families with food on each of the eleven estates throughout the strike and another common pot at San Miguel during the toma. They carried messages between estates, provided meals and lodging to campesinos from other counties who traveled to San Esteben offering solidarity, and solicited contributions to the union strike fund from community organizations in Los Andes and San Felipe.[83] While such activities did not make women central protagonists, they constituted for many a heady, educational first step in political activism. As Lucilia Flores, the former president of a local CEMA, recalled in an oral history, "For men it was dangerous, but for us women, it was very wonderful. Many women had never participated in anything before, and they knew absolutely nothing. And, nonetheless, there they were participating! They learned so much! They had to commit because their husbands were inside [the occupied estate.]"[84]

If, as Lucilia Flores suggested, women's activism flowed from the logic of familial solidarity, it acquired a new meaning following the mass arrest of San Miguel's campesino protestors. With San Esteben's local union leadership and a significant portion of union members in jail, women took front stage in subsequent attempts to resolve the conflict. Socialists and Communists, including regional and national Ranquíl leaders, took particular interest in mobilizing campesina women to represent men's cause outside prison walls. Labor organizers reemphasized the importance of women's support activities, hoping that the wives of imprisoned men would provide legitimacy and continuity to the lobby for the men's release and keep the strikers' cause alive. In oral histories, women in San Esteben remembered the reason for women's greater agency somewhat differently, attributing it to women's own initiative. According to Lucilia Flores, "when the men were arrested, the women took over. . . . [A] patrón came by after we heard the tremendous thunder [of the guns and tanks] and said, 'They've been arrested!' We immediately sent out a compañera to find out what was going on and took firm resolve to take over [the situation.]"[85]

On August 4, twenty women, all wives of imprisoned men, traveled to Valparaíso to protest outside the detention center. They called for the immediate release of their husbands and a renewal of negotiations between landowners, workers, and the government.[86] Some women marched with infants and children; others carried placards with phrases such as "Justice for the defenseless poor!" and "Shame on the government!"[87] Eliding the issue of campesino men's less than "defenseless" use of force during the San Miguel occupation, women insisted that the welfare of campesino families, not the legality of their husbands' actions, constituted the central issue. They held that the government's primary obligation was to pursue social justice, not disciplinary action. Lest such moral claims go unheeded, women also pursued more partisan forms of political pressure, sending a delegation of wives to meet with the Socialist senators Salvador Allende and Carlos Altamirano in Santiago.[88]

Back in Los Andes, women continued staffing the common pots, no longer to provide food to striking men, but to families who continued to struggle in men's absence.[89] When a provincial Christian Democratic congressman, Ernesto Iglesias, attempted to disband the common pots by offering women food and monetary assistance on an individual basis, they flatly rejected his overtures as an effort to break community solidarity. The women coldly informed him that the common pots would remain until their husbands were freed and the strike's demands for "family dignity" satisfactorily settled.[90] In interviews with both pro-government and pro-union leftist newspapers, women emphasized the misery in which whole campesino communities lived as justification for their ongoing struggle. They appealed to national sympathy for the welfare of women and children. Although such narratives bore the heavy mark of journalists well-versed in the trope of "suffering campesino women," they suggested women's own distinctive interpretation of class struggle. As campesina women running a soup kitchen replaced campesino men occupying an estate as the symbol of rural upheaval, protest goals were increasingly articulated with female accents. During the strike, the union leadership had equated social justice with empowering men as workers. After the arrests, women referenced social justice as a matter of community and family well-being. Although these concepts also figured into the labor movement's formulations of class solidarity, women almost exclusively referenced the ongoing struggle in these terms. However connected women saw improvements for male workers to broader campesino welfare, they conceptually subordinated men's empowerment to a more gender-inclusive project.

Campesina women counted on important urban allies, including women. In addition to the high-profile intervention of senators like Allende and Altamirano, María Elena Carrera, a Communist congress-woman whose own son had joined the San Miguel toma as a university student, became a fixed presence in San Esteben. According to several oral accounts, Carrera, more than any other high-ranking official, aggressively pressured the Christian Democratic government to concede to campesina demands and savvily finessed the constant media presence. Reportedly possessing a unique, gender-based ability to empathize with campesinas (enhanced by the fact that her son had been arrested along with the women's husbands), Carrera also explicitly encouraged militant female activism. Although couched within the paternalist rhetoric of women's conjugal duty, her stance and her prominence as an elected leader helped inspire female initiatives. As Lucilia Flores remembered fondly, "María Elena was remarkable. She could speak to the campesina woman in a way that campesinas understood. . . . She told them they had to back their men, put their shoulder to the wheel behind their husbands. . . . She went out at night door to door, urging us to go out and talk to other women. She came to my house and said, 'The only thing to do is to go out into the streets!'"[91] According to Flores, Carrera was also unusually responsive to profound class differences between poor and professional women's ability to devote themselves to politics. When questioned by several campesinas about who would care for their children while they were in the streets, Carrera organized female university students as volunteer babysitters.[92]

Direct participation and leadership within rural unions figured among the most important new roles compesina women assumed. With the San Esteben union leadership in prison and the Frei administration irate over its action, Ranquíl confederation made the diplomatic bid to ask a Christian Democratic, Triunfo-affiliated union in San Felipe to represent the detained workers in government negotiations.[93] Strikers' wives were requested to attend union meetings on their husbands' behalf; occasionally, women chaired the sessions and took active roles in restricting the involvement of obstructionist outsiders. In a reversal of the prevailing pattern of gender exclusion in union affairs, this involved women barring entrance to many men—including politicians, journalists, and even workers—deemed too conservative or otherwise considered obstacles to the cause. As Lucilia Flores recalled one of her own such experiences, "So many folks started arriving from the outside to take advantage of the situation—[right-wing] senators and congressmen. I remember a meeting [where] I had to kick them all out—I even had to kick out an uncle of mine [a campesino from Santa María]. They had no business there. It was our concern. We knew who was with us, and who was not."[94]

On August 8, women organized a rally in the Los Andes plaza to present new union demands. The six hundred people in attendance, a majority of them women, cheered as a spokeswoman listed the priorities: the release of the imprisoned men, a 33-percent salary raise, a doubling of family allowances, and guarantees against patrón retaliation.[95] Considerably watered down from workers' initial demands for 150-percent raises and land expropriations, the union's compromise reflected workers' vulnerability in the face of government opposition and an attempt to salvage minimum gains from a protracted struggle. Although women did not generate these demands themselves, they voted on them and gave them official approval and representation.

On August 13, the San Esteben conflict formally ended. The government decreed an end to the strike, released all detained workers, and gave them four days to return to their original jobs. Landowners were ordered to grant workers a 25-percent salary raise and were prohibited from firing participants in the conflict.[96] No changes were made regarding family allowances, regalías, or other patrón contributions to workers. The issue of expropriation was suspended altogether and would not gain CORA's attention until after Allende's election to the presidency in 1970.[97] By August 18, production in San Esteben had seemingly returned to normal with men cleaning ditches and women resuming their household labors.

Despite the defeat of most union goals, the two-month conflict had meaningfully reshaped gender dynamics within the local labor movement. On all eleven estates involved in the original strike, campesino men and women stood more united than before on the need to continue pushing for expropriation, and women remained integrated into union activities. If men viewed women as their temporary replacements, women proved unwilling to go back to the supportive sidelines. When the union regathered its forces in September to discuss submitting a formal petition to CORA re-requesting San Miguel's expropriation, dozens of wives showed up at the meeting.[98] Although several men objected that the women were not workers, women insisted that they had earned the right of inclusion, and other men present supported them.[99] Although the women could not vote, they were given seats and returned the following week. If their role in the San Esteben struggle had emerged out of a practical familial solidarity, it evolved into a sense of entitlement to participate in union struggles, even against the will of some men.[100] As one woman told the communist daily *El Siglo* on the day the common pot was disbanded, the end of the San Miguel struggle did not end women's struggle for recognition: "[Women] have to participate in [our men's union] problems. . . . We [were] in agreement with the strike for better salaries, but this is what you all call our tactics. We also believe that we need to help our husbands discuss [solutions]. From here on out, we are going to insist that our husbands give us the right to give opinions and participate in their decisions [about unions]."[101]

The reference to female support as "tactics" in a broader strategy is telling of how women reimagined labor activism as a heterosexual rather than masculine affair. While not overtly challenging the male composition and focus of unions, it suggested that women had distinct reasons for supporting unions and that they saw workable solutions as necessitating women's participation. The push to better life for male workers might be part of the "tactics" toward this end, but it was never enough on its own. "Men's problems and decisions" in unions might continue to predominantly deal with men, but the Agrarian Reform's broader goals of social justice could be reached only by women entering into the male terrain of labor struggles.

The extent of female participation in the San Esteben conflict undoubtedly owed much to the specific circumstances that led to men's mass arrest; but if the scale of women's involvement was unusual, it was not unique. Women routinely provided a range of support activities during strikes and land occupations elsewhere in the Aconcagua Valley and other parts of Chile.[102] If the situation in San Esteben afforded women rare leadership opportunities in unions, it was women's prior activism on behalf of men's strike and occupation that gave them a sense of entitlement to such roles. For the many other women who participated in less dramatic land and labor conflicts, the experience of running a common pot, attending a demonstration, or raising money for a union could similarly nurture a sense that the Agrarian Reform was not an exclusively male process and that women needed to participate. This is not to say that most women believed they should have equal footing as men in labor unions and asentamientos. Most married women, in particular, did not. Rather, it points to the significantly different meanings that support activities could have for men, women, and the labor movement. Union leaders may have welcomed women's help as a symbol of class solidarity, but for women, running a common pot could provide a sense of inclusion in a community struggle that allowed them to have opinions distinct from those of men. While it did not usually compel women to challenge the all-male nature of unions, it did enable them to define female participation as having a value beyond that of backing men.

The Legacy of Family Uplift

By 1970 the Christian Democrats had made great strides toward the goal of uplifting the rural family. Almost 20,000 families nationwide and 1,500 families in the Aconcagua Valley had been incorporated into asentamientos. Agricultural productivity had steadily grown, creating thousands of new jobs. Real incomes for campesino households had more than tripled. Illiteracy rates had halved; infant mortality had dropped by 60 percent; and housing conditions on all estates had greatly improved. The explosion in memberships of rural unions, CEMAS, and other popular organizations gave the rural poor effective vehicles for defending their interests and participating in national politics on a mass scale for the first time in Chile's history. As Eduardo Frei's tenure drew to a close, the San Felipe daily, *El Trabajo,* succinctly observed, "Aconcagua has been transformed, and our timid majority has benefited." [103]

Yet not all had benefited equally. Almost half of the rural population in the Aconcagua Valley still eked out subsistence livings on a minifundia sector left basically untouched by policies that focused on inquilinos and permanent workers. Asentados constituted a privileged minority, symbolizing both the Agrarian Reform's success and its limitations. The sharp rise in strikes and land occupations in 1969 and 1970 testified to other workers' impatience. Within all strata of the rural poor, men had benefited more than women.

The Christian Democratic Agrarian Reform institutionalized the male-headed family as the model for social mobilization and class uplift in the countryside. The nature and goals of rural labor unions, CEMAs, health care projects, education programs, and land reform policies all took shape from, and in turn formally legitimated, the assumption that rural men and women resided in households where husbands ideally had ultimate responsibility for wives and children. The state did not unilaterally create this model, but government policy contributed disproportionally to it. The rural labor movement, Catholic Church, private reform agencies such as APROFA, and most rural men and women applauded and abetted government efforts. Conflicts over the model largely revolved around the strategy and goals of gender-specific mobilization, not the model's gender distinctions or implicit gender hierarchy.

The Agrarian Reform's ethos of gender mutualism sought to minimize antagonisms between husbands and wives and to provide an impetus for women's greater involvement in civic life. Specific efforts through CEMA and INDAP programs encouraged women's support for the Agrarian Reform. They created unprecedented opportunities for women's contributions to labor struggles, acquisition of education, and collective representation of interests as wives and mothers. Some rural women seized on the logic of gender mutualism to expand the boundaries of acceptable female action. Wives made greater demands on husbands' obligations to families and emphasized themes of spousal cooperation and limits to men's unilateral authority. In a similar manner, women widened the scope of female activism to include nonlabor issues such as housing, and defined labor and land struggles as community concerns rather than strictly men's issues.

Despite women's new activism and frequent articulations of more gender-inclusive paradigms, the Agrarian Reform's model of family uplift solidified gender hierarchies that not only privileged men, but validated their social and sexual authority over women. Notwithstanding the significant rise in women's seasonal employment opportunities, gender divisions of labor as a whole changed only marginally. What changed was the meaning and value attached to work, with men's work alone defined as central to the mission of national development. This shift justified the logic of women's formal exclusion from unions and asentamientos—the Agrarian Reform's most radical accomplishments—and gave women significantly inferior access to political and economic power, deepening their dependence on men. However much gender mutualism may have tempered men's unilateral action and excesses toward women, the Agrarian Reform's equation of assertive masculinity and male class militancy with social transformation championed the desirability of increasing campesino men's authority. While this focus proved crucial to worker victories over landowners as well as to campesino men's sense of entitlement to citizenship and participation in national politics, it had more mixed implications for rural women. When paired with the official ideal of reconstituting male-headed families, the celebration of rural men's authority reinvigorated forms of popular patriarchy, including notions about the appropriateness of campesino men's stewardship of female sexuality.

Neither women's subordination to men nor male-headed families were new. What was new was the institutionalization of these relationships as state-sponsored, national goals. The difference is crucial. The Agrarian Reform was the most extensive state intervention into rural life in Chilean history. As a project aimed at nothing less than the creation of a socially just society, the Agrarian Reform set the parameters for future standards of equality and the means to achieve it. It was precisely the continuity with the past in the Christian Democratic model of family uplift—its claim to have roots in natural relations of gender and sexuality—that gave it such currency with political organizers, labor leaders, and most rural poor people. Its assumptions about sexuality and gender as they naturally were, in turn, translated gender inequalities and sexual hierarchies into national policy as natural facts. It was a model that would last.

chapter 6 Revolutionizing Women

Popular Unity and Female Mobilization

In September 1970, Chile surprised the world and many of its own citizens by democratically electing a president who vowed to take Chile down a peaceful and constitutional road to socialism. At the height of the Cold War pitting U.S. capitalist liberalism against Soviet socialist statism and a decade after the Cuban Revolution, the victory of veteran statesman Salvador Allende Gossens and his Popular Unity (UP) coalition of Socialists, Communists, Christian leftists, and social democrats proposed a fundamentally unique alternative: a Marxist economic program implemented through liberal democratic procedures using existing legal frameworks, without armed revolution or full control of state power. The UP was the culmination of almost a century of fitful political leaps and backslides by the Chilean Left as well as the more immediate result of expectations raised, but never fully met, by the Christian Democrats. Allende won the executive race against a leftleaning Christian Democrat, Radomiro Tomic, and a hardened National party leader, Jorge Alessandri, with a slim, 36.3 percent plurality of the vote rather than its majority. This result highlighted the degree of polarization in Chile and cast serious doubt on the UP's claim that there was an electoral mandate for socialism.[1] Nonetheless, Allende's triumph demonstrated the powerful presence of significant numbers of Chileans who applauded more radical solutions to the nation's inequality.

Accelerating the Agrarian Reform was central to the UP's plan for restructuring the Chilean economy. Along with the nationalization of banking and mining industries and the expropriation of key industrial sectors, the implementation of what Allende called a "real Agrarian Reform" was to serve as a primary tool for building socialism. In sharp contrast to the Frei administration's emphasis on increasing productivity and creating a new class of family farmers, the UP called for the eradication of all latifundia, efficient or not, and for more collective forms of ownership. It also moved in on medium-size producers, halving the size of private estates that would be exempt from expropriation, from eighty to forty hectares. While still allowing for individually owned property, it gave priority to creating large-scale enterprises farmed on a communal or cooperative basis. The UP also pledged to involve campesinos more directly in policy making and economic management by increasing the power of rural unions and placing workers on government agencies.

The UP's efforts met with considerable success. Although the Frei administration expropriated a majority of total land eventually included in the Agrarian Reform in the Aconcagua Valley, both the number of expropriated estates and the number of Reform-sector production units almost doubled under Allende (see Tables 14 and 15). In Chile as a whole, the UP incorporated 20 percent more land into the Reform sector in less than three years than had the Christian Democrats in six.[2] During Allende's first eighteen months in power alone, CORA expropriated over three thousand estates, accounting for 21 percent of all productive agricultural land in the country and almost all estates over eighty hectares of basic irrigated land.[3] National membership in rural unions practically doubled from 140,293 in 1970 to 241,081 by 1972, with significant numbers of the new members coming from the previously excluded ranks of afuerinos and seasonal workers (see Table 16).[4] The UP also established a new representative body called the campesino council (*consejos campesinos*), which expanded rural workers' formal advisory presence in the meetings of CORA, INDAP, and the Central Bank.

The UP inspired terrific enthusiasm and bitter animosity. Its promise to create a socialist society meant wildly different things to different constituencies. It raised and met the hopes of many poor and working-class Chileans for higher wages and access to health care, education, and land. At the same time, it enraged property owners of all sizes who either lost control over assets or feared that they would. While claiming to represent a unique coalition of the proletariat, peasantry, and petite bourgeoisie,

Table 14 Land Expropriations and Reform Production Units during the UP

Region	No. Estates Exprop.	Irrigated Hectares Exprop.	Non-irrigated Hectares Exprop.	Dry Hectares Exprop.	Total Hectares Exprop.	Ag. Reform Production Units
San Felipe	40	3,744	282	9,857	13,883	40
Los Andes	34	2,288	–	9,964	12,252	34
Aconcagua Valley	74	6,032	282	20,103	26,091	74
Chile	4,401	439,449	998,069	4,859,755	6,292,273	1,866

Hectare figures for Aconcagua Valley are compiled from fichas de expropriación, CORA. Hectare figures for Chile are compiled from ICADES, "La Reforma Agraria chilena: Rasgos definitorios," Santiago, 1977, qtd. in Huerta, *Otro agro para Chile,* 325. Figures for production units include asentamientos, CERAS, and CEPROS, qtd. in Manuel Barrera, *Chile: 1970–1972: La Conflictiva experiencia de los cambios estructurales* (Caracas: ILDIS, 1974), and Barraclough and Fernández, *Diagnóstico,* both qtd. in Huerta, *Otro agro para Chile,* 356.

Table 15 Land Expropriations and Reform under Frei

Region	No. Estates Exprop.	Irrigated Hectares Exprop.	Non-irrigated Hectares Exprop.	Dry Hectares Exprop.	Total Hectares Exprop.	Ag. Reform Production Units
Aconcagua Valley	37	12,004	32,046	199,893	243,983	37
Chile	1,412	290,601	602,065	3,200,673	4,093,339	826

Figures for Aconcagua Valley are compiled from fichas de expropriación, CORA. Hectare figures for Chile are from Barraclough and Fernández, *Diagnóstico,* 71. The figure for production units includes asentamientos only and is taken from Barrera, *Chile: 1970–1972,* qtd. in Huerta, *Otro agro para Chile,* 254.

Table 16 Campesino Union Membership by Confederation Affiliation, Chile, 1968–1973

Confederation	1968	1969	1970	1971	1972	1973
Libertad	17,421	23,132	29,132	34,715	43,260	44,260
Ranquíl	18,253	30,912	43,867	43,867	102,299	96,254
Triunfo	39,288	47,510	64,003	64,003	51,070	66,146
UOC*	n/a	n/a	n/a	29,355	39,675	14,199
Sargento	1,394	1,743	1,605	2,214	2,989	2,567
Provincias Ag.	n/a	355	1,686	1,219	1,788	2,181
Total	76,356	103,652	140,293	175,373	241,081	225,607

*Pro-UP splinter from Triunfo
Salinas, *Trayectoria.*

the UP's bold rhetoric about triumphing over the tyranny of private capital often left doubt about where those who owned humble amounts of property, such as shopkeepers and campesino farmers, fit into the category of *el Pueblo* (the people).[5] Chile's wealthy elite and a majority of the middle class found socialism, in whatever form, totally unacceptable. But feelings about Popular Unity were not simply determined by class. Allende represented salvation or despotism depending on one's vision of social justice and sense of inclusion in, or exclusion from, the revolutionary project. Within class, a person's past political experience, access to material resources, and perception of the risks and possibilities entailed in UP programs all mattered.

Gender mediated all of these factors, and the UP was deeply concerned about appealing to Chilean women. Allende campaigned on promises to expand protections for Chilean mothers, promote women's education, and defend the rights of female workers. Women were called upon to become protagonists in the struggle for social change, assume leadership roles, and enter the workforce. The General Secretary of the UP's Women's Front and later Minister of Labor, Mireya Baltra, proclaimed that the UP sought nothing less than women's "plain equality and equal opportunities."[6] The Chilean Left had embraced many of these goals in principle, if not always in practice, since the beginning of the century;

"The truth is that the economic policy of the UP has meant a significant increase in the buying power of workers. Salaries have risen and inflation has been arrested at half the rate of other years." Man tells woman: "Now there's enough money, Juanita!" Child exclaims: "Well done!"

"And this is only the start, imagine! It will get worse, soon you won't even be able to eat your own fingernails!" "How barbarous, dear!" UP pamphlet mocking elite complaints about consumer shortages, 1971.

Both cartoons from the UP pamphlet series NOSOTROS LOS CHILENOS, courtesy of the University of Wisconsin Land Tenure Center.

but by the 1960s, the Christian Democrats' overt courtship of female votes had forced the Left to launch a more concerted effort toward women. Both the Communist and Socialist parties as well as MAPU (a new, pro-UP party of radicalized former Christian Democrats) established female electoral committees and created special women's departments in unions, neighbors' councils, and other community organizations. In his speeches, Allende repeatedly stressed that socialism could not be accomplished without women, proclaiming that "women will be the pivot on which popular victory turns."[7]

Such overtures in large part stemmed from fear about female conservatism. In the 1970 presidential election, as in the 1964 election, significantly fewer Chilean women in both rural and urban areas voted for Allende than did men.[8] Although a majority of Chilean men also voted for candidates other than Allende, the UP felt it owed its slim victory margin to the support of working-class males.[9] But aggregate voting patterns are deceptive. Despite the fact that almost one third of all Chilean women *did* vote for Allende, the lower-than-hoped-for showing among women, combined with longstanding stereotypes of female religiousness and political apathy, created the view (shared both by contemporaries of the 1970s and later scholarship) that the Left had come to power without women's assistance. Such thinking not only obscured the real support that significant numbers of women gave the UP, but failed to note important differences across region, class, and political experience.

In the Aconcagua Valley, both men and women gave the UP proportionally less support than was the case nationally, a reflection of the strength of Catholic labor organizing since the 1950s and the Frei administration's initial focus on Aconcagua. However, the UP enjoyed solid support from both men and women in predominantly rural counties (all counties other than San Felipe and Los Andes) where the population was disproportionally poorer and more campesino. Counties with longstanding Communist and Socialist labor traditions, like Catemu, constituted pocket strongholds for the UP, with both men and women voting for Allende in numbers above the national average (see Tables 17, 18, and 19).

Support for Allende among rural women in the Aconcagua Valley and elsewhere in Chile may have been higher than the electoral roles indicate since a large portion of rural women never participated in the

Table 17 Female Voter Choice (percent of total female electorate),
Presidential Election, 1970, Aconcagua Valley and Chile

County or Region	Tomic	Alessandri	Allende
San Felipe	31.1%	41.4%	24.2%
Santa María	35.2%	37.1%	25.2%
Putaendo	36.3%	31.3%	31.1%
Catemu	32.8%	27.1%	38.2%
Panquehue	43.1%	36.1%	16.3%
Los Andes	27.6%	40.7%	24.2%
San Esteben	35.7%	36.4%	25.7%
Calle Larga	42.4%	33.3%	22.2%
Rinconada	32.2%	36.7%	30.2%
Aconcagua Valley–Total	34%	38%	26%
Acon. Valley Rural Counties*	36.6%	33.6.%	27.5%
Chile	30.2%	38.9%	30.5%

*Rural counties do not include those of San Felipe and Los Andes.
"Elección Ordinaria de Presidente, 1970," DRE.

1970 election. Male opposition to female involvement in politics and many women's acceptance of this position resulted in 25 to 30 percent fewer campesina women voting in 1970 than campesino men.[10] Although women's voter participation lagged behind men's throughout Chile, in the Aconcagua Valley, female participation ranked lowest in the rural counties where the UP won its highest support from rural men (see Table 19).[11] This suggests a certain correlation between the Left's political strength and the level of male opposition and/or female resignation to women's exclusion from formal politics. Yet it does not mean that such women opposed the UP. To the extent that political views were often (though certainly not always) shared within households, the UP might well have won a higher percentage of the female vote with less robust resistance to women's electoral participation. Perhaps the knowledge that the Left had failed to adequately turn out its own female constituency contributed most heavily to the UP's anxiety about women's support.

Nor did the overall lower showings for Allende in the Aconcagua Val-

Table 18 Male Voter Choice (percent of total male electorate), Presidential Election, 1970, Aconcagua Valley and Chile

County or Region	Tomic	Alessandri	Allende
San Felipe	27.3%	34.5%	35.8%
Santa María	25.7%	30.8%	39.8%
Putaendo	30.3%	25.8%	42.6%
Catemu	29.9%	18.6%	50.4%
Panquehue	41.0%	28.8%	28.7%
Los Andes	29.4%	32.8%	36.1%
San Esteben	30.6%	27.6%	40.6%
Calle Larga	39.9%	25.8%	33.2%
Rinconada	27.0%	30.9%	40.6%
Aconcagua Valley–Total	29.8%	30%	38%
Acon. Valley Rural Counties*	31.3%	26.4.%	40.6%
Chile	26.2%	31.7%	42.1%

*Rural counties do not include those of San Felipe and Los Andes.
"Elección Ordinaria de Presidente, 1970," DRE.

ley indicate the region's (or its women's) conservatism. As political scientist Lisa Baldez has argued, the female vote throughout Chile became more polarized along the political spectrum during the 1970 presidential election, not more right-wing in and of itself.[12] Nationwide, proportionally fewer women supported rightist candidates in 1970 (and later in 1972) than during elections in the 1950s.[13] In the Aconcagua Valley, most women in 1970, along with most men, solidly supported a more radical version of the Agrarian Reform. In predominantly rural counties, the Christian Democratic candidate Radomiro Tomic—who had campaigned for an Agrarian Reform almost identical to the UP's—received a significantly higher proportion of votes than he did nationally, and he was the highest vote winner among women. In contrast, Tomic won the smallest proportion of male votes and trailed far behind Alessandri in winning female votes nationally and in the more urban counties of San Felipe and Los Andes. Tomic's appeal in rural Aconcagua flowed from the Christian Democratic sympathies nurtured during the 1960s, but it also

Table 19 Gender Composition of Electorate, Presidential
Election, 1970, Aconcagua Valley

County or Region	Male	Female
San Felipe	49%	51%
Santa María	56%	44%
Putaendo	54%	46%
Catemu	58%	42%
Panquehue	59%	41%
Los Andes	48%	52%
San Esteban	57%	43%
Calle Larga	56%	44%
Rinconada	58%	42%
Aconcagua Valley	52%	48%
Acon. Valley* Rural Counties	57%	43%

*Rural counties do not include those of San Felipe and Los Andes.
"Elección Ordinaria de Presidente, 1970," DRE.

marked a positive response to Tomic's leftist departure from the Agrarian
Reform goals of Eduardo Frei. Like the UP, Tomic called for the elimination of latifundia, the incorporation of working-class organizations into
state power, and the creation of more collective forms of land tenure.
If more rural women in Aconcagua cast votes for the Christian Democrats than for the UP, women, like rural men, overwhelmingly supported
candidates pledging to accelerate and expand the Agrarian Reform.

The UP responded to the challenge of generating greater female support on multiple, at times contradictory, fronts. On one hand, it upheld
the maternalist tradition, shared across Chile's political spectrum, that
praised women's highest calling as that of a mother. Stressing its own
legitimacy as the true protector of the family in response to Christian
Democratic and the rightist accusations to the contrary, the UP expanded
and initiated numerous programs for mothers and children. It introduced
legislation to augment maternity leave, began additional free milk and
school lunch programs for infants and children, and amplified programs
to monitor the pre- and postnatal health of women and infants.[14] In mid-

1973, the government established the Ministry of the Family to "promote women and the family [as] the most basic and fundamental social cell, the primary agent forming mankind's personalities, and an organic entity in charge of transmitting experiences and values."[15] Even the UP's implementation of Chile's first national day-care policy (initiated under Frei), which aimed to facilitate women's productive activities outside the home, was championed as a measure that would assist women in fulfilling their primary family roles.

In his speeches, Allende commonly referred to Chilean women as wives and mothers, drawing parallels between traditional gender roles within the family and the contributions that women could make to the national good.[16] He simultaneously exhorted wives to cooperate with husbands and to set superior moral examples to which men might aspire. In particular, Allende praised women's capacity for sacrifice. In 1972, when the UP ran into production and distribution problems (resulting from the combined effects of manufacturer slowdowns, merchant hoarding, and a U.S.-imposed boycott), Allende suggested that women's self-abnegation in the family could provide a national model for resolving the crisis since "Chilean mothers know the suffering of hunger more than men . . . and [for them] the lack of meat doesn't mean anything."[17] Similarly, Allende applauded women's ability to reform men's character, encouraging husbands to embrace hard work and sober living. Joking once that he had decreed a law abolishing "Saint Monday" (the practice of not showing up to work after a weekend of heavy drinking), he told a group of campesinas, "You wives had better make sure that your husbands know that."[18]

If Allende celebrated women's wifely powers, he stressed the importance of men's responsibility for women's political education. As political scientist Elsa Chaney first noted, Allende was skeptical about women's capacity for understanding socialism and saw the remedy as resting in men's hands: Fathers, husbands, and boyfriends were to explain the logic of UP positions to daughters, wives, and girlfriends.[19] Allende admonished one crowd of men to entice women over to the UP's cause with feminine consumer pleasures and gentle persuasion:

> Whether the husband earns a little or a fair sum, he never gives [his wife] a bit of money to go to the movies, to buy a new dress. . . . The wives run around disheveled; they don't go to the beauty shop, they aren't able to

buy a lipstick. . . . Men have the obligation of understanding the woman and of making themselves understood. [You men] all go to the demonstrations alone, you don't even bring along your wives. You go home and you don't talk to them. You never say, 'Look here, Comrade Allende has declared such and such, etc.' You don't dialogue with the woman.[20]

Allende's paternalist affirmation of men's natural stewardship of women was closely wedded to a masculinist challenge that real Popular Unity men took on the heterosexual task of wooing women over to the right side. As he impatiently chided men in another speech, "Each one of you has a mother, a daughter, a [wife], a sister, a partner, or a friend. And he who doesn't—get him gone from the Popular Unity!"[21] As historian Sandra McGee astutely remarked, Allende likened men's political education of women to seduction, calling on men to "conquer women for the revolution, speaking to her with passion and a man's tenderness."[22] According to McGee, this suggested that "a type of domination akin to sexual subordination would be necessary to secure [women's] loyalty."[23]

But the UP's patriarchal stance toward women coexisted with visionary plans to revolutionize female roles. The UP's central platform called for equality between the sexes and for the emancipation of women. The coalition counted many feminists among its ranks—including veteran organizers, journalists, and other professional women—who argued that only a radical restructuring of society, including the home, would truly free women to realize their potential. Although the UP usually ducked issues of domestic divisions of labor in practice, it did assertively promote greater opportunities for women's paid employment and acknowledged the need to vastly expand childcare facilities if women were to participate in production on par with men.

The UP claimed to offer women an opportunity for personal, professional, and political growth unprecedented in Chilean history. The Coalition's Obligatory Social Service program, a reworked version of the Christian Democrats' Feminine Service program, called on the women it recruited for voluntary community service to help build a future that would "break with the *machista* and paternalist schemas of the past"[24] that had relegated women to "dependence and double exploitation," flattering them as subjects "only in their capacity as consumers."[25] A workers' government, it promised, would be completely different.[26] At an international seminar on "Women in Today's Latin America," Allende's wife,

First Lady Hortencia Bussi, stressed in her inaugural speech that women would help transform society not simply by entering the workforce, but through a profound cultural expansion that would unleash women's initiative and creativity at all levels: "The conditions of today's world demand women's participation in community life and production. This means not only incorporating women into different types of work that increase family budgets, but the widening of women's cultural horizons, [the involvement of women] in the advance of science, the development of new technologies . . . the creation of new possibilities."[27] Expressing this vision more succinctly, *El Siglo* gushed, "[With Allende], nothing is impossible for today's Chilean woman!"[28]

The UP's anticipation of fundamentally new and emancipatory roles for women flowed from a sincere belief in the transformative powers of socialism. Although Popular Unity built on policies shared by its political competition—most recently the Christian Democrats' campaign to "incorporate women into national processes"—it widened debates about the meaning of female emancipation and initiated approaches distinct from those of its predecessor. At the same time, the endurance of a strong maternalist and family ethic, which continued to assume both the desirablity of male-headed families and the primacy of men's productive roles, implied serious limits to such transformation. In an unwitting acknowledgment of this contradiction during a speech on infant-maternal health, Allende explained that women were equal to men except in their capacity as mothers, one fundamental to women's social nature and one that required dispensations from the norm: "We must give women full equality of possibilities before the Law and in life. But we cannot forget that women have a function in life—the most transcendental of the human race—to be mothers. Therefore, we need to understand that women, because they are mothers, need protection."[29]

The valuation of motherhood did not, in itself, mean that women had to come second to men. The ethos of gender mutualism—which continued and gained momentum under the UP—emphasized parity in men's and women's distinct social contributions and suggested curbs to men's authority over women. What limited the emancipatory ends of the UP's approach to women was the fact that men remained the normative standard for the citizen-worker the coalition aspired to nurture. Women were to be brought closer to this ideal as well. But as mothers or future mothers, they figured as exceptions—worker-citizens with responsibilities that exempted them from the same level of expectation advanced toward men. The UP's revolutionary vision understood transforming the means of production as the engine of social change, and it saw men as naturally less responsible for family than women. This double vision created repeated contradictions within the party's sometimes quite radical projects of gender equality.

Family Planning and Sex Education

The tension between the UP's goal to empower women and its claim to defend the Chilean family plainly surfaced in its approach to birth control and sex education. Popular Unity professed to offer a liberatory program of increased knowledge about, and access to, contraceptives that would counteract the sexual hypocrisy and coercion of bourgeois capitalism. Rhetorically distancing itself from the Frei administration's preference for couching birth control in terms of maternal-infant health, the UP began to emphasize limiting pregnancies as a matter of personal autonomy and social entitlement. In December 1970, a policy statement from the UP Commission on Health referred to family planning "as an inalienable right of women and the couple."[30] The Commission accused the Frei administration of pursuing a policy of population control under the guise of improving women's health and affirmed that, in contrast, Popular Unity would promote family planning in a way that "ensured every woman the possibility to have the number of children desired, when they were desired, in accordance with improving the fortune of the family."[31]

At the same time, UP policies heavily built on those of the Christian Democrats and continued to primarily emphasize family well-being and spousal cooperation. Adding to the changes that the Christian Democrats had already made to the SNS and continuing to work closely with APROFA, the UP put most of its efforts into broadening and decentralizing existing family planning projects. It expanded nutrition and vaccination programs and provided additional resources for pre-and postnatal examinations; regional SNS facilities were authorized to develop programs specific to their area's needs; rural neighborhood clinics made available contraceptives; and APROFA established eight new provincial headquarters. Family planning efforts continued targeting married couples and emphasized husbands' and wives' joint responsibility for limiting off-spring. The SNS continued to solicit men's consent to wives' contra-ceptive use and parental approval for adolescent girls. APROFA seminars maintained their focus on birth control as a means of improving men's abilities to adequately provide for their households.[32]

The strong continuities between UP and Christian Democratic poli-cies stemmed from political expediency as well as the UP's particular vision of working-class mobilization. Similar to the way that "Family Health" had conceptually aided the Frei administration in explaining its support for birth control to Catholics, the UP's family-centered approach aimed to neutralize accusations from both Christian Democrats and the Right that socialism was anti-family. Allende was particularly sensitive to allegations that the UP was immoral. His support for birth control dated from the 1930s when, as a young physician and Minister of Health, he had championed family planning as a rational tool for promoting public health. However, during the electoral campaigns of the 1960s, Allende avoided the subject and, as president, usually steered clear of publicly promoting contraceptives himself. The UP's family-centered programs also aspired to minimize objections to contraceptives from working-class men, the coalition's central base of support. They likewise furthered the idea of class uplift as a collective project involving the collaboration and mutual empowerment of men and women within individual house-holds. This complemented many leftists' assumption that the working-class family would serve as the basis for organizing socialism and that the interests of men and women within those families were always com-patible.

Yet if UP family planning policy affirmed spousal harmony within male-headed families, the coalition's simultaneous efforts to widen ac-cess to contraceptives and create a public dialogue about the connection between sex and human liberation considerably complicated this mes-sage. The UP launched new sex education programs that went far be-yond the "health information" previously provided in SNS clinics and APROFA workshops. The Office of Social Development (formerly Popular Promotion) and the Ministry of Education coordinated sex education, which included discussions about desire and satisfaction as well as physi-ology and reproduction, and they offered it at schools, unions, CEMAS, and other community organizations throughout the country.[33] In contrast to the Frei administration's tendency to equate sexual responsibility with sexual restraint, the UP's sex education programs connected birth control to issues of personal self-understanding and sexual fulfillment. In October 1971, a Ministry of Education conference on sex education resolved as one of its central goals "to help [couples] secure the right to separate reproduction from the exercise of their sexual lives."[34] By 1972, the Ministry of Education's sex education program had fourteen headquarters throughout the country and claimed that it could serve 500,000 students and 80,000 parents annually.[35] Praising the potential of sex education as a vehicle of working-class self-empowerment, Minister of Health Sergio Infante proclaimed that "family planning is crucial to the revolutionary process and the final objective of making socialist humanism a reality."[36]

Popular Unity's interest in sex education was part of a much broader and more ambitious effort to link all education to revolutionary liberation. As had the Christian Democrats before them, UP leftists understood that building a new society depended on profound cultural transformation, and they saw education as the chief engine for such change. But in contrast to the Christian Democratic insistent separation of "education" and "politics," the UP envisioned education as a site of active political struggle in a partisan quest to emancipate Chileans through socialism. Beginning in 1971, the Ministry of Education initiated conversations with an array of professional educators and political activists in what became known as the Congress on National Education to lay plans for the National Unified School, a national curriculum for all Chilean schools, public and parochial, which would pedagogically center around the concept of the "New Man."[37] Modeled on revolutionary Cuba's example, the New Man was explicitly political and essentially Marxist—a student who, through education, became conscious of society's problems and contradictions and who mobilized collectively to actively change his environment. As Allende described this new Chilean, "[The New Man] is a complete, harmonious being, autonomous and critical, yet fully socialized . . . an individual cognizant of, and responsible for, the national destiny which he himself builds and defends with his hands and his intelligence. . . . a Chilean who discovers and masters the laws of nature and takes advantage of her resources for the general welfare . . . [who] at the same time submits to the collective will the spontaneous tendencies of history."[38]

Although the UP did not formally propose plans for the Unified School until 1973, and never implemented them because of the coup, its vision of politically transformative education shaped many specific programs launched in anticipation of a national curriculum and intended to help pave the road to socialism. New sex education programs for youth particularly bore this mark. Proponents of the National Unified School envisioned sex education as a crucial component of any future emancipatory pedagogy in both primary and secondary schools. In early 1971, the Ministry of Education announced plans to develop a sex education curriculum that would "promote changes necessary to permit millions of children and adolescents to enter into a society where sex is a natural and happy fact, situated in a cultural context free of falsehoods, superstition, fear, and commercial exploitation."[39] In contrast to his usual hesitancy to speak openly on the subject, Allende heartily endorsed youth sex education, including information about birth control. Equating liberation with hygiene and rationalism, he preached that "it is time, breaking with an absurd and backward morality, to realize the importance of talking to our youth about the problems of sex. . . . The drama of the young woman who must suffer the consequences of her ignorance by seeking abortion can no longer be ignored. . . . [Education] and family planning should be the basis of a consciousness raising that lifts the moral level of our people."[40]

Although a national curriculum on sexuality was never implemented, sex education programs run by APROFA in conjunction with the Ministry of Education and the SNS operated throughout 1972 and 1973. Sex education intended to demystify sex for young people, not to challenge assumptions that matrimony was the appropriate place for sexual activity. Educators combined information on human development, sexual anatomy, dating, and attraction with warnings about the foolishness of adolescent pregnancy and admonishments that intercourse should be postponed until after marriage.[41] Although they gave information about how contraceptives worked, they usually did not give advice on where to obtain them. Still, the programs challenged longstanding Catholic associations of sex with prohibition and shame as well as the idea that procreation constituted the only acceptable expression of sexuality. They likewise questioned the idea that children's sexual education should be left to parents in the private domain of the family. Given that plans for the National Unified School envisioned both public and Catholic schools using the same curriculum, sex education represented a direct attack on Church authority over sexuality. Both sex and young people's sexual formation were defined as secular, public matters requiring open discussion and governmental involvement. As the director of APROFA summarized his organization's new approach under the UP, "We distinguish between *biological* responsibility and *social* responsibility . . . and social responsibility involves the community and the state" (emphasis original).[42]

The social and emancipatory message of UP family planning and sex education programs had particularly radical potential for women. Indeed, a feminist minority within the coalition linked birth control and sex education directly to women's liberation. A 1972 pamphlet entitled *La Emancipación de la mujer,* published by Popular Unity as part of a national education campaign on government objectives, asserted that "the sexual happiness [afforded by access to contraceptives and open discussions of sexuality] was fundamental to women's empowerment and therefore to class struggle and revolution."[43] Written by *El Siglo* journalist and Communist feminist Virginia Vidal, the pamphlet bemoaned the high rates of female frigidity and male impotence in the working class and blamed this sexual dysfunction for multiple social evils including machismo, sexual abuse, rape, and family violence.[44] Vidal called for a recognition that "sex was not only a physical relation, but also a spiritual one, especially for women" and proposed close connections between a woman's sexual fulfillment — especially orgasm — and her ability to be an assertive member of society. She also sharply criticized the heterosexual assumption that all Chilean women were (or should be) married or have children. Arguing forcefully that single and childless women also deserved sexual satisfaction and access to birth control, Vidal asserted that "not all women want to be mothers, not all women want to join their life with that of a man. Many single mothers are happy, but need better [economic] circumstances. . . . They are also entitled to happiness."[45]

Vidal blamed the political Right and the Christian Democrats for celebrating marriage and motherhood as a woman's highest and only place of achievement. She condemned this ideology of domesticity for fostering women's political passivity and subordination to men and argued that, in contrast, socialism could emancipate women by making motherhood and marriage a matter of choice rather than destiny.[46] This idea would entail structural as well as ideological transformations. The state could fully incorporate women into productive labor and political activism only by providing them with accessible birth control and childcare and by encouraging men to assume greater domestic responsibilities. Such change, Vidal cautioned, would be premised on a simultaneous cultural shift from men's perception of women as objects of their sexual domination to that of women as agents of their own sexuality.

Feminists like Vidal remained a minority voice within the UP. The coalition ultimately deemed Vidal's manifesto on female desire too critical of men and never distributed it. Instead, it continued circulating an earlier published pamphlet, *La Mujer chilena,* which limited itself to celebrating women's dual roles as mothers and workers and all but omitted any discussion of sexism.[47] Although UP family planning and sex education efforts recognized women's emancipation as a goal, they largely linked it to empowering families and couples and usually soft-pedaled the issue of male domination. Nonetheless, the very existence of Vidal's *La Emancipación de la mujer*—and the fact that it was originally published as part of a government series intended for mass consumption—testifies to the considerable debate within UP circles on the sexual nature of women's subordination as well as to the fact that connections between sexuality, marriage, and motherhood were being questioned in unprecedented ways. And other UP members joined Vidal in her criticisms. A prominent feminist sexologist, Felicitas Klimpel, headed the Ministry of the Family under Allende, and she staunchly advocated the importance of women's sexual fulfillment and criticized machismo as one of society's greatest ills.[48] Other feminists, female politicians, and labor leaders likewise agreed that the UP's liberatory agenda for women depended on ending men's sexual and social control of wives.[49]

In the spirit of Vidal's challenge, Popular Unity took a new approach to single women and unmarried mothers. It introduced legislation to fully equalize marriage relations and to legalize divorce.[50] Prominent UP women such as Felicitas Klimpel and Allende's wife hailed divorce as a tool for liberating women from the hypocrisy of Catholic annulments and extramarital affairs.[51] During the 1970 presidential campaign, Allende promised that his administration would "defend single mothers," a commitment later reiterated in the priorities of the UP's National Secretary on Women and its Ministry of the Family. In 1971, gynecological and contraceptive services were expanded to serve adolescent girls and single young women.[52] In 1972, the UP introduced legislation abolishing legal distinctions between illegitimate and legitimate births.[53] Although the government claimed as its primary motives the unfair discrimination against "innocent children," the policy in actuality lessened stigmas against adolescent girls and single women. The abolition of illegitimacy had particular significance for rural areas like the Aconcagua Valley, where over a quarter of all children were born out of wedlock and, of these, roughly one third had single adolescent mothers.[54] Although the UP fell short of Vidal's call to treat single women's nonmarital sexual activity as a positive norm, it did recognize that women were sexually active and bore children outside of marriage and showed a commitment to ensuring such women more parity with their married counterparts.

The coalition also took a novel approach to abortion. While never publicly condoning the procedure as legitimate, and downplaying calls by many feminists within its own ranks to have it legalized, the government permitted the performance of abortion in limited circumstances and significantly curtailed its criminal prosecution.[55] In 1970, the UP's Health Commission announced that, while education and accessible birth control would continue to be the cornerstones of the effort to reduce national abortion rates, the SNS also needed "to maintain the capacity to perform abortions in case such action should appear necessary or desired by the population."[56] Although this stipulation implied the use of abortion under special conditions such as saving a woman's life, it was, in practice, interpreted in a wider context. According to historian Ximena Jiles, Barros Lucos Hospital in Santiago regularly performed abortions for registered participants in the hospital's birth control program whose contraceptive methods had failed.[57] In San Felipe and Los Andes, occasional abortions were reportedly given in the public hospitals, and some SNS personnel administered abortions to women in their homes.[58] Even APROFA, which officially condemned the procedure on moral grounds, began publicly discussing the potential benefits of legal abortion and included information on clinical abortion techniques in the films and literature it disseminated to health care providers.[59]

The UP's more permissive stance on abortion had significant reper-

228 / *Partners in Conflict*

cussions for poor women's ability to safely terminate unwanted pregnancies. While the estimated rate of abortion in Chile remained stable
in relation to pregnancy between 1970 and 1973, maternal death from
abortion diminished by more than 25 percent.[60] Insufficient documentation makes it difficult to evaluate the extent to which more professional abortion procedures effected this decline. The decisions of medical professionals to administer abortions were arbitrary; in many rural
areas, traditional healers and nonmedically trained midwives probably
continued to perform the majority of such procedures. Yet the very fact
that the state health care system provided abortions in a limited capacity
certainly weakened SNS staff's anxieties about possible criminal prosecution and encouraged women of all ages and marital statuses to seek safer
conditions.[61]

The number of poor women demanding abortions did rise. A study
conducted by APROFA claimed that, while abortion had been three times
as frequent among poor women as among middle-class women prior to
1970, in 1972 the number was five times greater.[62] The report argued that
abortion had previously involved mainly older, married women between
the ages of twenty-five and thirty-five who had already had an average of
five children, but that it now increasingly involved younger women between the ages of eighteen and twenty-four who had two or three children.[63] The study also noted that campesinas, not just urban women, increasingly used abortion—a trend it attributed to rural women's greater
difficulties in securing their husbands' consent to contraceptives and to
campesinas' acquisition of the "urban value" of having a small family.[64]

Both poor rural and urban women had long used abortion in the absence or failure of contraceptives. Yet APROFA's assertions pointed to patterns directly related to the UP's family planning policies. First, abortion
became more accessible given the state's willingness to turn an at least
partially blind eye to its clinical practice. Second, given the SNS's continued insistence on a husband's consent to a wife's use of contraceptives
and the emphasis placed on the advantages of smaller families, abortion
became a more feasible option for women who wanted to limit pregnancies but could not secure their spouse's cooperation. Lastly, the availability of contraceptives declined by almost one third under the UP administration.[65] The United States had cancelled its health programs after
Allende's election, and the UP itself had terminated a contract with the

Rockefeller Foundation following a scandal in which the SNS alleged that doctors inserted IUDs without women's full knowledge of the consequences.[66]

But if the availability of contraceptives relatively decreased during the UP, overall infant and maternal health continued to improve. Women's use of medical birth control rose, if less dramatically than following the Frei administration's initiation of the first family planning programs. According to APROFA, 10 percent of all Chilean women between the ages of fifteen and forty-nine used medical contraceptives in 1970, but 12.4 percent did so in 1973.[67] In correspondence, the number of children that women bore during their lifetime continued to decline—down from a national average of 3.86 children in 1970 to an average of 3.59 in 1973.[68] Fertility declines were steepest for campesina women, falling from an average of 6.08 children in 1969 to an average of 5.6 by 1975.[69] Infant mortality declined by 18 percent.[70] If poor women sought abortions more frequently during the UP than under the Christian Democrats, they did so under safer circumstances. The numbers of women admitted to hospitals for abortion-related complications continued to drop (by an additional 4 percent nationally and 8 percent in the Aconcagua Valley); overall maternal death fell by another 27 percent.[71] In all, by 1973, Popular Unity had continued to improve infant-maternal health conditions, reduced the number of pregnancies among rural women in particular, and initiated a meaningfully new approach to sexuality, including the provision of reproductive health care to single and adolescent women, a candid sex education program for youths, and a tolerance of abortion.

Mobilizing Female Support

One of the main ways in which the UP sought to generate female support was by expanding women's participation in political and community organizations. The Left shared the Christian Democrats' faith in the connection between the poor's civic involvement and the pace of modernization. Marginality was seen as a drag on Chile's development, which popular mobilization would remedy. But the Left added its own twist to this formulation, defining popular organizations as vehicles for political education and class militancy. The UP called on women to involve themselves more fully in existing CEMAs and neighbors' councils as well as in the women's departments of unions.[72] Such activity, it argued, would teach women the merits of socialism, strengthen female class consciousness, and mobilize women to defend the government. The UP shared the Christian Democrats' tendency to consider women's public contributions as extensions of their roles as wives and mothers, but it differed in the meaning it attributed to housewife activism. Whereas the Christian Democrats had emphasized women's civic participation as a means of assisting families, contributing to the community, and deepening democracy, the UP stressed the importance of female activism to securing class interests and achieving human fulfillment under socialism. As Allende remarked in a speech about women's organizations in 1971, "The family of the working-class Chilean has suffered all of the consequences of capitalism. In a socialist society, on the other hand, everything will be at the service of the working-class family. . . . mothers' centers will be able to transform themselves into real centers of training, technical and cultural, allowing women to incorporate themselves into the struggle."[73]

The coalition emphasized class struggle, not just community uplift. It sought to foment a collective, female militancy that recognized that only a socialist reorganization of the economy and society would improve family welfare. The goal was not simply to bring women into the civic arena, but to make women more class conscious. If the UP feared female conservativism, it tried to put forth a confident face suggesting that the incorporation of more women into its institutions would solve the problem. In a 1972 article calling for the creation of women's departments within rural CUT offices and bemoaning the Communist Party's failure to foster adequate female leadership within its own ranks, *El Siglo* nervously reminded its readers that campesina women, in particular, potentially remained an untapped resource for class struggle: "We should remember that in many fights women have played an important role. There are hundreds of anonymous women who have been examples of courage in front of the latifundistas."[74]

The UP succeeded in meeting at least some of its organizational goals. Between 1970 and 1973, women's membership in CEMAs in the Aconcagua Valley doubled.[75] At the national level, CEMA membership reached one million.[76] Although both the Communist and Socialist parties had periodically criticized CEMAS as paternalistic, once in power, the Left sought to capitalize on the reality that CEMAs were by far the largest female organizations and were already closely tied to state bureaucracies.[77] Mothers' centers became vehicles for women's political education and direct involvement in UP programs. In Aconcagua, CEMAS oversaw the UP's milk distribution program, provided spaces for literacy classes and health education forums, and represented women at meetings on community development. Functionaries from INDAP made regular presentations at CEMAS on the Agrarian Reform, and delegates from the women's departments of UP political parties paid visits to explain government policies on education and housing.[78] Rural women's participation in neighbors' councils also grew. As the UP launched an ambitious plan in 1971 to build ten thousand new rural homes in Aconcagua, dozens of new neighbors' councils formed to assist campesino applications.[79] Although men usually continued to be the titular heads of these councils, women executed the bulk of the work involved, collecting signatures for petitions seeking electricity and water, and raising the modest financial quotas required for housing qualification.

Housing struggles grew particularly intense during the UP and often inspired female activism. Between 1970 and 1973, the local press in the Aconcagua Valley reported over three dozen housing-related property occupations in which protesters took over vacant land or buildings demanding a resolution of housing shortages. Such actions involved heavy female participation. Women physically seized buildings and set up encampments on disputed land, took part in delegations that met with government authorities, and formed common pots to sustain fellow protestors.[80] Although men were also present, housing-related tomas tended to have a female leadership since most men were employed on estates or asentamientos during the day. Officials from INDAP, CORA, and the Ministry of Housing pointed to the women's action as evidence of widespread female support for the UP's redistributive goals.

But housing struggles also involved women protesting the UP's delays and inadequacies. Most occupations involved takeovers of projects already under construction by the state agencies CORVI and CORHABIT. Protesters would illegally move into uncompleted buildings to urge faster construction and the immediate issue of legal titles. Such actions not only indicated the UP's efficiency, but also challenged the government's prerogative to unilaterally determine who qualified for residency. Moreover, housing struggles opened opportunities for the UP's political opponents to make inroads with women. In towns with municipal councils dominated by UP parties, such as Santa María and Los Andes, organizers from the Christian Democratic Party and Triunfo-affiliated unions helped initiate housing tomas to challenge local authorities. To the far left (outside the UP coalition), the Trotskyist Left Revolutionary Movement (MIR) organized at least three housing occupations in Rinconada county as part of its broader effort to encourage workers to take revolutionary action into their own hands.[81] Even in areas with widespread support for Popular Unity, such as Catemu and San Esteben counties, housing tomas were seen as a way of compelling the government to accelerate its pace.

In one of the largest housing occupations in Aconcagua, one hundred nominally homeless persons (*sin casas*) from the rural neighborhood of Villa España in Santa María occupied the adjacent property of a prominent landowner in May 1973. The protesters insisted that the land was abandoned and that the Ministry of Housing should use it to construct homes for a new neighborhood.[82] They also briefly occupied the town municipal building, demanding that the Socialist mayor, Gabriel Fernández, intercede on their behalf. Fernández recalled in an interview that he met with a delegation composed of CEMA members, whose leaders, Christian Democrats, he described as extremely insistent about their demands: "Oh, those women were fierce! . . . They said, 'Excuse us, Mr. Mayor, but we are tired of living like animals and tired of waiting for the government to hand us crumbs.' . . . Those women were much more militant than the tired old men who wanted to go home [after the meeting]. The women said, 'No sir! We are staying right where we are!'"[83] Although the protesters were convinced to leave the municipal building that afternoon, they remained camped on the land for the next four months and continued to meet weekly with Fernández and representatives from the Ministry of Housing. In July 1973, the UP announced its intention to purchase the land and to build permanent homes.[84]

Regardless of the political bent of a toma, housing struggles differed little in tactics and goals. Protesters shared a common outrage at the gap between their own living conditions and the UP's promises of equity. Increased female participation in CEMAs and neighbors' councils made women protagonists in these struggles, negotiating directly with housing authorities and political leaders as well as confronting landowners and elected officials. In 1972, a group of fifty families set up an encampment on the estate of a particularly notorious patrón in the Santa María county neighborhood of Calle Medio. They demanded that the UP immediately grant housing subsidies and residence titles to campesinos. Women from the local CEMA were placed in charge of meeting with leaders from the local union and with university students from Santiago helping to coordinate the action.[85] The women erected a Chilean flag and banner announcing, "This terrain has been seized by the People!" When the angry landowner passed by the occupation to threaten the protesters with armed eviction, the women reportedly slung mud at him and beat the side of his truck with sticks.[86]

The UP's organizing efforts had specific ramifications for adolescent girls. The coalition was eager to organize Chilean youth, both male and female.[87] It continued the Frei administration's policy of establishing coeducational agricultural schools and greatly increased the number of high school and university scholarships available to working-class youths.[88] Plans for the National Unified School envisioned rural secondary schools functioning as centers of campesino life, providing space for young people's artistic and cultural expression as well as for the development of academic and vocational skills.[89] The UP encouraged the formation of special youth departments (which included both girls and boys) in rural labor unions, political parties, and asentamientos as well as separate youth clubs in local neighborhoods. In contrast to the Christian Democratic youth programs' emphasis on promoting civic responsibility and preparing adolescents for adult family roles, the UP stressed adolescents' importance as current and future *workers* and suggested that Chilean youths had a revolutionary potential independent from that of adults and families. Viewing youths as inherently rebellious, CORA director David Baytelman urged the channeling of generational discontent into proper class consciousness: "The campesino masses are the authentic motors and actors of the Agrarian Reform. . . . if we do not achieve the real and positive participation [of rural youth] in the process, we run the risk that they will act in isolated forms."[90]

Rural youth clubs and education projects were meant to politicize and mobilize campesino adolescents whose frequent status as unwaged or seasonal laborers left them outside traditional union activities. In 1972, INDAP began working with labor leaders from UOC and Ranquíl to create theater and folklore programs aimed specifically at rural youths for the purpose of "changing values and culture [in order to] solidify the [political] changes being made by the UP."[91] Youth programs were also intended to build links with urban youth organizations and to enable rural adolescents' access to the leisure and educational opportunities currently available only in cities. Under Allende, the numbers of university students volunteering in the countryside expanded rapidly. Urban young people played significant roles in Agrarian Reform projects and labor struggles. Female students taught literacy courses, ran nutrition workshops at local CEMAS, and made banners and signs for strikes. Male students dug irrigation canals, explained rules of parliamentary procedure at union meetings, and joined male campesinos during estate occupations.

All of this exposed adolescent boys and girls to an emerging youth culture that celebrated a generation-specific politics and a heterosexuality independent of family life and adult control. Given girls' responsibilities at home and the greater tendency of campesino parents to restrict the social lives of daughters, it is doubtful that young women participated in political party youth branches and youth clubs to the same degree as did boys. Nonetheless, because political activities for young people centered around schools and vocational training, both of which were co-educational, youth organizations had a far more active female membership than did unions or political parties. Adolescent girls received the message that they should acquire technical knowledge about fruit production and farm machinery, not just homemaking. They also heard that creating an autonomous youth consciousness necessarily involved their spending more time in the company of peers (including boys) outside the parental gaze. Agricultural schools and neighborhood youth clubs regularly sponsored dances for young people where the *música internacionál* of the Beatles and Jimmy Hendrix and the *nueva canción* (new song) of Chilean folk and rock musicians such as Violeta Parra, Victor Jara, Quillapamú, and Los Jaivas displaced the traditional rhythms of cueca and *ranchero*.[92] By the early 1970s, Agrarian Reform production units and community organizations more frequently acquired televisions. They flashed images of young men with long hair and young women in miniskirts, replayed excerpts of popular music concerts in Santiago stadiums, and discussed the activities and political intrigues of university student governments.

Rural youths eagerly tracked the trends of their citified counterparts. A 1971 survey by IER of 1,200 rural youth in central Chile found that 70 percent of adolescent boys and girls listened to urban radio programs or viewed television on a regular basis and that they had a "great interest in accessing culture and information," especially on national political news and popular music.[93] The ability of campesino adolescents to consume urban-based culture through the purchase of a radio or magazine, or to participate in new forms of sociability, such as attending dances or the occasional movie, was facilitated by increased employment opportunities and higher wages, which put more spending money into the pockets of young men and a minimal amount into those of young women. The explicitly heterosexual impulses of urban youth culture became most immediately available in the presence of the university student volunteers housed on estates and asentamientos during their solidarity work. Youth brigades were coed, and male and female volunteers regularly gathered around campfires to discuss political strategies and share homemade wine. Rumors circulated that they shared the same tents for sleeping quarters.[94]

The celebration of youth heterosexuality simultaneously affirmed an expression of female sexuality and emphasized female bodies as objects of male desire. The popular leftist comic book *Firme,* widely read by youth audiences, depicted young female activists with enormous breasts protruding from tight sweaters "politicizing" men.[95] *Ramona,* a government-published magazine intended explicitly for young women, paired articles on choosing "the profession of your dreams" with beauty columns advising how to catch "the man of your dreams." One edition of the magazine, celebrating 1972 as the "year of the woman" with articles boasting the UP's success in catapulting women to leadership positions, sandwiched such female advancement between a cover featuring a naked girl draped in the Chilean flag.[96] Such imagery both expressed male anxiety about women's power to seduce (and deny) men and neutralized that threat by eroticizing women as natural sites of collective male longing. Women's contributions represented the fulfillment of the socialist nation, while the female body as nation figured heterosexual men as the citizen-machos being enticed to look and act.

But if youth magazines proved sexist, the celebration of heterosexuality by new youth programs and broader forms of emergent youth culture marked an expansion rather than a restriction of young women's lives. In contrast to the ways misogynist humor in the labor press helped justify women's exclusion from unions, the heterosexual emphasis of youth organizing accentuated women's inclusion in projects of social change. If young men's privilege and authority over young women was sexually affirmed, young women never figured merely as pawns of male heroics. They were called on to become politicized and to achieve education and jobs aimed at contributing to socialism, rather than to individual men or families. If motherhood remained one of their primary future roles as adults, their status as youth exempted them from the calling. In a youth culture that promoted autonomy from adults, the positive evaluation of heterosexual interaction also suggested greater independence from parents in young women's social and sexual dealings with men.

Women, Production, and Agrarian Reform Centers

The UP's call for women's greater incorporation into the workforce constituted the last main thrust of its overture to the female population. Reflecting the Left's faith in a causal relationship between wage labor and political radicalism, the UP proposed that women would acquire class consciousness fastest when involved in production. In addition, the coalition argued that women's wage work would enhance efforts to promote female equality and citizenship. As workers, women would participate in political and labor organizations on par with men and would make crucial contributions to national productivity. Such thinking shared much with the approach of socialist experiments in the USSR, China, and Cuba, where female emancipation was seen as an outcome of the socialization of productive relations. Women were being freed to perform labor for the national good. National productivity became a particular concern for the UP beginning in late 1971 as the effects of the U.S.-led boycott combined with employer sabotage and the government's own inefficiencies to depress industrial and agricultural output.[97] Calling on all Chileans to join in a "battle of production," the UP defined the full utilization of women's labor as a patriotic necessity for Chile's continued advance toward modernization and social justice. As a UP training pamphlet warned, "The country will be unable to emerge from underdevelopment and unable to achieve socialism until women are incorporated into productive activities."[98]

The call for women to join the battle of production generated great debate in UP circles about female roles. Men and women within minority ranks of the CUT, UP political parties, and government agencies offered explicitly feminist perspectives, including arguments that women's successful integration into the labor force was contingent on revolutionizing gender roles in the family. Socialist leader Arpad Pullai hailed the end of "the male breadwinner ideology," which he blamed for impeding "advances for women's equality." He contrasted the "possibilities for self-development" offered by the UP with capitalism's reductive view of women having only a "reproductive function."[99] In the pages of *El Siglo*, Virginia Vidal paraphrased and expanded on Friedrich Engles's argument that women's productive labor weakened female dependence on men and made a specific call for socializing housework to free women from the "slavery" of unpaid domestic labor.[100] Women labor leaders likewise recognized and condemned the link between housework and women's subordination as the primary reason for women's poor attendance at union meetings.[101] A 1972 article in *La Ultima Hora* blamed women's "tedious chores" at home for thwarting women's human development and condemned unpaid housework as hypermaterialist exploitation.[102] Minister of Justice Jorge Tapia labeled women's relegation to domestic routines a "semicolonial mentality" unfitting for a country that claimed a position as one of the most developed on the continent.[103] Marxist theorist Vania Bambirra warned that the privatized nature of housework, when combined with women's exclusive responsibility for it, impeded cross-class female solidarity. She argued that it made professional women's opportunities dependent on poor women's exploitation as domestic servants.[104] Feminist critiques of housework demanded an end of women's sole responsibility for children with particular vehemence. Although most cited state-provided day care as the solution, Virginia Vidal argued that it alone would prove insufficient and that women's true emancipation depended on men sharing equally in the many childrearing responsibilities that fell outside institutional purview.[105]

Despite this repeated feminist insistence on reorganizing the home, most UP efforts to promote women's employment did not call for men to perform more housework and childcare. On the contrary, the coalition often reconfirmed the sacredness of traditional maternity and house-wifery in response to accusations from the Right that women's work out-side the household threatened the family. This implied a double strategy of praising the ingenuity of female workers while insisting on women's primary role as mothers and homemakers with unique capacities for love and tenderness.[106] A 1972 article in *La Nación* on women textile workers expressed this logic precisely. Celebrating women's "conquest of the workplace" and ability to work "side by side with men," it reserved special praise for the fact that the women had "become leaders without abandoning their home and children."[107]

Still, the UP repeatedly stressed women's equality, connecting it to expanded work opportunities. The double celebration of women's pro-ductive labor alongside traditional family roles effectively asked women to work doubly hard; but it meaningfully widened visions of women's social capabilities as well. Pictures of women wearing hard hats and driv-ing trucks—common in newspapers from *El Siglo* and *Punto Final* to *La Nación*—titillatingly celebrated the new female workforce as capable of the most masculine jobs. That feminine employment in construction and transportation remained almost nonexistent did not lessen the power of that image. The UP's emphasis on women working defined women as central, rather than auxiliary, to processes of national transformation. However naive and teleological many UP leaders' belief in the link be-tween wage work and equality, female emancipation was proclaimed a national goal.[108] If men were not asked to do more housework, they were admonished to admire women's productive work and mocked for exag-gerated beliefs in male superiority. Praising women's equality as a sign of Chile's modernity as well as something women had earned through sacrifice, the president of the Confederation of Production and Com-merce, Jorge Fontaine, suggested that women's family responsibilities made women better workers and leaders than men.

> It's only logical that women have plain equality with men, now that they have demonstrated their capacity and sense of responsibility not only within the home, but in all work that they do in the countryside. . . .
> For centuries it was considered legitimate that women be relegated to the home, [but] modern life has demonstrated that this is absurd. . . .

I think that when women are in charge, things go better. Women have great intuition and a sense of responsibility. For so long there has existed a Latin American machismo purporting that men are superior to women even though [we see that] women surpass men in [the performance] of most tasks—industrial, agricultural, professional.[109]

The effort to incorporate women into productive processes took many forms. Day care centers were expanded, and plans for the National Unified School included proposals to make infant and toddler programs a permanent part of the Chilean school system.[110] Legislation expanding maternity leave to five months was introduced to encourage women's return to the workforce after childbirth. The UP's National Secretary on Women coordinated female professional and vocational training in medicine, law, dentistry, food processing, and garment manufacture.[111] The Obligatory Social Service program prepared adolescent girls and young women for careers as teachers, nurses, and social workers.[112] Laws introduced to regulate domestic service, women's largest source of paid employment, protected rights to an eight-hour day, overtime pay, vacation, and compensation for unjust firing. By 1972, almost 30 percent of all women worked in the formal labor force and almost 25 percent of the industrial workforce was female.[113]

In the countryside, the UP continued efforts begun by the Christian Democrats to expand women's income-generating capacities within the household. INDAP made new credits available to rural CEMAs for commercializing homemade textiles, canned produce, poultry, and rabbits.[114] Mothers' centers located near towns obtained financing to start small restaurants known as "popular kitchens" (*cocinas populares*).[115] But Popular Unity also emphasized the importance of women's labor in large-scale production, both in the Reform sector and on private estates. Photos of women harvesting grapes and peaches graced the front covers of INDAP and CORA publications, testifying to women's involvement in modern agribusinesses. Daily newspapers ran regular stories on campesina women's "new interest" in tractors, irrigation, and farm management, placing campesinas more firmly in the midst of "real" production (i.e., working for wages in the large-scale commercial sector).[116] And, indeed, in areas such as the Aconcagua Valley, women's participation in the paid agricultural labor force during the Agrarian Reform tripled. If these were exclusively seasonal jobs, they still evidenced the Agrarian Reform's success in expanding campesina women's agricultural employment.

The hallmark of the UP's effort to integrate campesina women into production was its attempt to replace the asentamiento with a new production unit known as the Agrarian Reform Center (*Centro de Reforma Agraria,* or CERA). The government explicitly designed these units to include women, as well as youths and seasonal workers, as full members. As one of their most constant advocates, Jacques Chonchol, UP Minister of Agriculture between 1971 and 1972, explained, CERAs were intended as transitional institutions for building socialism, and correcting problems created by asentamientos.[117] They aimed to increase production by incorporating entire families into the labor force as well as to promote identification with more communal forms of property by reducing the amount of land used by individual families. Most importantly, CERAs were meant to foment class solidarity rather than privileging a select few as the asentamiento did. The newly created units dispensed with the requirement that members be household heads with significant previous agricultural experience and extended the same entitlements to all residents regardless of marital status, occupation, or generation. Voting membership was open to all laborers, including afuerinos and seasonal workers, as well as to all women and youths over age sixteen, whether or not they were formally employed.

The UP hailed the inclusion of women in CERAS as an unprecedented achievement. The INDAP publication *Poder Campesino* gushed, "For the first time in Chilean history women have the right to participate with voice and vote in the leadership of campesino organizations, with the same rights and obligations [as men]. . . . it is now fully possible that a woman could even be elected president of the entire CERA general assembly."[118] The pamphlet carefully pointed out the inclusion of women both as workers and as housewives. The CERA general assembly, as well as its social welfare and vigilance committees, were open to "workers of both sexes" as well as to the nonworking "legitimate conjugal partners and family members of CERA workers." The remaining administrative body, the production committee, was open to all workers, "male or female."[119] INDAP's hopeful prediction that women would serve as CERA presidents was already a fact. In 1971, members elected María Contreras, a mother of six, as president of the Fidel Castro CERA in the southern county of Molina. Contreras received enormous publicity, appearing frequently as the subject of feature articles in the labor press and national dailies and receiving official visits both from her CERA's namesake, Fidel Castro, during the Cuban president's official visit to Chile in 1971 and from the first woman to enter space, Russian astronaut Valentina Tereshikova, in 1972.[120]

But despite their bold intentions, CERAS largely failed to generate either more employment for women or higher levels of female participation in administration. While women workers on CERAS were guaranteed a new say over matters of production, no directive to hire more women existed. Although women's agricultural employment increased, it was not in CERAS where women found work. Given that CORFO's National Fruit Production Plan was not formally launched until 1968, the majority of women who found jobs picking and processing fruit during the Agrarian Reform likely entered the workforce after Allende's election. But even during the UP, fruit and vegetable production was overwhelmingly concentrated on medium-sized private estates. Although a state-sponsored initiative directly resulted in changes in the private sector—something for which the UP could claim credit along with the Christian Democrats—this did little to mitigate the reality that, on the road to socialism, most campesina women found new work opportunities on private, not public, estates.

The vast majority of women gained CERA membership by virtue of being wives and daughters of male workers. Although this status still entitled women to vote in general assembly meetings, Patricia Garrett found that less than 5 percent of women living on CERAS actually voted and that most did not think of themselves as genuine members.[121] CERAS principally steered women toward the social welfare committee that oversaw issues of housing, education, food distribution, and culture. Despite INDAP's claim that social welfare committees offered unprecedented opportunities to women, their responsibilities closely resembled those of CEMAS, with one important difference: unlike mothers' centers, social welfare committees were administratively subordinated to the virtually all-male general assembly.[122] Moreover, because CERAS delegated little responsibility to social welfare committees, most functioned only irregularly.[123]

Male opposition to women's involvement in CERAS played a major role in marginalizing women within the UP's flagship institution for building socialist agriculture. In her interviews, Patricia Garrett found that over 90 percent of husbands discouraged their wives from participating in any administrative capacity in the Reform sector, and one of campesino men's most frequent criticisms of CERAs was their formal incorporation of women.[124] Of the handful of CERAs created in the Aconcagua Valley, women in Panquehue and Rinconada counties reportedly attended general assembly meetings, but no CERA seems to have allowed the voting participation of non–wage earning housewives.[125] Victor Acevedo, a member of a CERA in Los Andes county, recalled in an oral history that men found wives' participation inappropriate and that they resented efforts to change the status quo: "Fine, a woman could go to the assembly to be informed, to support her husband, but not to make decisions about the CERA. No. . . . That was the man's responsibility, and women were happy to let their husbands vote for them. . . . Women didn't want to work more, they had enough to do in the house, they were very sacrificing in the home. . . . You see, you can't just let women make decisions about men's work. . . . men don't run the home, and women shouldn't run men's things."[126]

It is unclear whether women were "happy" to have their husbands vote for them, but they seem not to have clamored for their own voice. In oral histories, most women recalled an interest in general assembly meetings, but said they did not have time to attend.[127] Others claimed no particular interest, regarding CERAs as men's business.[128] As in the case of asentamientos, most married women saw CERAs as benefiting them through the economic empowerment of male family members, not through expanded political and economic opportunities for themselves. Average real incomes for rural households more than doubled between 1970 and 1973, making married women's burdensome extra-household work unnecessary.[129] Victor Acevedo's observation that women worked hard at home, leaving little time for CERA committees, was to the point. Whereas Agrarian Reform labor legislation limited men's workday to eight hours and financially compensated men for workdays missed while attending political meetings, women received no such reprieve from, or compensation for, domestic tasks. Laundering, childcare, meal preparation, water hauling, and gardening continued requiring women's attention for daily averages of twelve hours. The UP's failure to respond to feminist calls within its own ranks for socializing or redividing domestic responsibilities hugely curtailed women's ability to participate fully in Agrarian Reform units.

But while gender divisions of labor limited female participation, men's sense that women's presence threatened masculine privilege cemented women's exclusion. Victor Acevedo's indignation that women might "run men's things" underscored male fears that CERAS would place women in structural parity with, or even authority over, men within the masculine world of work. This endangered the basis of the male-headed household, including the links between male sexual stewardship of wives, male breadwinning, and female domestic labor on behalf of men. It suggested that the UP's Agrarian Reform was backing away from a commitment to empower campesino men by reconstituting masculine authority.

The concerns of campesino men often found a sympathetic ear in the government functionaries responsible for implementing CERAS. If incorporating rural women into production and administration constituted an official UP goal enthusiastically promoted by national leaders such as Agricultural Minister Chonchol, Minister of Labor Baltra, and numerous outspoken feminists, the middle-class and professional men who staffed Agrarian Reform agencies often shared campesino men's sensibilities about the appropriateness of men providing for women and the dangers of women's extra-household activities. When explaining campesino resistance to women's participation in CERAS, CORA's Director of Campesino Development, Eduardo Placencio, emphasized all men's general investment in maintaining female fidelity, positing it as a natural reaction about which state agencies could do little: "Men fear for their security. The thing that a man just can't stand is [the possibility] that his wife would bring home more money than him, that she would neglect the children, [and] that she would have relations with other men. . . . so the campesino opposes his wife working [in the CERA] because he considers it a woman's fundamental duty to raise his children, wash his clothes, and make his food."[130]

Other CORA functionaries similarly voiced the idea that expanding paid work opportunities for women posed a specifically sexual threat to campesino men. The sociologist and CORA subdirector, Hector Reyes, admonished women to understand why men felt besieged and blamed female liberation for breeding immorality. Inferring broad connections between women's wage work and sexual infidelity, he likened the latter to prostitution and condemned it as far more dangerous than the purportedly noncommercial affairs of men:

> Women should understand that any plan involving female liberation is seen, on the emotional level, as an attack on the man. . . . [And] women have committed many errors. One has only to look at women's magazines to see the problem of women's liberation. You plainly see the problem of [sexual] lasciviousness. It makes men fear for their security. That the majority of men have extramarital relations is not a social problem in the same way that prostitution is. Thus, the only place where [the woman] should really challenge men is through her incorporation into the work force—when she can go home with money in her hand, always taking care that she doesn't neglect the children or have relations with other men. This is valid and is satisfactory to most men.[131]

Reyes' association of female wage work with prostitution had an almost century-long genealogy in which anxiety about women leaving the supposed safety of their homes to perform bodily labor for money (in work other than domestic service in someone else's home) was bemoaned by unions, leftists, and Catholic social reformers alike as a blight on the family and a symbol of working-class male impotence.[132] Although Reyes endorsed women's incorporation into production under certain circumstances, he placed a heavy burden on women to ensure that men could accept it. Husbands would remain "secure" only if working wives continued performing household labors up to previous standards, earned less money than their spouses, and vigilantly shunned attention from other men. His claim that men's sexual infidelities did not merit the same concern as did the sexual dangers of women's work further implied that working wives would have to continue tolerating men's affairs. Far from Virginia Vidal's and others' claim that the UP would free women from domestic drudgery and sexual subordination, Reyes called for female incorporation into production with as little change in gender relations and male sexual privilege as possible.

Campesino men's resistance to women's participation in CERAS and many government functionaries' own patriarchalist assumptions overlapped to virtually stall any momentum that the formal structure of

CERAs might have generated within the UP's general commitment to women's political and economic progress. According to oral histories, CORA officials did not push men to bring wives to general assembly meetings, nor did they usually encourage women to join the more female-oriented social welfare committees.[133] In addition, government functionaries often told their social superiors that the inclusion of women in CERAs jeopardized male support for the UP's Agrarian Reform, weakening resolve even among those politicians who supported CERAS' structure to force the issue. As Juan Carrera, a provincial CORA officer in Santiago, explained this capitulation, goals for rural women had to be jettisoned because men, not women, were central to the Agrarian Reform's mission and the UP was anxious about maintaining working-class men's allegiance: "Campesino [men] weren't ready to have women sharing the stage. It violated their machismo. [CORA] had very little capacity to change these personal attitudes and was having enough trouble getting campesino [men] to cooperate, so incorporating women into the CERA really became a secondary priority."[134]

The equation of "machismo" with "personal attitudes" that lay beyond governmental powers for change belied the extent to which CORA officials like Carrera shared campesino understandings about the appropriateness of men's authority over women. The Agrarian Reform hardly shied away from enormous tasks of cultural transformation. Changing campesino attitudes about private property, employer authority, and state power lay at the heart of its mission to radically remake society. CORA threw up its hands at the impossibility of altering attitudes toward women because men across class shared these assumptions. They formed the basis of a masculine identity and integrity in which many CORA officials partially recognized themselves and which they understood could be violated by any fundamental parity in men and women's Agrarian Reform participation. The insistence on machismo as a personal trait lying outside the terrain of political struggle further evoked a strategy for exempting gender and sexuality from the list of relationships and ideas requiring radical overhaul. It meant an acknowledgement from within UP ranks that certain of its policies and goals, if fulfilled, implied profound changes in men's relationships to women. And it rejected the proposal.

Such rejection exemplified the divisive heterogeneity of UP positions on women rather than a unified decision to calculatingly sacrifice women's needs. Women's exclusion from CERAS resulted from struggles within the UP over competing visions about the centrality of women to the creation of socialism and about what socialism meant for relationships between women and men. It did not suggest the insincerity or abandonment of other UP proclamations and debates about gender equality. It meant that, in the case of CERAS, a particular vision won. Alternative ideals about women's emancipation and its connection to equality in work, politics, and the home remained vital to UP debates and policies. They provided points of friction within areas where men's authority was preserved and reconstituted. Still, the success of campesino men and Agrarian Reform functionaries at derailing attempts to make the Agrarian Reform more gender-inclusive mattered greatly. The practical result of CERAS maintained men and male-headed families as the Agrarian Reform's central subjects and main protagonists. If it did not eclipse all other meanings and messages about gender, it did make it far more difficult for campesina women and their feminist allies to lay claim to the UP's promises of inclusion and equality.

chapter 7 Coming Apart

Struggle, Sex, and Social Crisis

On February 14, 1972, Hilda Gutiérrez Sánchez, described in judicial records as an "older housewife" living on Las Varillas asentamiento in Catemu county, charged twenty-five–year-old Juan Pérez Hernández, an agricultural worker, of attempting to rape her while she was harvesting beans. She told the court that Pérez had passed under the barbed wire separating their places of work and propositioned her while four of his male coworkers watched; when she protested that she was a married woman, he threw her to the ground and ripped her clothes. Gutiérrez claimed she prevented the rape only by screaming, at which point all of the men fled, but not before Juan Pérez hit her and menaced, "You're lucky I don't have a knife!"[1]

All four of Juan Pérez's coworkers testified that Hilda Gutiérrez was lying. Despite their contradictory accounts, all of the men—joined by Juan Pérez's father—defended the accused's innocence on the basis of his upstanding male character, or honor.[2] One testified to Pérez's "shy and peaceful" nature; another to the fact that Pérez was a "responsible and hard worker, a man without vices"; and still another to Pérez as a man who "doesn't [sexually] play around and is incapable of this kind of behavior."[3] Hilda Gutiérrez also defended the veracity of her story on the basis of honor. She stressed her married status and attempts to resist even in the face of personal danger. In addition, she submitted a statement from her local CEMA testifying to her upstanding character. Marked with the thumbprints and signatures of seventeen comembers, the document sternly condemned Juan Pérez and called for swift punishment in order to protect young girls from future attacks. The CEMA statement also challenged the integrity of the investigation:

> We, the undersigned, wish to leave it clear that Sra. Hilda Gutiérrez Sánchez, who we have known for a long time, whose life is without reproach, who is [an elected leader] in this mothers' center, and who is an exemplary mother, has never been seen with a man other than her husband. . . . We want to clarify that the drunk Juan Pérez Hernández attempted to rape her . . . and ask that justice be done as we consider [this man] a grave danger to all young girls who have to cut beans on this road or pass by it on the way to school. . . . It is clear that [the Pérez Hernández family] has very bad antecedents, and we ask that they be expelled from the county. . . . We also have reason to believe that the official in charge of the investigation has been swayed by outside influential parties and ask for a new investigation.[4]

Juan Pérez responded to the CEMA proclamation with an attack on Hilda Gutiérrez's sexuality. While finally admitting that he had crossed over the fence to see her, he insisted this had been at her request: she had asked him if he had a girlfriend, insinuated that she wanted to have sex, and challenged his manliness when he honorably declined. As he told the court, "When I refused, she insulted me for being unmanly and threatened me. I would not do such a thing because I am very Catholic. I'm a friend of her husband's, and she is not desirable."[5]

This was an exceptional story.[6] The majority of rape cases that ended up in court in the 1950s and 1960s involved very young women, usually pre-pubescent girls, whose victim status relied on evidence of prior virginity, sexual ignorance, and mental incapacity.[7] Hilda Gutiérrez was older, married, a mother, and perfectly sane. She gambled that she might convince the judge to rule on different criteria. Significantly, the CEMA statement suggested that the court needed to recognize and vindicate an older woman's reputation in order to spare future dishonor to young girls. In a twist that both departed from traditional markers of female virtue and revealed a certain generational tension between older and younger women, Hilda Gutiérrez's defenders proposed that her very status as wife and mother made her honorable—an implicit contrast to the more sexually suspect predilections of single women and adolescents, whose virtue the CEMA simultaneously urged the court to protect.

The case was also exceptional because it became a public affair dividing the community. It was the only case, revealed either in judicial records or in oral histories used for this study, that involved an organized response from a women's organization, not only defending a woman's honor but questioning the ability of the court to protect it. The reference to "outside influential parties" corrupting the investigation may well have pertained to CORA or INDAP officials, union activists, or asentamiento leaders, potentially pitting a CEMA against a male union or representatives of the Popular Unity government. Probably in a compromise aimed at alleviating community tension, the judge suspended the case for lack of evidence, but without clearing Juan Pérez of the charges.[8] While not ceding to Hilda Gutiérrez's claims, the residual doubt appeared to accept arguments that the community should be forewarned of Pérez's reputation.

Whatever the missing details, this case illustrates the ways in which the Agrarian Reform had reshaped women's and men's self-understandings as well as how gendered expectations and grievances were understood in terms of sexual conflict. In their respective testimonies, Hilda Gutiérrez and Juan Pérez not only drew on longstanding definitions of male and female honor, but specifically mobilized the official gender ideals promoted by the Agrarian Reform. Gutiérrez presented herself first and foremost as a wife and mother, but added evidence of her seasonal work as a bean cutter and stressed her political activism and leadership within the CEMA. Pérez's defense built on arguments that he was an honest and hardworking laborer who respected and was respected by other men of his asentamiento or union. Efforts to discredit his accuser relied on allegations that she, rather than he, had been the sexually irresponsible and aggressive party. Invoking double meanings of manliness, Pérez suggested that while he had been man enough (respectful enough) to decline Hilda Gutiérrez's advances, out of loyalty to the sexual claims of her husband, his friend, he was also man enough (virile enough) to comply with the proposition were it not for his standards of sexual taste: Gutiérrez was not desirable. The women who defended Hilda Gutiérrez flatly rejected such masculine posturing. Through the collective voice of the CEMA, they affirmed the plaintiff's virtue and condemned men's sense of sexual license, as well as men's overindulgence in alcohol, as dangerous enough to merit Pérez's expulsion from the community.

Hilda Gutiérrez and Juan Pérez went to court in 1972, an exceptionally divisive time throughout Chile. The UP's socialist agenda had met with a ferocious and internationally backed opposition, deepening already profound class and partisan conflicts and setting off a wave of organized and often violent sabotage. At the same time, those Chileans best positioned to benefit from the UP, including hundreds of thousands of rural and urban poor people, aggressively pushed for faster state action. The ensuing clash proved explosive. Between Allende's November 1970 inauguration and mid-1973, more than 8,200 strikes and 6,000 property occupations occurred nationwide, nearly one third of which took place in the countryside (see Table 20).[9] By late 1971 production slowdowns, merchant hoarding, and the U.S. boycott combined with workers' unprecedented earning power to spur three digit inflation, shortages of some consumer goods, and rationing. In October and November 1972, an anti-UP strike launched by truckers paralyzed much of the economy and ignited massive street demonstrations both in protest and in defense of the government. Landowners grew more aggressive in efforts to expel campesinos from occupied territory at gunpoint. Fascist groups, such as Patria y Libertad (fatherland and freedom), attracted young male recruits from wealthy communities and openly paraded in Santiago parks, goose-stepping through paramilitary drills. In the Chilean congress, the Christian Democrats joined ranks with the Nationalist Party to all but shut down parliamentary process: they prohibited debate on most executive policy proposals from the UP, forcing Allende to rely on obscure, if usually still legal, unilateral presidential powers. In response, the center-right opposition passed resolutions condemning Allende for acting unconstitutionally and called for his impeachment.

In defense of the UP, the Left organized massive demonstrations of tens of thousands of persons, regularly clogging the streets of Santiago and physically clashing with opposition groups from Patria y Libertad and the Catholic University. Santiago and other cities were subdivided into discreet industrial zones, aimed at developing a factory-based defense system. Tractors and farm trucks were brought into urban areas from asentamientos to provide a rudimentary transportation replacement for striking bus services; alternative food distribution centers were established to bypass merchants and warehouses who refused to open their gates. The left wing of the Socialist Party and MAPU began discussing the need to arm workers, while students from the University

Table 20 Labor and Land Conflicts, 1970–1973

Year	All Strikes	Rural Strikes	Rural Land Occupations
1970	1,867	523	456
1971	2,576	1,580	1,128
1972	3,278	1,758	1,273
1973	2,048	317*	309*

*January through March, 1973
For strikes in 1970 and 1973, see *Estadísticas laborales*
(Santiago de Chile: INE, 1976), 96–100; for strikes in
1971 and 1972, see Barraclough and Fernández, *Diagnóstico,* 134; for land occupations, see Academia de
Humanismo Cristiano, Cuadro 1, *Historia del movimiento campesino.*

of Chile and the Technical University instructed campesinos and urban
slum dwellers in the construction of Molotov cocktails. Communists,
the more conservative wing of the Socialist Party, and social democrats
from the other partisan factions of the UP staunchly opposed such measures, urging that laws be vigilantly upheld and violence avoided in the
interest of shoring up the government's legitimacy and ability to act co-
herently. By early 1973, Allende faced widening fissures within his own
coalition, accusations that the UP was abetting civil war, and loud rumors
about the impatience of the armed forces.[10]

Women figured prominently in this political strife. The UP's opponents escalated an aggressive media campaign, with roots dating back
to the 1964 elections and partially financed by the CIA, to warn Chilean
housewives that Marxism would outlaw religion, make children wards
of the state, destroy the family, and otherwise bring hatred to civil
society.[11] Right-wing women's groups such as Poder Feminino (feminine
power) organized a number of highly theatrical anti-UP actions, including the waving of black flags outside congress to "mourn democracy's
death" and the creation of mock-common pots in elite neighborhoods
to protest shortages of food and fuel. In December 1971, women march-

ing against the UP banged empty pans with cooking utensils. They denounced the government as devastating for Chilean families and chastised oppositional political leaders for failing to avoid a national crisis. When the march was confronted by pro-UP demonstrators, ensuing violence resulted in one hundred injuries and Allende's designation of Santiago as an emergency zone.[12] Although such activities disproportionally involved middle-class and elite women, significant numbers of working-class women also participated. As Margaret Powers and Lisa Baldez have argued, despite the explicitly political and class-based nature of such protest, organizations such as Poder Feminino were effective, and especially alarming to the UP, because of their populist approach to mass mobilization and their apolitical invocation of female patriotism. Poder Feminino proposed that Chilean women shared a primary, unselfish, and nonpartisan love of the family—the basis of community and country—and that this endowed women with a moral authority, transcending partisan interest, to rebuke a government hostile to family interests.[13]

The Left responded with its own pro-UP demonstrations and rallies of women, challenging both the Right's appropriation of "family" and its depiction of women as apolitical and united. Publications such as *El Siglo* and *Punto Final* praised the success of UP *comandos femininos* (female command centers), which had been established within CEMAs, unions, and universities to mobilize women for marches defending the government's gains in family income, education, and maternal health care. Simultaneously, they denounced the hypocrisy and questioned the legitimacy of the female opposition. They depicted the women who organized anti-UP common pots and the infamous 1971 "march of the pots and pans" as vulgar, even masculinized, fur coat–clad and diamond-wearing *damas* (ladies) who had never missed a meal in their life and who had forced their domestic servants to join the protests against their will.[14]

In the countryside, women's support was also a marker of political legitimacy. Although Poder Feminino concentrated its efforts in cities, several of its main leaders were women from prominent landowning families whose properties had been expropriated during the Agrarian Reform.[15] In the Aconcagua Valley, the National Party organized at least three anti-UP women's marches in Los Andes in late 1972, claiming to have unspecified campesina support.[16] CEMA delegations from rural Putaendo and Santa María counties attended a San Felipe protest in solidarity with the national truckers strike.[17] Meanwhile, *El Siglo* reported that a pro-UP rally, organized in San Felipe in 1973 "to reject fascism and civil war," involved women from the most remote parts of the Aconcagua Valley, making it the largest women's demonstration in the region's history.[18] In general, however, the participation of campesina women in large, all-female demonstrations either in favor of or against the government was far less common than in cities. Lacking transportation, time, and often the formal connections to political organizations, campesinas remained among the most difficult women to bring to large-scale showdowns.

Nonetheless, the spiraling conflict had a deep impact on rural women, and they formed strong feelings about the UP, ranging from staunch support to vague unease and open hostility. Politics became unavoidable. In rural hamlets throughout Chile, daily life came to involve the constant negotiation of political events and shifting circumstances. Men and women would awake to news that a local factory or estate had been occupied during the night. Municipal plazas became permanent sites of rallies, and fresh political graffiti appeared almost nightly on adobe walls. Unions, CEMAs, and neighbors' councils met constantly to organize new actions. The intensified political climate excited many campesino men and women. Involvement in a strike or common pot could be a heady and emotionally satisfying experience, regardless of whether one was protesting or praising the government. But exhilaration coexisted with extreme tension. Politics increasingly extended into the most daily and intimate parts of peoples lives. Party affiliation through unions and other base organizations came to govern a man's or woman's access to concrete resources as well as one's choice of friends. As class and partisan animosities intensified, old alliances and comraderies within campesino communities broke down, undermining loyalties formerly central to survival.

The process of social polarization was experienced in personal and familial ways as well as institutional and occupational ones; it had significantly different ramifications for women and men. Men were far more likely to be on the front lines of the most physically confrontational and politically visible battles over land occupations and labor strikes. Women negotiated the increasing politicization of consumption, housing, and education issues, but were often isolated from the union meetings and general assemblies of asentamientos and CERAs where political strategies were most hotly debated. As factionalism within the labor movement grew bitter, men confronted the breakdown of male solidarity codes that had been important to mobilizing campesinos in the early Agrarian Reform years. At the same time, the UP's plan to socialize the agrarian economy threw assumed links between manliness and future land entitlement into question. For women, the risks also heavily involved grievances over masculine ideals, but theirs were located more within the family. The added pressure women felt in making ends meet led to widespread accusations that men were not fulfilling their roles as providers. Men's increased absences from home also escalated fears about male sexual loyalty.

Popular (Dis)unity and Male Militancy
in the Rural Labor Movement

Political division within the rural labor movement over the UP's Agrarian Reform occurred almost immediately. The Christian Democratic confederation, Triunfo, denounced what it called the UP's attack on private property and, in 1971, the Christian Democratic Party declared formal solidarity with the National Party in opposing the Popular Unity project altogether. This provoked Triunfo militants from MAPU and Left Democracy (a party less radical than MAPU that had also severed from the Christian Democrats to support Allende) to split and carry a majority of Triunfo's membership into a new confederation, Unidad Obrero Campesino (Worker Campesino Unity, or UOC). Now backed by the considerable resources of INDAP, UOC joined the Communist and Socialist confederation, Ranquíl, in an aggressive organizing effort that nearly doubled union membership between 1970 and 1973, bringing over half of all rural union members into pro-UP affiliation. Meanwhile, the independent Catholic confederation, Libertad, remained defiantly unattached to any party; but while never formally joining the opposition, it denounced UP leadership as demagogic and adamantly opposed CERAS and the expropriation of medium-sized estates.

In the Aconcagua Valley, the labor movement reflected these divisions. A majority of union members moved decisively leftward while the diverse partisan tendencies realigned more precisely into two polarized camps. As the number of unionized men expanded by over a third in 1971 and 1972, the proportion affiliated with Triunfo plummeted from 73 percent to under 10 percent. Ranquíl and UOC, on the other hand, claimed to lead fully 53 percent of union members, and Libertad said to head 37 percent.[19] Campesino allegiances tended to reflect men's different access to land and the past political focus of different organizing efforts. Members of asentamientos created under Frei largely stayed loyal to Triunfo and Christian Democracy's vision of individual family farmers, while inquilinos on medium and small estates were more sympathetic to Libertad's message of cross-class cooperation and patrón responsibility. Ranquíl and UOC drew support from inquilinos on the remaining larger estates and from seasonal workers, the latter of which became a particular rhetorical focus of UP efforts to create more inclusive organizations in CERAS and campesino councils.

The Popular Unity Agrarian Reform engendered enormous bitterness among already divided factions and ended the loose cooperation that had characterized the rural labor movement under Frei. At the heart of this conflict lay sharp disagreement over the pace of land expropriation and the ultimate tenure of property in the Reform sector. Bold proclamations from Allende and his ministers that "latifundia was dead" and socialism was in the making sparked hugely divergent interpretations. For many inquilinos and salaried workers, it fanned hopeful expectations of imminent inclusion; for members of asentamientos, it generated fear that the UP was abandoning Frei's promise to grant individual titles.[20] The introduction of CERAS and even larger-scale production units called centers of production (CEPROS) fed rumors that all future Reform sector land would be farmed collectively and managed by the state.[21] The designation of properties over forty hectares as subject to expropriation upped the ante still more by placing medium-sized agriculturists in the same class category as latifundistas and raising questions about the viability of any private holding under UP socialism.[22]

Landowners mobilized through SNA and CAS to actively encourage the most apocalyptic view, and they fanned rumors among minifundistas and workers on medium-sized estates that the UP planned to expropriate even the tiniest subsistence plots.[23] If landowners had seen some points of collaboration with the Christian Democratic Agrarian Reform, they took the UP's frank opposition to capitalism as a declaration of class war.[24] Local newspapers reported increased activities of armed "white guard" vigilante groups who evicted striking workers and destroyed campesinos' personal belongings.[25] By mid-1971, Patria y Libertad had a noticeable following throughout the Aconcagua Valley.[26] The SNS's monthly magazine *El Campesino* grew increasingly shrill in its denunciations of anarchist violence and production sabotage, which it accused the UP of sponsoring.[27]

But landowners also responded with conciliatory appeals to potential campesino allies. For the first time in their histories, the SNS and CAS downplayed their unabashedly elitist orientation to open their memberships to small farmers and even some minifundistas.[28] They also turned decisively away from earlier opposition to the Agrarian Reform's goal of creating small farmers to champion the redistribution of asentamiento property to individual members.[29] They sought alliances with the national Confederation of Asentamientos and continued efforts to expand the rightist campesino association Provincias Agrarias Unidas.

Struggles between campesinos and landowners, and among campesinos themselves, centered around the escalating estate occupations and accompanying strikes. In 1971, there were 1,106 estate tomas and 1,580 rural strikes nationwide, followed by 1,273 estate tomas and 1,758 rural strikes in 1972.[30] As before, a variety of actors initiated tomas, but after Allende's election they were most commonly launched by inquilinos and wage-earning workers with leftist, or what became known as "ultraleftist," sensibilities. Importantly, such actions by sympathizers with the Left flatly contradicted Allende's vision of a tightly managed and constitutional transition to socialism, a position shared by the Communist Party and the more conservative wing of the Socialist Party. Officially, both the Ranquíl and the UOC confederations condemned tomas as undermining the UP's legitimacy. They argued that tomas played to the opposition's arguments that the government would not uphold the rule of law. But others within Popular Unity saw things differently. The left wing of the Socialist Party and radicalized ex–Christian Democrats from MAPU, including Minister of Agriculture Jacques Chonchol, advocated swift expropriations and viewed estate occupations as a critical tool. Operating still further to the left and outside the UP coalition, the Trotskyist MIR advocated mass mobilization and criticized Allende's government for collaborating with capitalists.

Such divisions sent campesinos mixed messages and undermined the coherent implementation of UP Agrarian Reform policies. But ambiguity also had advantages. It enabled workers who organized and participated in land occupations against the directives of UP leaders to claim that their actions still remained within the spirit of the Popular Unity agenda. In contrast to the Frei administration, the UP generally refused to use force against mobilized workers, no matter how illegal the action. The coalition needed to maintain legitimacy among the working classes and relied on worker militancy to provide the energy and initiative for building socialism.[31] The de facto message that estate seizures would not be repressed opened a floodgate to campesino activism.

At the local level, campesinos' own desire for land and their interpretation of the Agrarian Reform's meaning overwhelmingly fueled land occupations. As historian Peter Winn has vividly illustrated in his compelling account of Santiago textile workers, many Chileans saw Allende's election as a green light to proceed with the socialization of their own workplaces, taking their *compañero presidente* at his word that the UP stood for the empowerment of the poor and the expropriation of excess wealth.[32] In the countryside, this sentiment resonated strongly with seasonal laborers on asentamientos and with many inquilinos and permanent workers on estates where expropriation had been stalled in appeals courts. Such workers hailed the Popular Unity victory with an urgent confidence that the rules of the game had now changed. In the Aconcagua Valley, local union leaders claimed that the number of worker petitions to CORA requesting expropriation more than tripled in the first months of 1971 alone, followed by more than two dozen estate occupations between 1971 and early 1973.[33] Armando Gómez, who became president of the UOC-affiliated union in Putaendo county, recalled in an oral history that the UP initiated nothing short of a grab from below: "After Allende became president, things changed overnight. All of a sudden there was an explosion. Workers wanted land and demanded that the government expropriate all of Aconcagua in a day!"[34]

If the demand for land came from the rank and file, estate occupations were not entirely spontaneous. Urban-based militants from MAPU and the Socialist Party were involved in most tomas in San Felipe and Los Andes counties, while the MIR had a significant presence in Rinconada county.[35] Some occupations were planned weeks, even months in advance, sometimes involving participation from UOC and Ranquíl national leaderships, despite these confederations' official stance against tomas.[36] Campesinos who participated in tomas mobilized out of a clear sense of what was at stake. If they understood land occupations as morally just, they also recognized the illegality and possible consequences of such actions. Often, campesinos bargained that tomas would produce conflict, which, in turn, would force subsequent government intervention and expropriation. As one campesino frankly explained the rationale for illegal occupations to Peter Winn in a 1972 interview, "We have to break the laws if we want a workers' government in the future. If we are not able to pass over this legal wall that the reactionaries [*momios*] have built, we will never be able to do anything because there is no law that favors the workers. In order to achieve justice, we have to go beyond the limits of the law."[37]

Such bravado defined new standards of working-class male heroism. Gone was the early Agrarian Reform caution to couch campesino activism within the technicalities of new labor laws and CORA procedures. Gone too was the appeal for state authorities to intercede on campesinos' behalf. Now, militant land occupations—precisely because they were illegal—were proclaimed necessary vanguard actions through which campesinos would push the UP to real victory. This change reversed notions of who led and who followed and considerably widened definitions of the class enemy. Reactionaries—or *momios* (mummies) as was the most common phrase—now included not only landowners and other elites who used a "legal wall" to repress workers, but also fellow workers who would defend that wall. For campesinos, momio connoted lack of masculine resolve and willingness to fight for justice, and usually it juxtaposed the moral weakness of the upper-class patrón with the virile steadfastness of the worker. But when extended to include campesino peers, the term fused disdain for unmanly cowardice with an accusation of class treason.

For those hurling the insult, momio applied to the significant numbers of campesino men who sharply opposed more extensive expropriations and the creation of more inclusive production units. This group included members of existing asentamientos as well as inquilinos and permanent workers on medium- and small-sized estates with decent wages and land entitlements. These men tended to be older, usually over age thirty, with families, and they strenuously objected to the term *momio* as well as their defamers' definition of masculine activism. Many had participated in strikes and tomas between 1964 and 1970 and saw themselves as having struggled for the resulting reforms enacted under Frei that now provided unprecedented security. They challenged the equation of manly courage with a willingness to push the limits of the law, countering that Agrarian Reform laws had empowered campesino men to begin with. Reasserting the earlier logic of Catholic and Christian Democratic unions, which held that good salaries and just working conditions constituted desired ends in themselves, they characterized the wave of land occupations as the actions of fools who recklessly jeopardized hard-won gains. Diego Rojas, an inquilino from Catemu county, bitterly recalled in an oral history his objections to the 1972 occupation and to the subsequent expropriation of the medium-sized estate where he worked: "It was crazy! You can't divide fifty hectares into parcels for twenty men. . . . We had a decent relationship with the patrón—he was so scared of the Communists that he gave into almost everything we wanted. . . . Sure, I would have liked to have been my own boss too, [but they] weren't thinking with their heads."[38]

The charge of being a momio especially vexed asentamiento members since it directly challenged their just recently acquired status as the envied embodiment of the Agrarian Reform ideal. Now faced with accusations that they lacked adequate militancy and opposed true Agrarian Reform, they held tight to the realpolitik voiced by Diego Rojas that there was only so much land to go around. They interpreted the uncertainty of UP land tenure goals as a betrayal of the early Agrarian Reform promise to make them family farmers and, therefore, also as an attack on their identity as men. They saw the radical inclusiveness inherent in mass land occupations and CERAS as disasters that would end either in a proliferation of pitiful subsistence plots, or worse, the conversion of campesino men back into peons. As a former asentado from Santa María county succinctly recalled in an oral history, "[There are] only so many ways to slice a loaf of bread before you end up with crumbs."[39]

Fantasies of becoming individual farmers also motivated men who rushed to join tomas and called other men momios. According to most researchers who interviewed campesinos in the early 1970s, a good majority of all rural workers (as high as three fifths in one study) favored owning their own land over collective forms of property.[40] But among campesinos, the risks and prospects of obtaining land differed

quite markedly. Seasonal workers and migrant afuerinos had never enjoyed the privileges of job security or subsistence plots; because they
were often unmarried, they usually automatically disqualified for asentamiento membership. Many permanent workers found themselves in
similar positions, lacking access to subsistence plots and having suffered
exclusion from asentamientos because of their youth, lack of family, or
secondary status to inquilinos. If most of these men still desired their
own land, they were more immediately concerned about inclusion in
the Reform sector and could more easily gamble that UP socialism would
include cooperatives of small farmers. In the meantime, they stood to
benefit from an accelerated Agrarian Reform that no longer linked access
to land to being a head of household.

Divisions over the UP's Agrarian Reform did not always break down
neatly into categories of older versus younger, asentado versus seasonal
wage worker. Some longtime inquilinos supported expropriation of
medium-sized estates, just as a number of seasonal workers preferred a
good relationship with their patrón to inclusion in the Reform sector.
Political experience in past organizing efforts mattered greatly. Asentamientos created in the aftermath of leftist organizing efforts in the 1960s,
such as the San Miguel conflict, often steadfastly backed the UP and
opened up membership to seasonal laborers who resided in the same
county.[41] But even campesinos sympathetic to the Left generally remained skeptical of CERAS. Although they advocated more inclusive
Agrarian Reform production units, they often objected to membership by afuerino migrants and, as discussed earlier, to the participation
of women. Despite their enthusiasm for socialism, many also opposed
CERAS' orientation toward communal land tenure. They particularly resented the fact that CERAS drastically reduced the size of land allotments
for individual family use to under half a hectare. As a result, the vast majority of Agrarian Reform production units created under Allende continued to function as asentamientos with expanded memberships, not
as CERAS.[42] Known as "campesino committees," these middling institutions extended membership privileges to more men, but retained barriers against the most marginal workers and continued to allot land for
individual use. By May 1973, of the 115 Agrarian Reform production units
in Aconcagua province, 62 were asentamientos, 37 campesino committees, 11 cooperatives, and only 5 CERAS.[43]

Scenes from tomas. All from UP pamphlet series, NOSOTROS LOS CHILENOS, courtesy of the University of Wisconsin Land Tenure Center.

Bottom two: Mock slaying of "injustice."

Signs, hats, and flag of arrested campesino demonstrators. One sign reads, "Policeman, you are exploited just [like us!]" UP pamphlet series, NOSOTROS LOS CHILENOS, courtesy of the University of Wisconsin Land Tenure Center.

The widespread campesino opposition to CERAS suggested an affinity between campesinos included in the Reform sector under Frei and those included under Allende; it also underscored the limits of leftist efforts to bring afuerinos into solidarity with other workers.[44] Nonetheless, as the mounting political conflicts among campesinos indicated, the UP's more accelerated and inclusive Agrarian Reform program involved different types of risks and opportunities than had that of its predecessor. It widened the Agrarian Reform's formerly exclusive focus on married men with dependents and their secure employment positions to include the incorporation and celebration of all campesinos and their potential as workers. If never a perfect match, generation, marital status, and occupation had a rough correlation to a campesino's political support or opposition to the UP. These categories came to signify the distinctions between political sides. They pitted the aggressive demands of younger male workers for more radical land reform against the caution of older family men bent on protecting a relative privilege.

Rivalries between masculine styles and political objectives fueled mutual accusations and open fights. Immediately following Allende's election, inquilinos from Lo Bonito estate in Panquehue county began complaining to Catholic labor leaders from Libertad that other permanent and seasonal workers sympathetic to the UP were destroying farm equipment and under-irrigating fields in order to sabotage production and force expropriation.[45] Charges of malice frequently paired with accusations that the perpetrators were also lazy. Drawing on notions that linked hard work and masculine integrity, the inquilinos proposed that campesinos pressuring for faster expropriations were unprepared to manage their own land. In response, the inquilinos were assailed by their coworkers as apatronados who sneaked around spreading false rumors.[46] Like the term *momio, apatronado* was an accusation of masculine inadequacy. It connoted both fear and false consciousness, and it invoked the infantile spectacle of a worker hiding behind the boss.

Asentamiento members came under a somewhat different attack. Theoretically their own bosses, they could not be apatronados. They were instead insulted as *momios-patroncitos* (bitsy bosses)—a term simultaneously ridiculing asentados' inflated notion of manly superiority and acknowledging asentamiento members' status as employers, which rendered questionable members of the working class. For men still on the outside of the Agrarian Reform looking in, the asentado as worker-boss remained a figure of desire. But the UP's criticism of asentamientos as elitist and divisive, as juxtaposed to the egalitarian model of CERAS, provided a logic within which campesinos could push asentados to share their privilege. On El Tártaro–Lo Vicuña asentamiento in Putaendo county, hired workers who comprised almost a third of the labor force petitioned the asentamiento's general assembly in 1972 to open membership to all permanent and seasonal workers on the property. Although no suggestion surfaced that the asentamiento be administratively reorganized as a CERA (but a campesino committee was eventually formed), the demand for inclusive membership took its cue from the latter's more radical vision. When met with initial refusal from the general assembly, the workers launched a strike, backed by UOC, in which they refused to enter the fields and disabled asentamiento tractors by hiding engine parts.[47] Resulting fights between campesinos turned physical and, on one occasion, two workers were reportedly taken to the San Felipe hospital for a broken arm and head wounds.[48]

Land occupations aimed at speeding expropriations bred even more division. Rowdy counter-demonstrators armed with shovels and sticks

now met workers from Ranquíl and UOC-affiliated unions who initiated tomas at estate. Local police, initially called to the scene to prevent
violence between landowners and workers, more frequently mediated
between feuding campesinos.[49] In 1972, when UOC-affiliated workers in
San Felipe county seized the forty-hectare El Mirador estate belonging
to a prominent Christian Democrat, the sixteen resident inquilinos immediately circulated a petition denouncing the toma organizers as Communist outsiders who did not even work on the property.[50] They also
initiated a lawsuit against UOC, accusing the confederation of stealing
money and members from the former Triunfo unions.[51] In Los Andes
county, at least a dozen inquilinos sided with their employer during
a 1972 occupation of the Santa Ester estate and repudiated the occupiers' tactics as debaucherous and unlawful.[52] According to an irate letter
written to CORA by the landowner and cosigned by inquilinos, "MAPU,
Socialist, and Communist infiltrators" held the patrón and his family hos-
tage in their house, broke into a vat of homemade wine, and "became
naturally out of control."[53] When the police and local CORA officials arrived, the owner was reportedly "forced to negotiate away [his] right
to a reserve" by drunkards.[54] In a reverse scenario, campesinos and labor
leaders on the Left claimed that Christian Democrats and independent
Catholics staged the most controversial tomas in secret agreement with
the landowner to undermine the UP's legitimacy.[55]

The prospect that some campesinos would not only share the patrón's
position, but would actively collaborate in defending it, sparked particular hostility. National landowners' societies tried to evince a more
populist position by affirming campesino rights to private property. Employers used scare tactics about UP intention to expropriate subsistence
plots. Such strategies combined with campesinos' own concerns to produce significant instances of anti-UP cross-class solidarity.[56] During the
1972 national truckers strike, private estates throughout the Aconcagua Valley suspended production and, according to one oral history,
hosted parties for their idled workers in gratitude for their loyalty.[57]
When groups of campesinos tried to keep an estate from occupation,
owners and administrators from neighboring estates joined them in their
efforts.[58] A national association of small growers and private estate employees closely associated with the SNA, CONSEMACH, joined with local
landowner associations to provide more formal delegations of anti-toma

support.[59] Likewise, when armed landowners attempted to retake occupied estates through threats of violence, loyal workers carrying shovels and hoes came to their support. In one of the largest counter-tomas in Aconcagua, an estimated one hundred men, many with guns, seized three recently occupied estates in San Esteben county in June 1973 and set fire to the occupiers' clothes and victory banner.[60] Although the local paper suggested that landowner societies from Los Andes led the assault, campesino witnesses of the eviction insisted that most of the participants were agricultural workers and members of oppositional unions.[61] More ominous still, Socialist and MAPU union leaders from San Esteben and Santa María counties claimed that area landowners conspired to have them assassinated and offered other campesinos money to do the job.[62]

Whether or not campesinos collaborated in murderous plots against peers is less important than the belief that solidarity among working-class men had deteriorated enough to where such actions became possible. Mutual suspicions between partisan factions hardened into volatile antagonisms that eroded former bonds of male camaraderie and common cause. Pascual Muñoz complained that the walls of his asentamiento in Santa María county were nightly painted with slogans such as "Death to the momios!"[63] But just down the road, campesinos occupying an estate accused Muñoz's asentamiento of supporting the activities of Patria y Libertad that raced trucks past the toma site in the middle of the night, firing guns into the air.[64] On a more everyday level, political disputes were taken as personal insult, provoking brawls in the fields and at soccer games.[65] As recalled in an oral history by Raúl Aguirre, a former officer of the Triunfo-affiliated union in Panquehue county, animosity among workers began to take precedence over campesino struggles against landowners: "The conflict wasn't so much with the patrón, but between us. . . . A hate among us, a hate among [union and political] leaders so strong—a deadly, deadly hate."[66] This sentiment reflected the official stance of Triunfo and Libertad, characterized by its more conciliatory attitude toward landowners and its charge that the UP fomented social hatred. But campesinos on the Left also voiced regrets that other workers, not just the patrón, had become the main concern. In an oral history, Bernardo Flores, a former Socialist union officer from San Esteben county, recalled the months leading up to Allende's overthrow as a battle against intransigent campesinos: "I lived in the streets, in meetings all the time. I was dying of being so tired, [but] we fought with the mo-mios until the end. . . . They wanted to accommodate until there was nothing left but crumbs."[67]

The tendency to view other workers as the principle enemy signaled a critical rupture with earlier Agrarian Reform understandings of cam-pesino militancy. During the 1960s some men had also sided with the patrón, but union manhood had been constructed explicitly against such timidity and lack of class consciousness. Despite significant differences between Leftist, Christian Democratic, and independent Catholic agen-das, the willingness to stand up to the boss and the courage to trust and defend one's fellow workers in the shared project of accelerating the Agrarian Reform commonly defined union masculinity. During the UP, half of the labor movement came to deride the other half as unmanly cowards and class traitors; those accused assailed their attackers as arro-gant thugs and threats to security. Both lay claim to the Agrarian Re-form's male ideal of sober responsibility and class militancy, but came to accept an only partial vision of class solidarity. Both emphasized that the willingness to stand up to and defeat other union men had now be-come a vital part of union masculinity. Ironically, under Frei, collabora-tion among men was enabled by the limited and unfinished nature of the Christian Democrats' land reform project, which had allowed campesi-nos of very different political tendencies and relationships to the rural economy to interpret the Agrarian Reform as something on which they could project fantasies of inclusion. Under Allende, the definition and possibility of realizing a particular utopian project became much more concrete. Whatever its internal divisions and inconsistencies, the Popu-lar Unity government had a socialist goal. Its encouragement of popu-lar mobilization, acceleration of land expropriations, and emphasis on communal land tenure moved things rapidly in this direction. In part, the UP's very success exposed the profound differences and conflicting interests among campesinos. Coupled with a fierce and internationally backed counterattack by its opposition, such divisions forced a choosing of sides.

Friction on the Home Front

Campesina women also chose sides. Female community organizations in Aconcagua splintered along lines similar to those of the male labor movement. Mothers' centers that previously had incorporated members sympathetic to both leftist and Christian Democratic tendencies divided into separate organizations, and women boycotted meetings led by rival partisan factions.[68] Even the common pot ceased as a point of solidarity. During a toma led by Ranquíl sympathizers on the El Róque estate in Panquehue county in July 1972, women running the common pot accused several wives of workers who opposed the occupation of attempting to sabotage their efforts by stealing provisions and hoarding firewood.[69] Escalating tensions also ruptured everyday networks of reciprocity. Women accused each other of vandalizing personal property; neighbors who traditionally borrowed from each other or minded each other's children declined to do so with women from families of the wrong partisan color.[70] While animosities among rural women had long characterized rural life, conflicts during the UP appeared to have political motivation.

Partisan divisions among women were heavily conditioned by the occupational status and union affiliations of male family members, reflecting both women's economic dependence on men and the disproportional role of the labor movement in shaping popular political culture. But women had gender-specific understanding of political risks and conflicts and did not merely echo male concerns. Some of the rawest tensions among women occurred in struggles over the government-run *juntas de abastecimiento popular* (popular food provision councils, or JAPs), created in 1971 to distribute consumer goods and control prices. These councils functioned on the basis of neighborhoods, allowing each family to purchase a basic daily allowance of items such as bread, oil, milk, tea, meat, cheese, kerosene, paper, and yarn. Despite providing rural families with a steady supply of subsidized goods, JAPs symbolized scarcity to many women because they underscored the disparity between the rural poor's vastly increased purchasing power and the relative lack of consumer options. Consumption rose by 22 percent between 1970 and 1972, thanks to unprecedented working-class wages; but production, while increasing, rose less than 10 percent.[71] Aggravated by the international boycott, merchant hoarding, and industrial slowdowns, the imbalance created effective shortages at the very moment when the rural poor enjoyed higher incomes. "We had lots of money, and nothing to buy with it," many women recalled in oral histories.[72] Although families were free to buy at private stores, some shopkeepers' unwillingness to sell produce at official rates and, many times, to sell any goods at all, left JAPs and the black market as the only options. While campesina women blamed the situation on merchant greed and the general tendency of the rich to steal from the poor, they deeply resented the government's inability to prevent it.[73]

Popular Unity price control and distribution policies also constrained campesina women's productive activities. Many rural women raised animals and vegetable crops in their gardens, subsistence plots, or on small farms; they sold in town markets produce not consumed at home. State requirements that small producers sell to the government at official prices, and the labeling of all other activity as the illegitimate black market, placed a special burden on women whose agricultural labor was most concentrated in the non–wage-earning, minifundista, and small farming sectors. They were obliged either to abide by lower prices than their produce commanded (at a time when neighbors had cash to spare) or to sell on the sly. Both options bred resentment and created tension between women who illicitly sold and women who illicitly bought. Accusations that campesina producers gauged their neighbors and retaliatory threats of reporting informal sales to the authorities abounded.

But JAPs kindled particular ire. Women complained that JAP administrators allotted inadequate rations, or smaller portions than stipulated by the certificates, and that they periodically made unavailable certain items altogether. Rumors that JAP administrators kept back goods to sell on the black market, and that they gave larger and better portions of food to families sympathetic to the UP, fueled a sense of outrage. The fact that JAPs often employed campesina women as administrators could provoke particular conflict since it placed female acquaintances and neighbors in positions of control over the welfare of each other's families.[74] Angélica Saéz, the wife of a seasonal agricultural worker in Santa María county, recalled in an oral history that buying bread became a daily struggle with a woman who used to be her best friend:

Running the JAP really went to her head. It made her crazy. She thought she was so superior, but she was just very greedy and wanted everyone to know that she ran things in the neighborhood. I would say, "María, I have seven children, I need three kilos of bread." She would say, "No, you get only two," and then she would weigh me out only one and three quarters! If she had two chickens, she would always give me the small one. . . . She thought her family deserved more than mine. But I knew her, she was no better than me.[75]

Many women, whether or not they sympathized with the Popular Unity government, criticized JAPs for antagonizing relations between neighbors by making consumption beholden to partisan politics. To avoid this situation, some women opted to make purchases on the black market at triple the JAP price. Others illegally purchased from multiple JAPs to acquire quantities of goods larger than those officially allotted.[76] In 1972, members of a CEMA in Panquehue county submitted a letter to the local JAP protesting the lack of respect that a particular female administrator showed for other housewives. While such collective criticism appears to have been exceptional, the incident was notable for the degree of collaboration between women of different political tendencies and for women's insistence that food distribution be free of political patronage. As Olivia Ibacache, one of the signatories to the letter, remembered in an oral history, "I supported the Popular Unity [and] I was a Socialist, so I never had any problem at the JAP. [But] others did. Older señoras would be insulted, cheated a little on their bread. Oh, it was very disagreeable! I couldn't stand that. Politics is politics, and [should] have nothing to do with how a family is treated, or how [one] is respected. . . . JAPs should not be involved in political messiness."[77]

According to Ibacache, women's objections to JAPs sprang less from deprivation than from the personal indignities and conflicts the councils produced. The emphasis on "respect" and insistence that politics "have nothing to do with how a family is treated" underscored an anxiety that political divisiveness was going too far. Women's desire to insulate family survival and neighborhood relations from "political messiness" flowed from the specific dangers that neighborly conflicts posed for women's ability to make ends meet. Networks of female reciprocity provided women's families with crucial material and emotional support; daily exchanges with other women provided the main source of adult contact, information, and camaraderie. The fractiousness generated by JAPs jeopardized these links without offering alternative security.

For young and single campesina women the situation differed somewhat. Political mobilization and the ensuing social polarization proved less unnerving and more exciting for them than for most married women. In particular, single women and adolescent girls who were agricultural workers often became more directly involved in the land and labor struggles at the heart of the Agrarian Reform's mission. Although many married women provided moral and material support for these conflicts, the younger and single women who disproportionally made up ranks of female workers on private estates more often joined men in striking, signing petitions for expropriation, and occupying property.[78] In exceptional cases, women's concentrated numbers in the expanding fruit industry positioned them to push the boundaries of the types of property to be included in the Agrarian Reform and to take leading roles in tomas. According to oral histories, women workers on estates with sizeable apricot and peach cultivation seized small fruit-processing factories located on the property and demanded their expropriation along with the rest of the estate in at least four cases in the Aconcagua Valley.[79] Since CORA usually expropriated only land, leaving manufacturing facilities in the possession of landowners, such action directly challenged official policy.

In one incident, women employed at a small conserve factory on the Bucalemu estate in San Felipe county occupied the facility in May 1973, demanding its expropriation.[80] CORA had expropriated Bucalemu's agricultural land the previous month, but had left the conserve factory in the owner's control. After the owner locked out his seventy female employees in retaliation for the loss of his land, several dozen women workers broke into the factory and occupied it.[81] For over four months the women held the establishment against the objections of CORA that their action was illegal. The women took turns sleeping in the factory, providing each other with food and negotiating with government officials. According to participants, female workers who had assisted in strikes and land occupations led by the local UOC-affiliated union organized the toma. Male union leaders encouraged the action (despite the national confederation's formal stance against tomas) and lent the women material and organizational support in the form of transportation and contacts within CORA. However, according to male and female eye-witnesses alike, the decision to take over the factory and demand its expropriation came exclusively from women. María Trujillo, a worker at the factory who was eighteen at the time of the conflict, insisted that issues of gender parity, namely the fact that the expropriation of estate land alone would not benefit female workers, especially concerned the women. As she recalled in an oral history, "We were all workers on the estate, men and women. Many of us [women] had been assistants to men in their fights, so we understood the importance of workers controlling the industry. When CORA took possession of Bucalemu, it seemed only right that [women] not get left behind. . . . Everyone agreed! Some women were stronger than others, but everyone felt the factory should be passed into the control of the workers."[82]

Trujillo further explained that both married and single young women involved themselves in the toma, but that single women took a larger role both in the physical occupation and in negotiations. In part, she attributed this to some older single women's greater dependency on wages and more extensive exposure to union activities. But she maintained that the most significant limitation on such women's participation was husbands' sexual jealousy. She remembered, "Men couldn't bear the thought of their wives staying overnight in a factory—especially since there were male [union] compañeros around to protect us. Of course, single women also had problems with this, but it was easier to win over the father or uncle."[83] Men also worried about the consequences of female leadership for men's traditional protagonism in labor struggles. As Carlos Navarro, a former permanent worker on Bucalemu, recalled, "Even though [men] agreed that the factory should be expropriated, it was too much for some to watch their wives, sisters, and daughters occupying it . . . to see women standing guard, sleeping overnight. It was strongly felt that women should be in their homes, that a confrontation like that would turn them into men."[84]

Women's activism challenged contemporary notions of campesino manhood on two fronts. First, women's overnight presence in the factory weakened men's right to expect certain labors from wives and daughters at home, and, in particular, to monitor female sexuality. Second, women's specific actions in the factory toma closely mirrored those of men during land occupations, demonstrating both symbolically and practically that labor militancy was not exclusively masculine. Fears that women might be "turned into men" flowed from the ways that women assuming political roles usually filled by men called into question one of the main bases for male activism during the Agrarian Reform—a household head's struggle on behalf of dependent wives and children. The Bucalemu occupation also indicated that some women workers saw opportunities in the UP's efforts to accelerate expropriations and to encourage collective holdings. Given the UP's positive vision (if less than fully realized in practice) of incorporating women into political processes and the workforce, women felt enabled to challenge both contemporary notions about proper feminine conduct and the Agrarian Reform's ongoing concern with empowering male workers. They demanded the extension of the Reform sector's advantages to women, not on the basis of their status as men's family members, but on the basis of their status as workers entitled to the same benefits as their male counterparts. And they insisted that it should be women, not men, who physically wrested and won these victories.[85]

Sex and Social Crisis

As the conflicts of Agrarian Reform grew, married campesina women worried more about family dynamics. Men were increasingly absent from home, spending more time on occupied estates and in endless meetings; the more frequent and violent labor clashes provoked alarm about their husbands' physical safety. Wives also worried about men's ability and willingness to fulfill obligations at home. Would a prolonged strike end in the loss of a job? Would a husband suffer injuries, even death, in a toma? What were men doing during their absences, and when would they return? There was similar, if less acute, alarm about adolescent children. Would children, daughters in particular, who worked in agriculture become involved in labor conflicts? Was it appropriate for girls to attend youth club meetings? What were the risks of heterosexual camaraderie?

Such anxieties flowed from campesina women's marginalization from the daily negotiation of labor politics. Excluded from most union meetings and general assemblies, most women could not participate in the heated debates over union strategy and land occupation that kept most men abreast of—and protagonists in—a rapidly changing political climate. Husbands' unwillingness to keep wives informed of their activities exacerbated the situation. In oral histories, many women professed to know little about why their husbands changed unions or participated in certain tomas or strikes. Their spouses rarely told them why they spent the night away from home or how many days they expected to be away. As one woman described the problem, "[My husband] never told me anything. He insisted that I stay at home. I became afraid because I didn't know what was going on. . . . I never participated in anything with him, he was just gone a lot."[86]

As a whole, married campesina women experienced the impact of political polarization during the Popular Unity years in isolated and family-centered ways, in contrast to the vastly more collective and institutional spaces afforded men. While both men and women felt the strain of escalating conflict, wives were less well positioned than male family members to see such conflict as connected to specific political projects they could directly influence. Mothers' centers connected important numbers of women to political processes, but these organizations rarely made decisions about strikes and tomas. However significant, they only ever involved a minority of women, with the exception of women's activism in struggles for housing. But even housing tomas involved far lower proportions of rural women than labor unions did of rural men. Still defined as family issues, housing tomas came second to men's struggles over the means of production.

The more family-centered nature of married women's relationship to the Agrarian Reform encouraged women to evaluate the impact of political mobilization during the UP in terms of authority within the household. As tensions mounted and communities polarized, women equated the negative cost of class conflict with family crisis. Beyond the everyday struggles of consumption, such crisis involved a perceived breakdown in women's authority as wives and mothers and, in particular, an association with male negligence and sexual infidelity. Indeed, recollections of men's sexual betrayals during the late Agrarian Reform years figured prominently in the stories of over two thirds of the women interviewed for this study as well as in those collected elsewhere.[87] Most commonly, wives accused husbands of shirking their financial obligations and becoming involved with other women. The two usually were seen as inseparably linked. A husband's basic loyalty to his wife cemented his gendered obligations to the family. In turn, men's failures as responsible providers and respectful partners were seen as indicative of sexual promiscuity. Men's long absences and secretive activity often sparked accusations of male inadequacy. Women often suspected "union business" as camouflage for affairs and saw "politics" as a possible sexual threat.

Campesina women had reason to worry. The rural labor movement had long celebrated men's sexual prowess as an integral part of worker militancy, and the heightened political mobilization of the late 1960s and early 1970s provided men with ample opportunities to avoid the scrutiny of wives and to meet other women. During strikes and tomas, husbands could be away from their wives for several days, even weeks. Solidarity actions involved traveling to other counties, where men might lodge in another señora's home and enjoy the host community's modest festivities of drinking and dancing, usually in the presence of other women. Men with leadership positions had still greater extrafamilial demands and opportunities. While attending meetings in Santiago or Talca they were given small financial allowances, often used to wander the streets and visit local taverns; festive parties, complete with chicha and female company, lightened the intensity of education seminars.[88] Interactions with women ranged from jocular flirting to full affairs. In exceptional cases, men took more permanent lovers and started second families.[89] Men discovered that they not only had increased opportunities to pursue female company, but that their status as union or asentamiento leaders heightened their sexual cachet in women's eyes. As Armando Gómez recalled, "A lot of men took advantage of being out of the house, traveling to San Felipe and even to Santiago, to meet women and be with them. There were so many women, and they liked you a lot for being a leader, for being proud. . . . Men found this very exciting. It made them feel they could go around getting lots of women."[90]

But if campesino men understood extramarital sex as part of union manliness, it violated the Agrarian Reform's simultaneous promotion of gender mutualism and manly responsibility to family. Men acknowledged this conflict and admitted that it did not come without its price. Even husbands professing total loyalty returned from regional conferences or land occupations to accusations of infidelity. In women's eyes, the culpability of some men and the heightened sexual possibilities for all men cast doubt on most husbands. According to Armando Gómez, such suspicion ultimately cost men women's support for the Agrarian Reform. He lamented, "Lots of men had troubles with their women. They'd arrive home, and there would be a big fight because the wife thought he had been out going around town [with other women]. A lot of women didn't give their support to the Agrarian Reform for this reason."[91] Jorge Tejedo, an elected officer in San Felipe's Triunfo-affiliated union, had similar recollections, but apportioned blame along more partisan lines: "The conflict during the UP was really hard on women. Men would leave the house at four in the afternoon and not come back until three in the morning. . . . Or sometimes, these family men would leave for three or four days when occupying an estate. . . . And you can imagine what women thought of men spending nights out of the house! I saw many marriages broken into pieces over this."[92]

Tellingly, both Armando Gómez and Jorge Tejedo professed to have enjoyed their wives' full support, inferring that, although other men abused their absences from home, they had not. But their wives remembered things quite differently. Jorge Tejedo's wife, Ana Saavedra, remembered that her husband could become physically violent when she complained about his nighttime absences, and she accused him of sexual affairs with female clerical staff at union headquarters.[93] Faced with such recollections by his wife, Tejedo reiterated his claim of fidelity but admitted to flirting with other women and to "being hard on his wife."[94]

Armando Gómez's wife, Elena Vergara, had memories similar to Ana Saavedra's. She maintained that Gómez had numerous affairs on his trips as union president and that, in 1971, he left her to live with a lover he had taken in the city of San Felipe. He ceased to take an interest in their three children and only erratically passed by their home on El Tártaro–Lo Vicuña asentamiento to leave her money. She was finally forced to approach the Christian Democratic president of the asentamiento—her husband's political enemy—to plead that he allow her to purchase goods on credit that would later be charged to Gómez. She recalled, "Those were terrible years for me really. . . . It was so difficult . . . he ran around in all that politics—oh, it was chaos, so much fighting. . . . And it made me ashamed to go to [Gómez's political rival], but he gave me no choice. I had the children, and he made me do all the sacrificing."[95]

Women's memories of male infidelity and violent domestic conflicts in the late Agrarian Reform are substantiated by the significant rise in wife-beating charges women filed against men. During the UP, the number of cases in the San Felipe courts involving male violence against women more than tripled as compared to the Christian Democratic years, jumping from an average of twelve cases to an average of thirty-eight cases.[96] In 1973 alone, women brought a record number of fifty charges against men.[97] Whether this increase reflected a rise in the incidence of wife beating, women's heightened sense of entitlement to report it, or both, there was clearly a greater public acknowledgment of such violence. Women's reasons for filing charges also appear to have shifted slightly. As in the past, most cases involved men's objections to wives' interactions with other men and fights over the quality of women's housekeeping. However, in a notable increase from earlier years, almost a third of the available cases involved quarrels sparked by a wife's accusation of a husband's infidelity.[98]

Despite escalating conjugal conflicts, women like Elena Vergara and Ana Saavedra supported the Agrarian Reform. Although Saavedra, a Christian Democrat, shared her husband's antipathy for the UP, Elena Vergara professed loyalty to Allende, and both women praised the Agrarian Reform's general goal of empowering the rural poor. Both women saw their husbands' affairs, which had so jeopardized their security, as related to "politics" (men's involvement in unions and labor struggles) and to the "chaos" of the UP years (strained and openly conflictive relations within the rural community). This connection reflected neither a simple hostility toward politics as a whole nor a rejection of the Agrarian Reform's goals. Rather, it pointed to women's sexually inscribed vulnerability within the process of political struggle. Women expected and needed husbands' loyalty, and they bitterly resented and fought other claims on male fidelity. The Agrarian Reform's promotion of domesticity and decision to make women's benefits contingent on a sexual alliance with a participating male sustained this arrangement. A husband's affair entailed the danger that he might divert his income or land opportunities to another woman, leaving a wife to fend for herself.

Married women's fears about the connection between political conflict and family crisis also involved alarm over the sexual lives of daughters. There was a growing sense both that adolescent girls were more likely to become prey to sexually irresponsible men and that such young women would more willingly defy parental restrictions on their sexual lives. Fathers also worried, but because women were left ever-more responsible for campesino households and were already concerned about men's loyalties, women worried more. The Agrarian Reform ethos of youth independence and its encouragement of heterosexual opportunity undercut campesina mothers' sense of parental authority in general and their sense of control over daughters in particular. In oral histories, women recalled that their daughters attended youth functions without parental permission and regularly violated curfews, offering broken down buses or visits to relatives as excuses.[99] Anita Hernández, who had two adolescent daughters in the early 1970s, complained that the university student volunteers set a particularly harmful example for her children because female brigadistas socialized so openly with their male comrades.[100] María Galdámez and Katarina Antimán, also campesina mothers from Santa María county, corroborated the alarm in stories commonly relayed in daily newspapers such as *El Trabajo* and *La Aurora* that young people increasingly smoked cigarettes and marijuana, and that they nosily roamed country roads in the evening, painting estate walls with graffiti.[101] Although newspaper accounts indicated such problem youths as all male, women insisted in oral histories that they included female adolescents as well.

And daughters did challenge their mothers' authority and draw on new ideas about youth culture to justify their actions. In the most dramatic instances, they ran away from home. During the Popular Unity years, the number of home abandonment charges filed by parents in San Felipe against daughters more than doubled as compared to the number under the Christian Democratic administration.[102] As in the late 1950s and early 1960s, most young women seem to have run away in order to override parental opposition to a marriage, but a number of cases now involved girls who temporarily ran away from home for reasons of escape or leisure. Strikingly, these young women testified that they had no intention of marrying the men with whom they fled or of making such flight permanent.

Typical of these instances was seventeen-year-old Luisa Fernández, who ran away from home in September 1972 with her girlfriend, Susana Guerra, also age seventeen, and their *pololos* (boyfriends) to Valparaíso.[103] Fernández's mother accused the boyfriends of abducting the girls in order to have sex with them and otherwise "have a good time." But Luisa Fernández and Susana Guerra insisted that they had run away from home because their parents beat them and forbade them to go out with friends. They testified that while they had smoked marijuana on two occasions, they had never had sex with their boyfriends and had not planned to remain in Valparaíso past the end of the month. Similarly, in June 1973, the mother of seventeen-year-old Olivia Contreras filed charges against her daughter for running away to live with her boyfriend Nicanor Urgueta on an asentamiento.[104] The mother requested that the judge either force the couple to marry or demand her daughter's return. Five days later, Olivia Contreras returned home, stating that she had gone to the asentamiento just for a party and that, although she had had sex with her friend, she did not have a relationship with him. Her mother agreed to drop the legal request that the couple get married when a doctor determined that Contreras was not pregnant.

In both cases, and others like them, adolescent girls asserted the prerogative to escape parental homes for short-term periods of leisure and casual sexual-romantic liaisons. Mothers objected that such action placed daughters in moral danger and insisted on their right as parents to prohibit sexual activity not directed toward marriage. The young women's actions marked a challenge to contemporary parent-daughter relationships as well as to popular perceptions of the link between female sexuality and male authority. In most home abandonment cases of the late 1950s and the 1960s, daughters escaped parental households by trading parental stewardship of their sexuality for that of a husband. In contrast, by the early 1970s some young women argued that freedom from their parents was not contingent on forming permanent unions with men and that not all heterosexual and romantic activity necessarily had to end in marriage. Young women defended their associations with men in terms of their right to activities independent of parental desires, rather than as a general license to be sexually active. While daughters insisted that heterosexual interactions be decoupled from marriage, they saw freedom from parents rather than freedom with men as the central issue. Whereas these two relationships had been causally linked as a trade-off a half a generation earlier, some young women now maintained their separateness.

Adult campesina women's anxiety about their daughters' sexuality also surfaces in court records involving rape. The number of charges filed against men for rape in the San Felipe courts rose sharply during the Popular Unity years, tripling from an average of five cases between 1964 and 1970 to an average of fifteen cases between 1971 and 1973.[105] As was true of the preceding decade, most rape cases during the late Agrarian Reform years involved very young girls whom parents alleged had been raped by neighbors or strangers. In court, parents substantiated their charges by producing medical evidence of the girl's "deflowering," often arguing that their child was mentally retarded. In contrast, between 1969 and 1973, almost a third of cases involved adolescent girls, many of whom had much more difficulty using the traditional markers of female innocence. In at least three cases, young women denied charges filed by their parents that they had been raped.[106] In 1971, fourteen-year-old Silvia Tapia flatly repudiated her mother's testimony that she had been "kidnapped and raped, but too ashamed to tell." Instead, she told the judge that she had been "going with" the accused for six months "against the wishes of [her mother]," and that the couple had engaged in "voluntary sexual relations" on three occasions.[107]

Young women's negation of rape charges filed on their behalf by parents, most often by mothers, reveals deep disagreements between mothers and daughters over the appropriate sexual behavior of unmarried female adolescents. It also highlights the different meanings that mothers and daughters could attribute to sexual intercourse, and the frustration of some mothers at the inability to control a daughter's sexual conduct. There may have been instances in which parents filed formal rape charges over and above the will of their daughter out of a belief that their child was incapable of denouncing sexual violence. Yet the firm testimony of daughters like Silvia Tapia suggests that parents sometimes appealed to a judge to condemn a young woman's willfully consensual sexual activity. In such instances, parents turned to the courts for an authority that they felt they no longer possessed.

Rape cases in which the alleged victim denied the existence of rape were rare however. A far more common scenario depicted in court records from the late 1960s and early 1970s involved adolescent girls raped by boyfriends or acquaintances with whom they willingly socialized. In such cases, it became almost impossible to establish a young woman's victimhood according to the traditional indicators of virginity, social reclusiveness, and childlike ignorance of men. Instead, any evidence suggesting that a young woman had willingly sought the company of the accused man in other social (and possibly sexual) circumstances immediately compromised her qualification as victim, and, therefore, also her standing as a good daughter.

In June 1973, the mother of fourteen-year-old Elisa Saavedra filed charges of kidnapping and rape on her daughter's behalf against a bus driver and an agricultural worker.[108] In her original testimony, Saavedra's mother claimed that her daughter had been "forced to board a bus by two unknown men" and was taken to the "outskirts of town, held down, and raped." She further testified that her daughter "had never dated," "was not coquettish with men," and had been "so traumatized" by the incident that she did not admit the rape to her mother "until after her soiled underpants were discovered." Over the next two months of court hearings, however, this traditional picture of female victimization became more complicated. Elisa Saavedra herself told the judge that she had "voluntarily boarded the bus," and other passengers testified that the bus had not departed for the "outskirts of town" but, rather, had continued on its route to town "full of people." Saavedra continued to maintain that she had been raped, but altered her mother's story to say that, once in town, the men had "locked her in the bus." Yet this story was undermined when two of her school friends alleged that she was "crazy for young men" and "everybody knew it." Finally, the rape charges were dropped altogether when Saavedra confessed that the men were "not strangers," that she had formerly "gone with" the agricultural worker, and that she had accompanied the men to town "in order to have a drink."

Elisa Saavedra's connection to the accused disqualified her from judicial redress for rape—she could not claim sexual violence at the hands of company she had solicited. Yet one of the most interesting things about cases like Saavedra's is its illustration of the much wider social opportunities enjoyed by rural adolescent girls in the early 1970s, and the problems and anxieties that such opportunities produced. Expanded education options and improved transportation systems enabled by the Agrarian Reform allowed at least some young campesinas the chance to take un-chaperoned trips to town and to pursue heterosexual friendship and romance. "Going to town to have a drink with male friends" would have constituted an almost impossible scenario for an unmarried campesina a generation earlier. Such new forms of socializing also proved problematic. Cultural assumptions that unescorted single women were both sexually vulnerable and sexually available to men persisted alongside new ideas about youth independence. Young women's casual or romantic contact with men could involve danger and violence as well as pleasure. Yet as judicial records indicate, both the courts and many parents refused to recognize that women could be victimized within consensual relationships. This refusal not only placed blame for unwanted advances and sexual violence on young women themselves, it confirmed parental fears that the new opportunities for young people allowed daughters to pursue risky behavior.

Women's fears about daughters' expanded social opportunities were closely wedded to alarm over the increased separation of sexual activity and (men's) marital obligations. Longstanding concerns that sexually active daughters would suffer abuse and/or become material burdens on the young woman's family now combined with suspicions of men's greater sexual irresponsibility and parental loss of control. Daughters not only seemed to move more freely outside of their homes, but they seemed increasingly disinterested in using sexuality to secure marriage. The significant rise in adolescent pregnancy and single motherhood reinforced parental anxiety. By 1972, the number of women giving birth outside marriage in the district of San Felipe had jumped 22 percent from its 1964 level, while the number of unmarried adolescent mothers had also risen by 17 percent.[109] Although the percentage of adolescent girls who married had risen slightly by 1970 and women were marrying at slightly younger ages than they had in the 1960s, the numbers of single adolescent mothers still increased.[110] Given the connection between conjugal unions and most women's ability to benefit from the Agrarian Reform, combined with married women's growing sense of their own husbands' unreliability, daughters appeared at a higher risk of becoming unmarried mothers at precisely the moment marriage seemed ever more vital to a woman's survival.

Gender, Loyalty, and Crisis

Campesina women did not stop supporting the Agrarian Reform. They continued to applaud its redistributive goals and lay claim to its message of gender cooperation. Yet many complained about specific Popular Unity policies, and the enthusiasm of even some of the most pro-UP supporters dimmed as the countryside became wracked with conflict and uncertainty. Campesino men were also deeply divided over the merits of Popular Unity, with over 40 percent openly self-identifying with oppositional unions. Yet women seem to have criticized the UP in proportionally larger numbers than men and, in retrospect, to have lamented the 1970–1973 period more as a time of hardship. This greater female dissatisfaction was a matter of degree whose causes were deeply gendered in origin. It was not a polarized gender division that set rural women's political sensibilities apart from and in opposition to those of rural men's.

In the late 1970s and 1980s, many scholars came to argue that Chilean women opposed Allende, an idea that quickly became conventional wisdom about women generally and that was accepted as an official contributing factor to the UP's overthrow.[111] Yet most studies on the subject focused on voting patterns and centered on urban women. They did not differentiate by class and offered little explanation about where the almost one third of women who did vote for UP candidates fit into the category of "Chilean women." Reliance on electoral records as an indication of political sensibility proves particularly vexed in the case of rural women since, as already noted, for reasons that have more to do with sexism than political alienation, campesinas in the Aconcagua Valley were almost half as likely as men to vote. Moreover, as Lisa Baldez has astutely observed, given that throughout the late 1970s and 1980s the military regime aggressively championed the idea that "women had asked the army to step-in," the scholarly consensus about female opposition to the UP suggests a certain ideological victory by authoritarianism even among the regime's most ardent critics.[112]

But even in the context of how the debate about women and the UP has already been cast, it is worth reiterating that, of those campesina women who did vote in elections between 1970 and 1973, many overwhelmingly supported an accelerated Agrarian Reform. Women's electoral support for the UP, like that of men, significantly increased throughout Allende's tenure. In the 1971 city council elections, 36.7 percent of women in the Aconcagua Valley cast votes for UP candidates— in contrast to the merely 26 percent who had voted for Allende the year before.[113] In rural counties and leftist strongholds such as Catemu and Rinconada, 50 percent of all women who voted did so for the UP (see Table 21).[114] In the 1973 congressional deputy elections, in which Chris-

Table 21 Voting Preference by Gender, City Council Elections, 1971, Aconcagua Valley (in percentages)

County-Region	Popular Unity			Christian Democrat			National		
	M	F	T	M	F	T	M	F	T
San Felipe	39.2	30.6	34.6	27.5	36.9	32.3	16.8	17.7	17.5
Santa María	48.2	36	42.9	17.3	28.9	22.3	25.6	26	25.9
Putaendo	47.8	37.9	43.4	21.9	28.8	25	19.1	25.3	21.9
Catemu	57.8	50.1	54.2	22.3	24.6	23.2	16.9	22.4	19.2
Panquehue	44.5	32.9	39.6	32.2	32.9	32.5	21.4	32.7	26.1
Los Andes	49.4	40.1	44.6	20.3	24.7	22.4	16.8	25.5	21.5
San Esteban	46	32.7	–	22.9	31	26.4	22.9	31.4	26.6
Calle Larga	41.5	32.3	37.5	23.8	27	25.2	28.9	34.9	31.6
Rinconada	58.5	48.8	54.2	14.6	17.5	15.9	26	32.4	28.9
Aconcagua Valley Total	47	36.7	41.9	22.7	29.3	25.8	19.4	24.4	21.9
Aconcagua Valley 1970 Presidential Election	38	26	–	29.8	36.6	–	30	38	–

M=male, F=female, T=total
"Elección Ordinaria de Regidores, 4 de Abril, 1971," DRE.

tian Democrats and the Right ran on a single ticket, 36.2 percent of women in the Aconcagua Valley voted for the UP; in the predominantly rural counties, between 40 and 50 percent of women supported the coalition (see Table 22).[115] Similar results occurred in other rural areas of central Chile.[116] Although rural men's (also increasing) electoral support for the UP continued to outpace that of women, rural female enthusiasm for Popular Unity grew stronger, not weaker, with the acceleration of the Agrarian Reform.

Still, there was a difference. Although both campesino men and women became divided over the UP, campesina women felt proportionally more fearful and antagonistic. And this mattered. If the UP was making gains among women, it was not making them fast enough to win a full majority of the popular vote. While there is no evidence that

Table 22 Voting Preference by Gender, Congressional Elections (Deputies), 1973, Aconcagua Valley (in percentages)

Comuna-Region	Male		Female		Total	
	CD	UP	CD	UP	CD	UP
San Felipe	53.6	41.7	63.8	32.4	58.9	36.9
Curimon	39.5	58	54	43.4	46.3	51.2
Santa María	46.5	50.1	60.8	35.7	52.9	43.7
Putaendo	45.9	51.5	58.3	39	51.6	45.9
Catemu	35.2	61.3	46.3	51.8	39.8	57.3
Panquehue	43.3	53.5	54.3	42.9	47.9	49.1
Los Andes	53	43.9	65.9	32.1	59.6	37.9
San Esteben	41.4	54.2	60.6	37.2	49.7	46.8
Calle Larga	44.7	52.5	57.8	40.1	50.7	46.8
Rinconada	40.1	58.3	53.4	45.4	45.9	52.7
Aconcagua Valley Total	47.8	48.7	61.1	36.2	54.2	42.7
Aconcagua Valley 1970 Presidential Election	–	38	–	26	–	–

CD=Confederación de la Democracia [Christian Democratic–Right alliance]
"Elección Ordinaria Parlamentaria (Diputados), 4 de Marzo, 1973," DRE.

rural women as a group opposed Allende (and even less that they applauded the UP's overthrow), Popular Unity support in the Aconcagua Valley and many other rural areas was more male than female. Campesina women's greater reticence did not spring—as is often inferred by arguments that Chilean women opposed the UP—from a conservatism borne of women's greater religiousity. In Aconcagua, most rural women were not politically conservative nor were they particularly religious. Neither did women's reaction result from the Agrarian Reform "ignoring women." Although certainly men received the bulk of attention and resources, both the Christian Democrats and the UP were concerned with women's civic and political transformation and addressed them as part of the broader project of creating modern campesinos. Instead, rural women's more tepid response to the UP sprang from the ways the Agrarian Reform had actually already addressed them: It had re-figured women's sexual and social vulnerability to men and unequally positioned women and men to participate in the political struggles that reached crisis proportion after Allende's election. Importantly, these unequal gender configurations resulted from policies initiated by Christian Democracy in the 1960s. Although the UP built on the precedent and shared many of its predecessor's assumptions, it also attempted to institute more egalitarian and gender-inclusive policies with regard to women's productive labor, youth education, and political mobilization. That these efforts failed to produce a fundamentally new model does not make Popular Unity the model's sole architect. Because the UP would come to be seen as paying a fatal price for its Agrarian Reform, it would alone be held responsible for what went wrong. But women's marginalization within the Agrarian Reform sprang as much, and arguably more, from the family-centered strategies passionately urged by independent Catholics and Christian Democrats as it did from the Left's inability or unwillingness to imagine different strategies.

Most women in the Aconcagua Valley did not reject the gendered parameters of the Agrarian Reform. In the early 1970s, most women who became more skeptical of the UP did not resent the coalition's failure to make them land recipients or union members, nor did they widely oppose accelerated expropriations. What women feared was the way class conflict threatened certain gender ideals and material benefits that the Agrarian Reform, including the UP version, had created. In both its Christian Democratic and Popular Unity forms, the Agrarian Reform had urged married women to expect husbands to be able providers, respectful partners, and loyal heads of family. Women welcomed this ideal as an improvement on the already existing dynamic of female dependence, and largely did not challenge the fact that Agrarian Reform policies deepened married women's material dependence on men. Wives struggled with men over the meaning of respect and responsibility in husbands rather than over access to land and higher wages themselves. And women enjoyed a certain success. The ethos of gender mutualism emboldened women to object to men's sexual license both within and outside of marriage and to insist on an equivalent fidelity in men's material support. Men's own associations of masculinity with breadwinning often complemented women's interests.

But for men, the ideal of the responsible husband existed in tension with the requirements of other masculine signifiers necessitated and promoted by the Agrarian Reform, including worker militancy, male combativeness, loyalty to fellow men, and a general sexual prowess with women. Conflicts between women and men over the entitlements and meanings of these ideals and their relationship to male family responsibility were negotiated on a daily basis. But during the Popular Unity years, masculine ideals came under extraordinary stress. As men's energies were ever more absorbed by political conflicts away from the household, men's commitment to other men seemed to take precedence over their family commitments, frustrating women's needs at home and fueling a sense of abandonment. Men also felt this rupture, but they were primarily alarmed and consumed by the breakdown in male solidarity. Militancy now privileged combativeness against fellow workers, making loyalty to fellow campesinos only partial. As men were summoned to ever bolder acts of political confrontation, they entered into new alliances against one other. But whereas men assessed the cost of social struggle in terms of the courage to withstand and win fights against other male workers as well as the patrón, women saw the price more ominously in terms of their own men's abandonment, family dysfunction, and an insecure future.

Women's exclusion from the primary vehicles of political struggle heavily shaped their responses. The contentious fullness of men's hugely expanded involvement in unions and Agrarian Reform production units contrasted sharply with most women's social isolation and daily struggles to navigate increasingly fragile and combative relations with neighbors and shopkeepers. Despite the vital and transformative support work women did in CEMAs, women's organizations remained on the margins of the political whirlwind. This was not the case for all women. Female workers, such as those of the Bucalemu conserve factory, occupied private property side-by-side with men; housewives such as those active in the 1968 San Miguel conflict assumed men's roles in political negotiation; and hundreds of women seized land in demands for housing. Many women of course participated in heated debates about strategy and negotiated directly with state authorities and political parties. Likewise, adolescent girls who joined political youth groups or attended agricultural school were positioned to more directly partake in political discussions and actions. But if unions involved up to 90 percent of all campesino men, no equivalent level of institutional incorporation of rural women existed. A majority of women of all generations and marital statuses relied on secondhand information from male family members and neighborhood rumors. Family and neighborhood were far more likely than union or political party to be the spaces in which campesina women experienced and reacted to the ensuing polarization. Women's fears of crisis flowed from a sense that families were being adversely affected by forces beyond women's control at the same time that family continued to be central to female survival and still loudly touted by the UP as the foundation of social uplift.

epilogue   1973–1988

On the afternoon of September 11, 1973, army vehicles rolled into the principal towns of the Aconcagua Valley's nine counties, occupying their municipal plazas. The armed forces had already seized Santiago in a coup that began at dawn and were rapidly gaining control over the rest of Chile. By the time campesinos in San Felipe and Los Andes heard soldiers pounding on their doors, the military had taken thousands of prisoners throughout the country, the National Palace was in flames, and Salvador Allende was dead.[1] The armed invaders of Aconcagua encountered deserted streets and empty fields—there was no overt resistance. Contrary to widely believed rumors that the UP had "armed the masses," the military's furious search of campesino homes and union buildings uncovered only a handful of hunting shotguns and a rifle from Chile's 1890 civil war.[2] Most rural men and women had been advised of the coup by radio and, in fear, had heeded the Supreme Military Junta's declared curfew. A few people scrambled to burn lists of union memberships and to hide leaders and activists.[3] The majority waited in shock.

In an oral history twenty years later, Angélica Sáez, a campesina housewife from Santa María who had spent much of the UP period sympathetic to the Christian Democrats, recalled the day of Allende's overthrow as an epic tragedy for Chile's entire working class. In a gesture common to other interviews with campesinos in the 1990s and illustrative of the new meanings that the Popular Unity project would acquire during the subsequent military dictatorship of the 1970s and 1980s, Sáez recited from memory long parts of Allende's final speech on the morning of the coup in which he spoke prophetically about a coming authoritarianism and passionately about a day when all workers would march down Santiago's principal avenue to create a better world. In a narrative that rearranged the social antagonisms of the early 1970s to elide the bitter political divisions within campesino communities as well as her own opposition to Allende, she proclaimed the traumatic events of September 11 to be exclusively about the triumph of the rich over the poor: "When I heard [Allende's] speech, I knew the time for the poor to have voice and dignity was over. The rich would not allow it. . . . They had come to take away our land. . . . We knew it was over."[4]

It was indeed over, and with it, the Agrarian Reform—not only the UP's experiment with socialism, but Chile's general commitment to empowering the rural poor, begun almost a decade earlier under the Christian Democrats. During the next seventeen years of military rule, campesinos experienced a devastating erosion of the material and political gains won between 1964 and 1973. The military junta immediately returned over one third of expropriated land to former owners and dismantled CERAS and many asentamientos. Agricultural wages plummeted amid a severe recession induced by stiff monetary policies and did not recover their 1972 value until the late 1980s. Nationally, the regime closed congress, censored the press, and imposed martial law; locally, it took over mothers' centers and neighbors' councils, and replaced town councils and mayors with pro-military appointments. Leftist political parties and unions were outlawed as treasonous, and all collective bargaining and strike activity was banned.[5] Known activists and leaders belonging to factions of the UP suffered imprisonment, torture, and, in many cases, death. Even Christian Democratic labor leaders and campesinos who had opposed Allende came under surveillance and persecution. All things working-class, especially organized labor, became suspect in a war to purge Chile of the "Marxist scourge."

Military dictatorship brought authoritarianism to the countryside, but it did not reinstate the old order. Instead of returning to latifundia and inquilinaje, the junta fashioned an agrarian economy according to a radical neoliberal capitalist model based on market efficiency and temporary wage labor.[6] A third of the land in the Reform sector was auctioned to elite and middle-class entrepreneurs who reconstituted it into medium-sized agribusinesses producing luxury crops such as grapes and peaches for export. Another third of the Reform sector land was distributed to individual campesinos in the military's own version of land reform; but in less than a decade, almost three quarters of these peasant farmers were forced to sell their parcels to larger growers due to debts and lack of credit and technical support.[7] Throughout the dictatorship, the junta showed little interest in sustaining small farmers. By the mid-1980s, the structure of fruit production throughout central Chile closely resembled California's agri-industry, and fruit exports constituted Chile's third most important source of foreign revenue. Chile's fruit industry built on the fruit production initiatives sponsored by the Agrarian Reform, but it abandoned the latter's commitment to balancing foreign exports with domestic production. It also redirected proceeds into private hands and decisively restored employers' control over workers.

In the Aconcagua Valley, which quickly became one of Chile's most lucrative fruit regions, a majority of campesinos lost access to land and became dependent on seasonal and badly paid wage labor. By the late 1970s, temporary agricultural jobs outnumbered permanent jobs five to one, and rural unemployment seasonally hovered between 20 and 30 percent. Most remarkably, rural women entered the paid labor force in droves. Sharp declines in campesino household income, combined with the rural poor's heightened dependence on cash wages and the fruit industry's seasonal labor demands, pushed women into gender-specific jobs cleaning and weighing fruit in packing plants, or pruning and harvesting in orchards and vineyards. By the early 1980s, women comprised almost half of Chile's estimated 300,000 temporary fruit workers and numbered roughly 5,000 workers in the Aconcagua Valley.[8]

Increases in women's agricultural employment had begun with the Agrarian Reform's promotion of fruit and vegetable cultivation, but under military rule, women not only entered temporary wage labor in large numbers—temporary work became one of the only means of survival for both men and women. Jobs became more insecure and far more exploitative: employment lasted an average of two to five months. Temporary workers earned below the military's own declared minimum wage, working long shifts without overtime pay and for piecerates that placed the burden of production solely on workers. Employer coercion was commonplace as the military's overt repression of organized labor and the general climate of fear stifled resistance. In all, the soaring productivity of Chilean agriculture—soon hailed as an economic miracle in U.S. financial centers—was built squarely on the hyperexploitation of rural labor and the strangling of democratic institutions.

The changes under dictatorship struck at the heart of all that the Agrarian Reform had sought to accomplish. They were particularly devastating for campesino men. The Agrarian Reform's masculine ideal of political agency, productive independence, and patriarchal duty became absurd. Not only did the campesino man not become his own patrón; in most cases he lost all claims to land and acquired a new employer-boss who controlled workers with impunity. The repression of rural unions smashed the vehicles by which working-class men had challenged the authority of elite men, participated in national politics, and fostered a sense of masculine camaraderie and class militancy. In the weeks immediately following the coup, police sacked union halls and set fire to asentamiento banners proclaiming liberated territory. The rural strikes and land occupations so symbolic of campesino men's growing leverage between 1964 and 1973 disappeared overnight, as did the pro-worker stance of labor tribunals and government functionaries. The daily excitement of incessant meetings and negotiations gave way to a somber and isolated routine of going to work, appeasing employers, and avoiding activities that could be construed as political. In 1993, Armando Gómez, the former union leader from Putaendo county, reflected on the disparity between his life before and after Allende's overthrow. He equated the dictatorship's assault on rural labor with the loss of manhood: "[Military rule] broke us and reduced us to infants."[9]

Beyond the erasure of workers' political power, such infantilization was, for many rural men, closely linked to the fruit industry's impact on their work and the roles of women. The Agrarian Reform's ideal of men providing for wives and children withered in the 1970s and 1980s as temporary jobs replaced permanent ones, wages fell, seasonal demand for women's labor rose, and campesino households became dependent on female as well as male breadwinning. The very meaning of work radically shifted from a positive association with masculine self-realization and empowerment to a symbol of men's degradation and women's exploitation.

But shared hardships suggested new kinds of gender parity and a decrease in some forms of male control over women.[10] Women's shifts in fruit packing plants, which often lasted late into the night, eroded husbands' ability to curtail and monitor women's activities outside the home and resulted in some minimal male responsibility for childcare and meal preparation during women's absences. Employment in the fruit industry also gave women more direct control over household budgets since women workers usually insisted on retaining control over at least part of their wages, however inadequate. Women played prominent roles negotiating their families' survival within a burgeoning consumer economy fostered by the military's dramatic tariff reductions and the poor's growing reliance on cash income. They frequently made financial decisions without prior male consent. All of this fostered men's sense that they had become less materially essential to women than before—that "worker" could no longer serve as the basis for an exclusive masculine identity or "wages" the means by which men ensured female loyalty. Rumors about female fruit workers' sexual promiscuity abounded and domestic fights about sex increasingly focused around men's accusations of women's affairs and women's criticisms of men's failure to earn enough money. The basis of male authority over women was thrown into question.[11]

But military rule hardly liberated rural women. If the Agrarian Reform had empowered men more than women, most campesina women had materially and politically benefited in ways that became painfully clear in the immediate aftermath of the coup. Popular Unity's fall did not bring polarized communities closer together; it accelerated their fragmentation. If some women (as well as men) were momentarily relieved that the coup ended painful fights between neighbors over politics, they received little solace from the harsh reality that police and army officials now regularly harassed and detained any campesino/a, regardless of past political activities, or that some neighbors sought self-protection or retaliation by reporting one another to the authorities. The military takeover of mothers' centers ended women's ability to collectively address problems on a gender-specific basis and to be politically active as women. Although women's incorporation into politics during the Agrarian Reform had been far weaker than that of men, the onset of military rule made women's lives even more politically isolated.

The impossibility of realizing the Agrarian Reform's vision of domesticity also hurt women. Many campesinas had come to expect that their husbands would be the family's principal economic provider and that rising rural wages and access to land would yield ever higher standards of living. Although this ideal had ignored the needs of single women and reinforced female dependence, most campesinas had welcomed the economic empowerment of men as benefiting families and easing tensions within marriage. If the Agrarian Reform had bolstered men's sexual authority over women, it had also validated women's contributions to society and provided an ideal, if not always a practice, of mutual respect and curbs on male power.

Under military rule, women's greater access to paid work in the fruit industry was part of an economy that impoverished campesino families and made daily life for both men and women more difficult and unstable. Despite some men's modest participation in domestic labor, the vast majority of childcare and household work still fell to women, creating exhausting double burdens. Men's loss of land and permanent jobs greatly strained marital relationships and spurred male seasonal migration to other parts of the country, increasing incidences of men's home abandonment. By 1986, over 25 percent of households in Aconcagua were headed by women, almost triple the level of 1970.[12] Women's own low wages and only short terms of annual employment in the fruit industry made the survival of single and separated women extremely precarious. If women's ability to earn cash wages gave them heightened bargaining power in their relationships with male family members, it did so under increasingly difficult material conditions.

Moreover, jobs inside the fruit industry were oppressive. Female workers in the packing plants underwent far closer supervision than did male workers, most of whom labored in orchards or vineyards. During peak season, packing shifts lasted up to sixteen hours. Women labored standing, with minimal breaks and inadequate meals. They were subjected to humiliating pregnancy tests and fired when a pregnancy was discovered. Exposure to pesticides and toxic gases escalated incidences of miscarriage, stillborn children, and birth defects. Sexual harassment and threats from employers and supervisors were commonplace. If access to work widened some women's opportunities beyond those of the Agrarian Reform, it hardly freed them from sexual coercion or male dominance.

But women's entry into wage work nonetheless profoundly altered campesino gender dynamics and positioned women to play prominent roles negotiating the contours of authoritarian rule. The Agrarian Reform's legacy proved important to women's agency in both.[13] As the ideal of the male breadwinner gave way to the necessity of female wage work, women laid their own claims to the worker radicalism of the 1960s and early 1970s. Women fruit workers took pride in their labor, despite its acute exploitation, and welcomed the camaraderie that packing plant jobs afforded with female (and male) coworkers. They similarly valued their ability to provide crucial income to families. As had men during the Agrarian Reform, women linked their wages to certain rights in financial decisions at home as well as to a more general sense of authority within the household and limited autonomy outside of it.

Women's sense of themselves as workers, and the entitlements this implied, fused with older notions of reciprocity, particularly the Agrarian Reform's vision of gender mutualism. When wives defended to husbands their choice to spend wages on a kitchen pot or children's clothing (and occasionally on a lipstick or a pair of stockings), they did so not only as workers, who should have control over their wages, but as women, whose labor and decisions men should respect. When women returned home late from a work shift or socialized with friends at weekend dance functions and soccer games, they countered the sometimes jealous reactions of male family members with reminders that, as workers, they had earned some respite, and that, as women, they should share with men in the modest leisure of rural life. Gender relations were certainly not equal, and the need to renegotiate rights and obligations caused heightened, sometimes violent, conflict between men and women. But the relative parity in men and women's labor, and women's ability to re-articulate Agrarian Reform notions of worker entitlement and gender mutualism, eroded important parts of the patriarchal authority that the Agrarian Reform's promotion of male-headed households had sustained.

Women's ability to re-articulate the Agrarian Reform's legacy also proved crucial to challenging the realities of dictatorship. Despite the repression of rural labor organizing, the Aconcagua Valley in the late 1980s was a site of open resistance to the fruit industry's exploitative conditions and, by implication, to the military regime. Women's resurrection of the common pots that had sustained worker militancy during the strikes and land occupations of the Agrarian Reform emerged as one of the first displays of defiance. In the 1980s, common pots were established with backing from the Catholic Church to help provide meals for fruit workers' families during the winter months of unemployment. Beyond their practical function, they symbolized the denunciation of the military's economic "miracle" and provided one of the few spaces where workers could safely gather in groups to discuss their plight. Common pots evoked the class solidarity of the 1960s and early 1970s, but centered around female, rather than male, action.

Women also took direct action against fruit industry employers. In the mid-1980s, women fruit workers in the Aconcagua Valley carried out several successful lightening strikes.[14] Grievances focused on unacceptable working conditions (supervision in the bathroom, rancid sandwich meat served in packing plant cafeterias) as well as systemic exploitation (low piecerates, production quotas). Appealing directly to managers in ways reminiscent of male campesinos' petitions to landowners in the early 1960s, women argued that they deserved dignity as workers and adequate compensation as providers for families. In the dictatorship's final year of 1989, women from Santa María county surmounted the prohibitive obstacles imposed by the military's 1979 Labor Code by joining with male workers to form Chile's first union of temporary fruit workers. Women comprised over half of the union's five-hundred-plus membership, and two women served on the five-person executive council.[15] In oblique reference to the Agrarian Reform as well as to anti-dictatorship sentiments, the union's mission statement pledged to unite workers and strive for a just society.

Such activism faced huge limits. Unlike the male labor movement of the Agrarian Reform, the Santa María union had a fierce enemy, rather than a willing ally, in the national state. It struggled under a cloud of intimidation that fully legitimated employer prerogative over workers, rather than under a mandate to create a "revolution in liberty" or "constitutional socialism." The Santa María union forced few, if any, significant structural changes in the fruit industry, and, nationwide, the power of the rural labor movement remained weak. The Agrarian Reform's most fundamental goal—redistributing land—no longer even figured as part of rural workers' demands. Illustrative of the military's ideological victory, by the 1980s, this seemed unimaginable.

But worker activism in the Aconcagua Valley was highly meaningful. It marked radical shifts in women and men's understanding of themselves as workers as well as the transformation of the Agrarian Reform's masculinist rural union tradition into a labor movement decidedly more gender-inclusive.[16] Women's involvement in the Santa María union was crucial to this process. At union meetings and events, women raised issues specific to the situation of female workers—night shifts, lack of day care, pregnancy tests, sexual harassment—and stressed the importance of non-workplace-based struggles for housing and food. These emphases served as a model for nationally reinvigorating the rural labor movement that reemerged from clandestinity in the mid-1980s, eager to mobilize an increasingly female labor force and attracted to issues not directly aimed at employers.[17]

Women in Santa María also challenged union sexism. Drawing on the Agrarian Reform's tradition of union democracy and the language of broader antidictatorship struggles, they argued that women's prominence within the fruit industry be reflected in female leadership within the union, not just rank-and-file membership. Invoking the older logic of gender mutualism, women called for greater male respect for working women and criticized the machismo of husbands who refused to allow wives to attend union meetings.[18] Combating male dominance, they suggested, should be a central part of union struggle.

Women made connections between their current situation as workers under authoritarianism and an older political culture that had stressed justice, solidarity, and egalitarianism. They laid claim to a labor movement that had previously excluded them, and in doing so, redefined that movement for their own times. If the Agrarian Reform had meant unequal uplift for men and women, many of its goals became crucial to surviving and resisting military rule in more equitable ways. It would remain vital to rebuilding democracy once the dictatorship was over.

notes

Introduction

1 For example, see Jacques Chonchol, *El Desarrollo de América Latina y la reforma agraria* (Santiago de Chile: Editorial del Pacífico, 1964); Pablo Ramírez, *Cambio de las formas de pago a la mano de obra agrícola* (Santiago de Chile: Instituto de Capacitación e Investigación en Reforma Agraria 1968); Raúl Atria Benaprés, "Actitudes y valores del campesino en relación a las aldeas de la reforma agraria," *Cuaderno de sociología* 2 (1969); David Alaluf et al., *Reforma agraria chilena: Seis ensayos de interpretación* (Santiago de Chile: Instituto Capacitación e Investigación Reforma Agraria, 1970); Jaime Gazmuri, *Asentamientos campesinos: Una Evaluación de los primeros resultados de la reforma agraria en Chile* (Buenos Aires: Ediciones Troquel, 1970); Solon Barraclough and Almino Affonso, *Critical Appraisal of the Chilean Agrarian Reform* (Santiago de Chile: Instituto de Capacitación e Investigación en Reforma Agraria, 1972); Solon Barraclough et al., *Chile: Reforma agraria y gobierno popular* (Buenos Aires: Ediciones Periferia, 1973); Solon Barraclough and José Antonio Fernández, eds., *Diagnóstico de la reforma agraria chilena* (Mexico City: Siglo Veintiuno Editores, 1974); Hugo Ortega Tello, *Efectos de la reforma agraria sobre las técnicas de producción, 1965–1970* (Santiago de Chile: Centro de Estudios de Planificación Nacional, Universidad Católica, 1975).

2 See William C. Thiesenhusen, *Chile's Experiment in Agrarian Reform* (Madison: Univ. of Wisconsin Press, 1966); Robert R. Kaufman, *The Chilean Political Right and Agrarian Reform* (Washington, D.C.: Institute for the Comparative Study of Political Systems, 1965); and Kaufman, *The Politics of Land Reform in Chile, 1950–1970* (Cambridge, Mass.: Harvard Univ. Press, 1972); F. Broughton, "Chile: Land Reform and Agricultural Development" (Ph.D. diss., University of Liverpool, 1970); Wayne Ringlen, "Economic Effects of Chilean National Expropriation Policy on the Private Commer-

cial Farm Sector, 1964–1969" (Ph.D. diss., University of Maryland, 1971); James Petras and Robert LaPorte Jr., *Cultivating the Revolution: The United States and Agrarian Reform in Latin America* (New York: Random House, 1971); Clifford Smith, ed., *Studies in Latin American Agrarian Reform* (Liverpool: Centre for Latin American Studies, 1974).

One of the largest sets of studies on Chile's Agrarian Reform by U.S.-based scholars was coordinated through the University of Wisconsin's Land Tenure Center (LTC). For example, see William Thiesenhusen, *The Possibility of Gradualist Turnover of Land in Agrarian Reform Programs in Chile* (Madison: LTC, 1966); Thiesenhusen, *Grassroots Economic Pressures in Chile: An Enigma for Development Planners* (Madison: LTC, 1968); University of Wisconsin Land Tenure Center, *Chile's Experiments in Agrarian Reform* (Madison: LTC, 1967); Terry McCoy, *The Politics of Structural Change in Latin America: The Case of Agrarian Reform in Chile* (Madison: LTC, 1969); David Stanfield, *Methodological Notes on Evaluating the Impact of Agrarian Reform in Chile's Central Valley* (Santiago de Chile: LTC, 1973); David Stanfield and Marion Brown, *Projecto de cámbios socio-economicos en cien prédios del sector rural en Chile* (Santiago de Chile: LTC, n.d.); Tom Bossert and David Stanfield, *The Role of Participation and Campesino Consciousness in the Chilean Agrarian Reform* (Madison: LTC, 1974).

3 Barraclough and Fernández, *Diagnóstico;* José Bengoa, *Historia del movimiento campesino* (Santiago de Chile: Grupo de Investigacíones agrarias, 1983); Jorge Echeníque, *La Reforma agraria chilena* (Mexico City: Siglo Veintiuno Editores, 1975); Sergio Gómez, *Los Empresarios agrícolas* (Santiago de Chile: Instituto de Capacitación e Investigación en Reforma Agraria, 1972); Gómez, *Organizaciones rurales y estructura agraria* (Santiago de Chile: Facultad Latinoamericana de Ciencias Sociales, 1981); Gómez, "Los Campesinos beneficados por la reforma agraria chilena: Antecedentes, diferenciación, y percepción campesina," *Estudios rurales latinoamericanos* 4 (1981): 69–88; Brian Loveman, *Struggle in the Countryside: Politics and Rural Labor in Chile, 1919–1973* (Bloomington: Indiana Univ. Press, 1976); Kyle Steeland, *Agrarian Reform under Allende: Peasant Revolt in the South* (Albuquerque: Univ. of New Mexico Press, 1977); Ian Roxborough, "The Political Mobilization of Farm Workers during the Chilean Agrarian Reform, 1971–1973: A Case Study" (Ph.D. diss., University of Wisconsin-Madison, 1977); Ian Roxborough, Philip O'Brien, and Jackie Roddick, *Chile: The State and Revolution* (New York: Holmes and Meir, 1977); Peter Winn and Cristóbal Kay, "Agrarian Reform and Rural Revolution in Allende's Chile," *Journal of Latin American Studies* 6, no. 1 (1974): 135–59; Cristóbal Kay, "Agrarian Reform and the Class Struggle in Chile," *Latin American Perspectives* 18 (1978): 117–37. Also see James Petras and Hugo Zemelman Merino, *Peasants in Revolt* (Austin: Univ. of Texas Press, 1972); Peter Marchett, "Workers Participa-

tion and Class Conflict in Worker-Managed Farms: The Rural Question in Chile, 1970–1973" (Ph.D. diss., University of Michigan, 1977).

4 For more recent overviews of the scholarship on Chile's Agrarian Reform, see José Garrido, ed., *Historia de la reforma agraria en Chile* (Santiago de Chile: Editorial Universitaria, 1988); María Antonieta Huerta, *Otro agro para Chile: Historia de la reforma agraria en el proceso social y político* (Santiago de Chile: CISEC-CESOC, 1989); Cristóbal Kay and Patricio Silva, eds., *Development and Social Change in the Chilean Countryside: From the Pre-land Reform Period to the Democratic Transition* (Amsterdam: CEDLA, 1992). For comparative evaluations of agrarian reforms throughout Latin America, see William C. Thiesenhusen, *Broken Promises: Agrarian Reform and the Latin American Campesino* (Boulder, Colo.: Westview, 1995); Cristóbal Kay, "El Fin de la reforma agraria en América Latina? El Legado de la reforma agraria y el asunto no resuelto de la tierra," *Revista Mexicana de Sociología* 60, no. 4 (1998): 61–98.

5 Patricia Garrett, "Growing Apart: The Experiences of Rural Men and Women in Central Chile" (Ph.D. diss., University of Wisconsin-Madison, 1978); and Garrett, "La Reforma agraria, organización popular y participación de la mujer en Chile," in *Las Trabajadoras del agro: Debate sobre la mujer en América Latina y el Caribe*, ed., Magdalena León (Bogota: Asociación Columbiana para el Estudio de la Poblacion, 1982); Ximena Valdés S., *Mujer, trabajo y medio ambiente: Los Nudos de la modernización agraria* (Santiago de Chile: Centro de Estudios de la Mujer, 1992).

6 Other studies of rural women conducted in the 1960s and early 1970s likewise highlighted the Agrarian Reform's gender disparities. See Armand and Michèle Mattelart, *La Mujer chilena en una nueva sociedad Un Estudio exploratorio acerca de la Situación e imagen de la mujer en Chile*, trans. Isabel Budge de Ducci (Santiago de Chile: Editorial del Pacífico, 1968); M. Ferrada and Y. Navarro, "Actitúd del hombre y la mujer campesinos frente a la participación de la mujer en cooperativas campesinas" (master's thesis, Escuela de Trabajo Social, Universidad Católica, Santiago de Chile, 1968); M. A. Giróz and A. M. López, "Evaluación del proceso de integración de la mujer campesina en las organizaciones de base, cooperativas y sindicatos" (master's thesis, Escuela de Trabajo Social, Universidad Católica, Santiago de Chile, 1969).

7 Garrett, "Growing Apart," 255.

8 Carmen Diana Deere and Magdalena León, eds., *La Mujer y la política agraria en América Latina* (Mexico City: Siglo Veintiuno Editores, 1986); and Deere and León, eds., *Rural Women and State Policy: Feminist Perspectives on Latin American Agricultural Development* (Boulder, Colo.: Westview, 1987).

9 For examples of early optimistic analyses of socialism's possibilities for women, see Ruth Sidel, *Women and Childcare in China* (Baltimore: Pen-

guin, 1972); Sheila Rowbotham, *Women, Resistance, and Revolution* (New York: Vintage, 1974); Margaret Randall, *Examen de la opresión y la liberación de la mujer* (Bogota: América Latina, 1976); Claudie Broyelle, *Women's Liberation in China* (Atlantic Highlands, N.J.: Humanities Press, 1977); Nicole Murray, "Socialism and Feminism: Women and the Cuban Revolution," *Feminist Review* (1979): 57–73, 99–106; Margaret Randall and Lynda Yanz, eds., *Sandino's Daughters* (Vancouver: New Star, 1981).

10   For critiques of socialist projects and their attitudes toward rural women, see Norma Diamond, "Collectivization, Kinship, and the Status of Women in Rural China," *Bulletin of Concerned Asian Scholars* 7, no. 1 (1975): 25–32; Kay Ann Johnson, *Women, the Family, and Peasant Revolution in China* (Chicago: Univ. of Chicago Press, 1983); Judith Stacey, *Patriarchy and Socialist Revolution in China* (Berkeley: Univ. of California Press, 1983); Elisabeth Croll, *Women and Rural Development in China* (Geneva: International Labor Office, 1985); Susan Bridger, *Women in the Soviet Countryside* (New York: Cambridge Univ. Press, 1987); Laura Enríquez, *Harvesting Change: Labor and Agrarian Reform in Nicaragua* (Chapel Hill: Univ. of North Carolina Press, 1991); Beatrice Farnsworth and Lynne Viola, eds., *Russian Peasant Women* (New York: Oxford Univ. Press, 1992); Margaret Randall, *Gathering Rage: The Failure of Twentieth-Century Revolutions to Develop a Feminist Agenda* (New York: Monthly Review, 1992); Elizabeth Wood, *Baba and the Comrade: Gender and Politics in Revolutionary Russia* (Bloomington: Indiana Univ. Press, 1997); Aviva Chomsky and Aldo Lauria-Santiago, eds., *Identity and Struggle at the Margins of the Nation-State: The Laboring Peoples of Central America and the Hispanic Caribbean* (Durham, N.C.: Duke Univ. Press, 1998.)

11   Delia David, *Woman-Work: Women and the Party in Revolutionary China* (Oxford: Clarendon, 1976); Vivienne Shue, *Peasant China in Transition: The Dynamics of Development toward Socialism, 1949–1956* (Berkeley: Univ. of California Press, 1980); Bridger, *Women in the Soviet Countryside;* Roberta Manning, "Women in the Soviet Countryside on the Eve of World War II, 1935–1940," in *Russian Peasant Women,* ed., Farnsworth and Viola, 206–35.

12   Beatrice Farnsworth, "Village Women Experience the Revolution," in *Russian Peasant Women,* ed., Farnsworth and Viola, 145–66; Lynne Viola, "Bab'i Bunty and Peasant Women's Protest during Collectivization," in *Russian Peasant Women,* ed. Farnsworth and Viola, 189–205; Muriel Nazarri, "The Woman Question in Cuba: Material Constraints on Its Solution," *Signs* 9, no. 2 (1983): 246–63; Maxine Molyneux, "Mobilization without Emancipation: Women's Interests and the State in Nicaragua," *Feminist Studies* 11, no. 2 (1985): 227–54; and Molyneux, "The Politics of Abortion in Nicaragua: Revolutionary Pragmatism or Feminism in the Realm of Necessity?" *Feminist Review* 29, no. 17 (1988): 114–31.

13   Stacey, *Patriarchy and Socialist Revolution.*

14 One scholar has recently challenged the thesis put forth by Stacey and others. See Neil Diamant, *Revolutionizing the Family: Politics, Love, and Divorce in Urban and Rural China, 1949–1968* (Berkeley: Univ. of California Press, 2000).

15 Susan K. Besse, *Restructuring Patriarchy: The Modernization of Gender Inequality in Brazil, 1914–1940* (Chapel Hill: Univ. of North Carolina Press, 1996). Mary Kay Vaughan, "Modernizing Patriarchy: State Policies, Rural Households, and Women in Mexico, 1930–1940," in *Hidden Histories of Gender and the State in Latin America*, ed. Elizabeth Dore and Maxine Molyneux (Durham, N.C.: Duke Univ. Press, 2000); and Vaughan, *Cultural Politics in Revolution: Teachers, Peasants, and Schools in Mexico, 1930–1940* (Tucson: Univ. of Arizona Press, 1997).

16 Ester Boserup, *Women's Role in Economic Development* (New York: St. Martin's, 1970).

17 For examples of other scholars of the Chinese and Russian revolutions who deal with changes in marriage dynamics, see Bridger, *Women in the Soviet Countryside;* Farnsworth and Viola, eds., *Russian Peasant Women;* Johnson, *Women, the Family and Peasant Revolution;* Diamond, "Collectivization, Kinship and the Status of Women"; Wood, *Baba and Comrade;* David, *Woman-Work;* Shue, *Peasant China.*

18 This consideration of sexuality draws on earlier feminist materialist discussions of sexuality. See various essays in Annette Kuhn and AnnMarie Wolpe, eds., *Feminism and Materialism: Women and Modes of Production* (London: Routledge and Paul, 1978); Christine Delphy, *Close to Home: A Materialist Analysis of Women's Oppression*, trans. and ed. Diana Leonard (London: Hutchinson, 1984); Michèle Barrett, *Women's Oppression Today: Problems in Marxist Feminist Analysis* (London: Verso, 1980); Carole Pateman, *The Sexual Contract* (Stanford, Calif.: Stanford Univ. Press, 1988).

19 For example, see Steve J. Stern, *The Secret History of Gender: Women, Men, and Power in Late Colonial Mexico* (Chapel Hill: Univ. of North Carolina Press, 1995); Besse, *Restructuring Patriarchy;* Eileen Findlay, *Imposing Decency: The Politics of Sexuality and Race in Puerto Rico, 1870–1920* (Durham, N.C.: Duke Univ. Press, 1999); Ximena Valdés S. and Kathya Araujo K., *Vida privada: Modernización agraria y modernidad* (Santiago de Chile: CEDEM, 1999); Sueann Caulfield, *In Defense of Honor: Sexual Morality, Modernity, and Nation in Early-Twentieth-Century Brazil* (Durham, N.C.: Duke Univ. Press, 2000); Dore and Molyneux, eds., *Hidden Histories of Gender;* Karin Alejandra Rosemblatt, *Gendered Compromises: Political Cultures and the State in Chile, 1920–1950* (Chapel Hill: Univ. of North Carolina Press, 2000).

20 For example, see John D. French and Daniel James, eds., *The Gendered Worlds of Latin American Women Workers: From Household and Factory to the Union Hall and Ballot Box* (Durham, N.C.: Duke Univ. Press, 1997); Thomas

Miller Klubock, *Contested Communities: Class, Gender, and Politics in Chile's El Teniente Copper Mine, 1904–1948* (Durham, N.C.: Duke Univ. Press, 1998); Ann Farnsworth-Alvear, *Dulcinea in the Factory: Myths, Morals, Men, and Women in Colombia's Industrial Experiment, 1905–1960* (Durham, N.C.: Duke Univ. Press, 2000); Elizabeth Quay Hutchison, *Labors Appropriate to Their Sex: Gender, Labor, and Politics in Urban Chile, 1900–1930* (Durham, N.C.: Duke Univ. Press, 2001).

21 For example, see Johnson, *Women, the Family, and Peasant Revolution;* Stacey, *Patriarchy and Socialist Revolution;* Molyneaux, "Mobilization without Emancipation."

22 For example, see Stern, *The Secret History of Gender;* Besse, *Restructuring Patriarchy;* Findlay, *Imposing Decency;* Caulfield, *In Defense of Honor;* Dore and Molyneaux, eds., *Hidden Histories of Gender;* Rosemblatt, *Gendered Compromises.*

23 This distinction was first emphasized by Joan Scott in Joan Wallach Scott, *Gender and the Politics of History* (New York: Columbia Univ. Press, 1988).

24 Vaughan, "Modernizing Patriarchy," 195, and *Culture and Revolution.* The historical literature on hegemony and state power is large. See Antonio Gramsci, *Selections from the Prison Notebooks,* ed. and trans. Quintin Hoare and Geoffrey Nowell Smith (London: Lawrence and Wishart, 1971); Philip Corrigan and Derek Sayer, *The Great Arch: English State Formation as Cultural Revolution* (Oxford: Blackwell, 1985); Gilbert M. Joseph and Daniel Nugent, eds., *Everyday Forms of State Formation: Revolution and the Negotiation of Rule in Modern Mexico* (Durham, N.C.: Duke Univ. Press, 1994); Ana María Alonso, *Thread of Blood: Colonialism, Revolution, and Gender on Mexico's Northern Frontier* (Tucson: Univ. of Arizona Press, 1995); Florencia E. Mallon, *Peasant and Nation: The Making of Postcolonial Mexico and Peru* (Berkeley: Univ. of California Press, 1995); Klubock, *Contested Communities;* Rosemblatt, *Gendered Compromises.*

25 Aconcagua province's third department is Petorca, which lies outside the Aconcagua Valley and is not considered in this study.

26 In 1993 Chile formally opened a government archive for the twentieth century, Archivo Siglo XX, which includes records for the post-1960 period. However, this archive was still in formation in 1991 and 1992 when I carried out most of the research for this project. Ministerial records from the departments of labor, agriculture, housing, and economy have since been made available and will undoubtedly yield much useful information on the Agrarian Reform.

27 In the 1980s and early 1990s, ministerial records from the entire twentieth century were housed in a warehouse at San Alfonso, Santiago.

28 At the time this book was researched, CORA's records were housed at the

Sociedad de Agricultura y Ganado (SAG), a subdivision of the Ministry of Agriculture.

29 Research was conducted at the Ministerio de Salud and Chile's national health organization, the Sociedad Nacional de Salud. Some records for the Instituto de Desarrollo de Agricultura (INDAP), the major campesino education agency, were found at the Ministry of Agriculture. Records for campesino community organizations and mothers' centers promoted by Promoción Popular were found at the Ministry of Housing and Office of the Presidency. Studies and documents published by the Instituto de Capacitación e Investigaciones en Reforma Agraria (ICIRA) were also abundantly used.

30 Research was conducted at the Catholic agencies Instituto Pastoral Rural (INPRU), the Instituto de Educación Rural (IER), and the Obizpado de San Felipe.

31 This included the nongovernmental organizations Asociación de Protección de la Familia (APROFA); Centro de Estudios de la Mujer (CEM); Facultad Latinoamericana de Ciéncias Sociales (FLACSO); Grupo de Investigaciones Agrarias (GIA); ISIS International; and Programa de Economía y Trabajo (PET). University libraries consulted included those of the Universidad Católica and of the Universidad de Chile.

32 The various newspapers listed in the bibliography are located at the Biblioteca Nacional, Santiago.

33 I read criminal case court records from the Aconcagua Valley at the Juzgado de Crimen, San Felipe. Birth and baptism records were read at the Registro Civil, San Felipe and Santa María parishes.

34 Because my interviews were conducted in the immediate aftermath of military dictatorship and dealt with leftist politics as well as deeply personal stories, as a matter of course I told campesino informants that I would use a pseudonym when referring to their testimony in my written text. By the time this book went to print, almost a decade after the interviews, many informants would probably not have objected to the use of their real names and may have actually welcomed it, but it was impractical for me to recontact all of them about this issue. I therefore honor my original policy.

35 See Hayden White, *The Content of Form: Narrative Discourse and Historical Representation* (Baltimore: Johns Hopkins Univ. Press, 1987); James Clifford, *The Predicament of Culture: Twentieth-Century Ethnography, Literature, and Art* (Cambridge, Mass.: Harvard Univ. Press, 1988).

36 See Richard Bauman, *Story, Performance and Event: Contexual Studies and Oral Narrative* (New York: Cambridge Univ. Press, 1986); Luisa Passerini, *Fascism in Popular Memory: The Cultural Experience of the Turin Working Class,* trans. Robert Lumley and Jude Bloomfield (New York: Cambridge Univ. Press,

1987); Marie-Francoise Changrault-Duchet, "Narrative Structures, Social Models, and Symbolic Representation in the Life Story," in *Women's Words: The Feminist Practice of Oral History,* ed., Sherna Berger Gluck and Daphne Patai (New York: Routledge, 1991), 77–93; Alessandro Portelli, *The Death of Luigi Trastulli, and Other Stories: Form and Meaning in Oral History* (Albany: State Univ. of New York Press, 1991); Charlotte Linde, *Life Stories: The Creation of Coherence* (Oxford: Oxford Univ. Press, 1993); George M. Gugelberger, ed., *The Real Thing: Testimonial Discourse and Latin America* (Durham, N.C.: Duke Univ. Press, 1996); Farnsworth-Alvear, *Dulcinea in the Factory;* Daniel James, *Doña María's Story: Life History, Memory, and Political Identity* (Durham, N.C.: Duke Univ. Press, 2000).

chapter 1. *Patrón* and *Peón*

1 Instituto Nacional de Estadísticas (INE), *Censo de población: Aconcagua, 1960,* Cuadro 18.

2 According to a prominent study conducted by the Comité Interamericano de Desarrollo Agrícola (CIDA) and used to evaluate conditions for the Agrarian Reform, workers in Aconcagua were employed between forty and sixty days longer per year than workers elsewhere in central and southern Chile (CIDA, *Chile: Tenencia de la tierra y desarrollo socio-economico del sector agrícola* (1966, Cuadro XII-4, 183).

3 INE, *Censo de población: Aconcagua, 1960.*

4 For details on the impoverishment of rural households in Aconcagua, see Armand Mattelart, *Altas social de las comunas de Chile* (Santiago de Chile: Editorial del Pacifico, 1965).

5 According to the CIDA study, annual per capita incomes in central Chile in 1960 ranged from 4,492 escudos for the upper class to 331 escudos for agricultural workers (CIDA, *Chile: Tenencia de la tierra,* Cuadro IV-4, 33).

6 Arnold Bauer, *Chilean Rural Society from the Spanish Conquest to 1930* (Cambridge: Cambridge Univ. Press, 1975).

7 INE, *Censo agropecuario: Aconcagua, 1954–1955,* Cuadro 1 and 4.

8 Ibid.

9 According to Mario Góngora, Chilean inquilinaje has its origins in the colonial *merced* (a land grant) rather than in the *encomienda* (a grant to indigenous labor); but inquilinaje shared much with encomienda in that inquilinos were obliged to provide labor to their land's actual owners (Mario Góngora, *Origen de los "inquilinos" en Chile Central* [Santiago de Chile: Universidad de Chile, Seminario Historia Colonial, 1960]).

10 Código Laboral, 1931, art. 79.

11 According to CIDA's study, inquilinos in central Chile received only 13 percent of their earnings as a cash wage in the 1950s (CIDA, *Chile: Tenencia de la tierra,* Cuadro VIO-12, 59).

12 Inquilinos who had regalías between five and twenty hectares were technically classified as *inquilino-medieros* (from the Spanish word "half") whose labor arrangement was similar to sharecroppers in the southern United States.

13 Bauer, *Chilean Rural Society;* José Bengoa, *Historia social de la agricultura chilena* (Santiago de Chile: Edicones Sur, 1990).

14 This is the central argument put forth by Brian Loveman. See Loveman, *Struggle in the Countryside;* and Loveman, *Chile: The Legacy of Hispanic Capitalism* (New York: Oxford Univ. Press, 1988).

15 Loveman, *Struggle in the Countryside,* 197.

16 On the development of Chile's rural labor legislation, see Loveman, *Struggle in the Countryside;* Almino Affonso et al., *Movimiento campesino chileno* (Santiago de Chile: Instituto de Capitacion e Investigación en Reforma Agraria, 1970); Jean Carriere, *Land Owners and Politics in Chile: A Study of the Sociedad Nacional de Agricultura* (Amsterdam: Centrum Voor Studie en Documentatie van Latins-Amerika, 1981).

17 INE *Censo agropecuario: Aconcagua, 1964–1965,* Cuadro 6.3.

18 Ibid. For purposes of clarity, this book refers to both temporary and occasional workers as "seasonal" workers, as distinct from "permanent" and "inquilino" laborers.

19 Ibid.

20 On the demographic composition and labor obligations of permanent, temporary, and occasional workers, see CIDA, *Chile: Tenencia de la tierra,* 52–53.

21 CIDA, *Chile: Tenencia de la tierra,* Cuadro A-5, 71.

22 CIDA, *Chile: Tenencia de la tierra,* Cuadro B-1, 73.

23 Author's estimate based on interviews with former inquilinos and fifty-five surveys of Aconcagua estates conducted by CORA between 1965 and 1969 (CORA, "Fichas de expropriación, Aconacagua").

24 INE, *Encuesta de hogares,* 1968.

25 This percentage includes both inquilinos and permanent workers (INE, *Censo agropecuario: Aconcagua, 1964–1965,* Cuadro 6.3).

26 Ibid.

27 See Ximena Valdés S., "Una Experiencia de organización autónoma de mujeres del campo," in *Cuadernos de la mujer del campo* (Santiago de Chile: Grupo de Investigaciones Agrarias, 1983), 60.

28 Ibid.

29 Ibid.

30 INE, *Censo agropecuario: Aconcagua, 1964–1965,* Cuadro 6.3.

31 According to the 1964–1965 census, out of a total nonremunerated agri-cultural labor force of 8,073 workers in the Aconcagua Valley, 16 percent were women, and almost 90 percent of these were permanent workers (INE, *Censo agropecuario: Aconcagua, 1964–1965,* Cuadro 6.3). Census figures substantially underestimate the number of women workers. In every oral history conducted for this study, men and women insisted that campesina women from families with access to land "helped out" with seasonal har-vest tasks and had primary responsibility for family-owned livestock. That the census did not record such labor probably results from census takers' failure to ask rural women about the full range of their duties as well as the assumption that "helping out" did not constitute "work."

32 Florencia E. Mallon, *Defense of Community in Peru's Central Highland: Peasant Struggle and Capitalist Transition, 1860–1940* (Princeton, N.J.: Princeton Univ. Press, 1983); and Mallon, "Gender and Class in the Transition to Capitalism: Household and Mode of Production in Central Peru," *Latin American Per-spectives* 48, no. 1 (1986: 147–74); Carmen Diana Deere, *Household and Class Relations: Peasants and Landlords in Northern Peru* (Berkeley: Univ. of Cali-fornia Press, 1990).

33 See Garrett, "Growing Apart;" Ximena Valdés S., *La Posición de la mujer en la hacienda* (Santiago de Chile: Centro de Estudios de la Mujer, 1988); Ximena Valdés and Kathya Araujok, *Vida privada: Modernización agraria y modernidad* (Santiago de Chile: CEDEM, 1999).

34 Valdés, "Una Experiencia de organización autónoma," 61.

35 Various oral histories, including Jorge Tejedo, San Felipe, 20 Oct. 1992; René Aguirre, Santa María, 25 Oct. 1992; Raúl Fuentes, Santa María, 15 Nov. 1992; Raúl Aguirre, Panquehue, 21 May 1993; Armando Gómez, Putaendo, 22 May 1993.

36 For a fascinating discussion of campesina views of life on the large estates based on campesina artwork, see Loreto Rebolledo, *Fragmentos: Oficios y percepciones de las mujeres del campo* (Santiago de Chile: CEDEM, 1991).

37 Mattlelart, *Altas social.*

38 Consejería Nacional de Promoción Popular, *Encuesta nacional socio-económica en poblaciones marginales,* 1968, MV.

39 INE, *Censo de población: Aconcagua, 1960,* Cuadro 30; INE, *Encuesta de hogares 1966,* Cuadro 9.3.

40 INE, *Censo de población: Aconcagua, 1960,* Cuadro 5.

41 Five percent of women were widowed, and 2 percent were separated.

42 Information on gender and land titles in the minifundia sector comes ex-clusively from oral sources since it was not possible to survey Bienes Raices records on this subject. Informants overwhelmingly cited men as the prin-

ciple titleholders, although women did hold titles in cases where spouses had died or daughters were sole heirs to parents.

43 INE, *Censo de población: Aconcagua, 1960,* Cuadro 16.

44 Of those women who did engage in wage labor, single women over age twenty-five accounted for over 60 percent (INE, *Encuesta de hogares,* Cuadro 9.3; INE, *Censo de población: Aconcagua, 1960*).

45 INE, *Censo de población: Aconcagua, 1960,* Cuadro 12.

46 Various oral histories, including María Galdámez, Santa María, 20 Apr. 1993; Elena Vergara, Putaendo, 4 June 1993.

47 INE, *Censo de población: Aconcagua, 1960,* Cuadro 30. In census and demographic studies, the term "household head" was a vaguely defined category referring to the person who took ultimate responsibility for household decisions. The household head might or might not also be the household's primary economic provider. Given what was probably a propensity of census takers to assume that any woman who lived with a man was not a household head, the small proportion of female-headed households probably considerably underestimates the number of women who assumed primary household responsibilities.

48 The 1960 census reported that 26 percent of all Aconcagua households (urban and rural) in which a woman engaged in domestic service were headed by women. This figure was, respectively, 10 percent and 8 percent for households where women worked as venders and artisans (INE, *Censo de población: Aconcagua, 1960,* Cuadro 30).

49 In 1960, the average age of marriage for men in Aconcagua was 27.5. (INE, *Demografía,* 1960). The 1960 census listed 68 percent of men between the age of twenty and twenty-nine as single (INE, *Censo de población: Aconcagua, 1960,* Cuadro 5).

50 INE, *Censo de población: Aconcagua, 1960,* Cuadro 5.

51 Various oral histories, including Anita Hernández and Jacobo Fernández, Santa María, 18 Oct. 1992; Katarina Antimán, Santa María, 25 Oct. 1992; María García, Santa María, 22 Nov. 1992; Nancy Silva, Panquehue, 7 Apr. 1993.

52 Christine Delphy and Diana Leonard, *Familiar Exploitation: A New Analysis of Marriage in Contemporary Western Societies* (Cambridge: Polity, 1992), 196–225.

53 Ibid.

54 Danisa Malic and Elena Serrano, "La Mujer chilena ante la ley," in *Mundo de mujer: Continuidad y cambio* (Santiago de Chile: Centro de Estudios de la Mujer, 1988), 53–71.

55 Ibid.

56 Ibid.

57 A study conducted by Father Alberto Hurtado, a prominent progressive priest and campesino advocate, found that only 9 percent of rural women and less than 3 percent of rural men regularly attended mass (Alberto Hurtado and Humberto Muñoz, "Es Chile un país católica?" and Hurtado and Muñoz, "Sociología religiosa de Chile," qtd. in Brian H. Smith, *The Church and Politics in Chile: Challenges to Modern Catholicism* (Princeton, N.J.: Princeton Univ. Press, 1982], 98).

58 According to parish registries from the 1950s and 1960s in Santa María county, over 90 percent of births and marriages registered with the state (as mandated by law) were also registered in Church baptismal and marriage records (SMRC, "Nacimientos," 1950–1973; SMIC, "Bautismos y matrimonios," 1955–1965).

59 Bengoa, *Historia Social;* Loveman, *Struggle in the Countryside;* Smith, *The Church and Politics in Chile.*

60 The alliance between landowners and clergy was criticized in Father Hurtado's essay "Es Chile un país católica?"

61 Oral histories of Anita Hernández; Katarina Antimán; María Galdámez.

62 For an analysis of gender divisions of labor on the haciendas, see Valdés, *La Posición de la mujer en la hacienda.*

63 This builds on the arguments of Christine Stansell, *City of Women: Sex and Class in New York, 1789–1860* (Urbana: Univ. of Illinois Press, 1987) and Jeanne Boydston, *Home and Work: Housework, Wages, and the Ideology of Labor in the Early Republic* (New York: Oxford Univ. Press, 1990).

64 Loosely translated, *patrón* is the Spanish word for "boss." In the context of inquilinaje, *patrón* also connotes "master."

65 Historian George McBride argued that campesinos in central Chile shared a mestizo culture as early as 1900. See George McCutche McBride, *Chile: Land and Society* (New York: American Geographical Society, 1936).

66 See Thomas Miller Klubock, "Nationalism, Race, and the Politics of Imperialism: Workers and North American Capital in the Chilean Copper Industry," in *Rethinking the Political: A View from the North,* ed. Gilbert Joseph (Durham, N.C.: Duke Univ. Press, forthcoming); Rosemblatt, *Gendered Compromises.* Also see Gabriel Salazar and Julio Pinto, eds., *Historia contemporánea de Chile. Vol. 1, Estado, legitimidad y ciudanía* (Santiago de Chile: Ediciones LOM, 1999); Sonia Montecinos, *Madres y hauchos: Alegorías del mestizaje chileno* (Santiago de Chile: CEDEM, 1991); and Julio Pinto, *Trabajos y rebeldías en la pampa salitrera: El ciclo del salitre y la reconfiguración de las identidades populares (1850–1900)* (Santiago de Chile: Editorial: Universidad de Santiago, 1998).

67 Jeffrey L. Gould, *To Die in This Way: Nicaraguan Indians and the Myth of Mestizaje, 1880–1965* (Durham, N.C.: Duke Univ. Press, 1998).

68 For descriptions of the variety of landowning families in Aconcagua, see Sergio Gómez, "Transformaciones en una area de minifundio: Valle de Putaendo, 1960–1980," Documento de trabajo, Facultad Latinoamericano de Ciencias Sociales, Santiago de Chile, 1980. Also see Bauer, *Chilean Rural Society;* Bengoa, *Historia social;* Gómez, *Los Empresarios agrícolas;* Maurice Zeitlin and Richard Earl Ratcliff, *Landlords and Capitalists: The Dominant Class of Chile* (Princeton, N.J.: Princeton Univ. Press, 1988).

69 On the nationalist and Chilean identities of landowners, see McBride, *Chile: Land and Society,* 38–39, 150–70.

70 On landowners' Spanish identifications, see McBride, *Chile: Land and Society,* 150.

71 Anita Hernández, oral history.

72 Roger N. Lancaster, *Life is Hard: Machismo, Danger, and the Intimacy of Power in Nicaragua* (Berkeley: Univ. of California Press, 1992), 231.

73 Various oral histories, including Jacobo Fernández; Armando Gómez; and Pascual Muñoz, Santa María, 20 Nov. 1992. Also see interviews with campesinos from Putaendo county, in Gómez, "Transformaciones." Similar attitudes toward afuerinos and Indians were also reported in McBride's account of Chile in the 1930s. See McBride, *Chile: Land and Society,* 150.

74 Miguel Acevedo, oral history, San Esteben, 7 Sept. 1997.

75 Emilio Ibáñez, oral history, Santa María, 10 Nov. 1992.

76 For an extensive analysis of rural domestic service, see Garrett, "Growing Apart," 158–160.

77 Irene Campos, oral history, Santa María, 4 Sept. 1997.

78 Various oral histories, including Pascual Muñoz; Rosa Tolosa, Santa María, 11 Oct. 1992.

79 Jacobo Fernández, oral history.

80 Wives or other female family members increasingly held legal titles to land in the late 1950s, but this was often the result of attempts to legally subdivide property into smaller units in response to rumors of impending land reform, rather than an indication of women's authority over estate production. Sergio Gómez's study of landowners in central Chile found women's managerial and political roles as landowners to be insignificant (Gómez, *Los Empresarios agrícolas*).

81 According to a sample survey of estates in the Aconcagua Valley conducted by CORA between 1965 and 1967, only six of fifty estates had absentee landowners (CORA, "Carpetas de la reforma agraria, Aconcagua," CORA).

82 Irene Campos, Susana Tapia, Adriana Rojas, Anita Hernández, and Elba Herrera, oral histories, Santa María, 4 Sept. 1997.

83 According to the Central Bank of Chile, annual salaries of agricultural workers in 1961 Escudos were valued at 275,22 escudos in 1953; 165,41 escu-

dos in 1957; 146,33 escudos in 1958; and 177,92 escudos in 1960 (qtd. in Oscar Domínguez, *El Condicionamiento de la reforma agraria* [Louvain, 1963]: 15).

84 CIDA, *Chile: Tenencia de la tierra,* 56–57.

85 Oral histories of Anita Hernández; Jacobo Fernández; Jorge Tejedo; René Aguirre; Katarina Antimán; Nancy Silva; Raúl Aguirre; Armando Gómez.

86 Anita Hernández, oral history.

87 Elena Vergara, oral history.

88 This scene was recounted in various oral histories. Also see interviews in *Hombres y mujeres en Putaendo: Sus Discursos y su visión de la historia* (Santiago de Chile: Centro de Estudios de la Mujer, 1988).

89 Goméz, "Transformaciones," 53.

90 Anita Hernández, oral history.

91 Gómez, "Transformaciones," 57.

92 Miguel Acevedo and Raúl Fuentes, oral histories.

93 Ibid.

94 María Galdámez, oral history.

95 *El Trabajo,* 6 Feb. 1958.

96 Bernardo Flores, oral history, San Esteben, 14 Sept. 1997.

97 Ibid.

98 Emilio Ibáñez, oral history.

99 Raúl Fuentes, oral history.

100 Sexual violence was also directed at male workers. Unfortunately, its extent and nature are difficult to assert both because of the author's failure to adequately pursue the subject during the initial phase of research for this book and because, where it was pursued, informants hesitated to discuss it. Rape was defined both legally and in broader social understandings as a strictly heterosexual act involving vaginal penetration, while male/male sex and sexual violence (usually considered synonymous) were categorized as "sodomy" or "dishonest acts."

101 According to Brian Loveman, the Department of Labor received 1,389 labor petitions from rural workers nationwide between 1940 and 1950 (Loveman, *Struggle in the Countryside,* 130. Also see Loveman, *El Campesino chileno le escribe a su excelencia,* [Santiago de Chile: Instituto de Capacitación e Investigación ed Reforma 1971]).

102 See Almino Affonso et al., *Movimiento campesino;* Bengoa, *Historia social;* Loveman, *Struggle in the Countryside.*

103 The Communist party claimed to have organized twenty-five rural unions, including five thousand members, by 1924 (Affonso et al., *Movimiento campesino,* 52).

104 Jorge Tejedo, oral history.

105 Loveman, *Chile: The Legacy of Hispanic Capitalism.*

106 Luís Salinas, *Trayectoria de la organización campesina* (Santiago de Chile: AGRA, 1985), 12.

107 Daniel San Martín, interview by author, Santiago, Chile, 15 Nov. 1992.

108 Affonso et al., *Movimiento campesino,* 81–82. On the genesis and activities of Catholic Action and the Rural Education Institute, see Smith, *The Church and Politics in Chile.*

109 This anecdote was recounted to Sergio Gómez in an oral history (Gómez, "Transformaciones," 59).

110 James C. Scott, *Domination and the Arts of Resistance: Hidden Transcripts* (New Haven, Conn.: Yale Univ. Press, 1990); and Scott, *The Moral Economy of the Peasant: Rebellion and Subsistence in Southeast Asia* (New Haven, Conn.: Yale Univ. Press, 1976).

111 Gómez, "Transformaciones," 54.

112 Eduardo Ahumada and Sebastián Matthei, interviews, San Felipe, 26 Mar. 1993.

113 Ibid.

114 Various oral histories and interviews, including Raúl Fuentes; Eduardo Ahumada and Sebastián Matthei; Jorge Ovalle, oral history, La Higuerra, 19 Oct. 1992.

115 *El Trabajo,* 14 July 1958.

116 Rafael Baraona, Ximena Aranda, and Roberto Santana, *Valle de Putaendo: Estudio de estructura agraria* (Santiago de Chile: Instituto de Geografía de la Universidad de Chile, 1961), 265.

117 Ibid.

chapter 2. Binding Ties

1 Collantes' study was first printed in *La Nación* and republished in an anthology on the Agrarian Reform. See *La Nación,* 27 Nov. 1966; and Collantes, "La Adolescente se descubre a si mísma: Cambios e inquietudes de la pupertád," in *Antología chilena de la tierra,* ed. Antonio Corvalán (Santiago de Chile: Instituto de Capitación e Investigación en Reforma Agraria, 1970), 175–83.

2 Collantes, "La Adolescente se descubre a si mísma," 176.

3 Ibid., 180.

4 Pateman, *The Sexual Contract;* Delphy, *Close to Home;* Dephy and Leonard, *Familiar Exploitation.*

5 Anita Hernández, oral history.

6 María Galdámez, oral history.

7 María García and Irene Campos, oral histories.

8 Olivia Torres, oral history, Panquehue, 18 Jan. 1993.

9 Armand and Michèle Mattelart's 1968 survey claimed that 84 percent of the 250 rural women they interviewed said that the most important reason why some women should not have more children was economic (Mattelart, *La Mujer chilena*, 80).

10 The Mattelarts found that less than 14 percent of rural women in their sample claimed to have ever used medical birth control and that, of those who did, fully 75 percent used the "rhythm method" (ibid., 92).

11 In oral histories, women named a variety of different nonmedical contraceptive methods. Similar methods were reported to researchers from the Universidad de Chile, Valparaíso (José Cancino et al., "Habitos, creéncias y costumbres populares del puerperio y recién nacido," unpublished paper, Departmento de Obstétfica y Ginecolia, Universidad de Chile, Valparaíso, 1978).

12 Women mentioned infanticides in oral histories, and throughout the 1950s and 1960s, the local press annually reported one or two cases of infanticide. See *La Aurora*, 7 July 1959; and 22 Sept. 1962.

13 Throughout the late 1950s and early 1960s, the local press annually published three or four stories reporting the discovery and arrest of abortionists. For examples, see *La Aurora*, 2 Feb. 1962; and *El Trabajo*, 5 May 1959.

14 Abortion was a criminal offense for both practitioners and recipients. But between 1950 and 1964, all of the cases recorded at the San Felipe Juzgado de Crimen involved accusations against abortionists rather than recipient women.

15 Various oral histories and interviews, including Anita Hernández; Angélica Saéz, Santa María, 14 Nov., 1992; Rita Hernández, San Felipe, San Felipe, 1 June, 1993.

16 SNS, "Engresos hospitalarios," *Estadísticas de salud*, 1976.

17 APROFA, *Estadísticas 1960–1992*. This figure may overestimate the number of abortion-related deaths in rural Aconcagua since it is a composite of both rural and urban populations and APROFA maintained that abortion was more widely practiced in cities. The San Felipe and Los Andes hospitals reported an annual average of five abortion-related deaths throughout the 1950s and early 1960s. However, this figure probably underestimates the real numbers of deaths from abortion since it notes only those deaths officially reported to authorities or recognized by the hospital.

18 Norma Cárdanes, oral history, Santa María, 10 Mar. 1993.

19 Violeta Ramírez, oral history, San Esteben, 14 Oct. 1992.

20 Iván Gómez, oral history, Catemu, 24 Mar. 1993.

21 Emilio Ibáñez, oral history.

22 Stern, *The Secret History of Gender*.

23 This approach to wife beating builds on the excellent historical scholarship

on domestic violence. See Linda Gordon, *Heroes of Their Own Lives: The Politics and History of Family Violence: Boston, 1880–1960* (New York: Penguin, 1989); Stern, *The Secret History of Gender.*

24 SFJC, Regístro de Crimenes.

25 Of 135 cases of lesiones between 1951 and 1963, 49 were available for this study and of these, 35 involved women and men from poor, agricultural backgrounds.

26 The sections of this chapter on wife beating have previously been published as part of longer articles on domestic violence. See Heidi Tinsman, "Los Patrones del hogar: Esposas golpeadas y control sexual en Chile rural, 1958–1988," in *Disciplina y desacato,* ed. Godoy et al.; and "Household Patrones: Wife Beating and Sexual Control in Rural Chile, 1958–1988," in *The Gendered Worlds of Latin American Women Workers,* ed. French and James.

27 Case file S254;20951, SFJC. For purposes of privacy, many names cited in judicial records used in this book have been altered.

28 Marta Ramírez, oral history, San Esteben, 10 Oct. 1992.

29 Anita Hernández, oral history.

30 Case file S319;25030, SFJC.

31 Sonia Cárdanes, oral history, Santa María, 12 Apr. 1993.

32 Various oral histories, including Sonia Cárdanes; Anita Hernández; Elena Vergara; Raúl Fuentes; Armando Gómez; Jorge Ovalle.

33 Ibid.

34 Ibid.

35 Case file S356;27066, SFJC.

36 Elena Vergara, oral history.

37 Various oral histories, including Jorge Ovalle; Raúl Fuentes; Armando Gómez.

38 Untitled cueca rhythm dating from the mid-twentieth century and possibly much earlier, performed and explained by Anita Hernández and Ramón Martínez, Santa María, 18 Sept. 1992.

39 See Gabriel Salazar, "Ser niño huacho en la historia de Chile," *Proposiciones* no. 19 (1990): 55–83; Sonia Montecinos, *Madre y huachos: Alegorías del mestizaje chileno* (Santiago de Chile: CEDEM, 1991).

40 Malic and Serrano, "La Mujer chilena ante la ley," 60–66.

41 Anita Hernández, oral history.

42 The Mattelarts reported that 75 percent of the women and men they interviewed (separately) said that household decisions were made collaboratively by both husbands and wives, but that men exercised ultimate authority (Mattelart, *La Mujer chilena,* 75).

43 Patricia Carreras, oral history, San Esteben, 6 Apr. 1993.

44 Beliefs about the evil eye were regularly mentioned in oral histories (see,

for example, Anita Hernández; Katarina Antimán; Elena Vergara). They were also recorded by researchers in the Aconcagua Valley (Garrett, "Growing Apart," 52–53; Cancino et al., "Hábitos y creéncias).

45 Garrett, "Growing Apart," 53.

46 Various oral histories, including Anita Hernández; Katarina Antimán; Elena Vergara.

47 Elena Vergara, oral history.

48 Angelica Saéz, oral history.

49 Victoria Ibacache, oral history, Santa María, 14 Nov. 1992.

50 Nancy Silva, oral history.

51 See the rich literature on honor and its transformation from colonial times through the early twentieth century. For example, Verena Martinez-Alier, *Marriage, Class, and Color in Nineteenth-Century Cuba: A Study of Racial Attitudes and Sexual Values in a Slave Society* (Ann Arbor: Univ. of Michigan Press, 1974); Asunción Lavrin, ed., *Marriage and Sexuality in Colonial Latin America* (Lincoln: Univ. of Nebraska Press, 1989); Patricia Seed, *To Love, Honor, and Obey in Colonial Mexico: Conflicts over Marriage Choice, 1574–1821* (Stanford, Calif.: Stanford Univ. Press, 1988); Ramón Gutiérrez, *When Jesus Came the Corn Mothers Went Away: Sexuality and Marriage in Colonial New Mexico* (Stanford, Calif.: Stanford Univ. Press, 1991); Stern, *The Secret History of Gender;* Eileen Findlay, *Imposing Decency;* Sueann Caulfield, *In Defense of Honor.*

52 Various oral sources, including Anita Hernández; Katarina Antimán; René Aguirre; María Trujillo, Santa María, 26 Oct. 1992; Diego Hernández, San Felipe, 10 Oct. 1992; Leandro Herrera, Santa María, 22 Oct. 1992; Rita Galdámez, Santa María, 20 Apr. 1993.

53 The San Felipe Regístro de Crimenes listed an average of six rape cases per year between 1950 and 1964. Roughly half of these involved women from campesino families. In all of these cases, the accused man also came from a campesino or poor, urban working-class family.

54 For a discussion of rape and the idea of female sexual consent, see Pamela Haag, *Consent: Sexual Rights and the Transformation of American Liberalism* (Ithaca, N.Y.: Cornell Univ. Press, 1999).

55 Rapes of women over age twenty were reported (and dismissed) in two of the judicial cases reviewed. Rapes of older adolescents and young women were also reported in oral histories.

56 RCSF and RCSM; SNS, San Felipe, "Memoria, 1975."

57 The percentage of unmarried women with children in rural Aconcagua during the 1960s may have been as high as 25 or 30 percent, depending on a woman's age. According to the 1960 census, almost 40 percent of women between the ages of twenty and twenty-nine were unmarried,

whereas 23 percent of rural women between the ages of thirty and thirty-nine remained unmarried (INE, *Censo de población: Aconcagua, 1960*, Cuadros 5A, 5B).

58 Lilia Muñoz, oral history, Catemu, 14 Oct. 1992.

59 Elena Vergara, oral history.

60 Ibid.

61 Ibid.

62 This analysis builds on Christine Stansell's discussion of young women's sexual encounters with men (Stansell, *City of Women*).

63 INE, *Demografía: Aconcagua, 1960*, 1960.

64 According to the census, the percentage of women under age twenty with children was 7 percent in rural Aconcagua and 12 percent in Santiago (INE, *Censo de población: Aconcagua, 1960*, Cuadro 7. INE, *Censo de población: Chile, 1960*).

65 Olivia González, oral history, Santa María, 17 May 1993.

66 "Registro de Crimen," SFJC.

67 The dynamics of home abandonment cases are reminiscent of court trials involving "honor" elsewhere in Latin America. See literature cited in endnote 51 for this chapter.

68 Case file S293;23468, SFJC.

69 Ibid.

70 Case file S254;20828, SFJC.

71 Case file S293;23437, SFJC.

72 Case file S23455, SFJC.

73 Case file S293;23423, SFJC.

chapter 3. Making Men

1 *La Nación*, 20 July 1965.

2 Daniel San Martín, interview.

3 Salinas, *Trayectoria*.

4 *La Nación*, 20 July 1965.

5 Ibid.

6 Ibid

7 Constantine Christopher Menges, "Chile's Landowners' Association and Agrarian Reform Politics," Memorandum, Rand Corporation, Santa Monica, 1968.

8 Michael Fleet, *The Rise and Fall of Chilean Christian Democracy* (Princeton, N.J.: Princeton Univ. Press, 1985).

9 For a history of politics and culture during the Popular Front, see Rosemblatt, *Gendered Compromises;* Klubock, *Contested Communities;* Loveman,

Chile: The Legacy of Hispanic Capitalism; Paul W. Drake, *Socialism and Populism in Chile, 1932–52* (Urbana: Univ. of Illinois Press, 1978).

10 Loveman, *Struggle in the Countryside.*

11 Loveman, *Chile: The Legacy of Hispanic Capitalism,* 261–62.

12 "U.S. Aid: The Carrot and the Stick," *New Chile* (1972). Qtd. in Barbara Stallings, *Class Conflict and Economic Development in Chile, 1958–1973* (Stanford, Calif.: Stanford Univ. Press, 1978), 106.

13 Jerome Levinson and Juan de Onís, *The Alliance That Lost Its Way* (Chicago: Quadrangle, 1970).

14 Garrett, "Growing Apart," 176.

15 Cristóbal Kay, "Comparative Development of the European Manorial System and the Hacienda System" (Ph.D. diss., Univesity of Sussex, 1971), 221.

16 Other types of land that could be legally expropriated included land owned by the state, private property put up to repay debts, uncultivated land owned by public or private corporations, property necessary to complete a project being executed by CORA, farms under five hectares, and land bordering bodies of water.

17 Law 15.020 gave workers the option to be paid only in cash and specified that at least 35 percent of all wages would be paid in cash until 1964, after which point 50 percent would be paid in cash. The law limited landowners' ability to unilaterally determine the value of in-kind payments and stipulated that workers employed for one year or more on public or semipublic land were entitled to compensation for terminated contracts.

18 For details on Law 15.020, see Loveman, *Struggle in the Countryside,* 225–40.

19 Gómez, *Empresarios agrícolas;* Menges, "Chile's Landowners' Association."

20 Loveman, *Struggle in the Countryside,* 235.

21 Armando Gómez; Bernardo Flores, oral histories.

22 Loveman, *Struggle in the Countryside,* 176–77.

23 *Nuevo Campo,* Feb. through June, 1967.

24 Barraclough and Fernández, *Diagnóstico,* 178; Garrett, "Growing Apart," 186.

25 Barraclough and Fernández, *Diagnóstico,* 178.

26 *Tierra y Libertad,* May 1962.

27 Ibid.

28 *Tierra y Libertad por la Reforma Agraria* (Santiago de Chile: 1961), 15; various issues of *El Siglo,* 1961–1962.

29 For a discussion of rural labor petitions, see Affonso et al., *Movimiento campesino,* vol. 2, 122.

30 Armando Gómez, oral history.

31 Antonio Gramsci, *Selections from the Prison Notebooks of Antonio Gramsci,* eds. Quintin Hearne and Geoffrey Nowell Smith (New York: International Publishers, 1971), 265.

32 This builds on Roger Lancaster's discussion of the cochón in contemporary Nicaragua (Lancaster, *Life is Hard,* 253–54).

33 Various periodical sources, including *Tierra y Libertad,* April, 1963; *La Nación,* 15 July, 1964; *El Siglo,* 5 Feb. 1966.

34 Raúl Fuentes, oral history; Pedro Reyes, oral history, San Esteben, 10 Mar. 1993. Also see *Tierra y Libertad,* May 1963.

35 *El Trabajo,* 26 August 1965.

36 Various oral histories, including Armando Gómez and Jorge Tejedo.

37 See Klubock, *Contested Communities.*

38 Emilio Ibáñez, oral history.

39 Law 16.250 required rural employers to make monetary contributions (equal to 2 percent of each worker's monthly wage) to the state Foundation for Union Education and Assistance (FEES) that ran various education and organizing projects and directly financed unions according to membership size. Workers were required to give 2 percent of their salaries either to the union of their choice or to FEES.

40 Salinas, *Trayectoria.*

41 The MCI constituted a 1964 offshoot of the UCC, formed to support Eduardo Frei's campaign.

42 An indication of the magnitude of INDAP's organizing efforts lies in the fact that, in 1965, the agency spent 249,045 escudos on union organizing in the combined provinces of Aconcagua and Valparaíso; in 1970, the agency spent 1,018,927 escudos on organizing in this zone (INDAP, "Resumen de gestión creditaria, 1962–1972").

43 Salinas, *Trayectoria.*

44 Two very small confederations accounted for the remaining 2 percent of the total unionized rural labor force in 1970. The religious Catholic confederation, Sargento Candelaria, had a membership of 1,605 members, and the landowner-sponsored confederation, Provincias Agrarias Unidas, had a membership of 1,686 (Salinas, *Trayectoria*).

45 FEES, "Descripción numerica de la organización sindical campesina chilena, 1968–1969," 1971.

46 Ibid.

47 Ibid.

48 At the national level, the total number of petitions submitted by rural workers between 1964 and 1967 was 2,119. In 1968, the number of petitions submitted was 1,852 (Academia de Humanismo Cristiano, Cuadro 1, *Historia del movimiento campesino*).

49 Affonso et al., *Movimiento campesino,* vol. 2, 22.

50 Gómez, "Transformaciones," 34.

51 Ibid., 84.

52 Chile, Central Bank, *Boletín Mensual,* cited in Kay, "Comparative Development of the European Manorial System," 216.

53 Gómez, "Transformaciones," 84.

54 *La Nación,* 16 Jun. 1965, 11.

55 Nationally, there were only three rural strikes in 1960, seven in 1961, and five in 1963. In constrast, in 1965 there were 142 rural strikes nationally, and 586 strikes in 1966 (Academia de Humanismo Cristiano, *Historia del movimieto campesino,* Cuadro 1).

56 Affonso et al., *Movimiento campesino,* vol. 2, 58.

57 Loveman, *Struggle in the Countryside,* 257.

58 Gómez, "Transformaciones," 37.

59 *La Nación,* 16 Jun. 1965.

60 Affonso et al., *Movimiento campesino,* vol. 2, 135.

61 Daniel San Martín, interview; Ricardo Leigh, interviews, Santiago, Chile, 10 Nov. 1992.

62 Gómez, "Transformaciones," 41.

63 Ibid.

64 Armando Gómez, oral history.

65 For a detailed description of several tomas in the mid-1960s, see Affonso et al., *Movimiento campesino,* vol. 2, 107–33.

66 Affonso et al., *Movimiento campesino,* vol. 2., 123.

67 Armando Gómez, oral history.

68 CORA, "Fichas de expropriación," 4729, 4727, 3241, 3261; Armando Gómez, oral history.

69 Daniel San Martín, interview.

70 Pascual Muñoz, oral history.

71 David Montgomery, *Workers' Control in America: Studies in the History of Work, Technology, and Labor Struggles* (Cambridge: Cambridge Univ. Press, 1979); Stern, *The Secret History of Gender;* Klubock, *Contested Communities.*

72 According to CORA estate surveys in Aconcagua, by the late 1960s at least half of private estates were meeting legal requirements and paying wages in excess of those on the Reform sector.

73 All issues of *El Campesino* between 1964 and 1973 gave reports on union membership, strikes, and land expropriations. For declarations of the Aconcagua Association of Agriculturalists, see *El Trabajo,* 8 Oct. 1965; 28 Oct. 1965; 1 Dec. 1965.

74 Armando Gómez, oral history.

75 *El Trabajo,* 8 Aug. 1965; *La Aurora,* 19 Mar. 1966.

76 Pascual Muñoz, oral history; various editorials in *El Trabajo* and *El Campesino.*

77 Pascual Muñoz, oral history. This story was also mentioned by Emilio Ibañez.

78 Pascual Muñoz, oral history.

79 "Triunfo Campesino, Capacitación," manual for union education, ca. 1969. Author's photocopy from original manual belonging to former Triunfo union president Jorge Tejedo, San Felipe.

80 Undated pamphlet published by Ranquíl. Personal collection of Emilio Ibáñez, Santa María.

81 Ossa Pretot spoke on behalf of Promoción Popular, an agency discussed in chapter 4 (*La Nación*, 18 Sept., 1966).

82 *La Nación*, 18 Sept., 1966.

83 Ibid.

84 *Campo Nuevo*, March 1967.

85 A study conducted by the University of Wisconsin Land Tenure Center and ICIRA in the central valley in 1970 maintained that only 7 percent of workers living in an area where a union existed did not belong to it. The study also alleged that 67 percent of these men had been involved in submitting a labor petition and that 47 percent had participated in a strike (University of Wisconsin Land Tenure Center, "Proyecto de cambios socio-economicos en cien prédios del sector rural en Chile," 1970; qtd. in Garrett, "Growing Apart," 192).

86 Klubock, *Contested Communities.*

87 Daniel San Martín; Armando Gómez; Raúl Fuentes, interviews and oral histories.

88 According to the University of Wisconsin–ICIRA study, almost 50 percent of all male workers in the central valley played on soccer teams in 1970 (qtd. in Garrett, "Growing Apart," 192).

89 Raúl Fuentes; Raúl Aguirre; Armando Gómez, oral histories.

90 Armando Gómez; Emilio Ibáñez, oral histories.

91 Armando Gómez, oral history.

92 See Affonso et al., *Movimiento campesino,* Vol. 1, 206–10.

93 Pedro Reyes, oral history.

94 "Triunfo Campesino, Capacitación."

95 Emilio Toledo, oral history, Santa María, 25 May 1993.

96 Pedro Muñoz, oral history, Catemu, 14 June 1993; Raúl Fuentes; Emilio Toledo; Armando Gómez, oral histories and interviews.

97 Pedro Muñoz, oral history.

98 For examples, see *El Siglo,* 27 Jan. 1963; 28 Apr. 1963; *Tierra y Libertad,* Apr. 1963, 2.

99 Stansell, *City of Women.*

100 In the 1958 presidential election, 34 percent of the female vote in the Aconcagua Valley went to Alessandri, 25 percent to Frei, and 21 percent to Allende. Of the male vote, Allende received 32 percent, Alessandri 29.5 percent, and Frei 19 percent. In 1964, Frei received 63 percent of the female

vote in the Aconcagua Valley, whereas Allende received 32 percent (author's calculations from DRE, Regístro Electoral, 4 de Septiembre 1958 and Regístro Electoral, 4 de Septiembre 1964).

101 *El Siglo,* 11 Oct. 1969.

102 Ricardo Leigh, interview.

103 For example, see *Nuevo Campo,* Sept. 1967; Oct. 1967; Apr. 1968; *Tierra y Libertad,* Jan. 1964.

104 *Tierra y Libertad,* Apr. 1963 and Nov. 1963; *El Trabajo,* 29 Nov. 1967.

105 *Campo Nuevo,* Mar. 1964.

106 *Tierra y Libertad,* May 1962.

107 For examples of Catholic and Christian Democratic visions of unions as vehicles of family uplift, see "El ABC del sindicalismo campesino," MCI pamphlet, ca. 1964, INPRU; "Tierra y libertad: la reforma agraria," ASICH pamphlet, 1961, INPRU; "Confederación nacional sindical campesina Libertad," Libertad pamphlet, ca. 1968, INPRU; "Triunfo Campesino, Capacitación."

108 For a discussion of the MCI, see Affonso et al., *Movimiento campesino,* vol.1, 204. For a discussion of INDAP, see INDAP, "Marco nacional de programación," 1968, 7.

109 Affonso et al., *Movimiento campesino,* vol.1, 233.

110 INDAP's training manuals specified female workers' rights, including the right to join a union. INDAP, "Manual de derechos campesinos," 1968.

111 See *La Nación,* 12 July 1965; Affonso et al., *Movimiento campesino,* vol. 1, 233. For information of the 1964 conference of sixty delegates, see *La Nación,* 13 Dec. 1964.

112 According to *La Nación,* over 400 women attended the conference in 1965 (*La Nación,* 12 July 1965).

113 Ibid.

114 "Conclusions of the Primera Asemblea General de Socios," typed memo, MCI archive, qtd. from Affonso et al., *Movimiento campesino,* vol. 1, 227.

115 For the text of FRAP's "Declarations on the Rights of Women Workers," see *El Siglo,* 13 July 1964.

116 There is a growing and excellent literature on the political mobilization of working-class women in the first half of the twentieth century. See Edda Gaviola Artigas et al., *Queremos votar en las próximas elecciones: Historia del movimiento femenino chileno, 1913–1952* (Santiago de Chile: Facultad Latinoamericana de Ciencias Sociales, 1986); Cecilia Salinas, *La Mujer proletaria: Una Historia para contar* (Concepción: Ediciones Literatura Americana, 1987); Lorena Godoy et al., *Disciplina y desacato;* Klubock, *Contested Communities;* Rosemblatt, *Gendered Compromises;* Hutchison, *Labors Appropriate to Their Sex.*

117 *El Siglo,* 1962.

118 *Unidad Campesina,* May 1962.

119 *El Siglo,* 23 July 1966.

120 In 1962, the FCI listed the protection of native women's entitlements to communal lands and cooperatives as one of its primary organizing goals for rural women (*Unidad Campesina,* May 1962).

121 *El Siglo,* 10 Feb. 1963.

122 Garrett, "Growing Apart."

123 *El Siglo,* 11 Jan. 1966.

124 *Unidad Campesina,* May 1962.

125 Jorge Tejedo; Bernardo Flores, oral histories.

126 *El Siglo,* 11 Dec. 1962; 30 May 1967; 16 Aug. 1969.

chapter 4. Promoting Gender Mutualism

1 This draws on Mary Kay Vaughan's discussion of revolutionary Mexico's attempt to modernize peasant patriarchy (Vaughan, "Modernizing Patriarchy," 194).

2 Acción Sindical Chilena, "Tierra y libertad por la reforma agraria," 1961.

3 Jacques Chonchol, *El Desarrollo de América Latina y la reforma agraria* (Santiago de Chile: Editorial del Pacífico, 1964), 73.

4 Garrett, "Growing Apart," 176.

5 Consejería Nacional de Promoción Popular, "La Población organizada se incorpora al poder," 1965, MV.

6 See the description of the Ley de Junta de Vecinos y Demas Organizaciones Comunitarias, qtd. in Garrett, "Growing Apart," 180–81.

7 Ibid.

8 *El Trabajo,* 22 July 1970; *La Nación,* 25 July 1969.

9 *La Nación,* 6 Oct. 1964.

10 *La Nación,* 24 Sept. 1967.

11 *La Nación,* 25 July 1969.

12 *La Nación,* 6 Oct. 1964.

13 *La Nación,* 24 Sept. 1967.

14 *La Nación,* 19 Mar. 1970.

15 *La Nación,* 30 May 1970.

16 For examples, see *La Aurora,* 10 Feb. 1967; and *La Nación,* 23 Mar. 1968. For historical accounts of female professionals also see Lorena Godoy, "Armas ansiosas de triunfo: Dedal, agujas, tijeras . . .": La Educación profesional feminina en Chile, 1888–1912," in *Disciplina y desacato,* ed. Godoy et al.; and Rosemblatt, *Gendered Compromises.*

17 Karin Alejandra Rosemblatt, "Domesticating Men: State Building and

Class Compromise in Popular-Front Chile," in *Hidden Histories*, ed. Elizabeth Dore and Maxine Molyneux.

18 Text of broadcast published in *La Nación*, 30 May 1970.

19 The legal voting age was lowered to eighteen in 1970.

20 For examples, see *El Trabajo*, 5 Jan. 1963; and *La Nación*, 24 Jan. 1965.

21 *Sucro y Semilla*, August 1964, 28.

22 *El Trabajo*, 9 Sept. 1967.

23 See Smith, *The Church and Politics in Chile*; Loveman, *Struggle in the Country-side*; Bengoa, *Historia Social*.

24 Hutchison, *Labors Appropriate To Their Sex*; M. Soledad Zárate, "Mujeres viciosas, mujeres virtuosas: La Mujer delincuente y la casa correccional de Santiago, 1860–1990," in *Disciplina y desacato*, ed. Godoy et al.

25 Klubock, *Contested Communities*; Rosemblatt, *Gendered Compromises*.

26 *La Aurora*, 30 July 1965.

27 *Sucro y Semilla*, June, August, and September 1964; *La Nación*, 7 Oct. 1964; and *El Trabajo*, 18 Nov. 1965.

28 *La Aurora*, 13 Apr. 1967.

29 For IER programs, see IER's annual reports, "Memoria del Instituto de Educación Rural," 1968, 1969, 1970, INPRU. Also see *La Nación*, 7 oct. 1964; 30 May 1965; and 13 Apr. 1967.

30 For additional references to the domestic agenda of early Catholic education programs for women, see periodical reports on MCI activities and Catholic agricultural schools (*La Nación*, 1 Sept. 1965; *El Trabajo*, 4 Aug. 1965; and 19 Aug. 1965).

31 Kathleen B. Fischer, *Political Ideology and Educational Reform in Chile, 1964–1976* (Los Angeles: UCLA Latin American Center, 1979), 46.

32 INE *Censo de Población: Aconcagua, 1960* and INE, *Censo de población: Aconco-gua, 1970*.

33 "Trayectoria del trabajo feminino en INDAP," INDAP, Santiago, typed memo qtd. in Garrett, "Growing Apart," 202.

34 INDAP, "Marco Nacional de Programación," 1968, 7.

35 Ibid., INDAP, "Manual de Derechos Campesinos," 1968, 12–15.

36 INDAP, "Memoria del Departamento de Educación y Economía del Hogar," 1967, 4.

37 *La Nación*, 11 Mar. 1965.

38 INDAP, "Memoria del Departamento de Educación y Economía del Hogar," 1967, 8; *La Nación*, 14 Jan. 1967.

39 For announcements and descriptions of education programs sponsored by CORA, INDAP, and INACAP, see *La Nación*, 13 Apr. 1967; 25 July 1969; 19 June 1970; *El Trabajo*, 27 June 1966; 1 Sept. 1966; and 18 June 1968. Also see INDAP, "Marco Nacional de Programación," 1968, 5–9.

40 *La Nación,* 28 July 1967.

41 *La Nación,* 19 June 1970.

42 Fischer, *Political Ideology and Educational Reform in Chile.*

43 "Capacitación Laboral," training manual for Triunfo Campesino, ca. 1969, author's photocopy, 10–11.

44 INDAP, "Memoria de INDAP, Año 1971," 1971; INDAP, "Marco Nacional de Programación," 1968, 8.

45 For examples of the extensive periodical coverage on youth programs, see *La Nación,* 16 Feb. 1970; 18 July 1965; *El Trabajo,* 10 May 1970; suplemento, 6 July 1968; *El Siglo,* 19 Aug. 1968; 19 Aug. 1969.

46 INPRU, "Memoria del IER, 1970–1971" (Santiago: IER).

47 INPRU, *Sucro y Semilla.*

48 INPRU, "Memoria del IER, 1970–1971"; monthly radio advertisements in *El Trabajo.*

49 INDAP, "Marco Nacional de Programación," 1968, 9–10.

50 CNPP, "Primer reunión nacional de institutos públicos y privados sobre el desarrollo de la comunidad," 1968, 22.

51 INDAP, "El Sindicato: La Organización del pueblo," publication for use by Confederación Triunfo, 1969; author's photocopy.

52 FEES, "Obstáculos e incenativos a la sindilicación campesina," 1970, 125.

53 M. A. Giroz and A. M. Lopez, "Evaluación del proceso de integración de la mujer campesina en las organizaciones de base: Cooperativas y sindicatos" (master's thesis, Escuela de Trabajo Social, Universidad Católica, Santiago de Chile, 1969), 10.

54 INDAP, "Marco de Programación," 1969, qtd. in Giroz and Lopez, "Evaluación del proceso de integración," 12.

55 Ibid., 16.

56 All contemporary and scholarly sources agree that real wages in the countryside increased significantly during Chile's Agrarian Reform. There is, however, disagreement over the extent of the increase. Some scholars have argued that real wages for campesinos increased between three and ten times between 1964 and 1970 (see Wayne Ringlein, "Economic Effects of Chilean National Expropriation Policy on the Private Sector, 1964–1969" [Ph.D. diss., University of Maryland, 1971]; and Loveman, *Struggle in the Countryside*). Other sources estimate that real rural wages during the 1964–1970 period increased between two and six times (see Ministerio de Trabajo y Previsión Social, Oficina de Planificación y Presupuesto, "Informe sobre asuntos laborales," 1969, 164; and Barraclough, "Reforma agraria en Chile"). According to published records from INE, real agricultural wages increased threefold between 1964 and 1970 (Comisión Central Mixta de Sueldos, *Estadísticas laborales,* 1976, 41).

57 María Ibacache, oral history, Santa María, 24 Apr. 1993.

58 Anita Hernández, oral history.

59 Sonia Araya, oral history, Los Andes, 2 June 1993.

60 Anita Hernández; Katarina Antimán; Elena Vergara, oral histories. Eugenia Flores, oral history, San Felipe, 22 Nov. 1992.

61 Emilio Ibáñez; Raúl Fuentes; Pascual Muñoz; Armando Gómez, oral histories.

62 Ricardo Leigh, interview.

63 Marta Castro, oral history, Putaendo, 22 May 1993.

64 Giroz and Lopez, "Evaluación del proceso de integración," 11.

65 "Esquema de clase no. 2: Organización sindical," Triunfo training manual, INDAP, ca. 1969, 2.

66 Article 87, Law 16.880 of Junta de Vecinos y Demás Organizaciones Comunitarias, 1968, qtd. in Edda Gaviola Artigas, Lorella Lopresti, and Claudia Rojas, "Los Centros de madres: Una forma de organización para la mujer rural," unpublished manuscript, ISIS, 1988, 2.

67 Ibid., 35–37.

68 Teresa Valdés et al., "Centros de madres, 1973–1989: Solo disciplinamiento?" (documento de trabajo, Facultad Latinoamericano de Ciencias Sociales, Santiago de Chile, 1989), 22–30; Edda Gaviola Artigas et al., "Los Centros de madres."

69 Valdés et al., "Centros de madres," 22–30.

70 See Rosemblatt, *Gendered Compromises;* Corinne Antezana-Pernet, "Mobilizing Women in the Popular Front Era: Feminism, Class, and Politics in the *Movimiento Pro-Emancipación de la Mujer Chilena* (MEMch), 1935–1950" (Ph.D. diss., University of California-Irvine, 1996).

71 Valdés et al., "Centros de madres, 1973–1989."

72 Ibid.

73 Most scholarship has analyzed CEMAS as organizations formed and controlled by the Frei administration. For examples, see Edda Gaviola Artigas, Lorella Lopresti, and Claudia Rojas, "Chile centros de madres: La Mujer popular en movimiento?" in *Nuestra memoria, nuestro futuro: Mujeres e historia: América Latina y el Caribe,* ed. Maria del Carmen Feijóo (Santiago de Chile: ISIS, 1988), 79–88; Garrett, "Growing Apart;" Teresa Valdés et al., "Centros de madres"; Valdés S., "Una Experiencia de organización autónoma," 25–80.

74 *Tierra y Libertad,* April 1963.

75 *El Trabajo,* 15 Dec. 1965.

76 Ricardo Silva, interview, Santiago, 22 Apr. 1993.

77 INDAP created the Department of Education and Home Economics to coordinate programs for and the distribution of resources to CEMAS. The De-

partment had three subsections: Health and Nutrition, Home Industries, and Rural Homemaking.

78 The activities of CEMAS were reported widely in the press. For examples, see *Nuevo Campo,* Nov. and Dec. 1968; May and June 1968; *La Nación,* 3 Jan. 1966; 2 July 1966; *El Trabajo,* 1 July 1969; 23 May 1970; 18 June 1970.

79 Garrett, "Growing Apart"; Valdés et al., "Centros de madres, 1973–1989"; Valdés S., "Una Experiencia de organización autónoma."

80 Silvia Herrera, oral history, San Esteben, 14 May 1993.

81 *El Trabajo,* 1966.

82 MCI, *Boletín Centro de Madres* 1, qtd. in Affonso et. al., *Movimiento campesino,* 228.

83 *La Aurora,* 26 April 1966.

84 Government-distributed sewing machines were not gifts. Through a financial agreement with the Banco de Chile, CEMAS made machines available to women on a credit they had to repay in twenty monthly installments.

85 Pedro Muñoz, oral history.

86 Patricia Carreras, oral history.

87 Garrett, "Growing Apart," 208.

88 Falaha, "Censo de organizaciones campesinas," qtd. in Garrett, "Growing Apart," 204.

89 Katarina Antimán, oral history.

90 See *El Trabajo,* 4 Oct. 1965; 25 Jan. 1966; 25 Oct. 1966; 2 July 1968; 9 Sept. 1968; *Campo Nuevo,* Mar. 1967; September 1967; February 1968; *Tierra y Libertad,* February 1967; Mar. 1967.

91 Violeta Ramírez, Patricia Carreras, Elena Vergara, oral histories.

92 Elena Vergara, oral history.

93 *Campo Nuevo,* Apr. 1968.

94 Anita Hernández; Katarina Antimán; Rita Galdámez, oral histories.

95 *El Trabajo,* 3 Feb. 1966.

96 *El Trabajo,* 10 Feb. 1966.

97 *El Trabajo,* 6 Jul. 1966.

98 Amanda Puz, *La Mujer Chilena* (Santiago de Chile: Editora Nacional Quimantú, 1972), 60.

99 *El Trabajo,* 2 May 1966.

100 *El Trabajo,* 21 Sept. 1967.

101 Medical birth control was promoted to a limited degree during the Popular Front. See Rosemblatt, *Gendered Compromises;* María Angélica Illanes D., *"En el nombre del pueblo, del estado y de la ciencia, (...)": Historia social de la salud pública, Chile 1880–1973* (Santiago de Chile: Colectivo de Atención Primaria, 1993).

102 *Boletín del Comité Chileno de Protección de la Familia,* July 1965 (hereafter cited as *Boletín APROFA*).

103 Figures are for 1964. APROFA, *Estadísticas APROFA,* 1980.

104 Figures are for 1965. SNS, "Defunciones y causas de muerte," 1960–1972; SNS, "Nacimientos," 1960–1972.

105 *Boletín APROFA,* July 1965.

106 American University Field Staff, "Births, Abortions, and the Progress of Chile," *Field Staff Reports* 19, no. 2 (1972).

107 APROFA, "Síntesis histórica de la planificación familiar en Chile," 1974.

108 Qtd. from Ximena Jiles Moreno, *De la miel a los implantes: Historia de las políticas de regulación de la fecundidad en Chile* (Santiago de Chile: Corporación de Salud y Políticas Sociales, 1992), 126.

109 Ibid., 131.

110 Ibid., 131–32.

111 INE, *Demografía,* 1985.

112 In 1965, 89.5 out of every 1,000 children born in San Felipe and Los Andes died within their first year of life. In 1970, the infant mortality rate was 68.8 per 1,000 live births, and in 1972 it fell to 67.7 (compiled from San Felipe-Los Andes SNS reports, "Defunciones y causas de muerte," 1972, and "Nacimientos," 1972). In 1966, 26.1 of every 1,000 women of fertile age died during pregnancy or childbirth from birth- or pregnancy-related complications. By 1970 this rate had fallen to 16.8 per 1,000 women, and by 1972 it was 16.3 (APROFA, 1980 *Estadísticas APROFA*).

113 Jiles, *De la miel a los implantes,* 135.

114 See *La Aurora,* 24 Oct. 1966.

115 According to agency records, APROFA published and distributed over 80,000 pamphlets, bulletins, and cartillas between 1966 and 1972 ("APROFA: Diez años de labor," *Boletín APROFA,* August 1972, 6–7).

116 *Boletín APROFA,* July 1969, 1.

117 The seminar was attended by fifty labor leaders, forty-eight of whom were male, and twenty-four SNS health workers (*El Trabajo,* 22 July 1969).

118 Anita Hernández; María Trujillo, oral histories.

119 Dr. Luís Ortega, interview, San Felipe, 16 Mar. 1993.

120 Anita Hernández; Patricia Carreras; Rosa Saá, Santa María, 20 Nov. 1992, oral histories.

121 Dr. Luís Ortega, interview.

122 APROFA, *Estadísticas APROFA,* 1984, 5.

123 "Atenciones y recursos: San Felipe-Los Andes SNS," Memo, SNS, San Felipe, 1968, 1969, 1972. This figure includes consultations by both urban and rural women of all classes.

124 Mattelart, *La Mujer chilena,* 89–90.

125 Nora Ruedi, "La Transición de la fecundidad en Chile," qtd. in Ana María Silva Dreyer, "Tendencias generales de la fecundidad en Chile, 1960–1987," Unpublished paper, Instituto de la Mujer, Santiago de Chile, July 1990, 3.

126 Ibid., 3; 15.

127 In 1964, APROFA estimated that there were 29.9 abortions and 10 abortion-related maternal deaths for every 1,000 women of fertile age. Total maternal deaths in 1966 numbered 26.1 per 1,000 women of fertile age. In 1970, APROFA estimated that there were 20.6 abortions and 6.6 maternal deaths per 1,000 women of fertile age. Total maternal deaths in 1970 numbered 16.8 per 1,000 women of fertile age (APROFA, *Estadísticas APROFA*, 1982).

128 According to SNS annual reports, there were 1,211 abortion-related hospitalizations in the departments of San Felipe and Los Andes in 1964. In 1970, the two departments reported 915 abortion-related hospitalizations (compiled from SNS, "Engresos hospitalarios," *Estadísticas de salud, 1976*).

129 APROFA, *Estadísticas APROFA, 1960–1992*, 1993. Also see Dreyer, "Tendencias generales de la fecundidad," 9–10.

130 Mattelart, *La Mujer chilena*, 89–90.

131 Rosa Tolosa; Katarina Antimán; María Galdámez, oral histories. Also see Mattelart, *La Mujer chilena*, 89–90.

132 Mattelart, *La Mujer chilena;* Garrett, "Growing Apart."

133 Victoria Antimán, oral history, Panquehue, 24 Jan. 1993.

134 Norma Reyes, oral history, San Esteben, 19 Jan. 1993.

135 Anita Hernández, oral history.

136 Emilio Ibáñez, oral history.

137 Raúl Ahumada, San Felipe, 18 May 1993; Sergio Contreras, Los Andes, 22 May 1993, oral histories.

138 Walter García, oral history, Santa María, 24 Oct. 1992.

139 Between 1964 and 1973, women in the Aconcagua department of San Felipe filed an annual average of twenty lesiones against husbands and permanent partners, and almost three quarters involved poor and campesina women. Of the 240 cases of physical harm filed between 1964 and 1973, 70 were available for study; of these, almost three quarters involved rural poor people, where at least one of the partners was listed as earning their livelihood in agriculture (JCSF, Registro de Crimen, 1955–1973).

140 See Tinsman, "Esposas golpeadas" and "Household *Patrones.*"

141 Case file S350;26768, SFJC.

142 Ibid.

143 Ibid.

144 Ibid.

145 Ibid.

146 Case file B27;27615, SFJC.
147 Ibid.

chapter 5. Struggling for Land

1 Author's calculations, based on CORA, "Fichas de expropriación," 50–185.
2 Ibid.
3 Ibid.
4 Barraclough and Fernández, *Diagnóstico,* 71.
5 CORA, "Fichas de expropriación," 169, 197.
6 Gómez, "Transformaciones," 36–41.
7 Ibid., 62.
8 CORA, "Fichas de expropriación," 1964–1970.
9 According to CORA, the Frei administration expropriated 45.7 percent of estates for abandoned or poor exploitation; 29.8 percent were voluntary transfers; 9.8 percent were improperly subdivided territories; and only 13 percent were in excessive size (CORA, *Reforma agraria chilena, 1965-1970,* 1970, 38).
10 See Loveman, *Struggle in the Countryside,* 252–54.
11 Various oral histories and interviews including Jorge Tejedo; Raúl Fuentes; Armando Gómez; Cristián Angelini, Santiago, 3 Mar. 1993; Miguel Merino, Santiago, 11 Mar. 1993.
12 Interview with "Juan," in *Hombres y Mujeres de Putaendo,* 38.
13 Garrett, "Growing Apart," 222.
14 According to studies conducted by Patricia Garrett and María Antonieta Huerta, between 1,200 and 1,500 asentados lived in the Aconcagua Valley by 1970 (Huerta, *Otro agro para Chile;* Garrett, "Growing Apart"). According to the INE's *Censo Agropecuario: Aconcagua, 1964-1965,* cuadro 6.1–6.3, the total male agricultural labor force (paid and unpaid) numbered 9,400 men.
15 CORA, "Fichas de expropriación," 1964–1970, 56, 124, 133.
16 Sergio Contreras, oral history.
17 Garrett, "Growing Apart," 154.
18 See Gómez, "Transformaciones," 43; 74; 80–81.
19 Emilio Ibáñez, oral history.
20 Estate case files 3248; 3250; 4729; and 5096, CORA.
21 Oral histories of Miguel Acevedo and Bernardo Flores. Miguel Merino, interview, Santiago, 11 March 1993.
22 Miguel Acevedo, oral history.
23 Jacobo Fernández, oral history.
24 Ibid.
25 See oral histories and interviews in *Obstáculos e incenitivos a la sindicalización campesina* (Santiago de Chile: FEES, 1970).

26 Miguel Merino, interview.

27 Miguel Acevedo, oral history.

28 Elena Vergara; María Trujillo; Rosa Saá, oral histories.

29 Various oral histories, including Elena Vergara; Katarina Antimán; Rita Galdámez; Rosa Saá; Victoria Antimán; and Claudia León, San Esteben, 21 June 1993.

30 Pedro Alvarez, Putaendo, 14 June 1993, oral history. Also see the interview with "Juan" in *Hombres y mujeres de Putaendo,* 45–46.

31 Pedro Alvarez, oral history.

32 Various oral histories, including Rosa Saá; Victoria Antimán; Claudia León; Elena Vergara.

33 Cristián Angelini interview, Santiago, 3 March 1993. Miguel Merino, interviews.

34 Patricia Garrett found that 96.3 percent of women in her sample never participated in any decision-making body (Garrett, "Growing Apart," 234).

35 Various oral histories, including Rosa Saá; Victoria Antimán; Claudia León; Elena Vergara.

36 Valdés S. and Araujo K., *Vida privada.*

37 Rosa Saá, oral history.

38 Pascual Muñoz, oral history.

39 Various oral histories, including Rosa Saá; Victoria Antimán; Patricia Carreras; Elena Vergara; Anita Hernández; Katarina Antimán; Rita Galdámez; Olivia González. Angelica Tejedo, oral history, Santa María, 24 Jan. 1993. See also Garrett, "Growing Apart"; and Valdés S., *Mujer, trabajo, y medio ambiente.*

40 The provincial records of CORA, which were unavailable for this study, might well include evidence of individual appeals and even more organized efforts by single women to challenge official policy.

41 Armando Gómez and Jorge Tejedo, oral histories.

42 Kay, "Class Conflict and Agrarian Reform," 135.

43 Macarena Mack, Paulina Matta, and Ximena Valdés, *Los Trabajos de las mujeres entre el campo y la ciudad, 1920–1982: Campesina, costurera, obrera de la costura, empleada doméstica, cocinera de fundo, temperera* (Santiago de Chile: Centro de Estudios de la Mujer, 1986); Valdés S. et al., *Sinópsis de una realidad ocultada;* Garrett, "Growing Apart."

44 INE, *Censo agropecuario: Aconcagua, 1964–1965,* Cuadro 6.3; INE, *Censo agropecuario: Aconcagua, 1975–1976,* Cuadro 11.A. Although the 1975–1976 agricultural census was conducted two years after the fall of the Popular Unity government, it is a close approximation of Chile's rural employment situation at the end of the Agrarian Reform. The military regime of 1973–1990 radically reorganized Chile's agriculture, but it did not begin dismantling asentamientos in full until after 1976.

45 Ibid.

46 INE, *Censo agropecuario: Aconcagua, 1975–1976,* Cuadros 25 and 28; INE, *Censo de población: Aconcagua, 1970,* Cuadro 9.

47 INE, *Censo agropecuario: Aconcagua, 1975–1976,* Cuadro 301.

48 W. Murray, "Competitive Global Fruit Export Markets: Marketing Intermediaries and Impacts on Small-Scale Growers in Chile," *Bulletin of Latin American Research* 16, no. 1 (1997).

49 See Murray, "Competitive Global Fruit Exports"; Sergio Gómez and Jorge Echeníque, *La Agricultura Chilena: Dos Caras de la Modernización* (Santiago de Chile: Facultad Latinoamericana de Ciencias Sociales, 1988); Lovell Jarvis, "Changing Private and Public Roles in Technological Development: Lessons from the Chilean Fruit Sector," in *Agricultural Technology: Policy Issues for the International Community,* ed. J. Anderson (Wellingford: CAB International, 1994).

50 INE, *Censo agropecuario: Aconcagua, 1964–1965,* Cuadro 18; INE, *Censo agropecuario: Aconcagua, 1975–1976,* Cuadro 15.A.

51 Ibid.

52 Fifty-two percent of women worked on properties between twenty and one hundred hectares in size, whereas only 19 percent worked on properties over one hundred hectares, most of which were asentamientos (INE, *Censo agropecuario: Aconcagua, 1975–1976,* Cuadros 22.B and 11.B).

53 See Mattelart, *La Mujer chilena;* Garrett, "Growing Apart;" *Hombres y mujeres de Putaendo;* Tinsman, "Unequal Uplift;" Ximena Valdés S. et al., eds., *Historias testimoniales de mujeres del campo* (Santiago de Chile: CEDEM, 1983).

54 Between 1964 and 1974, the number of women in the Aconcagua Valley permanently employed in agriculture reportedly fell from 113 to 111 (INE, *Censo agropecuario: Aconcagua, 1964–1965,* Cuadro 6.3; INE, *Censo agropecuario: Aconcagua, 1975–1976,* Cuadro 11.A).

55 Ibid.

56 Ibid.

57 David E. Hojoman, "Land Reform, Female Migration, and the Market for Domestic Service in Chile," *Journal of Latin American Studies* 21, no. 1 (1989): 105–32.

58 María Trujillo and María García, oral histories.

59 Figures from cuadros 1–3, appendix, qtd. Academia de Humanismo Cristiano, in *Historia del movimiento campesino.*

60 For example, *El Siglo* claimed that the Comité Coordenador de Confederaciones mobilized some 150,000 campesinos to participate in a one-day national strike protesting employer failure to make required monetary payments to FEES and the SNS (*El Siglo,* 13 May 1970).

61 Armando Gómez, oral history.

62 Gómez, "Transformaciones," 69.

63 According to *La Nación*, the Santa Marta estate had 1,000 hectares of irrigated land and more than 20,000 hectares of pasture and dry land. It had 180 permanent workers and inquilinos, 2,000 sheep, and 200 cattle. The estate had been the site of numerous labor conflicts since the 1950s and campesinos had formally requested its expropriation under Alessandri (*La Nación*, 15 Apr. 1998).

64 *La Nación*, 7 Mar. 1968; 8 Mar. 1968.

65 *La Nación*, 7 Mar. 1968; 8 Mar. 1968; 5 May 1968.

66 *La Nación*, 14 Jul. 1968.

67 Armando Gómez, oral history.

68 Various oral histories, including Jorge Tejedo; Raúl Aguirre; Pedro Muñoz; Jorge Ovalle; and Jorge Ríos, La Higuerra, 19 Oct. 1992.

69 Tanya Korovkin, "Neo-Liberal Counter-Reform: Peasant Differentiation and Organization in Tártaro Central Chile," in *Neo-Liberal Agriculture in Rural Chile*, ed. David E. Hojoman (New York: St. Martin's, 1990), 96.

70 Gómez, "Tranformaciones"; Kay, "Agrarian Reform and Class Struggle"; Kay and Silva, eds., *Development and Social Change;* Loveman, *Struggle in the Countryside.*

71 Interview with "Juan," in *Hombres y mujeres de Putaendo,* 37.

72 Armando Gómez, oral history.

73 Jacobo Fernández, oral history.

74 Susana López, oral history, Panquehue, 14 June 1993.

75 María García, oral history.

76 Jorge Tejedo, oral history.

77 *La Aurora*, 26 July 1968.

78 *La Aurora*, 1 Aug. 1968.

79 Estate case files 3259 and 3260, CORA.

80 According to newspaper accounts, a girl was killed by a government jeep that accidentally ran over her in the street (*El Siglo*, 19 Aug. 1968).

81 Claudia León and Sergio Contreras, oral histories.

82 Ibid.

83 *El Siglo*, 5 Aug. 1968; various oral histories, including Bernardo Flores; Miguel Acevedo; Lucilia Flores, oral history, San Esteben, 14 Sept. 1997.

84 Lucilia Flores, oral history.

85 Ibid.

86 Various oral histories, including Claudia León; Sergio Contreras; Lucilia Flores; Bernardo Flores.

87 Ibid.

88 *El Siglo*, 5 Aug. 1968.

89 Lucilia Flores, oral history.

90 *El Siglo,* 8 Aug. 1968.

91 Lucilia Flores, oral history.

92 Ibid.

93 *La Aurora,* 6 Aug. 1968.

94 Lucilia Flores, oral history.

95 *El Siglo,* 8 Aug. 1968.

96 *La Aurora,* 13 Aug. 1968.

97 San Miguel and several other estates involved in the 1968 strike were expropriated under the Popular Unity government in December 1972 and converted into an asentamiento of the same name (CORA, "Fichas de expropriación," 1964–1970, 188 and 189).

98 Claudia León and Sergio Contreras, oral histories.

99 Ibid.

100 This analysis draws on the important work of Temma Kaplan, "Female Consciousness and Collective Action: The Case of Barcelona, 1910–1918," *Signs* 7, no. 3 (1982): 545–63; and Maxine Molyneux, "Mobilization without Emancipation: Women's Interests and the State in Nicaragua," *Feminist Studies* 11, no. 2 (1985): 227–54.

101 *El Siglo,* 15 Aug. 1968.

102 Various oral histories, including Miguel Acevedo; Lucilia Flores; Angelica Saéz; and Rosa Saá.

103 *El Trabajo,* 14 June 1970.

chapter 6. Revolutionizing Women

1 Jorge Alessandri received 34.9 percent of the national vote; Radomiro Tomic 27.8 percent (Loveman, *Chile: The Legacy of Hispanic Capitalism,* 295).

2 Barraclough and Fernández, *Diagnóstico,* 71.

3 Solon Barraclough et al., *Chile: Reforma agraria y gobierno popular* (Buenos Aires: Ediciones Periferia, 1973), 11.

4 Ibid.

5 See Jaime Gazmuri, *Gobierno Popular: Reforma agraria* (Santiago de Chile: Centro de Estudios Agrarias de la Universidad Católica de Chile, 1972).

6 Qtd. from speech reprinted in *El Siglo,* 8 Mar. 1972.

7 For example, see text from a campaign speech by Allende for the 1964 elections, reprinted in *El Siglo,* 7 Oct. 1963; and *El Siglo,* 2 Aug. 1964.

8 Of all women who voted in the 1970 presidential election, 38.9 percent voted for Alessandri; 30.5 percent for Allende; and 30.2 percent for Tomic (DRE, "Elección ordinaria de presidente de la república, Septiembre, 1970"). For a gendered analysis of voting patterns, see Elsa Chaney, "The Mobilization of Women in Allende's Chile," in *Women in Politics,* ed. Jane S. Jaquette

(New York: Wiley, 1974); Michael Francis and Patricia A. Kyle, "Chile: The Power of Women at the Polls," in *Integrating the Neglected Majority: Government Responses to Demands for New Sex Roles,* ed. Kyle (Brunswick, Ohio: King's Court Communicating, 1976); Steven M. Neuse, "Voting in Chile: The Feminine Response," in *Political Participation in Latin America,* ed. John A. Booth and Mitchell A. Seligson (New York: Holmes and Meier, 1978–1979).

9 Of the entire male electorate, 42.1 percent voted for Allende; 31.7 percent for Alessandri; and 26.2 percent for Tomic. Scholars such as Norma Chinchilla, James Petras, and Maurice Zeitlan have argued that, in rural areas, (male) afuerinos and wage-earning workers provided the bulk of campesino support for Allende. For an overview of this literature, see Kay, "Agrarian Reform and the Class Struggle," 122.

10 Author's calculations from the "Elección Ordinaria de Presidente, 1970."

11 For a discussion of women's lower voter turnout nationwide, see Lisa Baldez, "In the Name of the Public and the Private: Conservative and Progressive Women's Movements in Chile" (Ph.D. diss., University of California-San Diego, 1997), 85; Neuse, "Voting in Chile," 130.

12 Baldez, "In the Name of the Public and the Private," 88–89.

13 Ibid., 86.

14 For a concise overview of UP policies toward women, see Sandra McGee Deutsch, "Gender and Sociopolitical Change in Twentieth-Century Latin America," *Hispanic American Historical Review* 71, no. 2 (1991): 292–306.

15 See *La Nación,* 2 Feb. 1973. Text qtd. from *El Siglo,* 16 Nov. 1972.

16 "La Politica agraria del gobierno de la UP: Discurso del compañero presidente Salvador Allende pronunciado en Valdivia el 7 de Octubre 1972," photocopied pamphlet, Wisconsin Land Tenure Center; CORA, "La Gran pelea entre lo nuevo y lo viejo," *Cuadernos campesinos para la unidad nacional,* 1971.

17 "La Politica agraria del gobierno de la UP," 28.

18 Ibid., 2.

19 Chaney, "The Mobilization of Women in Allende's Chile," 270.

20 Salvador Allende Gossens, *La Historia que estamos escribiendo: El Presidente en Antofagasta,* 1972, qtd. in Chaney, "The Mobilization of Women in Allende's Chile," 270.

21 Author's translation, qtd. in McGee Deutsch, "Gender and Sociopolitical Change," 298.

22 Ibid., 299.

23 Ibid.

24 *Puro Chile,* 7 Sept. 1972, qtd. in Baldez, "In the Name of the Public and the Private," 98.

25   La Nación, 5 Sept. 1972, qtd. in Baldez, "In the Name of the Public and the Private," 99.

26   Ibid.

27   Speech of Hortencia Bussi de Allende at the Segundo Seminario Latino-americano de Mujeres, Santiago. Reprinted in El Trabajo, 27 Oct. 1972.

28   El Siglo, 8 Mar. 1972.

29   Allende's speech from the press conference at the Concepción Intendencia on UP Infant-Child programs, El Siglo, 29 Mar. 1972.

30   Comité Sectorial de Salud, Unidad Popular, "Doctrina de salud: Pre-informe de la Comisión Central de Salud," reprinted in APROFA, Boletín APROFA, December 1970, 4.

31   Ibid.

32   Various oral histories and interviews, including Anita Hernández; Luís Ortega; Marta Danéa, interview, San Felipe, 19 Nov. 1992.

33   APROFA, Boletín APROFA, Jan. 1971, 1–2.

34   APROFA, Boletín APROFA, Nov. 1971, 2.

35   La Nación, 16 Apr. 1972.

36   Qtd. from Jiles, De la miel a los implantes, 157.

37   See Fischer, Political Ideology and Educational Reform,; Joseph P. Farrell, The National Unified School in Allende's Chile: The Role of Education in the Destruc-tion of Revolution (Vancouver: Univ. of British Columbia Press, 1986).

38   Qtd. in Fischer, Political Ideology and Educational Reform in Chile, 75.

39   APROFA, Boletín APROFA, Nov. 1971, 2.

40   APROFA, Boletín APROFA, Sept. 1971, 2.

41   APROFA, Boletín APROFA, Sept. 1972, 1–2.

42   APROFA, Boletín APROFA, Sept. 1971, 1.

43   Virginia Vidal, La Emancipación de la mujer (Santiago de Chile: Editorial Nacional Quimantú, 1972), 49–52.

44   Ibid., 49–50.

45   Ibid., 76.

46   Ibid., 87.

47   Puz, La Mujer chilena.

48   For an account of Klimpel's priorities as Minister of the Family, see inter-view in La Nación, 5 Feb. 1971. Also see Klimpel's 1960 study on the social conditions of Chilean women, La Mujer chilena: El Aporte femenino de Chile, 1910–1960 (Santiago de Chile: Editorial Andrés Bello, 1962).

49   For example, see an article by Chilean feminist Olga Poblete, La Ultima Hora, 9 Mar. 1971; speech by Arpad Pullai, El Siglo, 8 Mar. 1972; inter-view with women union leaders in La Nación, 6 Sept. 1972, and La Nación, 23 Mar. 1968.

50   McGee Deutsch, "Gender and Socio-Political Change," 301.

51   For Hortencia Bussi de Allende on divorce, see speech reprinted in El Tra-

bajo, 27 Oct. 1972. For Felicitas Klimpel and the Ministry of the Family on divorce, see *La Nación,* 5 Feb. 1971.

52   APROFA, *Boletín APROFA,* Dec. 1970, 2.

53   APROFA, *Boletín APROFA,* Nov. 1971, 2; and July 1972, 1.

54   Legislation abolishing the distinction between illegitimate and legitimate children was introduced, but not passed by the time of Allende's overthrow. Nonetheless, its very proposal already began to have an impact on the official recording of births. In the department of San Felipe, the Registro Civil stopped distinguishing between illegitimate, natural, and legitimate children in the beginning of 1971. In 1972, 23 percent of all women giving birth in the department of San Felipe were not married to the father of their child, and fully 27.5 percent of these mothers had not yet reached the age of twenty (author's study of RCSF Registro de nacimiento, San Felipe, 1964–1973).

55   Many Communists had been particularly longstanding proponents of legal abortion. For arguments, see *El Siglo,* 7 and 8 Nov. 1969.

56   "Citas de documentos de la Unidad Popular," *Boletín APROFA,* Dec. 1970, 2.

57   Jiles, *De la miel a los implantes,* 160.

58   Anita Hernández and Rosa Saá, oral histories.

59   "APROFA, 1962–1972: Diez años de labor," *Boletín APROFA,* Aug. 1972, 6.

60   APROFA estimated that between 1971 and 1973 the overall rate of abortion in Chile diminished by 2 percent, while the rate of abortion-related maternal death decreased by 26.5 percent (*Estadísticas APROFA,* 1980, 10–12). A 1972 report by American University claimed that while both abortion-related hospitalization and death declined between 1970 and 1972, the number of abortions relative to pregnancies remained the same (American University Field Staff, "Births, Abortions, and the Progress of Chile," *Field Staff Reports,* 19, no. 2 [1972]: 2–3).

61   Between 1971 and September 1973, no arrests for abortion were made in Aconcagua (SFJC, Registro de Crimenes).

62   Dr. Onofre Avendano, "El Aborto: Problema médico, social y jurídico," unpublished study by APROFA, Dec. 1972, 3.

63   Ibid., 4.

64   Ibid.

65   APROFA, "Síntesis historica de la planificación familiar en Chile," 1974, 18.

66   For a discussion of this conflict, see Jiles, *De la miel a los implantes,* 160.

67   Ana María Silva Dreyer, "Estadisticas sobre planificación familiar y aborto en Chile," unpublished paper, informativo no. 4, Instituto de la Mujer, Santiago de Chile, 1990, 5.

68   Nora Ruedi, "La Transición de la fecundidad," qtd. in Silva Dreyer, "Tendencias generales de la fecundidad en Chile, 1960–1987," 3.

69   According to Ruedi's study, family planning programs between 1965 and

1975 had the greatest proportional impact on women from the poorest agricultural sectors. Whereas fertility rates for poor rural women all rose between 1955 and 1965 (for the poorest campesina women by 17.12 percent), fertility between 1965 and 1975 declined by 39.65 percent for the poorest minifundistas, by 39.82 percent for the poorest rural and urban wage-earners, and by 31.92 percent for nonworking campesina women (ibid., 6–7).

70 According to SNS figures, Chile's infant mortality rate dropped from 79.3 deaths per 1,000 live births in 1970 to 65.2 deaths per 1,000 live births in 1973 (SNS San Felipe-Los Andes, "Defunciones y causas de muerte," 1972 and 1988; SNS San Felipe-Los Andes, "*Nacimientos,*" 1972 and 1988).

71 According to data compiled by Silva Dreyer, the number of women admitted to hospitals for abortion-related complications declined by 26 percent between 1965 and 1970 and by 13.5 percent between 1970 and 1975. She emphasizes that although abortion data included information on spontaneous miscarriages, most of the abortion-related hospitalizations indicated induced abortions (Silva Dreyer, "Estadisticas sobre planificación familiar y aborto en Chile," 16). Whereas 1,211 women were admitted to the San Felipe hospital for abortion in 1964, this number fell to 915 in 1964 and 849 in 1972 (compiled from SNS, "Engresos hospitalarios: Estadísticas de salud," 1976). According to APROFA, maternal death declined from 16.8 deaths per 1,000 women of fertile age in 1970 to 12.2 deaths per 1,000 women of fertile age in 1973 (APROFA, *Estadísticas APROFA,* 1980).

72 For examples of UP initiatives to mobilize women, see *La Nación,* 11 Feb. 1973; and 4 May 1973.

73 "Mensaje Presidencial, 21 de Mayo 1971," qtd. in Valdés et al., "Centros de madres," 23–24.

74 *El Siglo,* 31 Jan. 1972.

75 Gaviola Artigas, Lopresti, and Rojas, "Chile centros de madres," 79–88.

76 Valdés et al., "Centros de madres," 22.

77 See *El Siglo,* 30 Nov. 1970.

78 Various oral histories including María Trujillo; Emilio Ibáñez; Patricia Carreras; Elena Vergara.

79 Gabriel Fernández, interview, San Antonio, 28 May 1993.

80 Various oral histories, including María Trujillo; Emilio Ibáñez; Jorge Tejedo; Jorge Ríos; Anita Hernánez; Carlos Ordenas, Calle Medio, 7 Sept. 1997; María Ordenas, Calle Medio, 7 Sept. 1997.

81 Carlos Ordenas, oral history.

82 *El Trabajo,* 24 May 1973.

83 Gabriel Fernández, interview.

84 The transaction was not completed before the military coup in September

1973, when several leaders of the Villa España toma were reportedly taken prisoner.

85 Roberto Rojas, La Troya, 7 Sept. 1997; Luís Alberto Reinoso, La Troya, 7 Sept. 1997; Miguel Gutiérrez, Calle Medio, 7 Sept. 1997; Sebastián Tapia, Calle Medio, 7 Sept. 1997; Carlos Ordenas, oral histories.

86 Ibid.

87 "La Politica agraria del gobierno de la UP,"; CORA, "La Gran pelea entre lo nuevo y lo viejo."

88 For press coverage of various campesino scholarships offered by the UP, see *La Nación,* 7 May 1971; 23 Jan. 1972; 30 Jan. 1972; 30 Apr. 1972; 25 Jul. 1972; 14 Mar. 1973; *El Trabajo,* 22 Aug. 1973.

89 Farrell, *The National Unified School.*

90 *La Nación,* 1 Oct. 1971.

91 *La Nación,* 25 Jul. 1972.

92 Local newspapers frequently advertised youth club activities, including both educational and recreational events. For examples, see *El Trabajo,* 16 Apr. 1971; 15 June 1971; 14 July 1971; 14 June 1972; *La Aurora,* 11 Mar. 1971; 15 May 1971; 6 June 1973.

93 IER, *Memoria IER, 1970–1971,* 24.

94 Various oral histories including Carlos Ordenas; Miguel Acevedo; Lucilia Flores.

95 Chaney, "The Mobilization of Women in Allende's Chile," 271.

96 *Ramona,* 28 Mar. 1972, qtd. in Chaney, "The Mobilization of Women in Allende's Chile," 271.

97 Kay, "Agrarian Reform and Class Struggle," 125–27.

98 Interview with Eliseo Richards, Jefe de Capacitación, *La Nación,* 26 Apr. 1973.

99 *El Siglo,* 8 Mar. 1972.

100 *El Siglo,* 11 Mar. 1972.

101 *La Nación,* 20 Apr. 1971; 4 Nov. 1972; *La Ultima Hora,* 6 Oct. 1972; *El Siglo,* 29 Mar. 1972.

102 *La Ultima Hora,* 6 Oct. 1972.

103 *El Trabajo,* 10 Jul. 1972.

104 *Punto Final,* 22 June 1971; qtd. in Chaney, "Women in Latin American Politics," 108.

105 Vidal, *La Emancipación de la mujer,* 18.

106 For official UP discussions of incorporating women into the workforce, see Unidad Popular, *La Mujer en el gobierno de la Unidad Popular* (Santiago de Chile: Editorial Quimantú, 1970); Puz, *La Mujer chilena; El Siglo,* 13 Feb. 1972; 11 Mar. 1972; 10 Dec. 1972; *La Nación,* 20 Apr. 1971; 21 Nov. 1972; 9 Sept. 1972; *La Ultima Hora,* 6 Oct. 1972.

107 *La Nación,* 6 Sept. 1972.

108 *La Nación,* 2 Feb. 1973.

109 Interview with Jorge Fontaine, reprinted in *El Siglo,* 29 Mar. 1972.

110 Fischer, "Political Ideology and Educational Reform."

111 *La Nación,* 2 Feb. 1973.

112 For a description of the expansion of this program under the UP, see *El Trabajo,* 10 July 1972.

113 Adriana Muñoz, "Fuerza de trabajo feminina: Evolución y téndencias," in *Mundo de Mujer: Cambio y Continuidad* (Santiago de Chile: Centro de Estudios de la Mujer, 1992), 209.

114 INDAP, "Memoria del Departamento de Educación y Economía del Hogar," 1972, 1.

115 Rosa Saá, oral history.

116 *La Nación,* 9 Oct. 1972; *El Siglo,* 6 Apr. 1973; *La Ultima Hora,* 6 Nov. 1972.

117 See Loveman, *Struggle in the Countryside,* 291–98.

118 INDAP, "Poder Campesino: El Campesino en el Centro de Reforma Agraria," 1972, 5.

119 Ibid., 6.

120 *La Nación,* 12 Dec. 1971; *El Siglo,* 29 Mar. 1972.

121 Garrett, "Growing Apart."

122 INDAP, "El Centro de la Reforma Agraria," 1971, 2.

123 Garrett, "Growing Apart," 105.

124 Ibid.

125 Various oral histories, including María Trujillo; Raúl Fuentes; Miguel Merino; Victor Acevedo, oral history, Los Andes, 18 May 1993.

126 Victor Acevedo, oral history.

127 Various oral histories including Angelica Tejedo; Silvia Ahumada, Panquehue, 26 Apr. 1993.

128 Patricia Carreras and Nancy Silva, oral histories.

129 INE, *Estadísticas Laborales,* 1976, 41.

130 Interview with Eduardo Placencio, Gerente de Desarollo Campesino de CORA, 1972; qtd. in Vidal, *La Emancipación de la mujer,* 65.

131 Interview with Hector Reyes, reprinted in *El Siglo,* 29 Mar. 1972.

132 See Elizabeth Quay Hutchison, "El Fruto envenenado del arbol capitalista: Women Workers and the Prostitution of Labor in Urban Chile, 1896–1925," *Journal of Women's History* 9, no. 4 (1998): 131–52.

133 Various oral histories including Jorge Tejedo; Raúl Fuentes; Armando Gómez.

134 Juan Carrera, interview, Santiago, 3 May 1992.

chapter 7. Coming Apart

1 Case file S370;28128, SFJC.

2 Cases such as this suggest the endurance of honor as a marker of sexual and social respectability. See the rich literature on honor and its transformation from colonial to modern times, cited in endnote 51, chapter 2.

3 Case file S370;28128, SFJC.

4 Ibid.

5 Ibid.

6 Out of 114 rape cases filed at the San Felipe Juzgado de Crimen between 1958 and 1973, 70 were available for examination in this study. Thirty-six involved persons listed as "agricultural workers" or "campesinos," whereas another twelve involved very poor people who may have made part of their livelihood from agriculture. Only four cases involved married women or women under age twenty-five (SFJC, Regístro de Crimenes, 1958–1973).

7 Ibid.

8 Only a minority of rape cases (eleven of those studied) ended in a man's conviction, and in those that did not, it was customary for charges against the defendant to be dropped.

9 For strikes in 1970 and 1973, see INE, *Estadísticas Laborales,* 1976, 96–100; for strikes in 1971 and 1972, see Barraclough and Fernández, *Diagnóstico,* 134; for land occupations, see Academia de Humanismo Cristiano, *Historia del movimiento campesino,* Cuadro 1.

10 For discussion of the crisis leading to Allende's overthrow, see Paul E. Sigmund, *The United States and Democracy in Chile* (Baltimore: Johns Hopkins Univ. Press, 1993).

11 According to Paul Sigmund, Patria y Libertad received $38,000 from the CIA for anti-Allende activities (cited in Baldez, "In the Name of the Public and the Private," 86–89).

12 For a detailed discussion of oppositional organizing by women during the UP, see Baldez, "In the Name of the Public and the Private." Also see Chaney, "The Mobilization of Women in Allende's Chile"; Edda Gaviola Artigas, Lorella Lopresti, and Claudia Rojas, "La Participación política de la mujer chilena"; María de los Angeles Crummett, "El Poder Feminino: The Mobilization of Women against Socialism in Chile," *Latin American Perspectives* 4, no. 4 (1977): 103–13; Michèle Mattelart, "Chile: The Feminine Side of the Coup; or, When Bourgeois Women Take to the Streets," *NACLA's Latin America and Empire Report* 9, no. 6 (1975): 14–25; Margaret Power, "Right-Wing Women and Chilean Politics: 1964–1973" (Ph.D. diss., University of Illinois-Chicago, 1997).

13 Baldez, "In the Name of the Public and the Private"; Power, "Right-Wing Women and Chilean Politics."

14 *El Siglo,* 4 May 1972.

15 Baldez, "In the Name of the Public and the Private," 77; 113; 115.

16 *La Aurora,* 21 Mar. 1972.

17 Lucilia Flores, oral history.

18 *El Siglo,* 13 Jun. 1973.

19 Salinas, *Trayectoria.*

20 Loveman, *Struggle in the Countryside;* Kay, "Agrarian Reform and Class Struggle."

21 CEPROS were large state farms designed to remain collectively farmed and intended to maximize production. Few CEPROS were actually established and there were none in the Aconcagua Valley (see José Garrido, "Origen e alcances de la crisis alimentaria," in *Fuerzas armadas y seguridad nacional,* ed. [Santiago de Chile: Portada, 1973], 170).

22 For a discussion of this problem from within UP ranks, see Gazmuri, *Gobierno popular y reforma agraria.*

23 Gómez, *Los Empresarios agrícolas,* 41; 43.

24 Ibid.

25 Miguel Acevedo, oral history.

26 *La Aurora,* 25 Jun. 1973; 27 July 1973; *El Trabajo,* 4 Jun. 1972; 8 June 1972; *El Siglo,* 8 Apr. 1972.

27 *El Campesino,* Jan. 1972, Mar. 1972, Apr. 1973.

28 Gómez, *Los Empresarios agrícolas.*

29 Ibid.

30 Barraclough et al., *Chile: Reforma agraria y gobierno popular,* 134; Academia de Humanismo Cristiano, *Historia del movimiento campesino,* Cuadro 1.

31 Kay, "Agrarian Reform and Class Struggle," 127–29.

32 Peter Winn, *Weavers of Revolution: The Yarur Workers and Chile's Road to Socialism* (New York: Oxford Univ. Press, 1986).

33 Twenty-four accounts of land occupations during the 1971–1973 period were found in CORA files on individual estates in San Felipe and Los Andes (estate case files, CORA). Due to the careless maintenance of these records, however, it was impossible to survey records for all properties, and this figure probably significantly underestimates the number of land occupations.

34 Armando Gómez, oral history.

35 Various oral histories and interviews, including Jorge Tejedo; Daniel San Martín; Miguel Merino; Armando Gómez; Emilio Ibáñez.

36 Jorge Ovalle and Jorge Ríos, oral histories.

37 Interview by Peter Winn, Melipilla, 1972, cited in Kay, "Agrarian Reform

and Class Struggle," 134. Also see Winn and Kay, "Agrarian Reform and Rural Revolution in Allende's Chile."

38 Diego Rojas, oral history, Catemu, 25 May 1993.

39 Pascual Muñoz, oral history.

40 Norma Stoltz Chinchilla and Marvin Sternberg, "Reform and Class Struggle in the Countryside," *Latin American Perspectives* 1, no. 2 (1974): 106–28. Other researchers are less specific about quantifying the support, but share this conclusion. See Barraclough and Fernández, *Diagnóstico;* Echeníque, *La Reforma agraria chilena;* Garrett, "Growing Apart"; Gómez, "Los Campesinos beneficados por la reforma agraria"; Kay, "Agrarian Reform and Class Struggle in Chile"; Loveman, *Struggle in the Countryside.*

41 Loveman, *Struggle in the Countryside,* 235.

42 Loveman, *Struggle in the Countryside,* 291–96; Kay, "Class Struggle and Agrarian Reform," 130.

43 Garrido, "Origen e alcances de la crisis alimentaria," 170.

44 For internal UP discussions about the problem of organizing afuerinos see FEES, *La Organización sindical del sector afuerino,* 1971.

45 Raúl Aguirre, oral history.

46 Ibid.

47 Armando Gómez, oral history.

48 Ibid.

49 Various oral histories and interviews, including Jorge Tejedo; Emilio Ibáñez; Daniel San Martín; Raúl Aguirre.

50 Jorge Tejedo, oral history.

51 Ibid.

52 Estate case file 3248, CORA.

53 Ibid.

54 Ibid.

55 Emilio Ibáñez, oral history; Cristián Angelini, interview.

56 Raúl Aravena, interview, Santiago, 3 Mar. 1993.

57 Raúl Fuentes, oral history.

58 Miguel Acevedo and Bernardo Flores, oral histories.

59 Gómez, *Los Empresarios agrícolas.*

60 *La Aurora,* 27 July 1973.

61 *La Aurora,* 27 July 1973; Bernardo Flores and Lucilia Flores, oral histories.

62 Bernardo Flores and Armando Gómez, oral histories.

63 Pascual Muñoz, oral history.

64 Carlos Ordenas, oral history.

65 Raúl Aguirre, oral history.

66 Ibid.

67 Bernardo Flores, oral history.

68 Angélica Tejedo, oral history; Victoria Acevedo, oral history, Putaendo, 4 May 1993.

69 Susana López, oral history.

70 Elena Vergara and Susana López, oral histories.

71 Barraclough and Fernández, *Diagnóstico,* 7.

72 See, for example, Anita Hernández, oral history.

73 Angelica Saéz, oral history.

74 Anita Hernández and Angelica Saéz, oral histories.

75 Angelica Saéz, oral history.

76 Anita Hernández, oral history.

77 Olivia Ibacache, oral history, Panquehue, 23 May 1993.

78 Oral histories of María Trujillo; Patricia Carreras; and Lucilia Flores.

79 Oral histories of María Trujillo; Miguel Acevedo; Bernardo Flores; and Lucilia Flores.

80 Estate case file 4727, CORA.

81 María Trujillo and Miguel Acevedo, oral histories.

82 María Trujillo, oral history.

83 Ibid.

84 Carlos Navarro, oral history, San Felipe, 26 Feb. 1993.

85 The conflict was still unresolved when the military overthrew Allende in September 1973. According to María Trujillo, all occupants of the factory were arrested by the armed forces.

86 Qtd. from interview of "Inés," in *Hombres y mujeres de Putaendo,* 1986, 17–18.

87 Various oral histories, including Elena Vergara; Armando Gómez; Jorge Tejedo; Ana Saavedra, oral history, San Felipe, 15 April 1993. Also see *Hombres y mujeres de Putaendo;* and Valdés S. et al., eds., *Historias testimoniales.*

88 Various oral sources, including Raúl Fuentes; Armando Gómez; Emilio Toledo; Pedro Muñoz.

89 Raúl Fuentes; Armando Gómez; Elena Vergara; Anita Hernández, oral histories.

90 Armando Gómez, oral history.

91 Ibid.

92 Jorge Tejedo, oral history.

93 Ana Saavedra, oral history.

94 Jorge Tejedo, oral history.

95 Elena Vergara as she was interviewed as "Inés" in *Hombres y mujeres de Putaendo,* 119–20.

96 The number of "woundings" cases filed by women against men at the San Felipe Juzgado de Crimen was thirty-four in 1971, thirty in 1972, and fifty in 1973. Between 1964 and 1970, there was a total of eighty-four cases, or an annual average of twelve cases (*SFJC,* Registro de Crimenes).

97 Almost three quarters of the seventy-one wife-beating cases filed between 1971 and 1973 available for study involved women from poor rural families (SFJC).

98 Eighteen cases involved women's accusations of male infidelity.

99 Various oral histories, including Anita Hernández; María Galdámez; Katarina Antimán; Elena Vergara.

100 Anita Hernández, oral history.

101 María Galdámez and Katarina Antimán, oral histories, *El Trabajo,* 8 June 1971; 20 June 1973; *La Aurora,* 16 May 1971.

102 Between 1964 and 1970 an average of fifteen home abandonment cases occurred per year; between 1971 and 1973 there was an annual average of thirty-five such cases (SFJC, Regístro de Crimenes).

103 Case file S373; 28295, SFJC.

104 Case file S378; 28837, SFJC.

105 Author's calculations from SFJC, Regístro de Crimenes.

106 Case files S374; 27906; S370; 27835; S345; 27924, SFJC.

107 Case file S374; 27906, SFJC.

108 Case file S378; 28846, SFJC.

109 In 1964, 18 percent of all births registered in San Felipe corresponded to unmarried women whose children were either "illegitimate" or "natural." In 1972, this figure was 23 percent. In 1965, women under age twenty accounted for 23 percent of illegitimate births, whereas they accounted for 27.5 percent of such births in 1972 (author's calculations from SFRC, Regístro de Nacimiento, 1964–1973).

110 According to the national census in 1960, 11 percent of rural women under age twenty in Aconcagua were married. In 1970, this figure had risen to 12 percent. In 1960, 57 percent of all women between twenty and twenty-nine years of age were married. In 1970, this figure rose to 60 percent (INE, *Censo de población: Aconcagua, 1960* and *Censo de población: Aconcagua, 1970*). In 1970, the average age at which rural women in Aconcagua married was 22.8 years. In 1960 this figure rose to 24 years and it fell again slightly in 1968 to 23.6 (INE, *Demografía: Aconcagua, 1960; Demografía: Aconcagua, 1968; Demografía: Aconcagua, 1970*).

111 Gaviola Artigas, Lopresti, and Rojas, "La Participación de la mujer chilena"; Chaney, "Women in Latin American Politics" and "The Mobilization of Women in Allende's Chile"; Francis and Kyle, "Chile: The Power of Women at the Polls"; Neuse, "Voting in Chile: The Feminine Response"; Norma Stoltz Chinchilla, "Mobilizing Women: Revolution in the Revolution," in *Women in Latin America;* María de los Angeles Crummett, "El Poder Feminino"; Nathaniel Davis, *The Last Two Years of Salvador Allende* (Ithaca, N.Y.: Cornell Univ. Press, 1984).

112 Baldez, "In the Name of the Public and the Private," 88–89.
113 DRE, "Elección Ordinaria de Regidores, 4 de Abril 1971."
114 Ibid.
115 DRE, "Elección Ordinaria Parlamentaria (Diputados), 4 de Marzo 1973."
116 In the rural counties of Melipilla, María Pinto, El Monte, and San Antonio, the percentage of the female vote going to the UP in 1973 was, respectively: 32.1, 38.7, 35.4, and 46.7. In the departments of San Bernardo and Maipo, it was 39 and 36.1, respectively. The percentage of the male vote going to the UP in these regions was even higher: for Melipilla, 40.9; for María Pinto, 47.5; for El Monte, 46; for San Antonio, 56.2; for San Bernardo, 48; for Maipo, 46.1 (ibid.).

Epilogue: 1973–1988

1 Allende died during the bombing of the National Palace, and the cause of his death is hotly contested. Many believe he was killed by the military; others maintain that he committed suicide.
2 Daniel San Martín, interview.
3 Emilio Ibáñez and Armando Gómez, oral histories.
4 Angelica Sáez, oral history.
5 In 1979, the military instituted a labor code that formally reinstated the rights of unions to collectively bargain and strike. However, in the case of agricultural workers, the new law's restrictiveness effectively rendered collective bargaining and strikes illegal.
6 There is a substantial literature on the impact of military rule and neoliberal economic policy on the Chilean countryside. Major works include Sergio Gómez and Jorge Echeníque, *La Agricultura Chilena: Dos caras de la modernización* (Santiago de Chile: CIREN, 1988); Sergio Gómez, *Políticas estatales y campesinado en Chile (1960–1989),* (Santiago de Chile: Facultad Latinoamericano de Ciencias Sociales, 1989); María Elena Cruz and Cecilia Leiva, *La Fruticultura en Chile después de 1973: Una Area privilegiada de expansión del capitalismo* (Santiago de Chile: Grupo de Investigaciones Agrarias, 1987); Jaime Crispi, "Neo-liberalismo y campesinado en Chile," working paper no. 5, Grupo de Investigaciones Agrarias, Santiago de Chile, 1981; Lovell Jarvis, *Chilean Agriculture under Military Rule;* Arturo Saéz, *El Empresario frutícola chileno 1973–1985: Uvas y manzanas, democracia y autoritarismo* (Santiago de Chile: Ediciones Sur, 1986); Daniel Rodríguez and Silvia Venegas, *De praderas a parronales* (Santiago de Chile: GEA, 1989); Silvia Venegas, *Una Gota al dia . . . un chorro al ano: El Impacto social de la expancion fruitcola* (Santiago de Chile: GEA, 1992); Kay and Silva, eds., *Development and Social Change in the Chilean Countryside;* Patricio Silva, "The State, Politics, and Peasant Unions

in Chile," *Journal of Latin American Studies,* no. 20; Gonzalo Falabella, "Trabajo temporal y desorganización social," *Proposiciones* (Santiago, 1988).

7 In the Aconcagua Valley, approximately 1,200 men received land allotments from former asentamientos between 1976 and 1980. In the comunas of San Felipe, Los Andes, and Putaendo, almost three quarters of these recipients had sold their property by 1986 (CORA, "Proyecto de parcelización, Aconcagua," 1975–1988; Bienes Raices, San Felipe, Los Andes, and Putaendo, "Inscripciones de CORA," 1975–1988).

8 Falabella, "Trabajo temporal y desorganización social"; Ximena Valdés S., "Feminización del mercado de trabajo agrícola: Las Temporeras," in *Mundo de mujer: Cambio y continuidad* (Santiago de Chile, Centro de Estudios de la Mujer, 1988).

9 Armando Gómez, oral history.

10 There is a substantial literature on the impact of the fruit industry on rural women and rural gender roles. See Valdés S., *Mujer, trabajo y medio ambiente;* Valdés S., "Feminización del mercado de trabajo agrícola"; Valdés S., "Entre la crisis de la uva y la esperanza en crisis," paper presented at the 47th American Congress, New Orleans, July 1991; Valdés S. et al., *Sinópsis de una realidad ocultada;* Falabella, "Trabajo temporal y desorganización social"; Falabella, "Organizarse y sobrevivir: Democracia y sindicalización en Santa María," paper presented at the 47th American Congress, New Orleans, July, 1991; María Soledad Lago and Carlota Olavarria, *La Participación de la mujer en las economias campesinas: Un Estudio de casos en dos comunas frutícolas* (Santiago de Chile: Grupo de Investigaciones Agrarias, 1981); Pilar Campana, "La Problematica de la organización de la mujer rural en Chile," *Agricultura y Sociedad* (May 1987); Julia Medel, Soledad Olivos, and Verónica Riquelme, *La Temporeras y sus visión del trabajo* (Santiago de Chile: Centro de Estudios de la Mujer, 1989); Veronica Oxmán, "La Participación de la mujer campesina en organizaciones," unpublished paper, ISIS-Santiago, 1983.

11 For further elaboration on this argument, see Tinsman, "Patrones del hogar" and "Household *Patrones.*"

12 Estimates of the Servicio Nacional de la Mujer, qtd. in Venegas, *Una Gota al dia.*

13 For the changes in gender dynamics and women's political activism under authoritarian rule, as well as the relevance of the Agrarian Reform to anti-dictatorship struggles, see Heidi Tinsman, "Reviving Feminist Materialism: Neo-liberalism in Pinochet's Chile, 1973–1990," *Signs* 26, no. 1 (2000): 145–88.

14 Gonzalo Falabella, "Historia del Santa María sindicato inter-empresa de trabajadores permanentes y temporeros," unpublished manuscript, 1999, author's copy; and Falabella, "Organizarse y sobrevivir"; Valdés S., "Femi-

nización del mercado de trabajo agrícola" and "Entre la crisis de la uva y la esperanza en crisis."

15   Santa María Sindicato Inter-Empresa de Trabajadores Permanentes y Temporeros, Regístro de Socios, 1990.

16   See Veronica Schield, "Recasting Popular Movements: Gender and Political Learning in Neighborhood Organizing in Chile," *Latin American Perspectives* 21, no. 2 (1994): 59–76.

17   Author's notes from El Primer Encuentro Nacional de la Mujer Temporera, sponsored by the Comisión Nacional Campesina at Canelo de Nos, Santiago de Chile, June 6–8, 1993.

18   Various oral histories, including María Galdámez; Anita Hernández; Elena Muñoz, Santa María, 22 Nov. 1992; Sonia Gutiérrez, Santa María, 14 June 1993. Also, author's notes from meetings of the Santa María union directiva, June and July 1991 and February through December 1992.

selected bibliography

Archives and Public Records

Archive of the Asociación de Protección de la Familia, Santiago de Chile (APROFA)
Archive of the ex-Corporación de Reforma Agraria, Sociedad de Agricultura y Ganado, Santiago de Chile (CORA)
Archive of the Instituto de Desarrollo Agropecuario, Ministerio de Agricultura, Santiago de Chile (INDAP)
Archive of the Instituto de Educación Rural, Santiago de Chile (IER)
Archive of the Instituto Pastoral Rural, Santiago de Chile (INPRU)
Archive of the Ministerio de Vivienda, Santiago de Chile (MV)
Archive of the San Felipe Juzgado de Crimen, San Felipe, Chile (SFJC)
Archive of the Sociedad Nacional de Salud, Santiago and San Felipe, Chile (SNS)
Dirección Registro Electoral, Santiago de Chile (DRE)
Instituto Nacional de Estadísticas, Santiago de Chile (INE)
Land Tenure Center, University of Wisconsin, Madison (LTC)
Regístro Civíl, Los Andes, Chile (RCLA)
Regístro Civíl, San Felipe, Chile (RCSF)
Regístro Civíl, Santa María, Chile (RCSM)
Santa María Iglesia Católica (SMIC), Santa María, Chile

Government Documents and Reports

Chile, Comisión Central del Censo. *Censo Agropecuario, Aconcagua.* 1955; 1965; 1975.
———— *Censo de Población: Aconcagua.* Santiago de Chile, 1960; 1970.
Chile, Fundación de Educación Sindical. *Descripción numérica de la organización campesina chilena, 1968–1969.* Santiago de Chile, 1971.

Chile, Instituto Nacional de Estadísticas. *Demografía.* Santiago de Chile, 1960–1970.

———— *Encuesta de hogares.* Santiago de Chile, 1966; 1968.

———— *Estadísticas Laborales.* 1964–1976.

Chile, Ministerio de Trabajo y Provisión Social. "Informe sobre asuntos laborales." Santiago de Chile, 1969.

Comité Interamericano de Desarrollo Agrícola. *Chile: Tenencia de la tierra y desarrollo socio económico del sector agrícola.* Santiago de Chile, 1966.

Corporación de Formento de la Producción (CORFO). "Insumos físicos en la agricultura, 1961–1962." Santiago de Chile: Imprenta Arancibia, 1964.

Corporación de Reforma Agraria. *Reforma agraria chilena, 1965–1970.* Santiago de Chile, 1970.

Instituto de Capacitación e Investigación de Reforma Agraria. *Antecedentes para el estudio de conflictos colectivos en el campo.* Santiago de Chile, 1972.

Periodicals and Newspapers

La Aurora (Los Andes), 1957–1973
Boletín APROFA (Santiago de Chile), 1964–1973
El Campesino (Santiago de Chile), 1958–1973
Confederación Campesina (Santiago de Chile), 1966
Lucha Obrera (Santiago de Chile), 1964–1973
El Mercurio (Santiago de Chile), 1958–1973
La Nación (Santiago de Chile), 1957–1973
La Nueva Prensa (Santiago de Chile), 1967–1972
Nuevo Campo (Santiago de Chile), 1967–1968
Punto Final (Santiago de Chile), 1970–1973
La Reforma Agraria (Santiago de Chile), 1960–1962
El Siglo (Santiago de Chile), 1958–1973
Sucro y Semilla (Santiago de Chile), 1962–1972
Tierra y Libertad (Santiago de Chile), 1962–1964
El Trabajo (San Felipe), 1958–1973
Ultima Hora (Santiago de Chile), 1971–1972
Unidad Campesina (Santiago de Chile), 1962–1963

Published Sources

Academia de Humanismo Cristiano. *Historia del movimiento campesino.* Santiago de Chile: Grupo de Investigaciones Agrarias, 1983.

Acuña, Lila. *Hombres y mujeres en Putaendo: Sus discursos y su visión de la historia.* Santiago de Chile: Centro de Estudios de la Mujer, 1986.

Affonso, Almino, et al. *Movimiento campesino chileno.* 2 vols. Santiago de Chile: Instituto de Capacitación e Investigación en Reforma Agraria, 1970.

Alaluf, David, et al. *Reforma agraria chilena: Seis ensayos de interpretación.* Santiago de Chile: Instituto Capacitación e Investigación en Reforma Agraria, 1970.

Alonso, Ana María. *Thread of Blood: Colonialism, Revolution, and Gender on Mexico's Northern Frontier.* Tucson: Univ. of Arizona Press, 1995.

American University Field Staff. "Births, Abortions, and the Progress of Chile." *Field Staff Report* 19:(2), 1972.

Angell, Alan. *Politics and the Labour Movement in Chile.* London: Oxford Univ. Press, 1972.

Antezana-Pernet, Corrine. "Mobilizing Women in the Popular Front Era: Feminism, Class, and Politics in the *Movimiento Pro-Emancipación de la Mujer Chilena* (MEMch), 1935–1950." Ph.D. diss., University of California-Irvine, 1996.

Aranda, Ximena. "Mujer, familia, y sociedad rural: El Valle de Putaendo." Ford Foundation: Santiago, 1981.

Aranda, Ximena, et al. "Organizaciones femininas del campo: Problemas y perspectivas." *Agricultura y sociedad* (1987).

Arteago, Ana María. "Politización de lo cotidiano y subversión del cotidiano." In *Mundo de mujer: Continuidad y cambio.* Santiago de Chile: Centro de Estudios de la Mujer, 1988.

Atria Benaprés, Raúl. "Actitudes y valores del campesino en relación a las aldeas de la reforma agraria." *Cuaderno de sociología* no. 2 (1969).

Baldez, Lisa. "In the Name of the Public and the Private: Conservative and Progressive Women's Movements in Chile." Ph.D. diss., University of California-San Diego, 1997.

———. *Nonpartisanship as Political Strategy: Women Left, Right, and Center in Chile.* Pittsburgh: Latin American Studies Association, 1998.

Baraona, Rafael, Ximena Aranda, and Roberto Santana. *Valle de Putaendo: Estudio de estructura agraria.* Santiago de Chile: Instituto de Geografía de la Universidad de Chile, 1961.

Barraclough, Solon, et al. *Chile: Reforma agraria y gobierno popular.* Buenos Aires: Ediciones Periferia, 1973.

Barraclough, Solon, and José Antonio Fernández, eds. *Diagnóstico de la reforma agraria chilena.* Mexico City: Siglo Veintiuno Editores, 1974.

Barrett, Michèle. *Women's Oppression Today: Problems in Marxist Feminist Analysis.* London: Verso, 1980.

Bauer, Arnold J. *Chilean Rural Society from the Spanish Conquest to 1930.* Cambridge: Cambridge Univ. Press, 1975.

Bengoa, José. *Historia social de la agricultura chilena.* Santiago de Chile: Ediciones Sur, 1990.

Berger Gluck, Sherna, and Daphne Patai, eds. *Women's Words: The Feminist Practice of Oral History.* New York: Routledge, 1991.

Bergquist, Charles. *Labor in Latin America: Comparative Essays on Chile, Argentina, Venezuela, and Colombia.* Stanford, Calif.: Stanford Univ. Press, 1986.

Besse, Susan K. *Restructuring Patriarchy: The Modernization of Gender Inequality in Brazil, 1914–1940.* Chapel Hill: Univ. of North Carolina Press, 1996.

Boydston, Jeanne. *Home and Work: Housework, Wages, and the Ideology of Labor in the Early Republic.* New York: Oxford Univ. Press, 1990.

Campana, Pilar. "Peasant Economy, Women's Labor, and Differential Forms of Capitalist Development: A Comparative Study in Three Contrasting Situations in Peru and Chile." Ph.D. diss., University of Durham, Great Britain, 1985.

Cancino, José, et al. "Hábitos, creencias y costumbres populares del puerperio y recién nacido." Unpublished paper, Departamento de Obstétrica y Ginecolia, Universidad de Chile, Valparaíso, 1978.

Carrière, Jean. *Land Owners and Politics in Chile: A Study of the Sociedad Nacional de Agricultura.* Amsterdam: Centrum voor Studie en Documentatie van Latijns-Amerika, 1981.

Caulfield, Sueann. *In Defense of Honor: Sexual Morality, Modernity, and Nation in Early-Twentieth-Century Brazil.* Durham, N.C.: Duke Univ. Press, 2000.

Centro de Estudios de la Mujer. *Notas sobre una intervención educativa: Escuela de mujeres rurales y almacén campesino.* Santiago de Chile: Centro de Estudios de la Mujer, 1988.

Centro para el Desarrollo Económico y Social de América Latina. "Fecundidad y anticoncepción en poblaciones marginales." Unpublished paper, Santiago de Chile, 1971.

"Los Centros de madres: Una Forma de organización para la mujer rural." Unpublished document, ISIS, Santiago de Chile, 1988.

Chaney, Elsa. "The Mobilization of Women in Allende's Chile." In *Women in Politics,* ed. Jane S. Jaquette. New York: Wiley, 1974.

———. "Women in Latin American Politics: The Case of Chile and Peru." In *Male and Female in Latin America,* ed. Anne Pescatello. Pittsburgh: Univ. of Pittsburgh Press, 1979.

Chaparro, N. *La Mujer y el desarrollo chileno: America Latina y la participación de la mujer.* San José, Costa Rica: CEDAL, 1973.

Chomsky, Aviva, and Aldo Lauria-Santiago, eds. *Identity and Struggle at the Margins of the Nation-State: The Laboring Peoples of Central America and the Hispanic Caribbean.* Durham, N.C.: Duke Univ. Press, 1998.

Chonchol, Jaques. *El Desarrollo de América Latina y la reforma agraria.* Santiago de Chile: Editorial del Pacífico, 1964.

Chuchryk, Patricia M. "Subversive Mothers: The Women's Opposition to the Military Regime in Chile." In *Women, the State, and Development,* ed.

Sue Ellen M. Charlton, Jana Everett, and Kathleen Staudt. Albany: State University of New York Press, 1989.

Collantes, Laura. "La Adolescente se descubre a si mísma: Cambios e inquietudes de la pupertád." In *Antología chilena de la tierra,* ed. Antonio Corvalán. Santiago de Chile: Instituto de Capacitación e Investigación en Reforma Agraria, 1970.

Collier, Simon, and William F. Sater. *A History of Chile, 1808–1994.* Cambridge: Cambridge Univ. Press, 1996.

Concurso de Autobiografías Campesinas. *Vida y palabra campesina: Primer concurso de autobiografías campesinas.* 6 vols. Santiago de Chile: Grupo de Investigaciones Agrarias, 1986.

Corrigan, Philip, and Derek Sayer. *The Great Arch: English State Formation as Cultural Revolution.* Oxford: Blackwell, 1985.

Covarrubias, Paz, and Rolando Franco. *Chile: Mujer y sociedad.* Santiago de Chile: UNICEF, 1978.

Crummett, María de los Angeles. "El Poder Feminino: The Mobilization of Women against Socialism in Chile." *Latin American Perspectives* 4, no. 4 (1977): 103–14.

Deere, Carmen Diana. *Household and Class Relations: Peasants and Landlords in Northern Peru.* Berkeley: Univ. of California Press, 1990.

Deere, Carmen Diana, and Magdalena León, eds. *La Mujer y la política agraria en America Latina.* Mexico City: Siglo Veintiuno Editores, 1986.

———. *Rural Women and State Policy: Feminist Perspectives on Latin American Agricultural Development.* Boulder, Colo.: Westview, 1987.

Delphy, Christine. *Close to Home: A Materialist Analysis of Women's Oppression.* Trans. and ed., Diana Leonard. London: Hutchinson, 1984.

Delphy, Christine, and Diana Leonard. *Familiar Exploitation: A New Analysis of Marriage in Contemporary Western Societies.* Cambridge: Polity, 1992.

DeShazo, Peter. *Urban Workers and Labor Unions in Chile, 1902–1927.* Madison: Univ. of Wisconsin Press, 1983.

Dore, Elizabeth, and Maxine Molyneux, eds. *Hidden Histories of Gender and the State in Latin America.* Durham, N.C.: Duke Univ. Press, 2000.

Dorsey, J. "*Empleo de mano de obra en las haciendas del Valle Central de Chile: VI Región, 1965–1976.*" Memorandum, Organización Internacional del Trabajo, Santiago de Chile, 1981.

Drake, Paul W. *Socialism and Populism in Chile, 1932–52.* Urbana: Univ. of Illinois Press, 1978.

Echeníque, Jorge. *La Reforma agraria chilena.* Mexico City: Siglo Veintiuno Editores, 1975.

"Un Estudio exploritorio de la participación social y productiva de la mujer en nueve asentamientos de la comuna de María Pinto." Master's thesis, Facultad de Ciencias Jurídicas y Sociales, Universidad de Chile, Santiago, 1972.

Farnsworth-Alvear, Ann. *Dulcinea in the Factory: Myths, Morals, Men, and Women in Colombia's Industrial Experiment, 1905–1960.* Durham, N.C.: Duke Univ. Press, 2000.

Farrell, Joseph P. *The National Unified School in Allende's Chile: The Role of Education in the Destruction of a Revolution.* Vancouver: Univ. of British Columbia Press, 1986.

Fawez, María Julia. "Los Trabajadores de los asentamientos y la nueva empresa agrícola." Master's thesis, Universidad Católica, Santiago de Chile, 1971.

Ferrada, M., and Y. Navarro. "Actitúd del hombre y la mujer campesinos frente a la participación de la mujer en cooperativas campesinas." Master's thesis, Escuela de Trabajo Social, Universidad Católica, Santiago de Chile, 1968.

Findlay, Eileen. *Imposing Decency: The Politics of Sexuality and Race in Puerto Rico, 1870–1920.* Durham, N.C.: Duke Univ. Press, 1999.

Fischer, Kathleen B. *Political Ideology and Educational Reform in Chile, 1964–1976.* Los Angeles: UCLA Latin American Center, 1979.

Fleet, Michael. *The Rise and Fall of Chilean Christian Democracy.* Princeton, N.J.: Princeton Univ. Press, 1985.

Foucault, Michel. *The History of Sexuality.* Trans. Robert Hurley. Vol. 1. New York: Vintage, 1990.

Fowler-Salamini, Heather, and Mary Kay Vaughan, eds. *Women of the Mexican Countryside, 1850–1990: Creating Spaces, Shaping Transition.* Tucson: Univ. of Arizona Press, 1994.

Francis, Michael, and Patricia A. Kyle. "Chile: The Power of Women at the Polls." *Integrating the Neglected Majority: Government Responses to Demands for New Sex-Roles,* ed. Patricia A. Kyle. Brunswick, Ohio: King's Court Communications, 1976.

French, John D., and Daniel James, eds. *The Gendered Worlds of Latin American Women Workers: From Household and Factory to the Union Hall and Ballot Box.* Durham, N.C.: Duke Univ. Press, 1997.

Garretón, Manuel Antonio, and Tomás Moulián. "Procesos y bloques políticos en la crisis chilena, 1970–1973." *Revista mexicana de sociología* 41, no. 1 (1979).

Garrett, Patricia. "Growing Apart: The Experiences of Rural Men and Women in Central Chile." Ph.D. diss., University of Wisconsin-Madison, 1978.

———. "La Reforma agraria, organización popular y participación de la mujer en Chile." In *Las Trabajadoras del agro:* Debate sobre la mujer en América Latina y el Caribe, ed. Magdalena León. Bogota: Asociación Colombiana para el Estudio de la Población, 1982.

Garrido, José, ed. *Historia de la reforma agraria en Chile.* Santiago de Chile: Editorial Universitaria, 1988.

Gaviola Artigas, Edda, et al. *Queremos votar en las próximas elecciones: Historia del movimiento femenino chileno, 1913–1952.* Santiago de Chile: Facultad Latinoamericana de Ciencias Sociales, 1986.

Gaviola Artigas, Edda, Lorella Lopresti, and Claudia Rojas. "Chile centros de madres: La Mujer popular en movimiento?" In *Nuestra memoria, nuestro futuro:* Mujeres e historia: América Latina y el Caribe, ed. Mariá del Carmen Feijóo. Santiago de Chile: ISIS, 1988.

———. "La Participación política de la mujer chilena entre los años 1964–1973." Unpublished document, ISIS-Santiago, 1987.

Gazmuri, Jaime. *Asentamientos campesinos: Una Evaluación de los primeros resultados de la reforma agraria en Chile.* Buenos Aires: Ediciones Troquel, 1970.

———. *Gobierno Popular: Reforma agraria.* Santiago de Chile: Centro de Estudios Agrarios, de la Universidad Católica de Chile, 1972.

Giroz, M. A., and A. M. Lopez. "Evaluación del proceso de integración de la mujer campesina en las organizaciones de base: Cooperativas y sindicatos." Master's thesis, Escuela de Trabajo Social, Universidad Católica, Santiago de Chile, 1969.

Godoy, Lorena. "'Armas ansiosas de triunfo: Dedal, agujas, tijeras . . . ': La educación profesional feminina en Chile, 1888–1912." In Godoy et al.

Godoy, Lorena, et al., eds. *Disciplina y desacato: Construcción de identidad en Chile, siglos* XIX *y* XX. Santiago de Chile: SUR/CEDEM, 1995.

Gómez, Sergio. "Cambios estructurales en el campo y migraciones en Chile." Documento de trabajo, Facultad Latinoamericana de Ciencias Sociales, Santiago de Chile, 1981.

———. "Los Campesinos beneficados por la reforma agraria chilena: Antecedentes, diferenciación, y percepción campesina." *Estudios rurales latinoamericanos* 4 (1981): 69–88.

———. *Los Empresarios agrícolas.* Santiago de Chile: Instituto de Capacitación e Investigación en Reforma Agraria, 1972.

———. *Organizaciones rurales y estructura agraria, Chile, 1973–1976.* Santiago de Chile: Facultad Latinoamericana de Ciencias Sociales, 1981.

———. *Políticas estatales y campesinado en Chile (1960–1989).* Santiago de Chile: Facultad Latinoamericana de Ciencias Sociales, 1989.

———. "Transformaciones en una area de minifundio: Valle de Putaendo, 1960–1980." Documento de trabajo, Facultad Latinoamericana de Ciencias Sociales, Santiago de Chile, 1980.

Góngora, Mario. *Origen de los "inquilinos" en Chile Central.* Santiago de Chile: Universidad de Chile, Seminario Historia Colonial, 1960.

Gordon, Linda. *Heroes of Their Own Lives: The Politics and History of Family Violence: Boston, 1880–1960.* New York: Penguin, 1989.

Gould, Jeffrey L. *To Die in This Way: Nicaraguan Indians and the Myth of Mestizaje, 1880–1965.* Durham, N.C.: Duke Univ. Press, 1998.

Gramsci, Antonio. *Selections from the Prison Notebooks.* Ed. and trans. Quintin Hoare and Geoffrey Nowell Smith. London: Lawrence and Wishart, 1971.

Haag, Pamela. *Consent: Sexual Rights and the Transformation of American Liberalism*. Ithaca, N.Y.: Cornell Univ. Press, 1999.

Hojoman, David E. "Land Reform, Female Migration, and the Market for Domestic Service in Chile." *Journal of Latin American Studies* 21, no. 1 (1989): 105–32.

Huerta, María Antonieta. *Otro agro para Chile: Historia de la reforma agraria en el proceso social y político*. Santiago de Chile: CISEC-CESOC, 1989.

Hutchison, Elizabeth Quay. "El Fruto envenenado del arbol capitalista: Women Workers and the Prostitution of Labor in Urban Chile, 1896–1925." *Journal of Women's History* 9, no. 4 (1998): 131–52.

———. *Labors Appropriate to Their Sex: Gender, Labor, and Politics in Urban Chile, 1900–1930*. Durham, N.C.: Duke Univ. Press, 2001.

Illanes O., María Angélica. *"En el nombre del pueblo, del estado y de la ciencia (...)": Historia social de la salud pública, Chile 1880–1973*. Santiago de Chile: Colectivo de Atención Primaria, 1993.

James, Daniel. *Doña María's Story: Life History, Memory, and Political Identity*. Durham, N.C.: Duke Univ. Press, 2000.

Jiles Moreno, Ximena. *De la miel a los implantes: Historia de las políticas de regulación de la fecundidad en Chile*. Santiago de Chile: Corporación de Salud y Políticas Sociales, 1992.

Joseph, Gilbert M., and Daniel Nugent, eds. *Everyday Forms of State Formation: Revolution and the Negotiation of Rule in Modern Mexico*. Durham, N.C.: Duke Univ. Press, 1994.

Kaplan, Temma. "Female Consciousness and Collective Action: The Case of Barcelona, 1910–1918." *Signs* 7, no. 3 (1982): 545–63.

Kaufman, Robert R. *The Politics of Land Reform in Chile, 1950–1970*. Cambridge, Mass.: Harvard Univ. Press, 1972.

Kay, Cristóbal. "Agrarian Reform and the Class Struggle in Chile." *Latin American Perspectives* 18 (1978): 117–37.

———. "Comparative Development of the European Manorial System and the Hacienda System." Ph.D. diss., University of Sussex, 1971.

———. "El Fin de la reforma agraria en América Latina? El Legado de la reforma agraria y el asunto no resuelto de la tierra." *Revista Mexicana de Sociología* 60, no. 4 (1998), 61–98.

Kay, Cristóbol, and Patricio Silva, eds. *Development and Social Change in the Chilean Countryside: From the Pre-land Reform Period to the Democratic Transition*. Amsterdam: CEDLA, 1992.

Kirkwood, Julieta. *Ser política en Chile: Las feministas y los partidos*. Santiago de Chile: Facultad Latinoamericana de Ciencias Sociales, 1986.

Klimpel Alvarado, Felícitas. *La Mujer chilena: El Aporte femenino al progreso de Chile, 1910–1960*. Santiago de Chile: Editorial Andrés Bello, 1962.

Klubock, Thomas Miller. *Contested Communities: Class, Gender, and Politics in Chile's El Teniente Copper Mine, 1904–1948.* Durham, N.C.: Duke Univ. Press, 1998.

———. "Nationalism, Race, and the Politics of Imperialism: Workers and North American Capital in the Chilean Copper Industry." In *Rethinking the Political: A View from the North,* ed. Gilbert Joseph. Durham, N.C.: Duke Univ. Press, forthcoming.

Kuhn, Annette, and AnnMarie Wolpe, eds. *Feminism and Materialism: Women and Modes of Production.* London: Routledge and Paul, 1978.

Lancaster, Roger N. *Life is Hard: Machismo, Danger, and the Intimacy of Power in Nicaragua.* Berkeley: Univ. of California Press, 1992.

Land Tenure Center Library, comp. *Agrarian Reform in Latin America: An Annotated Bibliography.* Madison, Wis.: The Center, 1974.

Lavrin, Asunción. *Women, Feminism, and Social Change in Argentina, Chile, and Uruguay, 1890–1940.* Lincoln: Univ. of Nebraska Press, 1995.

Lechner, Norbert. "Represión sexual y manipulación social." *Cuadernos de la realidad.* No. 12, 1972.

Loveman, Brian. *El Campesino chileno le escribe a su excelencia.* Santiago de Chile: Instituto de Capacitación e Investigación en Reforma Agraria, 1971.

———. *Chile: The Legacy of Hispanic Capitalism.* New York: Oxford Univ. Press, 1988.

———. *Struggle in the Countryside: Politics and Rural Labor in Chile, 1919–1973.* Bloomington: Indiana Univ. Press, 1976.

Mack, Macarena, Paulina Matta, and Ximena Valdés. *Los Trabajos de las mujeres entre el campo y la ciudad, 1920–1982: Campesina, costurera, obrera de la costura, empleada doméstica, cocinera de fundo, temporera.* Santiago de Chile: Centro de Estudios de la Mujer, 1986.

Malic, Danisa, and Elena Serrano. "La Mujer chilena ante la ley." In *Mundo de mujer: Continuidad y cambio.* Santiago de Chile: Centro de Estudios de la Mujer, 1988.

Mallon, Florencia E. *Defense of Community in Peru's Central Highland: Peasant Struggle and Capitalist Transition, 1860–1940.* Princeton, N.J.: Princeton Univ. Press, 1983.

———. "Gender and Class in the Transition to Capitalism: Household and Mode of Production in Central Peru." *Latin American Perspectives* 48, no. 1 (1986): 147–74.

———. *Peasant and Nation: The Making of Postcolonial Mexico and Peru.* Berkeley: Univ. of California Press, 1995.

Marchett, Peter. "Worker Participation and Class Conflict in Worker-Managed Farms: The Rural Question in Chile, 1970–1973." Ph.D. diss., University of Michigan, 1977.

Mattelart, Armand. *Altas social de las comunas de Chile.* Santiago de Chile: Editorial del Pacífico, 1965.

Mattelart, Armand, and Michèle Mattelart. *La Mujer chilena en una nueva sociedad: Un Estudio exploratorio acerca de la Situación e imagen de la mujer en Chile.* Trans. Isabel Budge de Ducci. Santiago de Chile: Editorial del Pacífico, 1968.

Mattelart, Michèle. "Chile: The Feminine Side of the Coup; or, When Bourgeois Women Take to the Streets." *NACLA's Latin America and Empire Report* 9, no. 6 (1975): 14–25.

McBridge, George McCutchen. *Chile: Land and Society.* New York: American Geographical Society, 1936.

McGee Deutsch, Sandra. "Gender and Sociopolitical Change in Twentieth-Century Latin America." *Hispanic American Historical Review* 71, no. 2 (1991): 259–306.

Menges, Constantine Christopher. "Chile's Landowners' Association and Agrarian Reform Politics." Memorandum, Rand Corporation, Santa Monica, 1968.

Molyneux, Maxine. "Mobilization without Emancipation: Women's Interests and the State in Nicaragua." *Feminist Studies* 11, no. 2 (1985): 227–54.

Montecinos, Sonia. *Madre y huachos: Alegorías del mestizaje chileno.* Santiago de Chile: CEDEM, 1991.

Montgomery, David. *Workers' Control in America: Studies in the History of Work, Technology, and Labor Struggles.* Cambridge: Cambridge Univ. Press, 1979.

Movimiento de Izquierda Revolucionaria. *La Política del MIR en el Campo: Una Respuesta a los ataques del partido comunista y declaración del Secretariado Nacional del MIR.* Santiago de Chile: Ediciones El Rebelde, 1972.

Nazarri, Muriel. "The Woman Question in Cuba: Material Constraints on Its Solution." *Signs* 9, no. 2 (1983).

Neuse, Steven M. "Voting in Chile: The Feminine Response." In *Political Participation in Latin America,* ed. John A. Booth and Mitchell A. Seligson. New York: Holmes and Meier, 1978–1979.

Oxmán, Veronica. "La Participación de la mujer campesina en organizaciones: Los Centros de madres rurales." ISIS, Santiago de Chile, 1983.

Passerini, Luisa. *Fascism in Popular Memory: The Cultural Experience of the Turin Working Class.* Trans. Robert Lumley and Jude Bloomfield. New York: Cambridge Univ. Press, 1987.

Pateman, Carole. *The Sexual Contract.* Stanford, Calif.: Stanford Univ. Press, 1988.

Pinto, Julio. *Trabajos y rebeldías en la pampa salitrera: El Ciclo del salitre y la reconfiguración de las identidades populares (1850–1900).* Santiago de Chile: Editorial Universidad de Santiago, 1998.

Portelli, Alessandro. *The Death of Luigi Trastulli, and Other Stories: Form and Meaning in Oral History.* Albany: State Univ. of New York Press, 1991.

Power, Margaret. "Right-Wing Women and Chilean Politics: 1964–1973." Ph.D. diss., University of Illinois-Chicago, 1997.

"El Problema agrario en 100 asentamientos del valle central." Record from Instituto de Capacitación e Investigacion de Reforma Agraria. Santiago de Chile: Biblioteca Nacional, 1972.

Puz, Amanda. *La Mujer chilena.* Santiago de Chile: Editora Nacional Quimantú, 1972.

Rebolledo, Loreto. *Fragmentos: Oficios y percepciones de las mujeres del campo.* Santiago de Chile: CEDEM, 1991.

Rivera A., Rigoberto. *Los Campesinos chilenos.* Santiago de Chile: Grupo de Investigaciones Agrarias, 1988.

Rosemblatt, Karin Alejandra. "Domesticating Men: State Building and Class Compromise in Popular-Front Chile." In Dore and Molyneux.

———. *Gendered Compromises: Political Cultures and the State in Chile, 1920–1950.* Chapel Hill: Univ. of North Carolina Press, 2000.

Roxborough, Ian. "The Political Mobilization of Farm Workers during the Chilean Agrarian Reform, 1971–1973: A Case Study." Ph.D. diss., University of Wisconsin-Madison, 1977.

Roxborough, Ian, Philip O'Brien, and Jackie Roddick. *Chile: The State and Revolution.* New York: Holmes and Meir, 1977.

Salazar, Gabriel. *Labradores, peones y proletarios: Formación y crisis de la sociedad popular chilena del siglo XIX.* Santiago de Chile: Ediciones Sur, 1985.

———. "Ser niño huacho en la historia de Chile." *Proposiciones* no. 19 (1990): 55–83.

Salazar, Gabriel, and Julio Pinto, eds. *Historia contemporánea de Chile.* Vol. 1, *Estado, legitimidad y ciudanía.* Santiago de Chile: LOM Ediciones, 1999.

Salinas, Cecilia. *La Mujer proletaria: Una Historia para contar.* Concepción: Editiones Literatura Americana Reunida, 1987.

Salinas, Luís. *Trayectoria de la organización campesina.* Santiago de Chile: AGRA, 1985.

Sbarisaro, Franzani, and Rubie Mufdi. "Análisis crítico sobre los centros de madres." Unpublished paper, Escuela de Orientación del Hogar, Universidad de Chile Chillán, Chillan, Chile, 1971.

Schejtman Mishkin, Alexander. *El Inquilino del valle central:* La Estructura actual de la empresa campesina y el proceso de cambio de la institución. Santiago de Chile: Instituto de Capacitación e Investigación en Reforma Agraria, 1968.

Scott, James C. *Domination and the Arts of Resistance: Hidden Transcripts.* New Haven, Conn.: Yale Univ. Press, 1990.

———. *The Moral Economy of the Peasant: Rebellion and Subsistence in Southeast Asia.* New Haven, Conn.: Yale Univ. Press, 1976.

Scott, Joan Wallach. *Gender and the Politics of History.* New York: Columbia Univ. Press, 1988.

Sigmund, Paul E. *The Overthrow of Allende and the Politics of Chile, 1964–1976.* Pittsburgh: Univ. of Pittsburgh Press, 1977.

Silva Dreyer, Ana María. "Estadísticas sobre planificación familiar e aborto en Chile." Unpublished paper, Informativo no. 4, Instituto de la Mujer, Santiago de Chile, 1990.

———. "Tendencias generales de la fecundidad en Chile, 1960–1987." Unpublished paper, Instituto de la Mujer, Santiago de Chile, July 1990.

Smith, Brian. *The Church and Politics in Chile: Challenges to Modern Catholicism.* Princeton, N.J.: Princeton Univ. Press, 1982.

Stacey, Judith. *Patriarchy and Socialist Revolution in China.* Berkeley: Univ. of California Press, 1983.

Stallings, Barbara. *Class Conflict and Economic Development in Chile, 1958–1973.* Stanford, Calif.: Stanford Univ. Press, 1978.

Stansell, Christine. *City of Women: Sex and Class in New York, 1789–1860.* Urbana: Univ. of Illinois Press, 1987.

Steeland, Kyle. *Agrarian Reform under Allende: Peasant Revolt in the South.* Albuquerque: Univ. of New Mexico Press, 1977.

Stern, Steve J. *The Secret History of Gender: Women, Men, and Power in Late Colonial Mexico.* Chapel Hill: Univ. of North Carolina Press, 1995.

Thiesenhusen, William C. *Broken Promises: Agrarian Reform and the Latin American Campesino.* Boulder, Colo.: Westview, 1995.

Tinsman, Heidi. "Household *Patrones:* Wife Beating and Sexual Control in Rural Chile." In French and James.

———. "Patrones del hogar: Violencia doméstica y control sexual en Chile rural, 1964–1988." In Godoy et al.

———. "Unequal Uplift: The Sexual Politics of Gender, Work, and Community in the Chilean Agrarian Reform, 1958–1973." Ph.D. diss., Yale University, 1996.

Townsend, Camilla. "Refusing to Travel *La Via Chilena.*" *Journal of Women's History* 4, no. 3 (1993): 43–63.

Unidad Popular. *La Mujer en el gobierno de la Unidad Popular.* Santiago de Chile: Editorial Quimantú, 1970.

Valdés, Teresa, et al. "Centros de madres, 1973–1989: Solo disciplinamiento?" Documento de trabajo, Facultad Latinoamericana de Ciencias Sociales, Santiago de Chile, 1989.

Valdés S., Ximena. "Una Experiencia de organización autónoma de mujeres del campo." In *Cuadernos de la mujer del campo.* Santiago de Chile: Grupo de Investigaciones Agrarias, 1983.

————. "Feminización del mercado de trabajo agrícola: Las Temporeras." In *Mundo de mujer: Cambio y continuidad.* Santiago de Chile: Centro de Estudios de la Mujer, 1988.

————. *Mujer, trabajo y medio ambiente: Los Nudos de la modernización agraria.* Santiago de Chile: Centro de Estudios de la Mujer, 1992.

————. *La Posición de la mujer en la hacienda.* Santiago de Chile: Centro de Estudios de la Mujer, 1988.

Valdés S., Ximena, et al. *Sinópsis de una realidad ocultada: Las Trabajadoras del campo.* Santiago de Chile: Centro de Estudios de la Mujer, 1987.

————, eds. *Historias testimoniales de mujeres del campo.* Santiago de Chile: CEDEM, 1983.

Valdés S., Ximena, and Kathya Araujo K. *Vida privada: Modernización agraria y modernidad.* Santiago de Chile: CEDEM, 1999.

Vaughan, Mary Kay. *Cultural Politics in Revolution: Teachers, Peasants, and Schools in Mexico, 1930–1940.* Tucson: Univ. of Arizona Press, 1997.

————. "Modernizing Patriarchy: State Policies, Rural Households, and Women in Mexico, 1930–1940." In Dore and Molyneux.

Verba, Ericka. "El Círculo de Lectura and the Club de Señoras (1915–1920)." *Journal of Women's History* 7, no. 3 (1995): 6–33.

Vidal, Virginia. *La Emancipación de la mujer.* Santiago de Chile: Editora Nacional Quimantú, 1972.

Winn, Peter. *Weavers of Revolution: The Yarur Workers and Chile's Road to Socialism.* New York: Oxford Univ. Press, 1986.

Winn, Peter, and Cristóbal Kay. "Agrarian Reform and Rural Revolution in Allende's Chile." *Journal of Latin American Studies* 6, no. 1 (1974): 135–59.

Zárate, M. Soledad. "Mujeres viciosas, mujeres virtuosas: La Mujer delincuente y la casa correccional de Santiago, 1860–1990." In Godoy et al.

Zeitlin, Maurice, and Richard Earl Ratcliff. *Landlords and Capitalists: The Dominant Class of Chile.* Princeton, N.J.: Princeton Univ. Press, 1988.

index

Heidi Tinsman is an Assistant Professor
in the Department of History at the University of
California at Irvine.

Library of Congress Cataloging-in-Publication Data

Tinsman, Heidi
Partners in conflict : the politics of gender, sexuality,
and labor in the Chilean agrarian reform, 1950–1973 /
Heidi Tinsman.
p. cm. — (Next wave)
Includes bibliographical references and index.
ISBN 0-8223-2907-7 (cloth : alk. paper) —
ISBN 0-8223-2922-0 (pbk. : alk. paper)
1. Gender role—Chile—History—20th century.   2. Land
reform—Chile—History—20th century.   3. Peasantry
—Chile—History—20th century.   I. Title.   II. Series.
HQ1075.5.C5 T56   2002
305.3'0983—dc21   2001007713